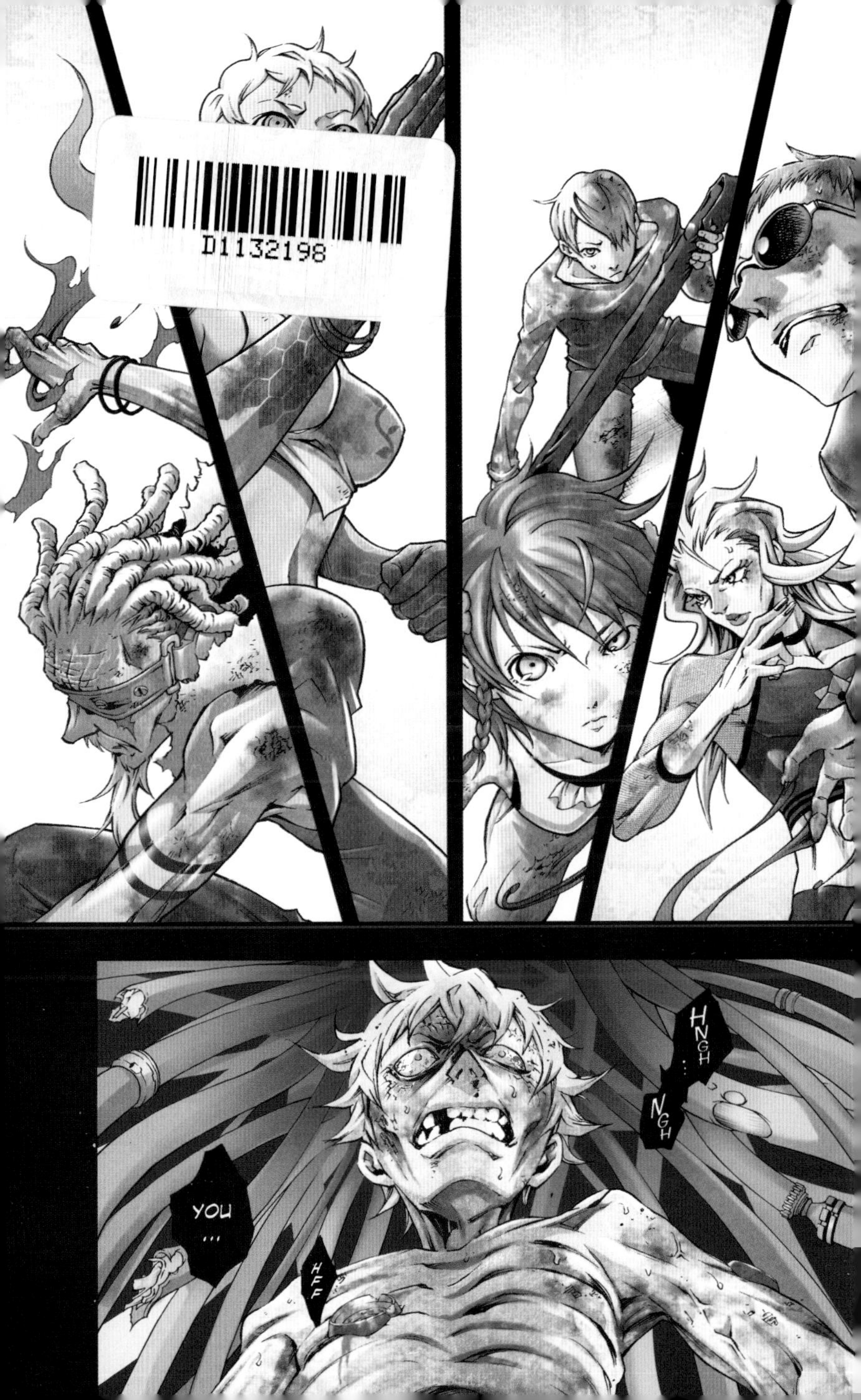
HNGH ... NGH
YOU ...
HFF

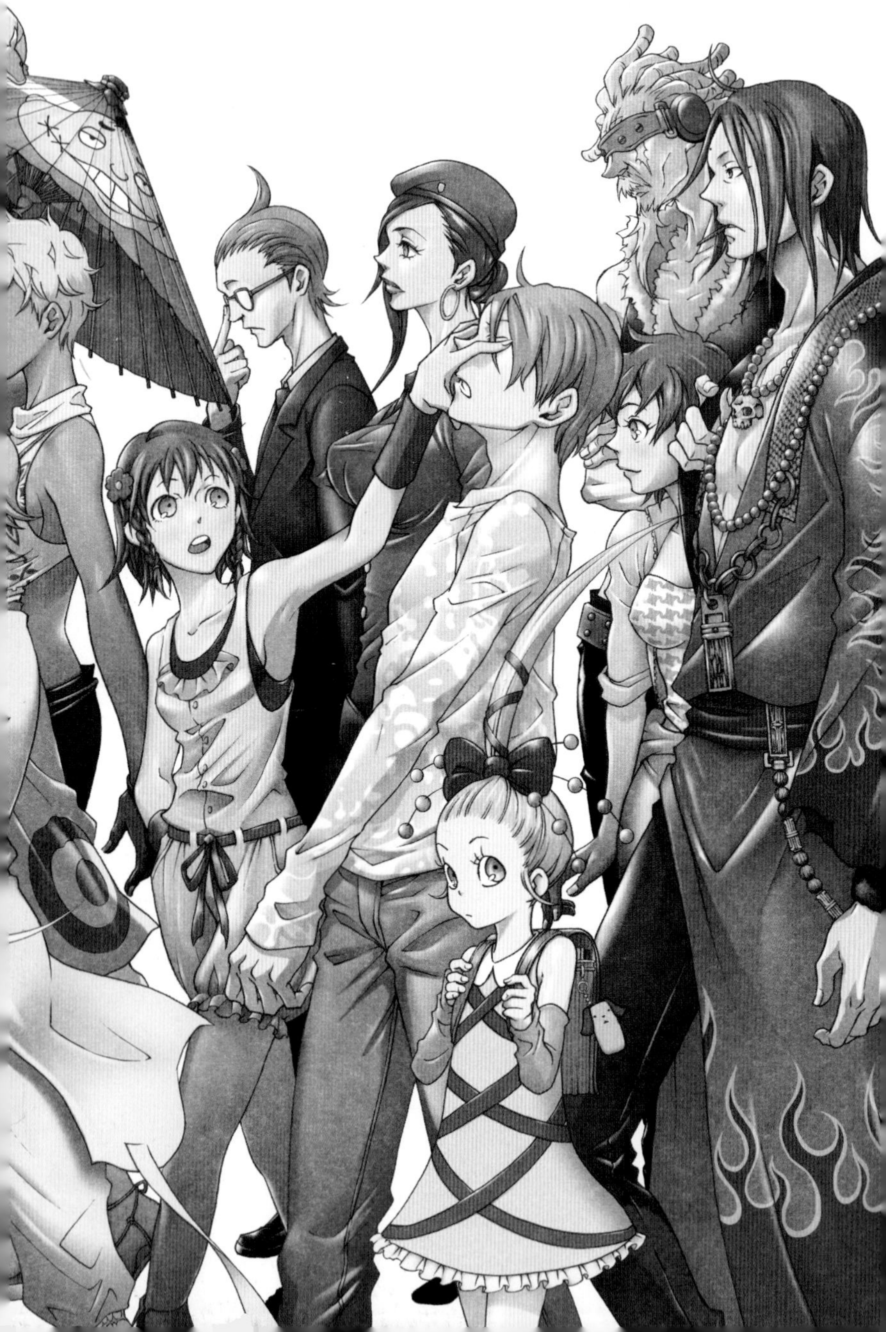

DEADMAN WONDERLAND

STORY & ART BY JINSEI KATAOKA, KAZUMA KONDOU

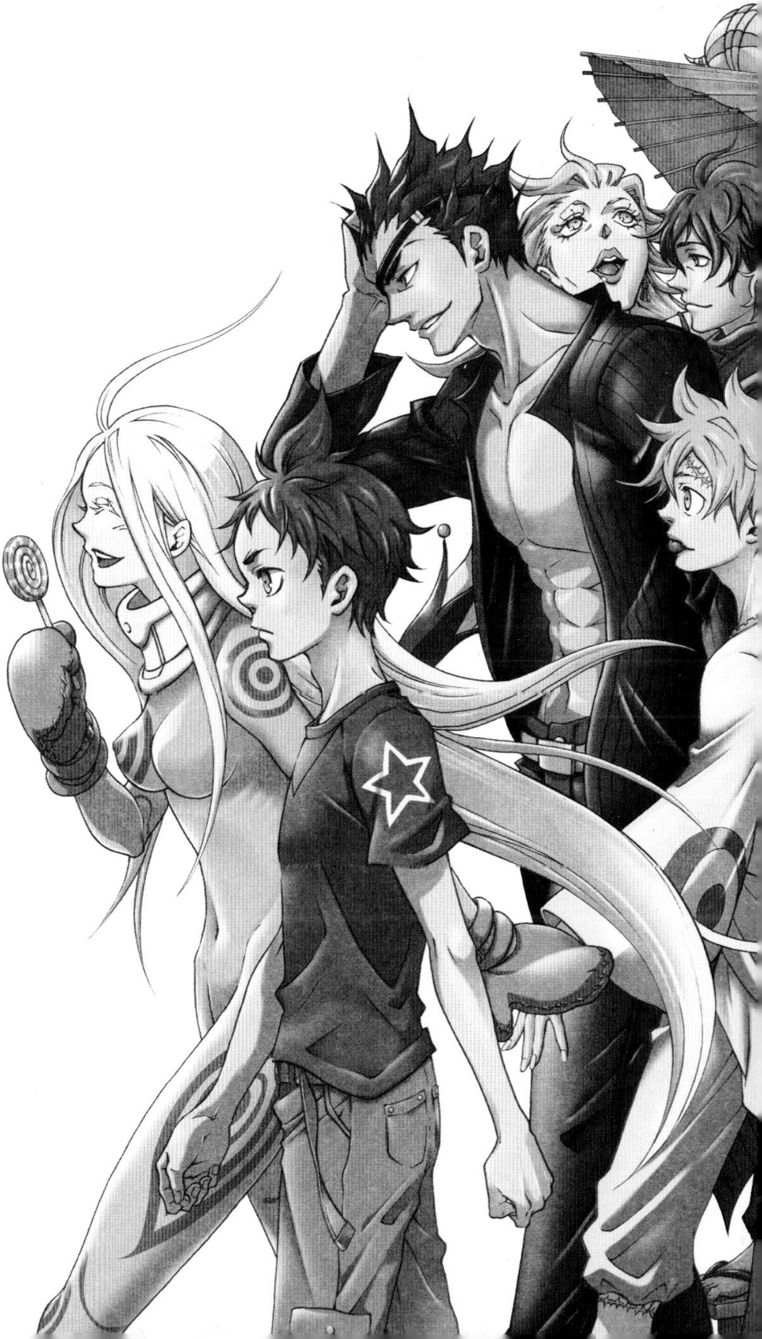

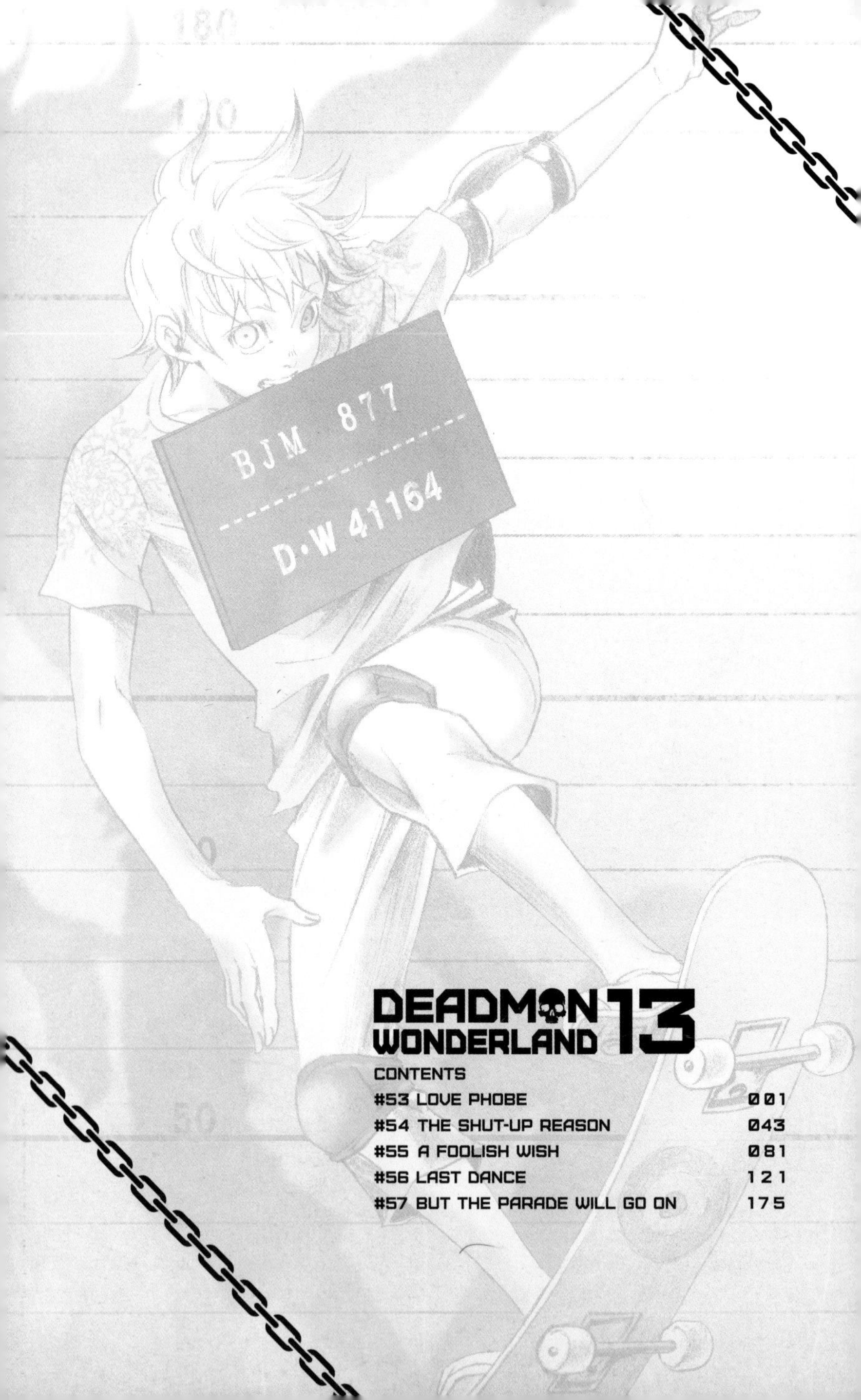
180
BJM 877
D·W 41164

DEADMAN WONDERLAND 13

CONTENTS

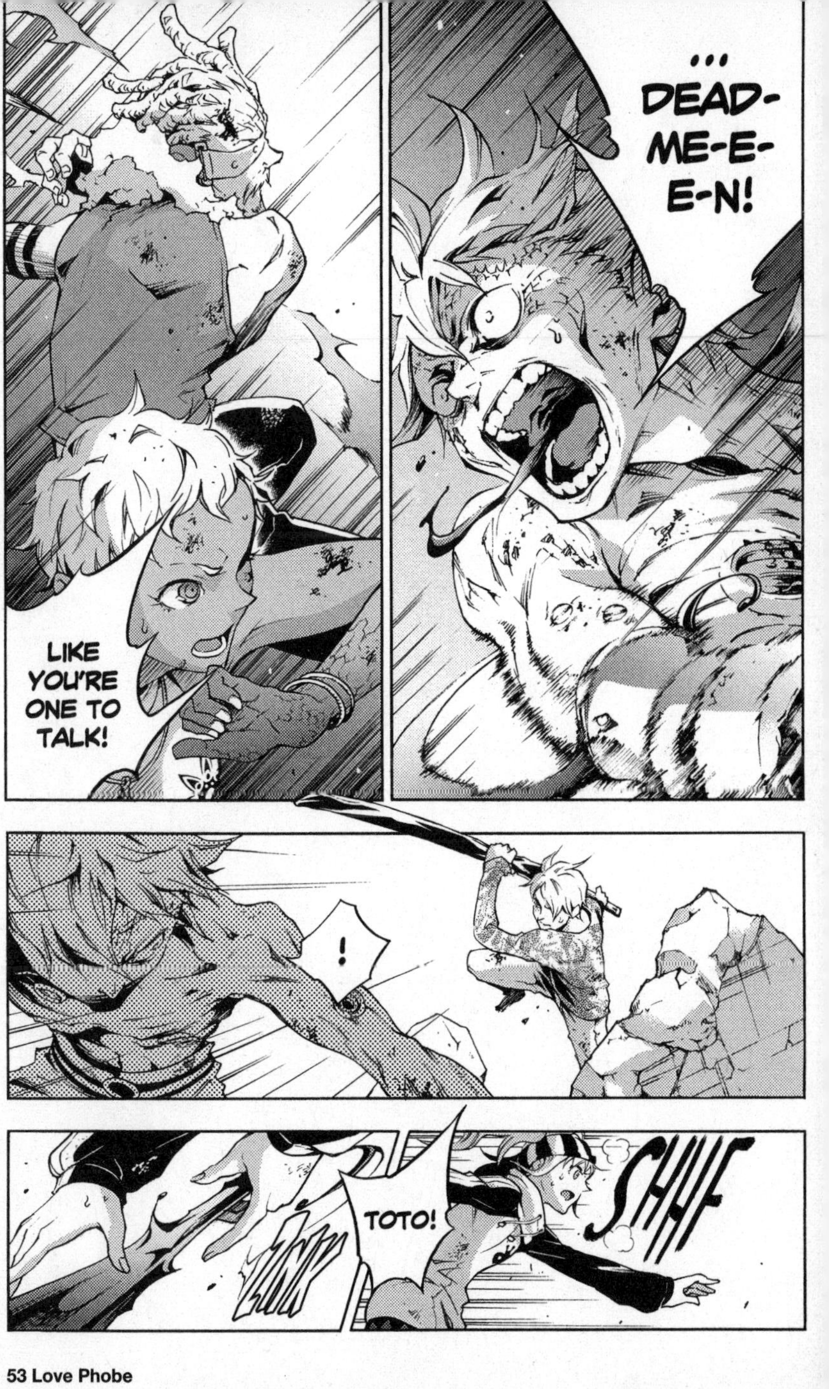
...DEAD-ME-E-E-N!
LIKE YOU'RE ONE TO TALK!
!
SHHF
TOTO!

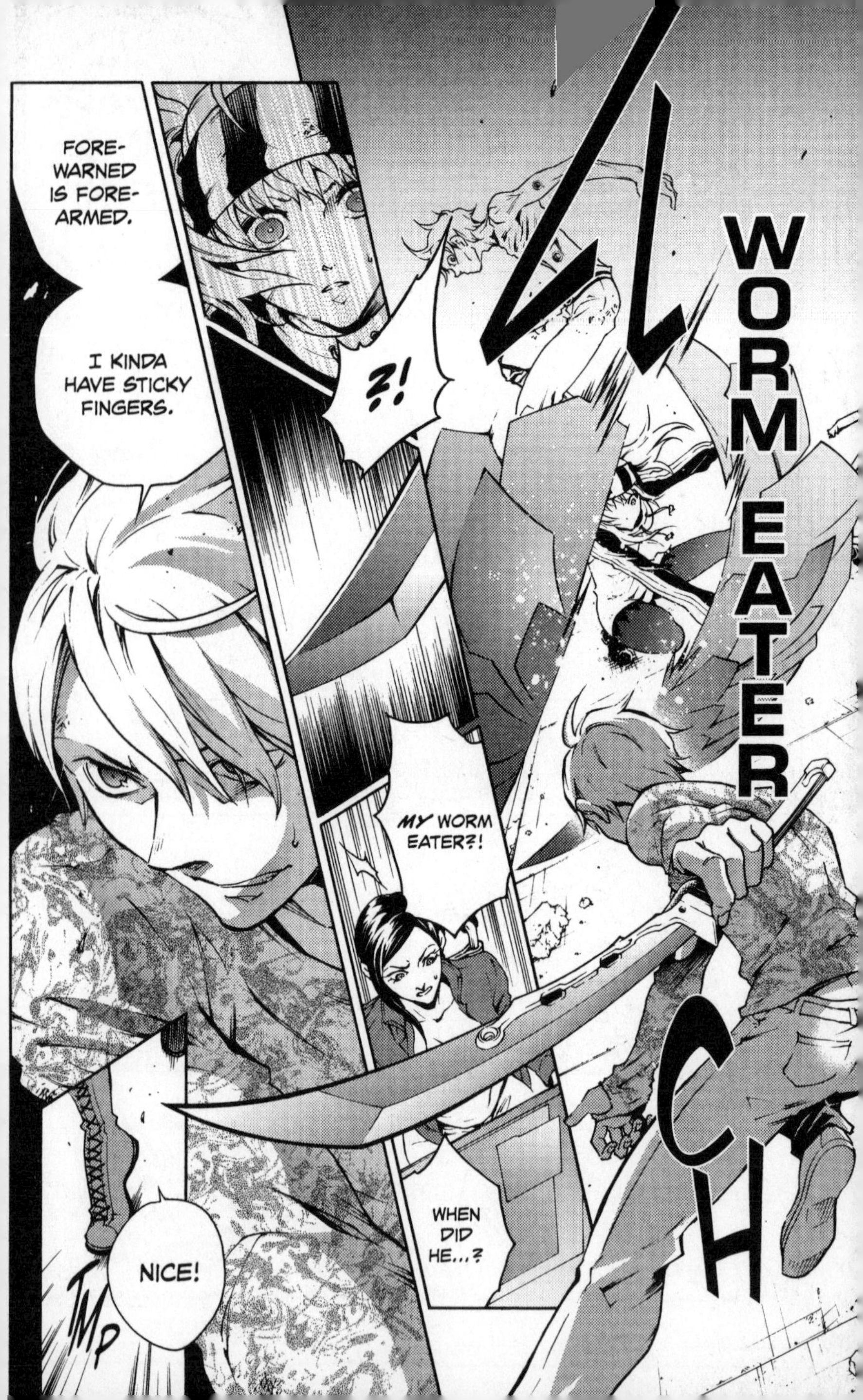
?!
WORM EATER
CH
MY WORM EATER?!
WHEN DID HE...?
FORE-WARNED IS FORE-ARMED.
I KINDA HAVE STICKY FINGERS.
NICE!
TMP

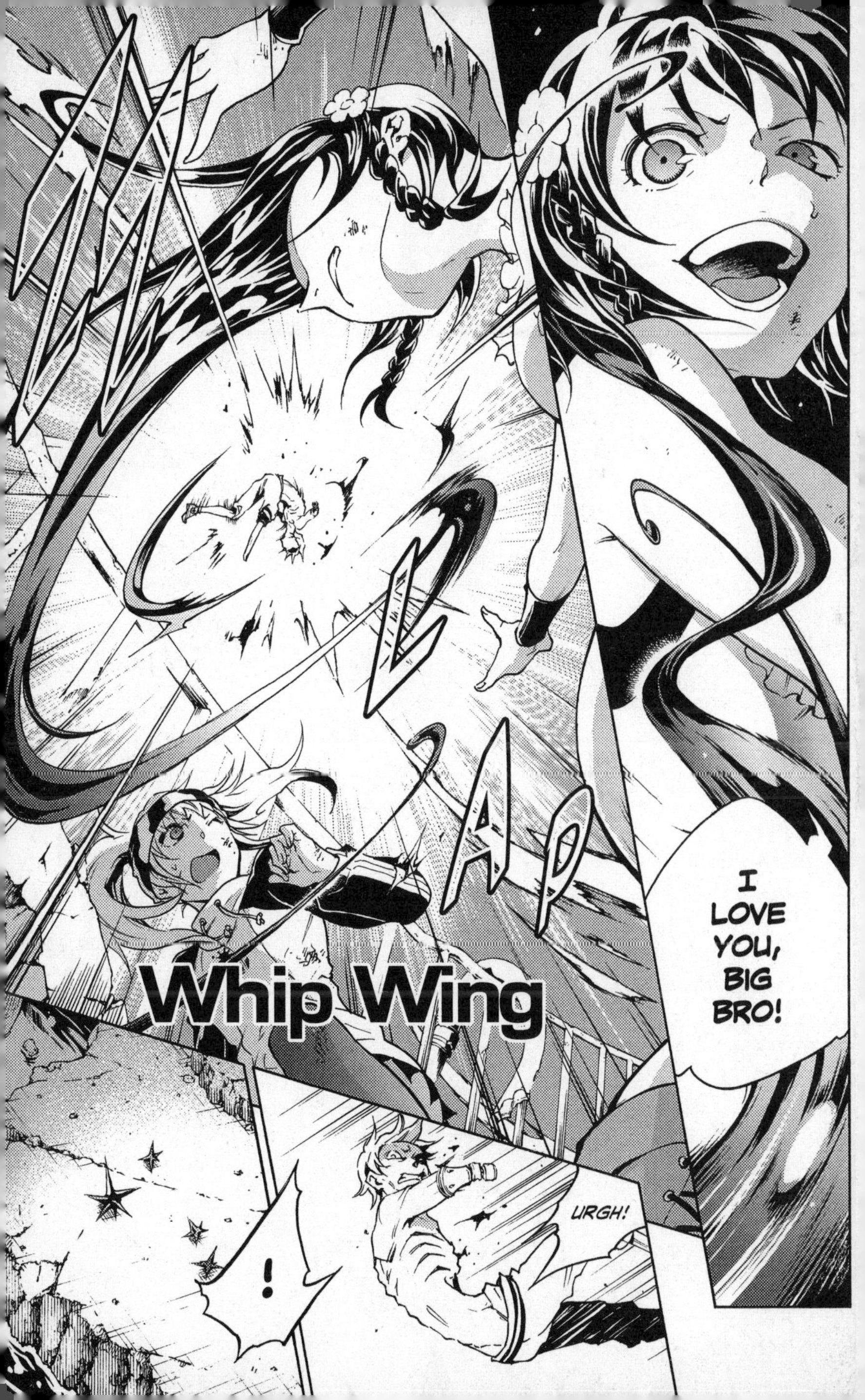
I LOVE YOU, BIG BRO!
ZAP
Whip Wing
URGH!
!

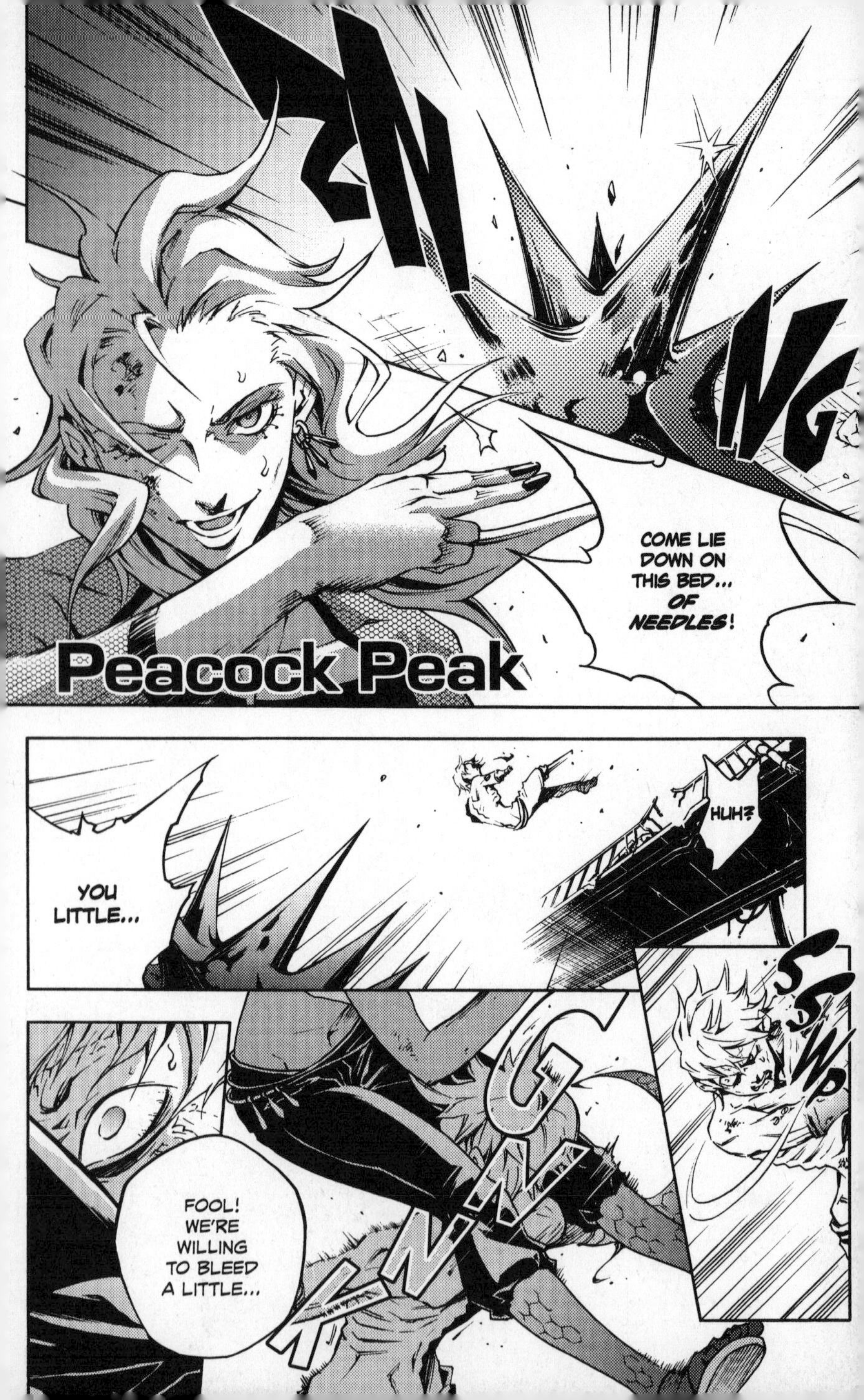
COME LIE DOWN ON THIS BED... OF NEEDLES!
Peacock Peak
HUH?
YOU LITTLE...
FOOL! WE'RE WILLING TO BLEED A LITTLE...

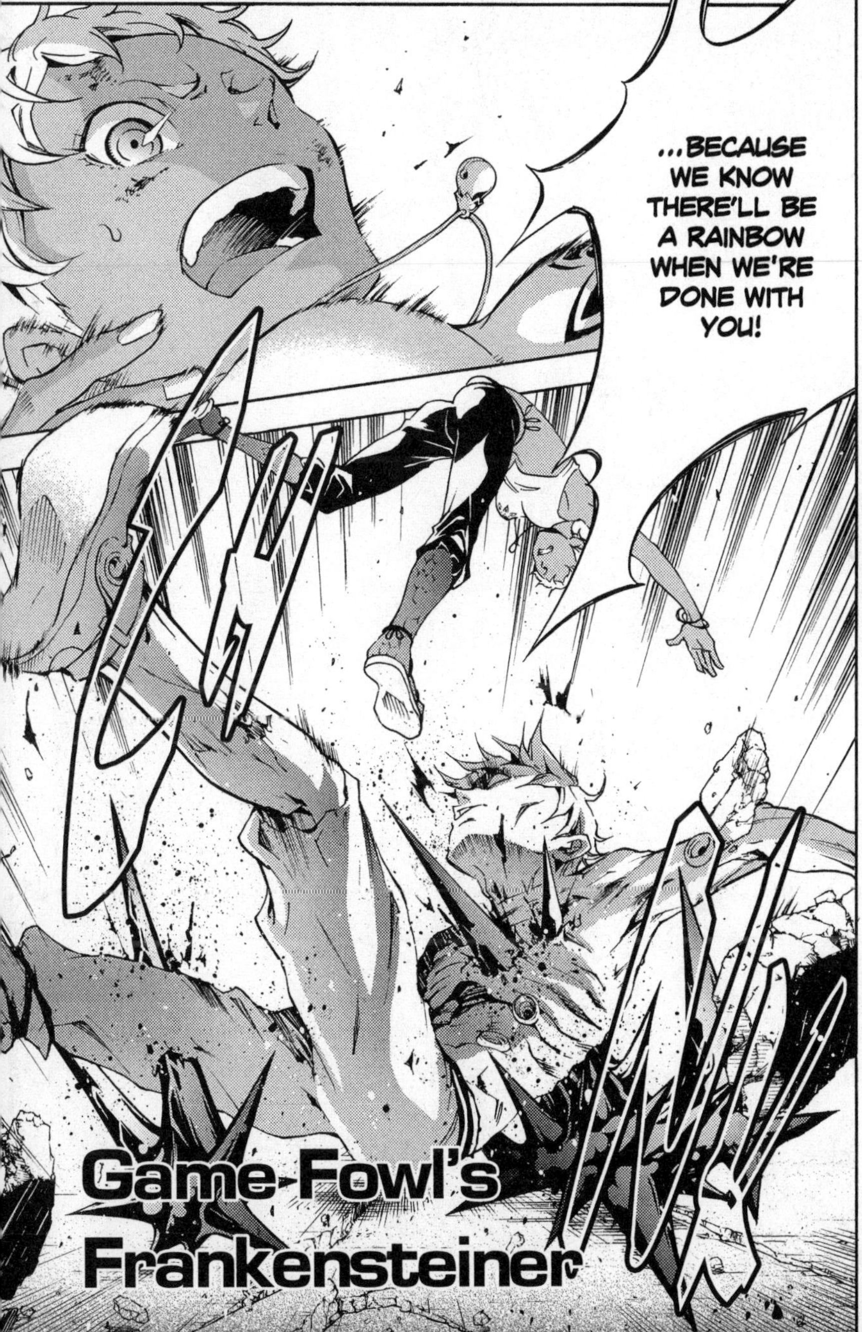
...BECAUSE WE KNOW THERE'LL BE A RAINBOW WHEN WE'RE DONE WITH YOU!
Game Fowl's Frankensteiner

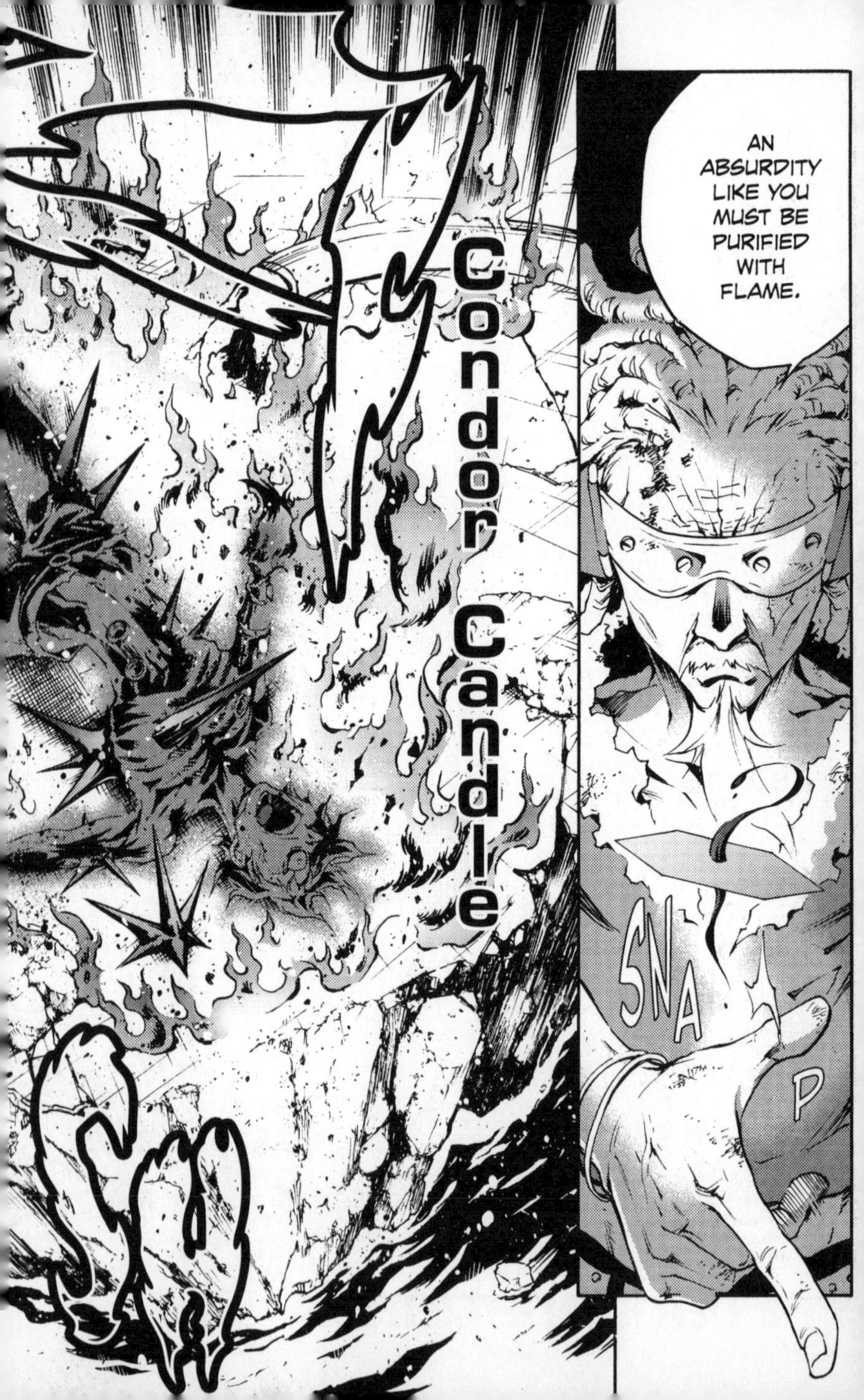
AN ABSURDITY LIKE YOU MUST BE PURIFIED WITH FLAME.
SNAP
Condor Candle

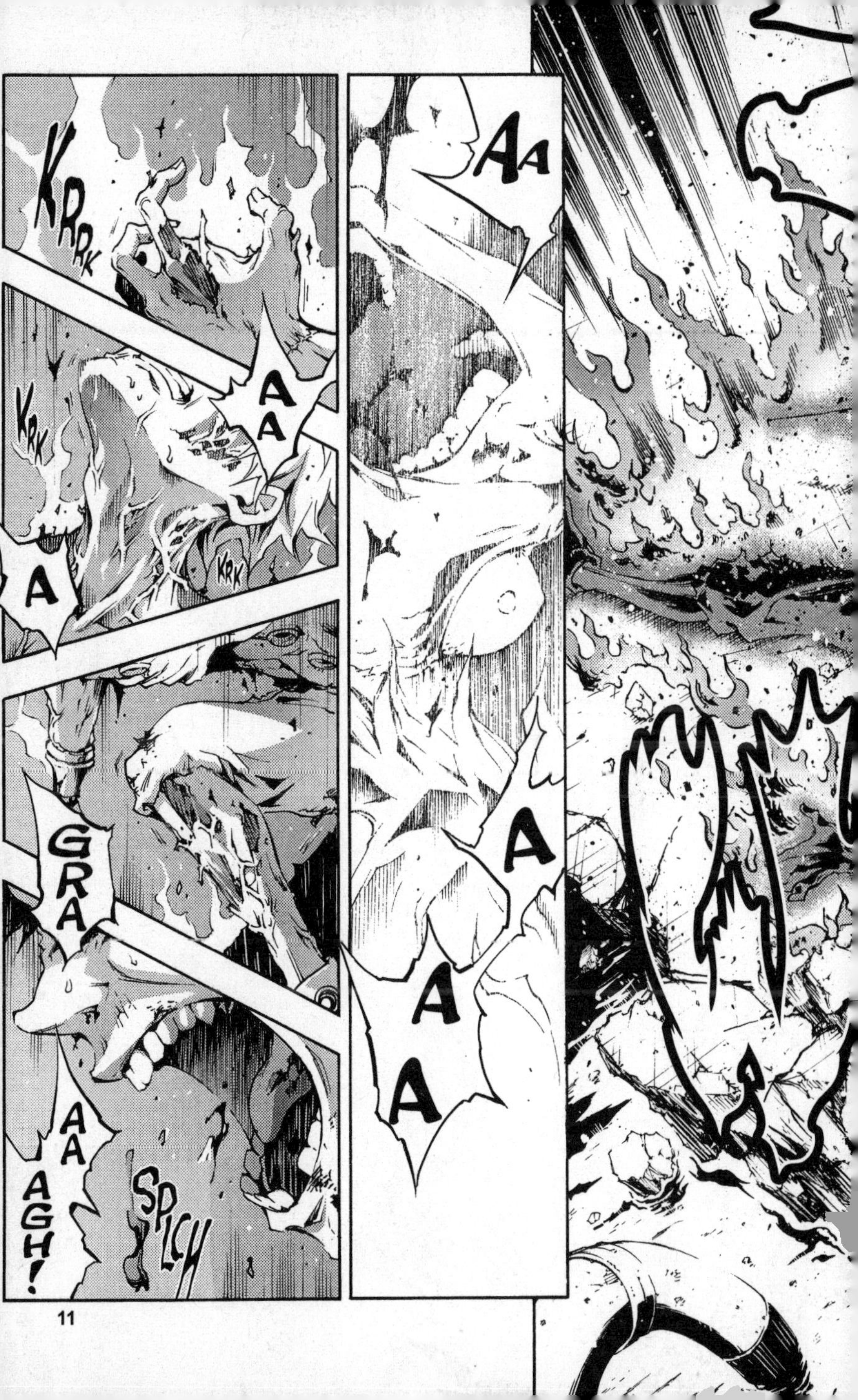
AA
A
A
A
KRRRK
AA
KRK
A
KRK
GRA
AAAGH!
SPLCH

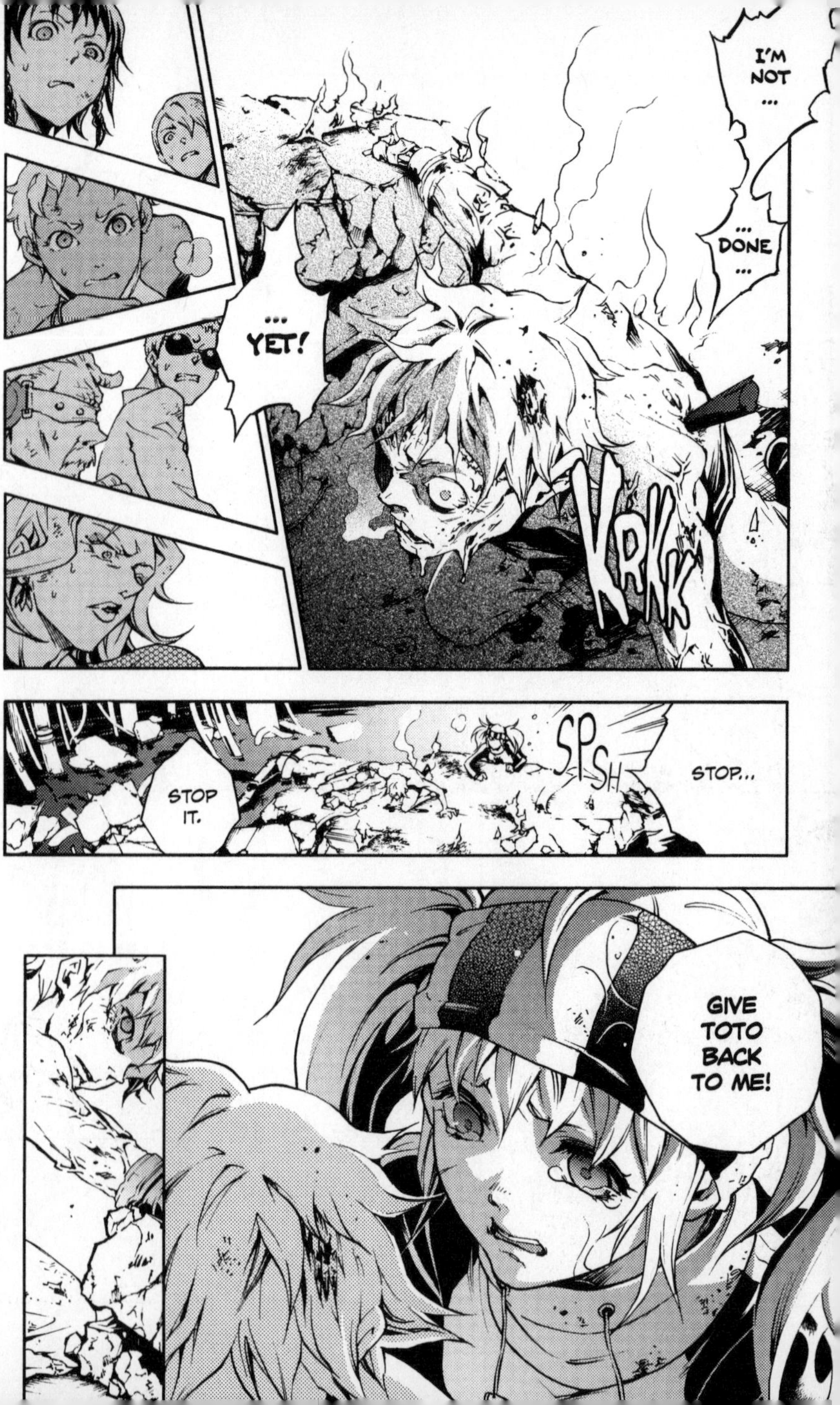
I'M NOT ...
... DONE ...
KRKK
... YET!
STOP...
SPSH
STOP IT.
GIVE TOTO BACK TO ME!

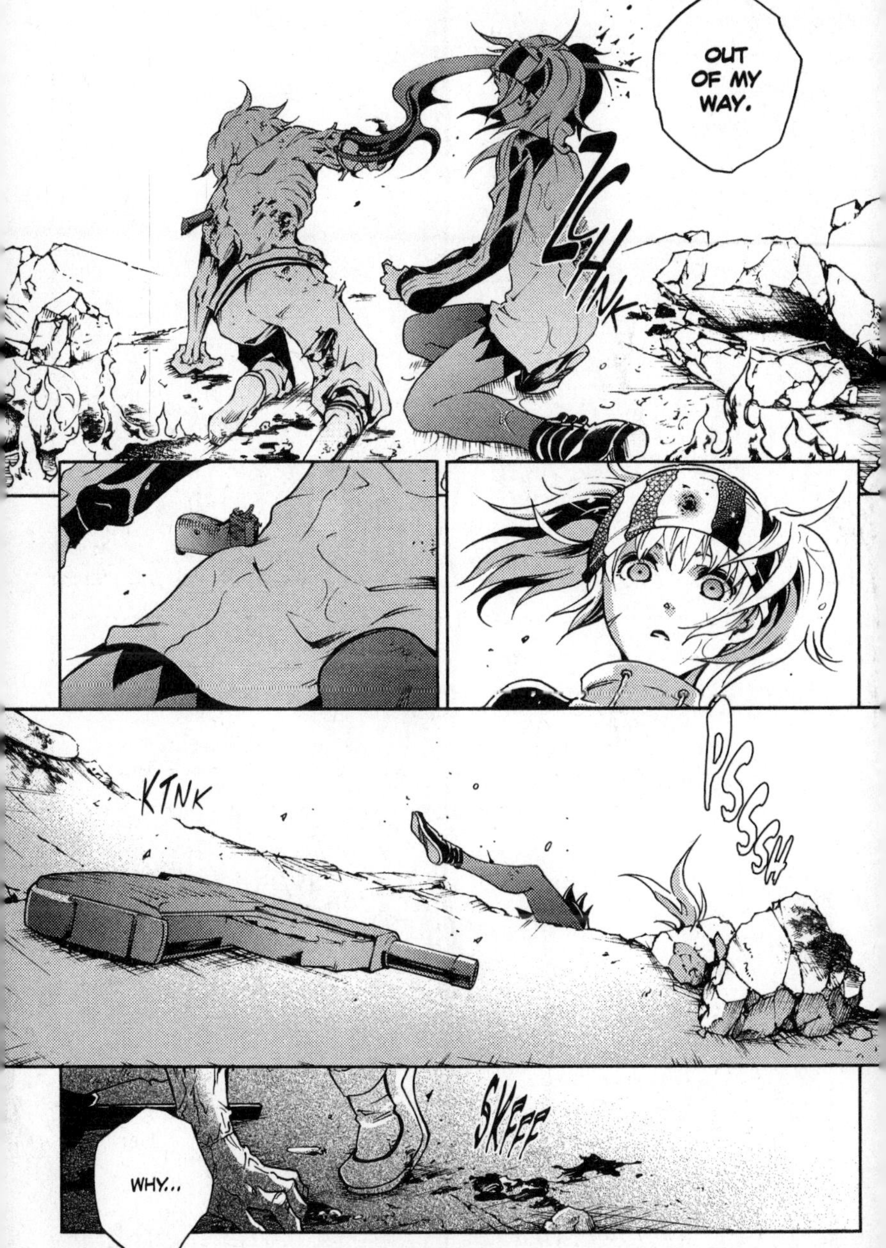
OUT OF MY WAY.
ZCHNK
PSSSSH
KTNK
SKFFF
WHY...

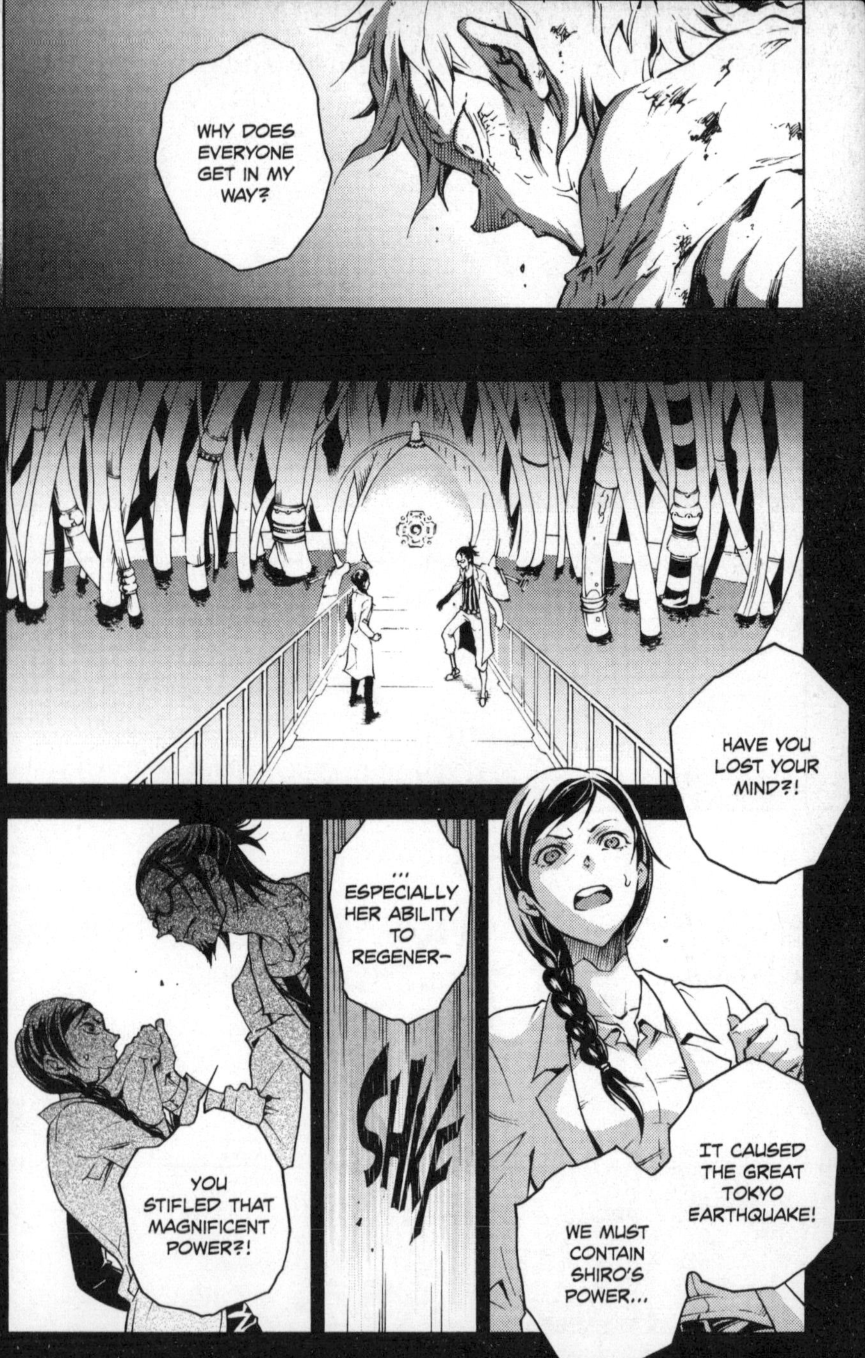
WHY DOES EVERYONE GET IN MY WAY?
HAVE YOU LOST YOUR MIND?!
IT CAUSED THE GREAT TOKYO EARTHQUAKE!
WE MUST CONTAIN SHIRO'S POWER...
...ESPECIALLY HER ABILITY TO REGENER—
SHAKE
YOU STIFLED THAT MAGNIFICENT POWER?!

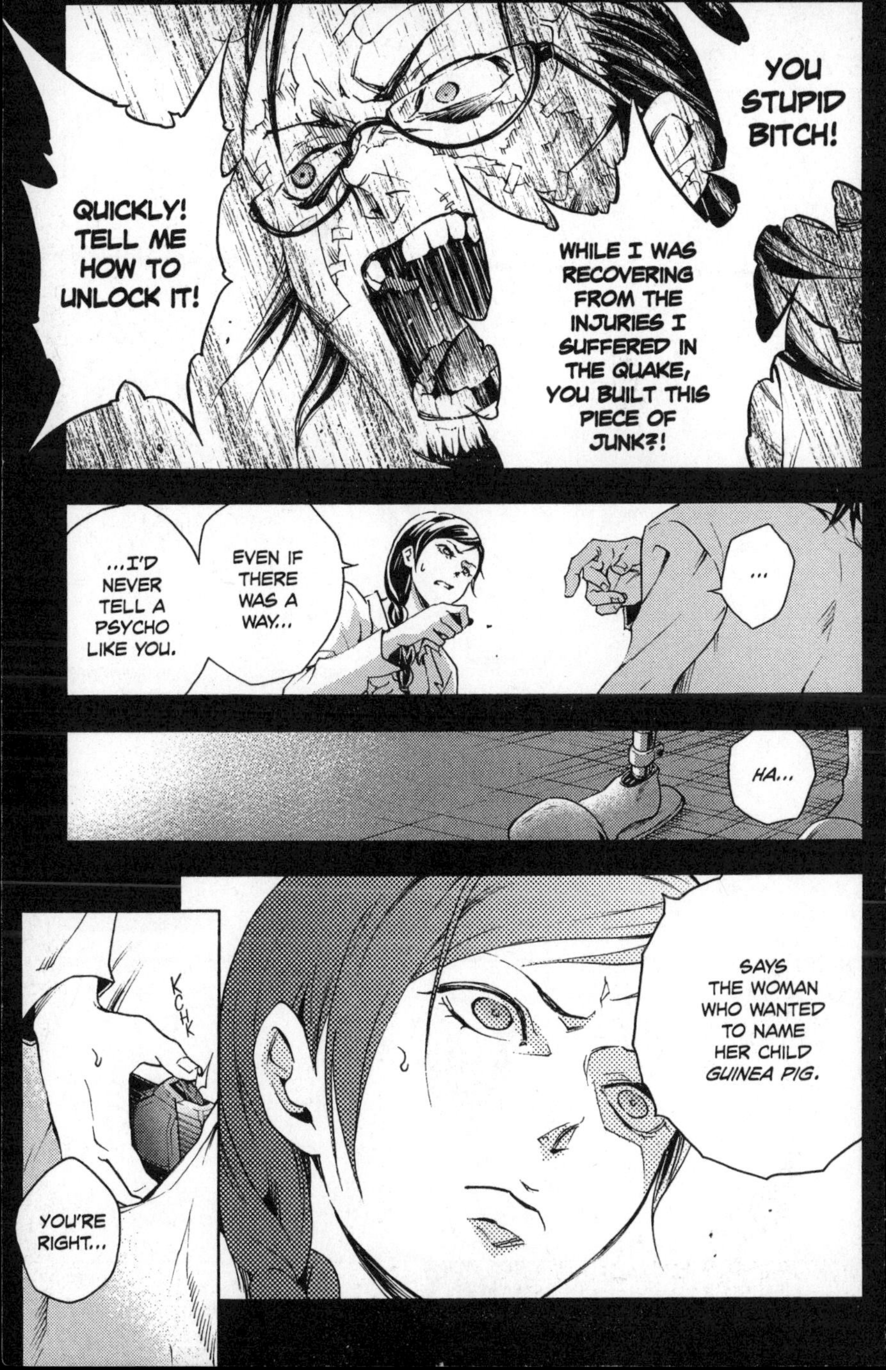
YOU STUPID BITCH!
WHILE I WAS RECOVERING FROM THE INJURIES I SUFFERED IN THE QUAKE, YOU BUILT THIS PIECE OF JUNK?!
QUICKLY! TELL ME HOW TO UNLOCK IT!
...
EVEN IF THERE WAS A WAY...
...I'D NEVER TELL A PSYCHO LIKE YOU.
HA...
SAYS THE WOMAN WHO WANTED TO NAME HER CHILD *GUINEA PIG*.
KCHK
YOU'RE RIGHT...

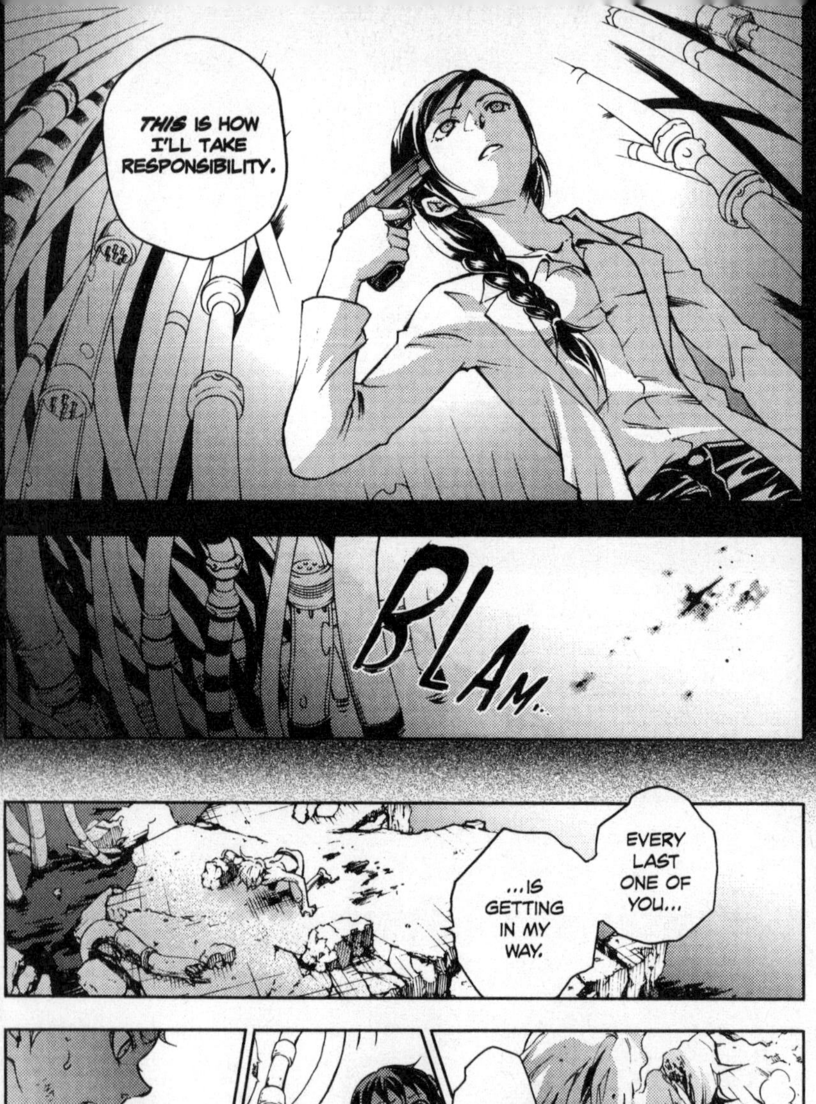
THIS IS HOW I'LL TAKE RESPONSIBILITY.
BLAM..
EVERY LAST ONE OF YOU...
...IS GETTING IN MY WAY.
SNIFF
WHY?
W...
WHY?!

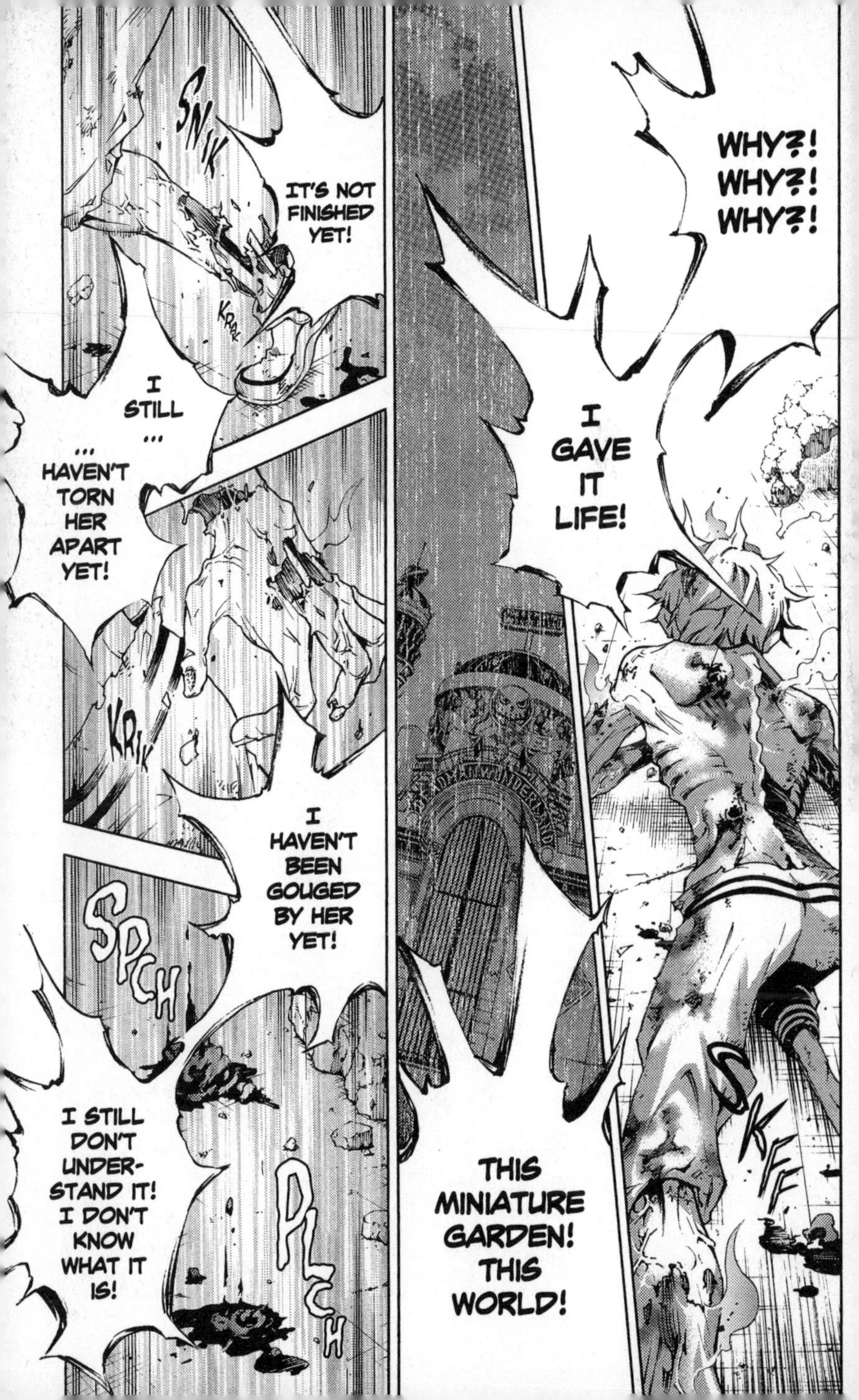
WHY?! WHY?! WHY?!
I GAVE IT LIFE!
THIS MINIATURE GARDEN! THIS WORLD!
SKFF
SNIK
IT'S NOT FINISHED YET!
KRAK
I STILL ...
... HAVEN'T TORN HER APART YET!
KRIK
I HAVEN'T BEEN GOUGED BY HER YET!
SPCH
I STILL DON'T UNDER-STAND IT! I DON'T KNOW WHAT IT IS!
PLCH

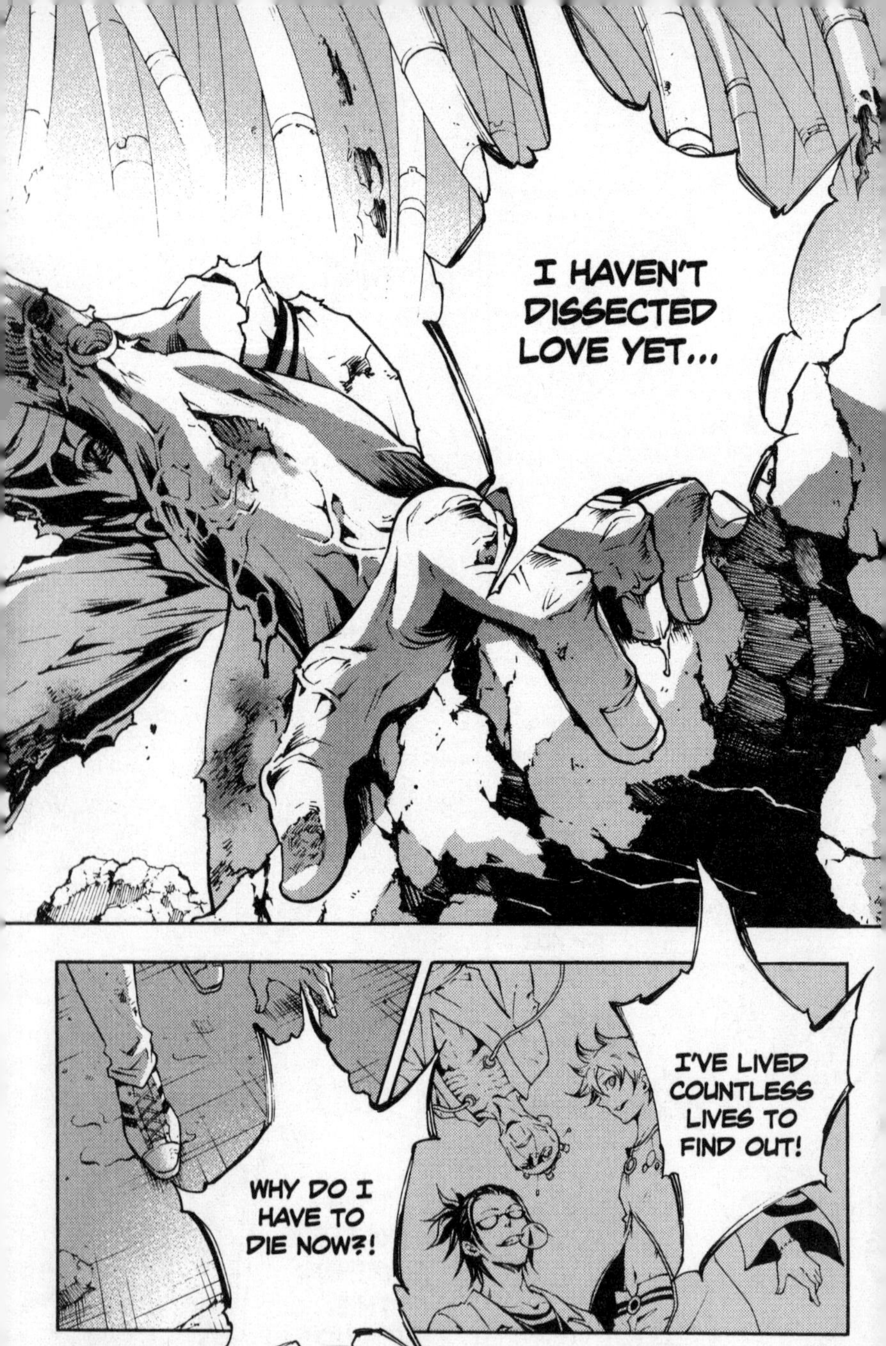
I HAVEN'T DISSECTED LOVE YET...
I'VE LIVED COUNTLESS LIVES TO FIND OUT!
WHY DO I HAVE TO DIE NOW?!

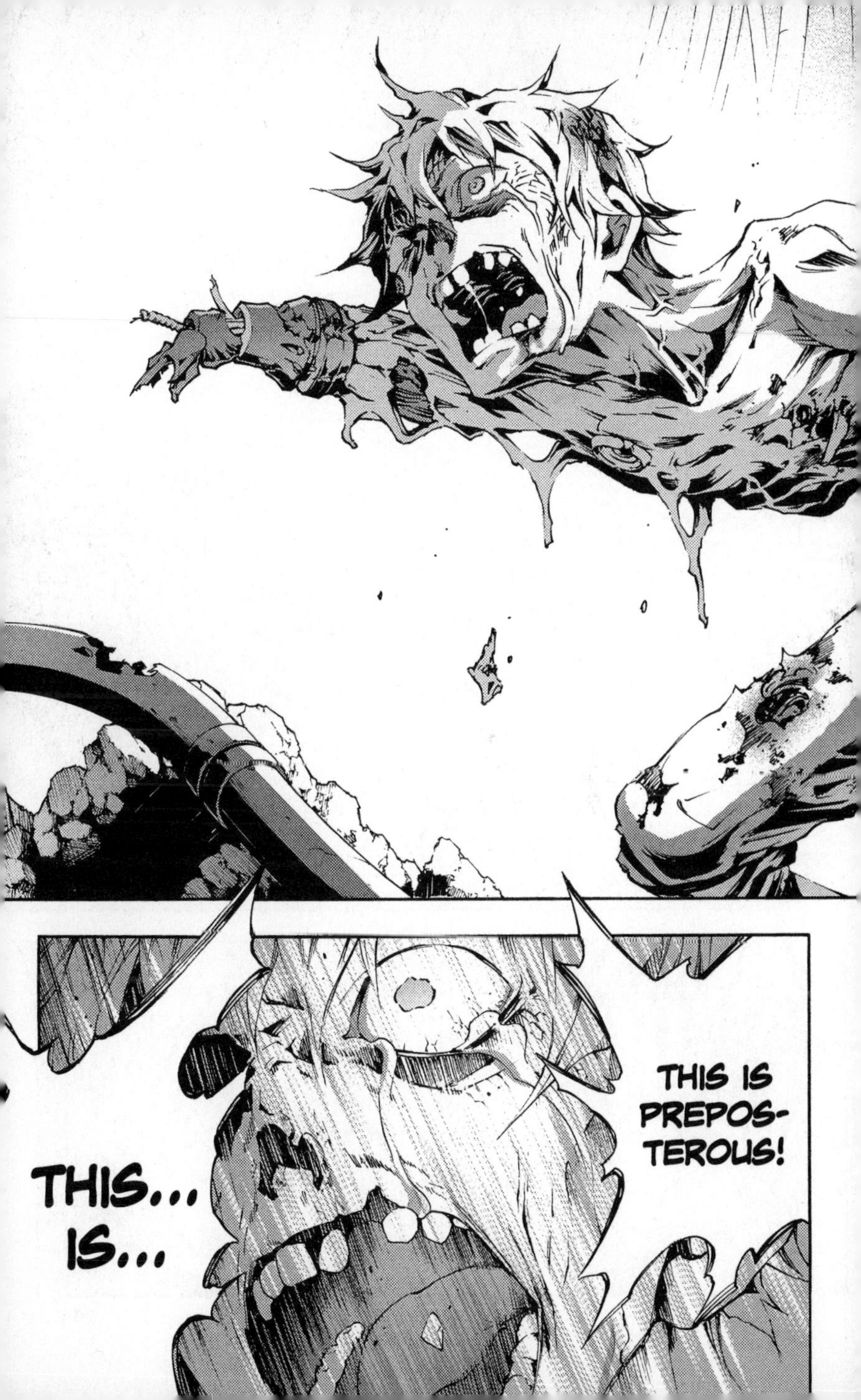
THIS IS PREPOS-TEROUS!
THIS... IS...

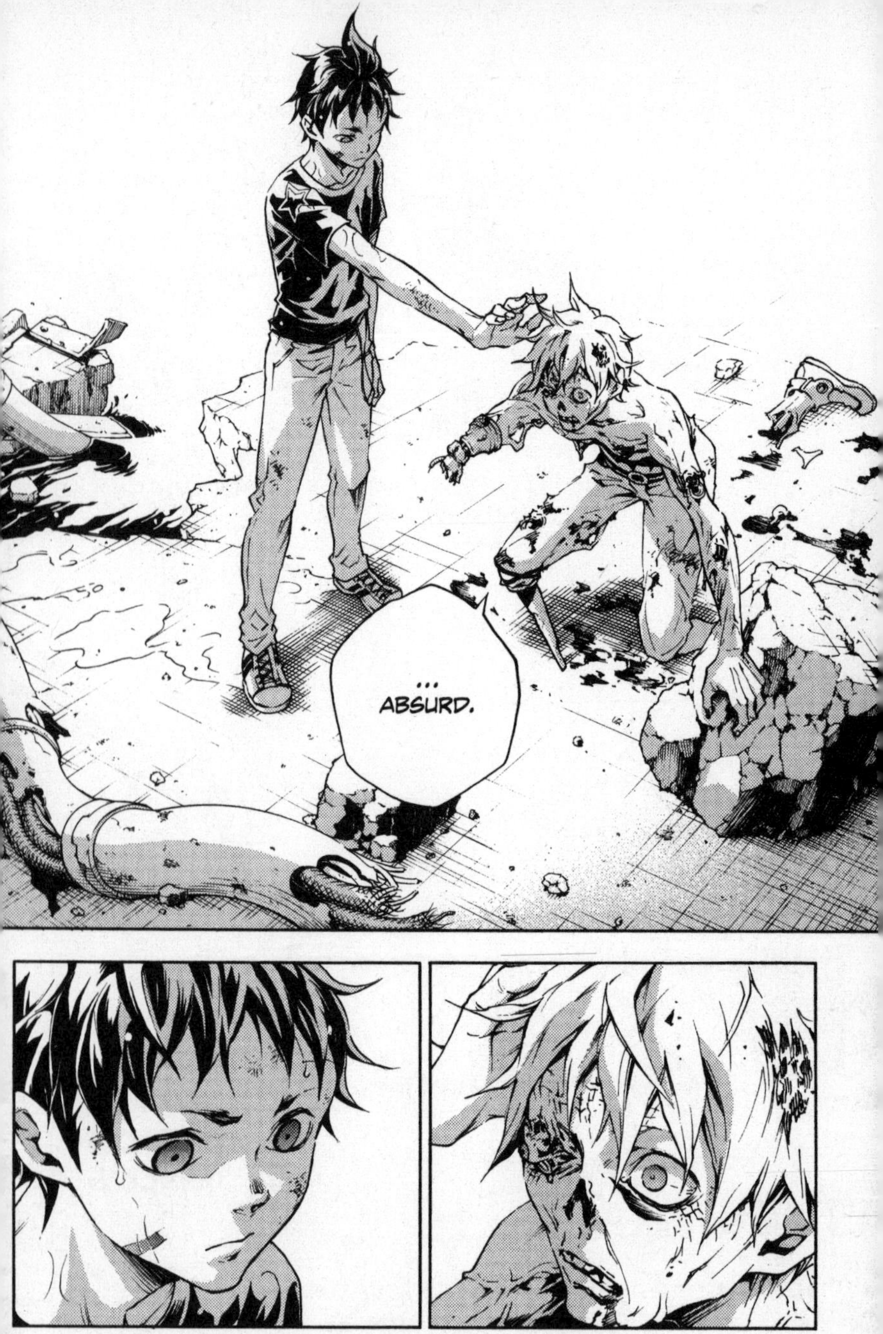
... ABSURD.

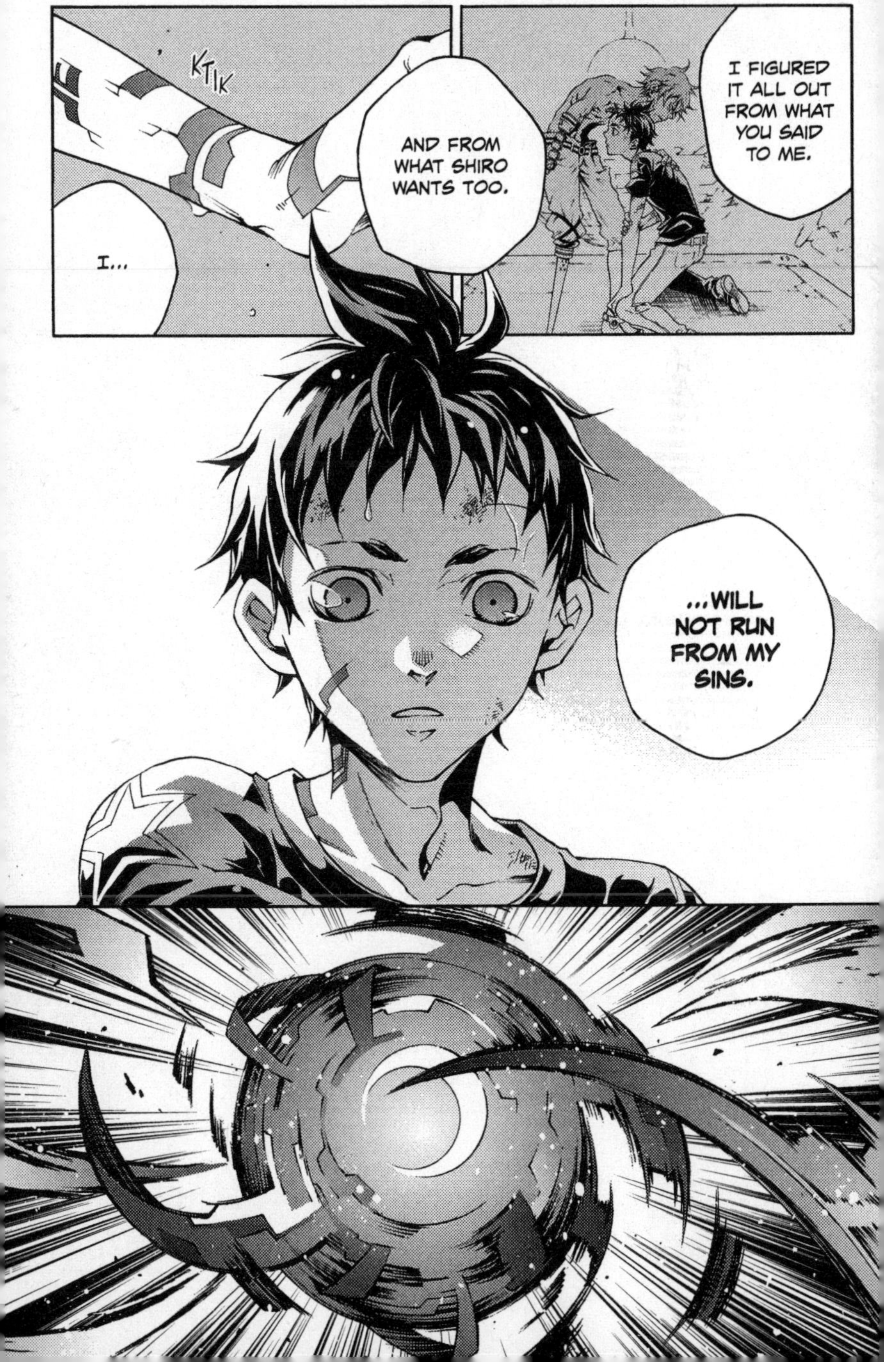
I FIGURED IT ALL OUT FROM WHAT YOU SAID TO ME.
AND FROM WHAT SHIRO WANTS TOO.
KTIK
I...
...WILL NOT RUN FROM MY SINS.

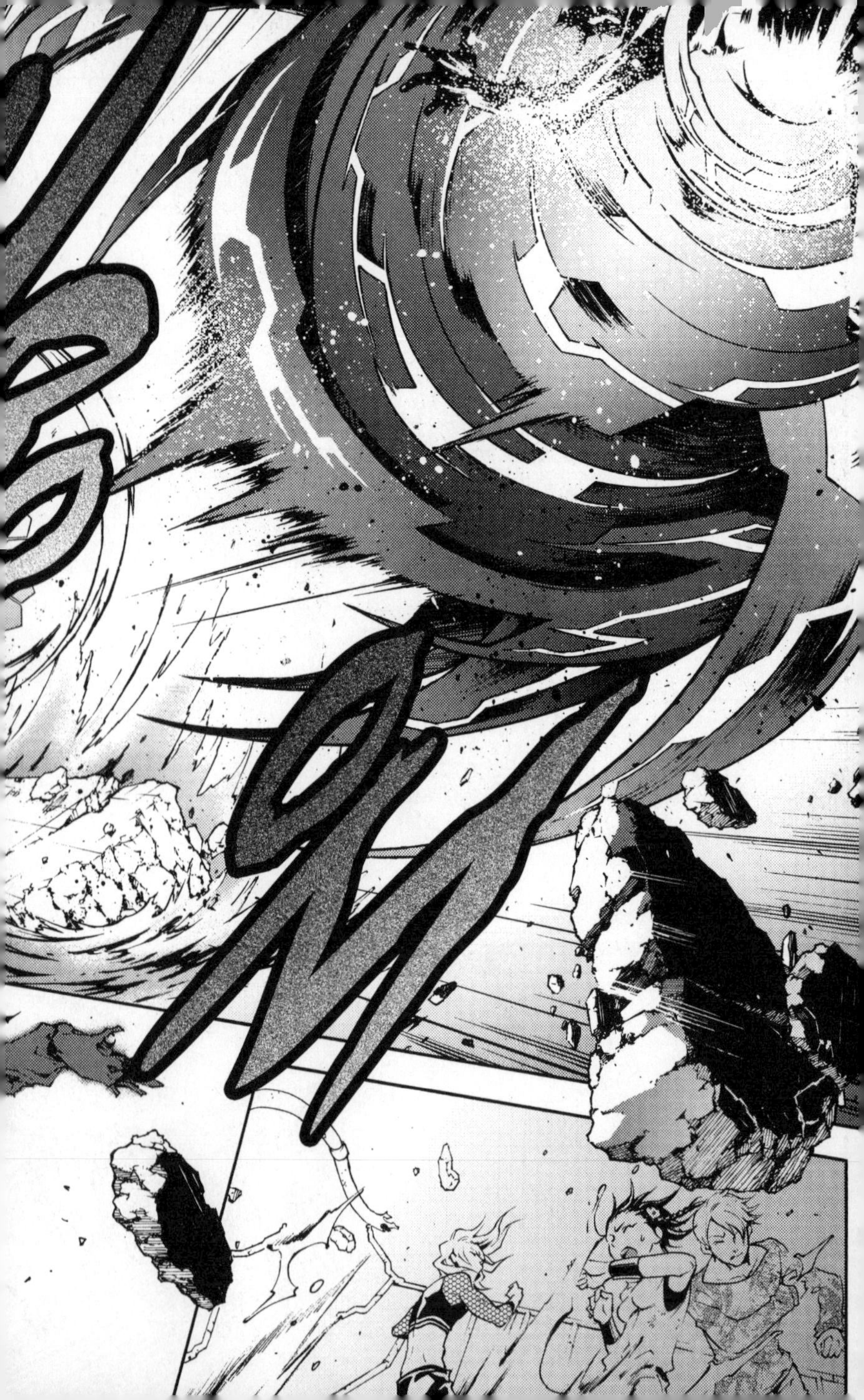

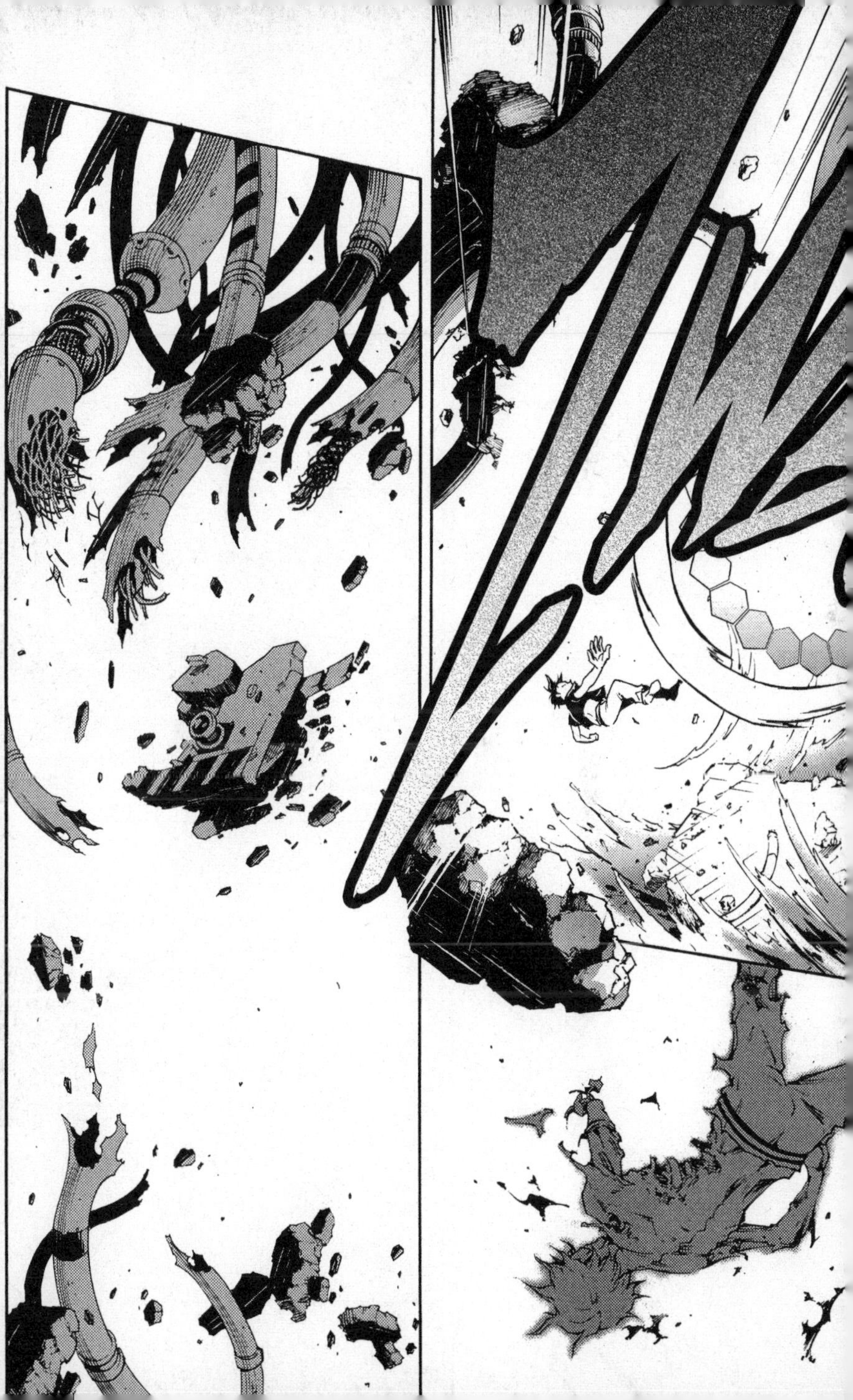

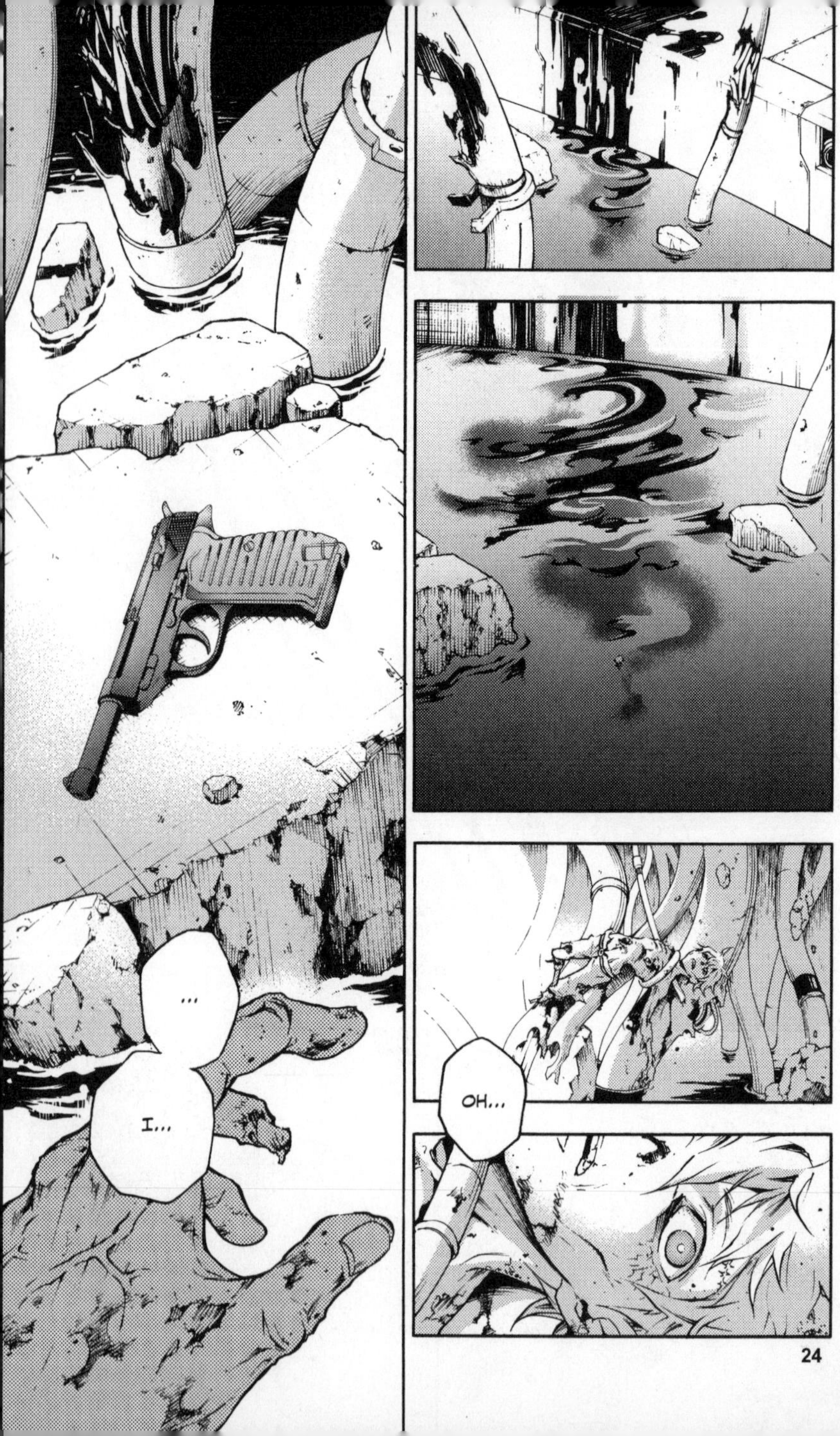
OH...
...
I...

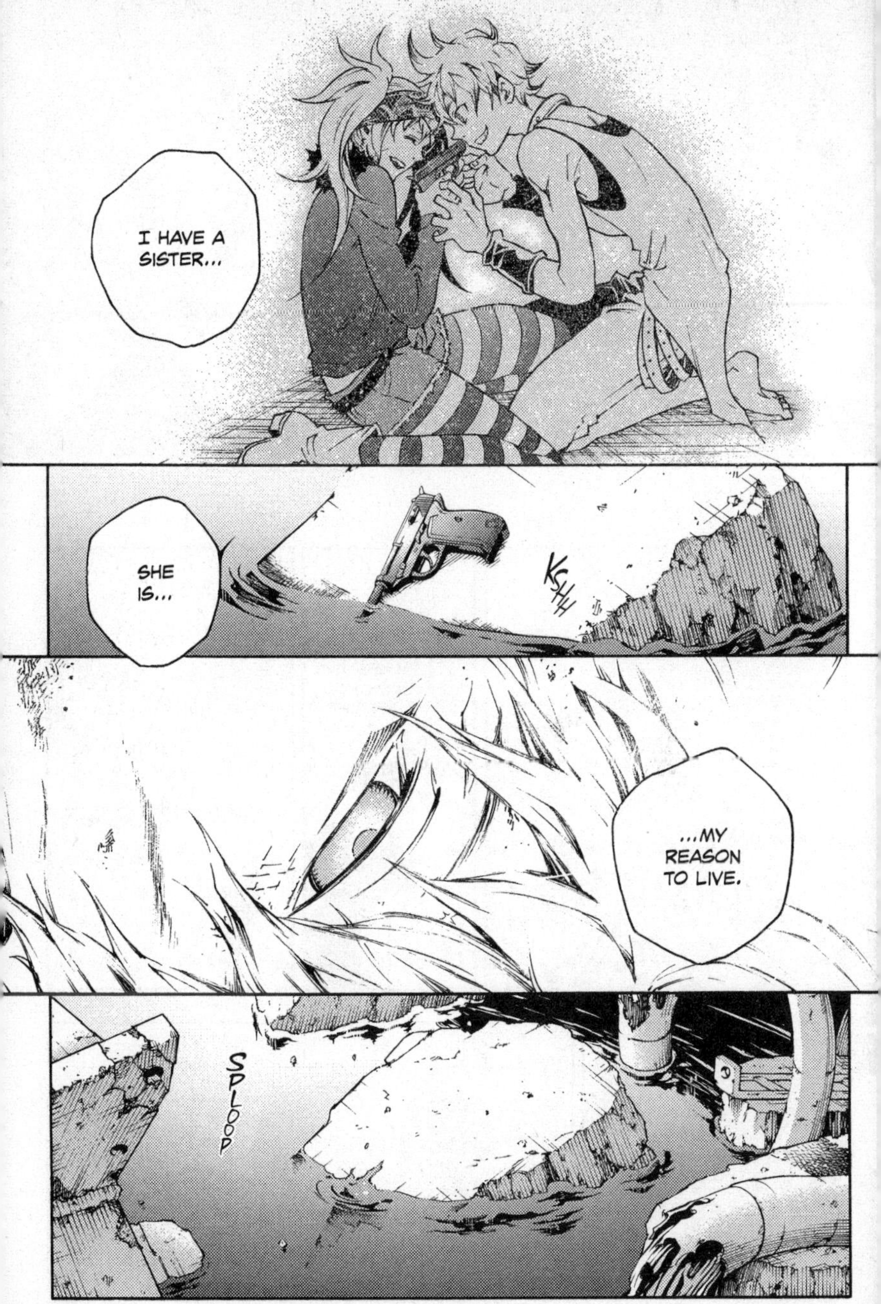
I HAVE A SISTER...
SHE IS...
KSHH
...MY REASON TO LIVE.
SPLOOP

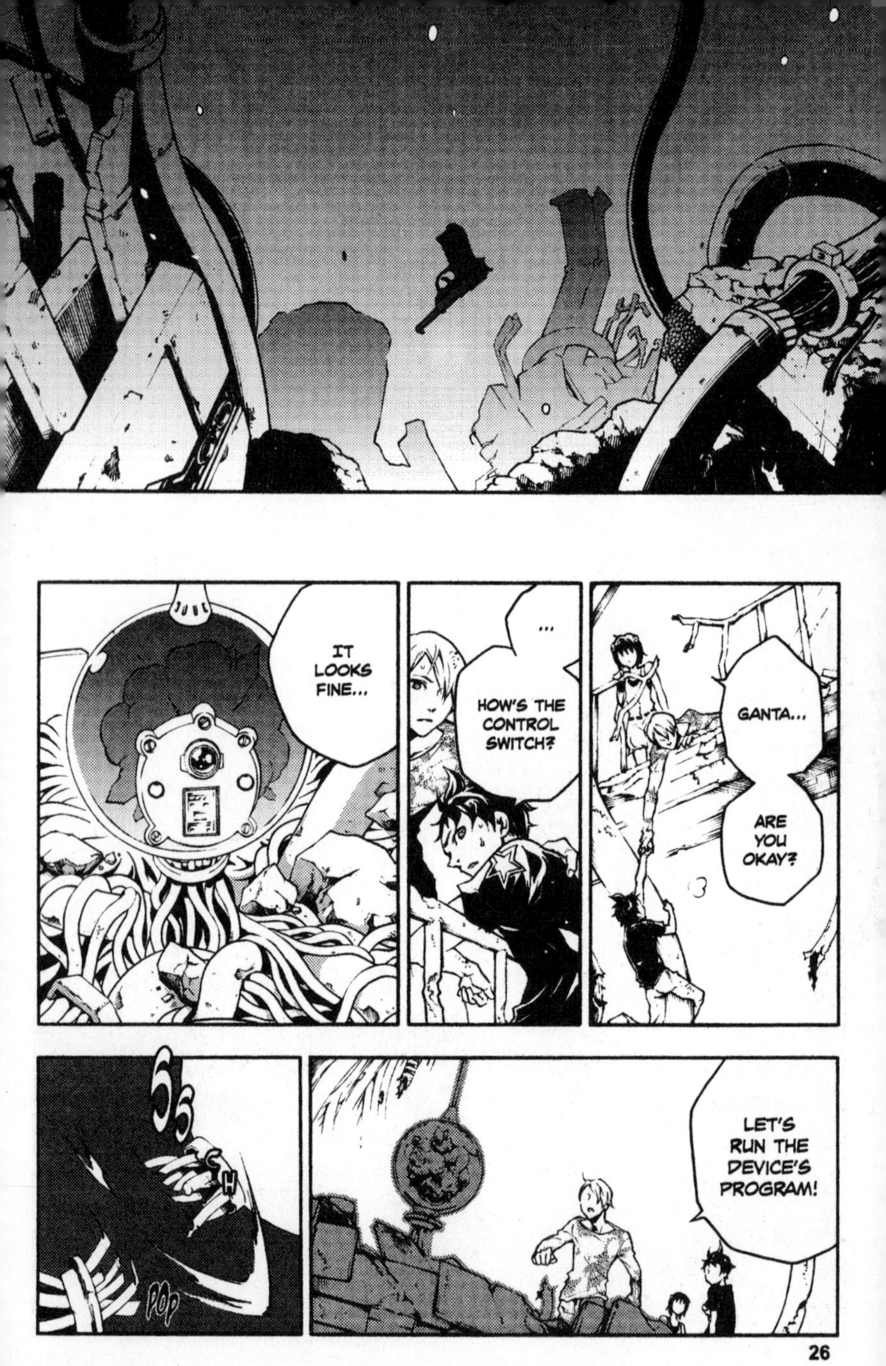
GANTA...
ARE YOU OKAY?
...
HOW'S THE CONTROL SWITCH?
IT LOOKS FINE...
LET'S RUN THE DEVICE'S PROGRAM!
POP

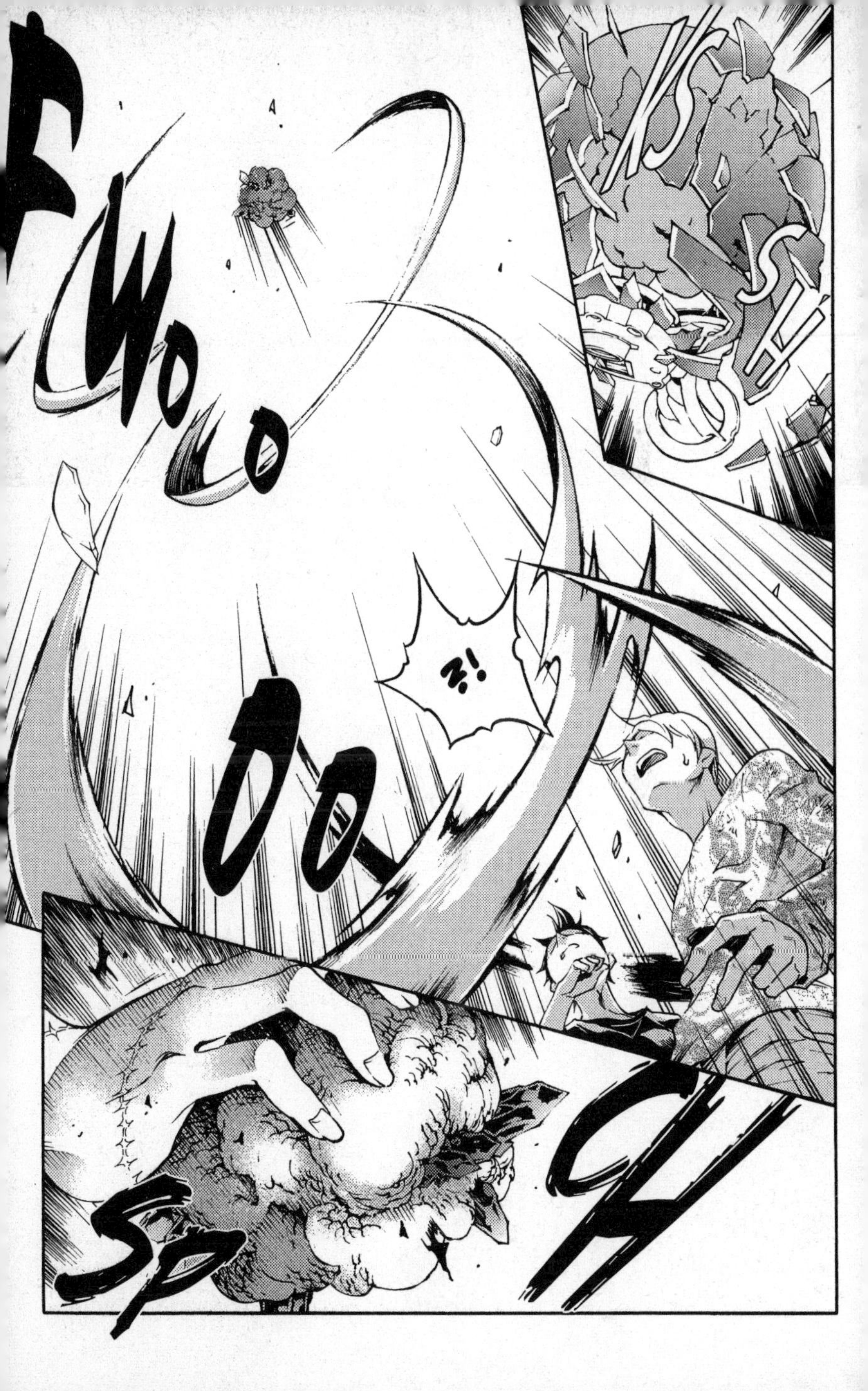
KSSH
?!

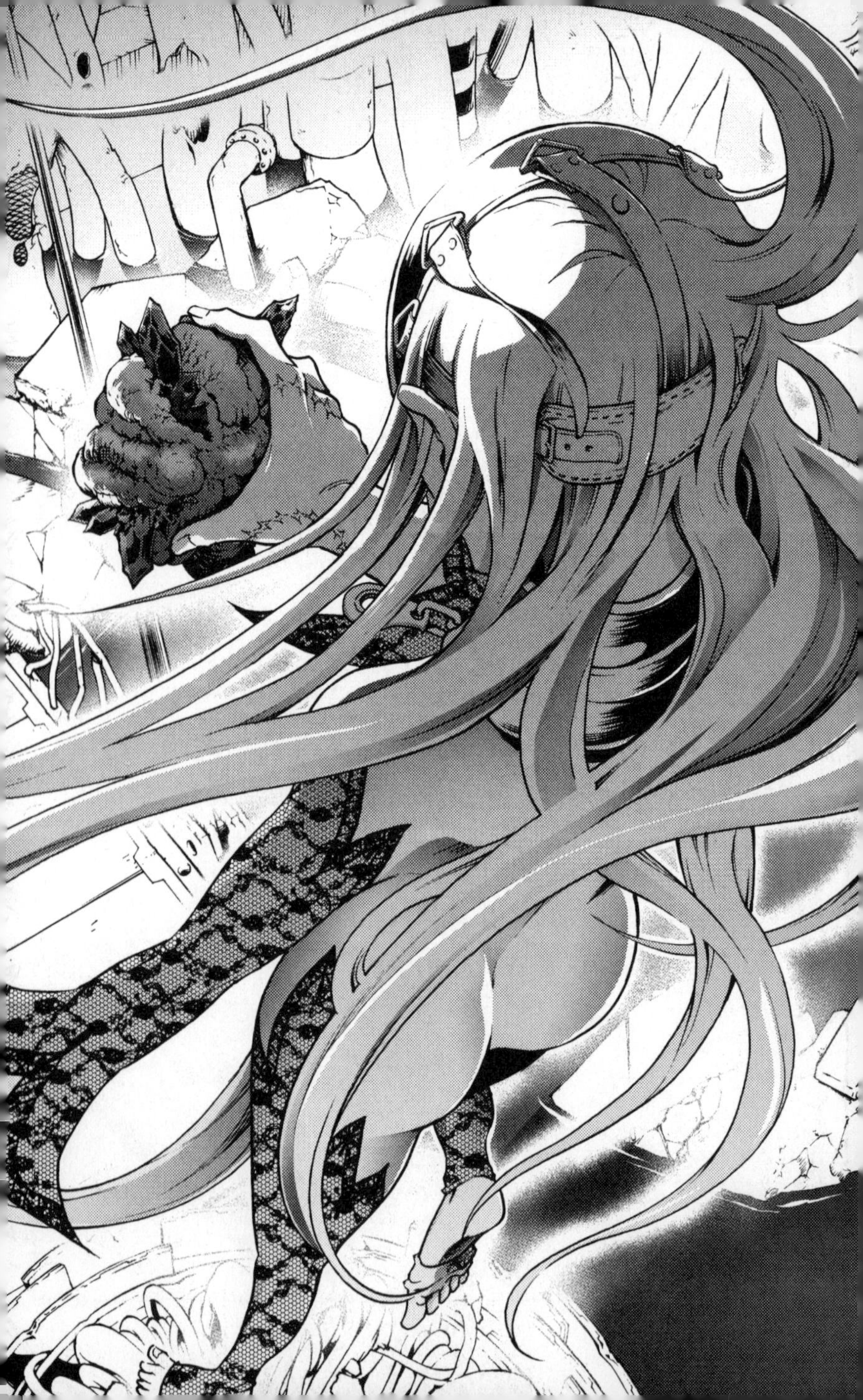

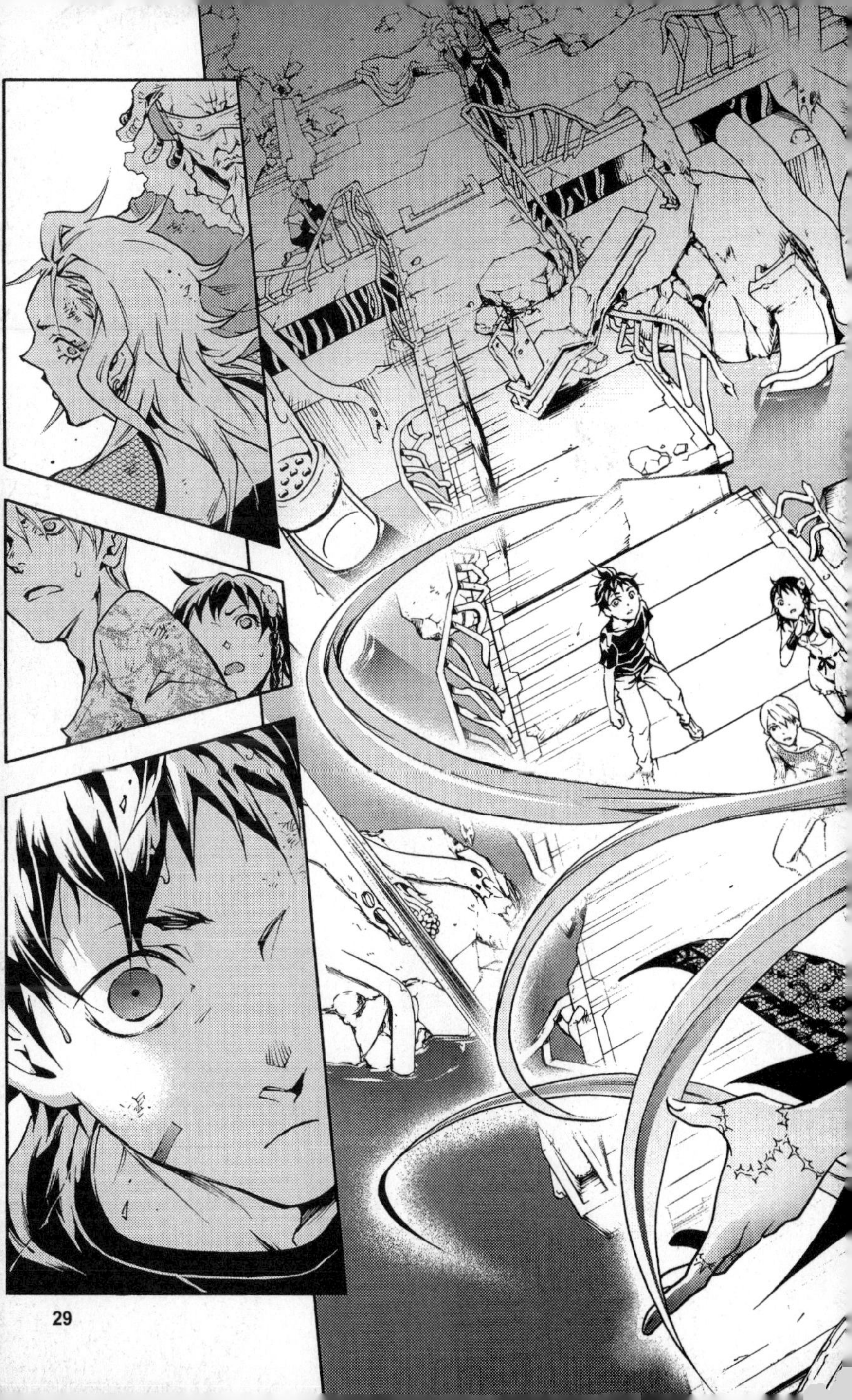

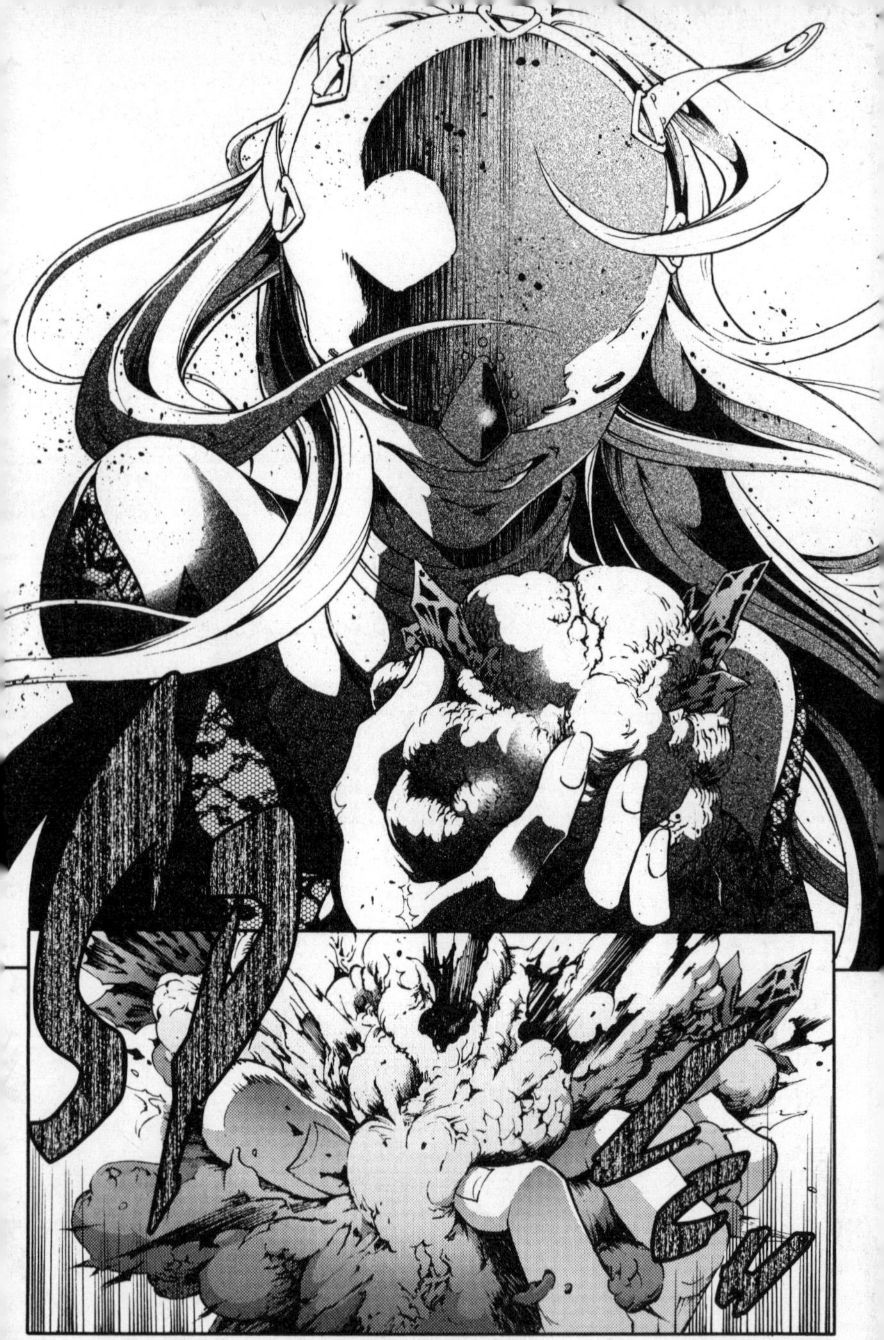

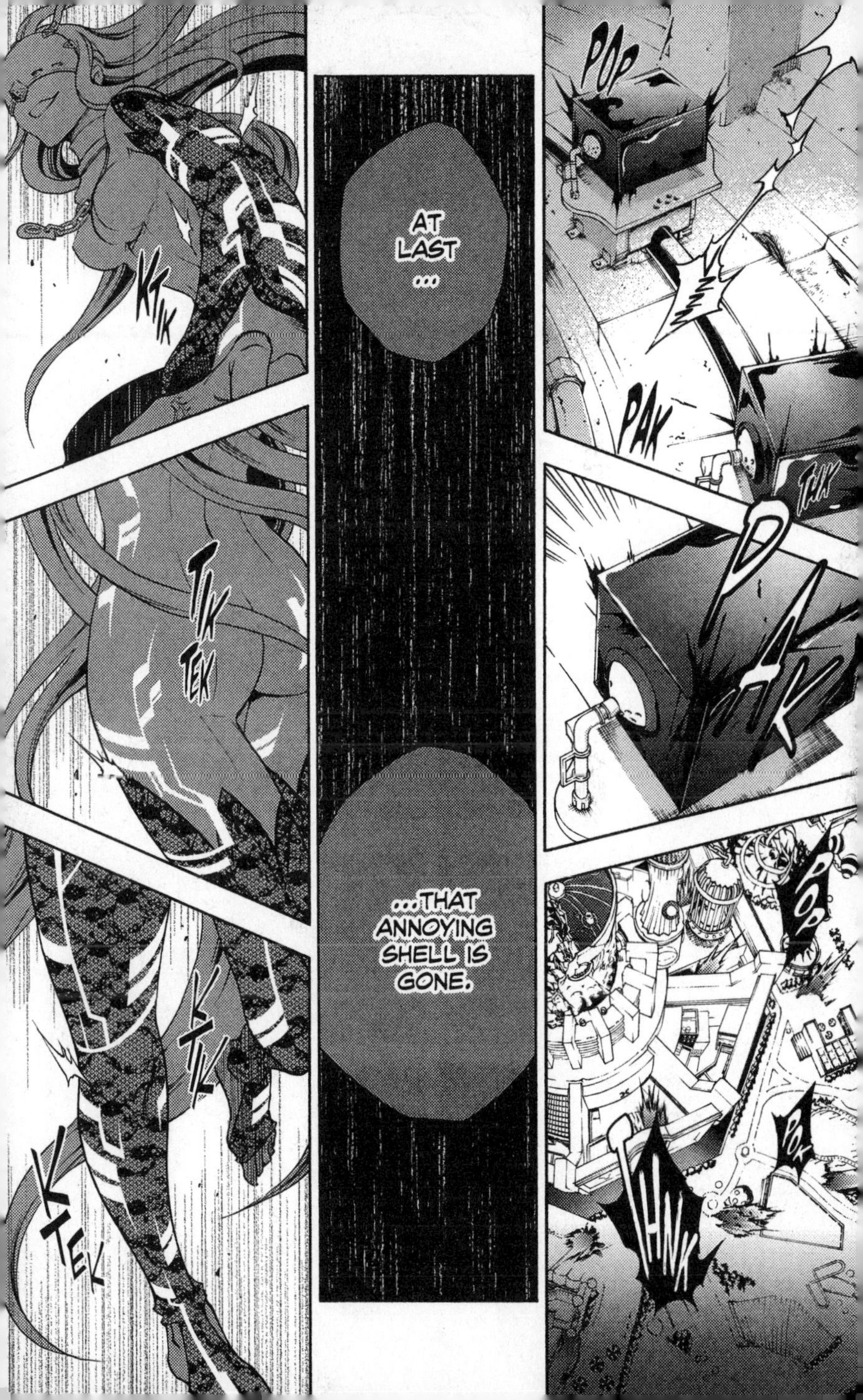
POP
PAK
TAK
PAK
POP
POK
THNK
AT LAST...
...THAT ANNOYING SHELL IS GONE.
KTIK
TIK TEK
KTIK
KTEK

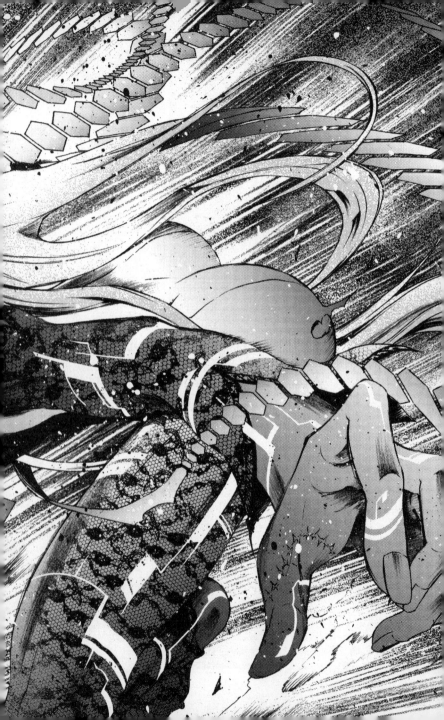

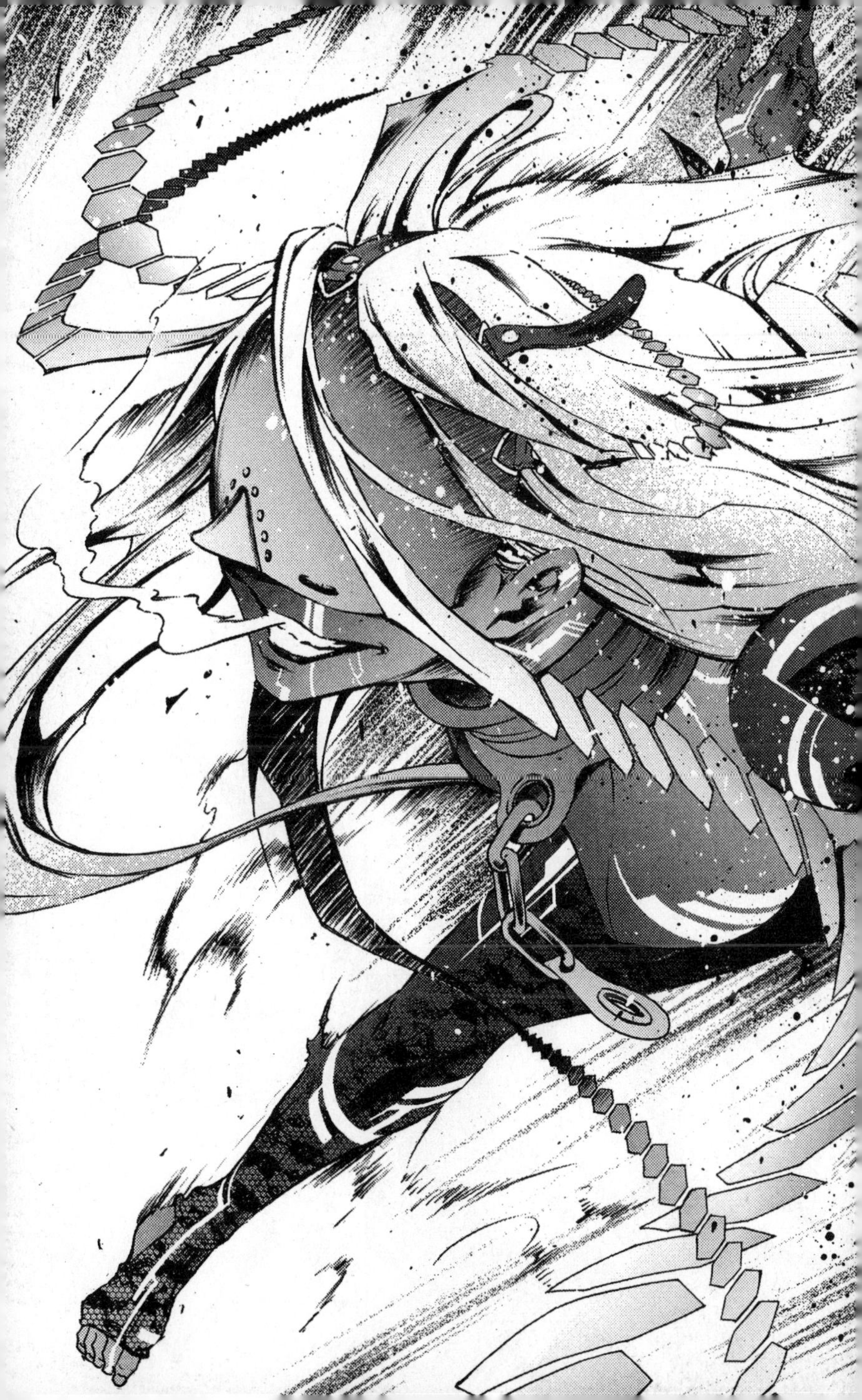

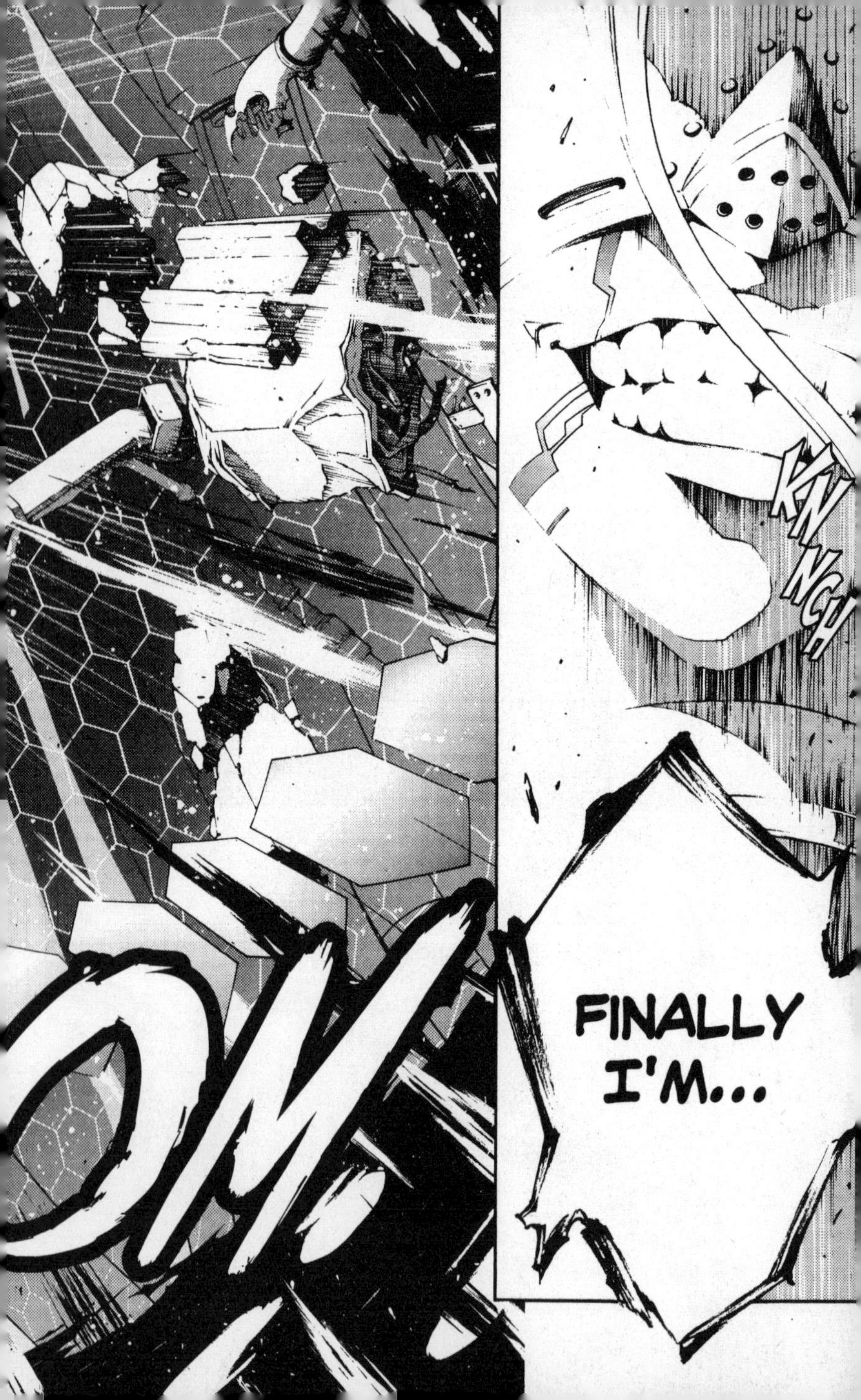
KNNCH
FINALLY I'M...

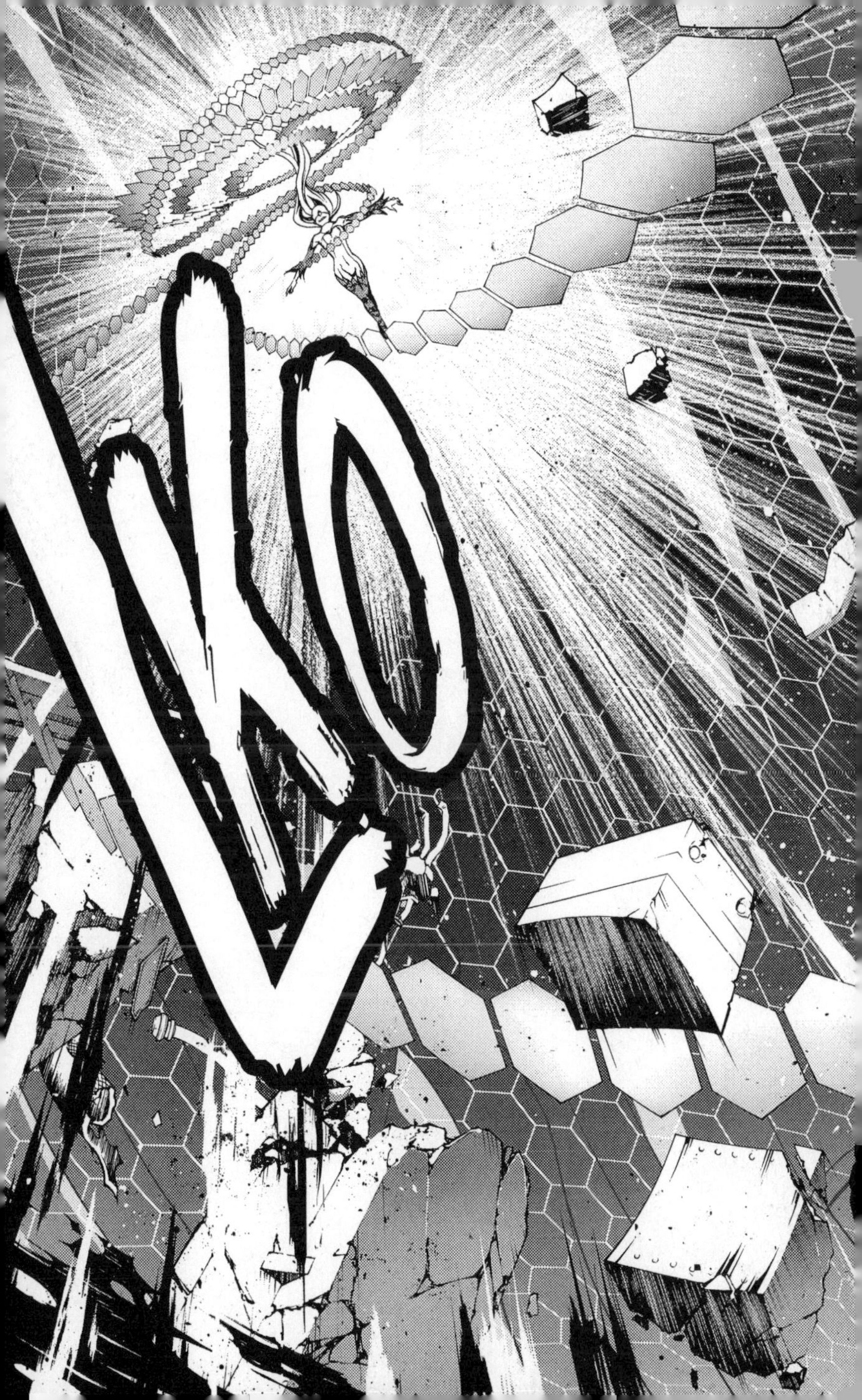
KO

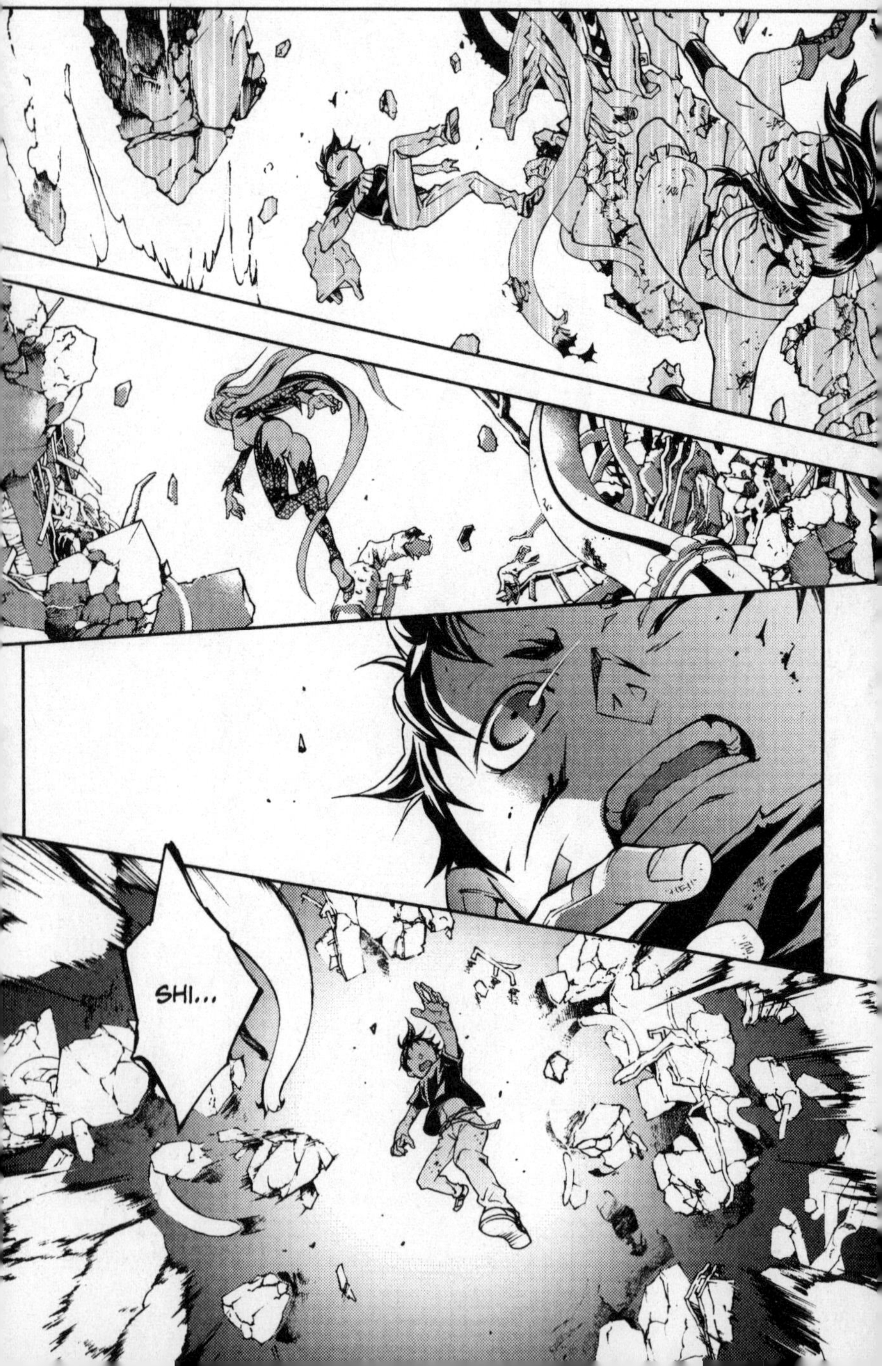
SHI...

BDOOOM

DOOM

DOOM

SHIROO-O!

WRETCHED EGG!

HER SEAL HAS BEEN REMOVED!

DREE

DREE

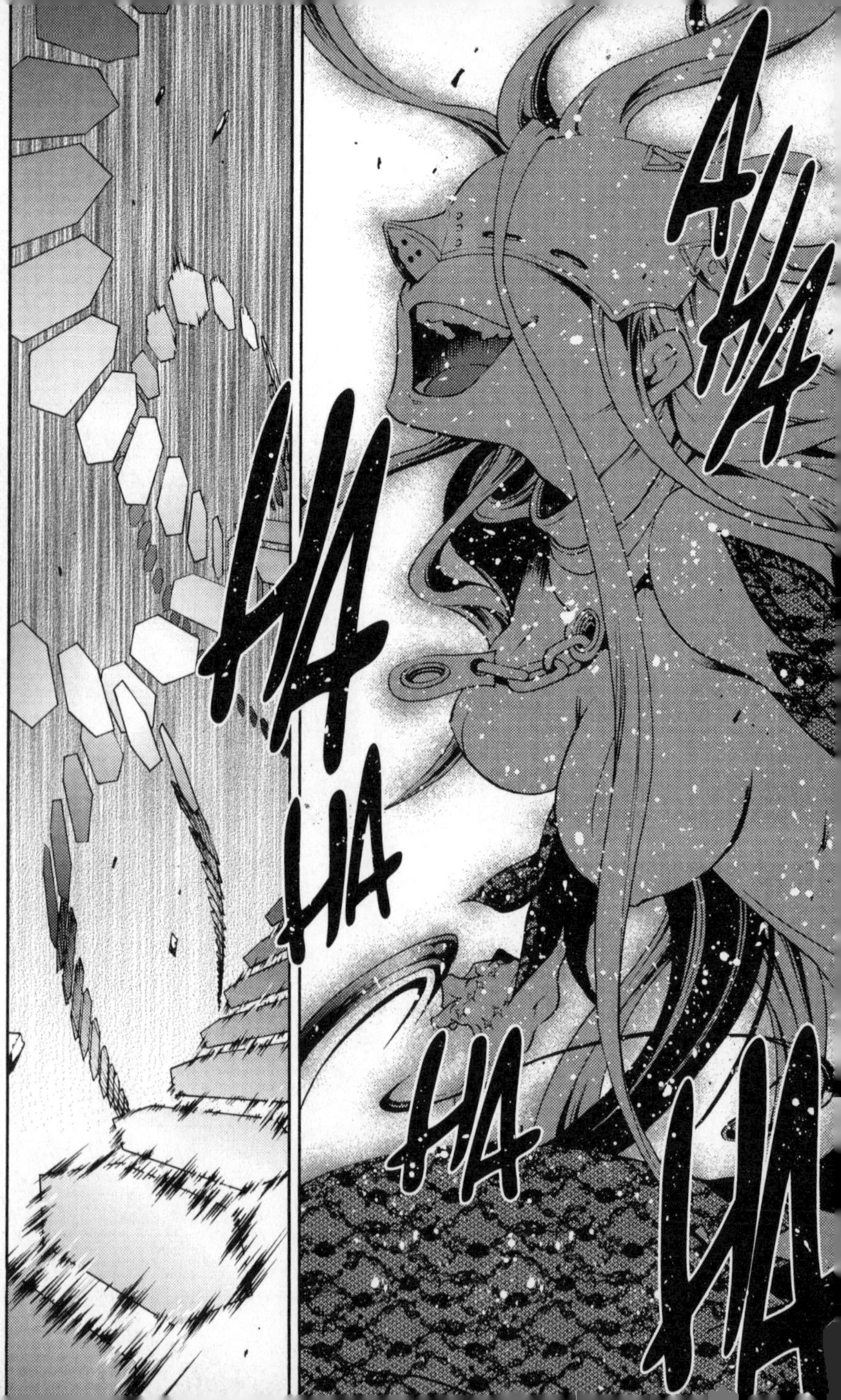
AHAHA
HA
HA
HA
HAHA

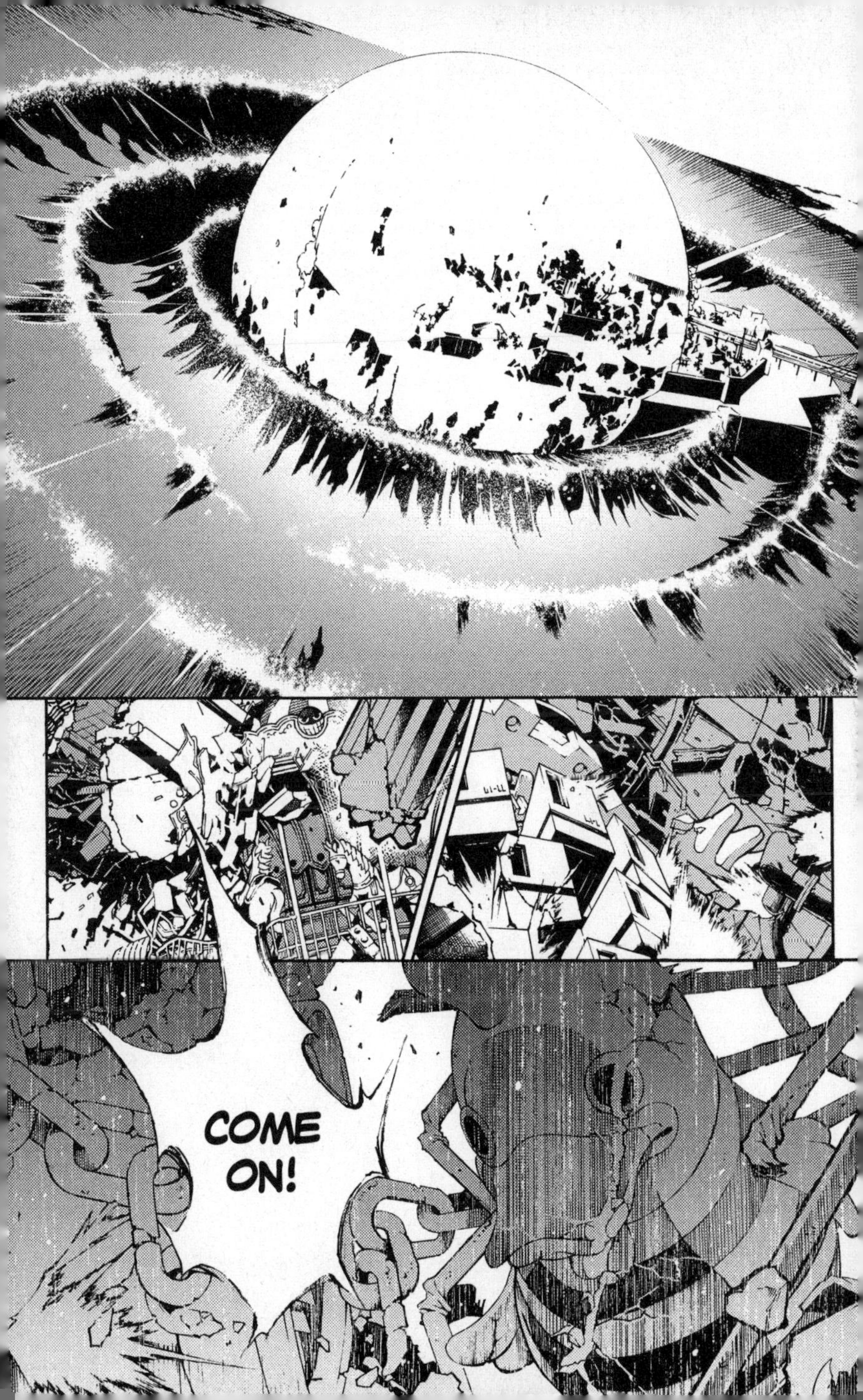
COME ON!

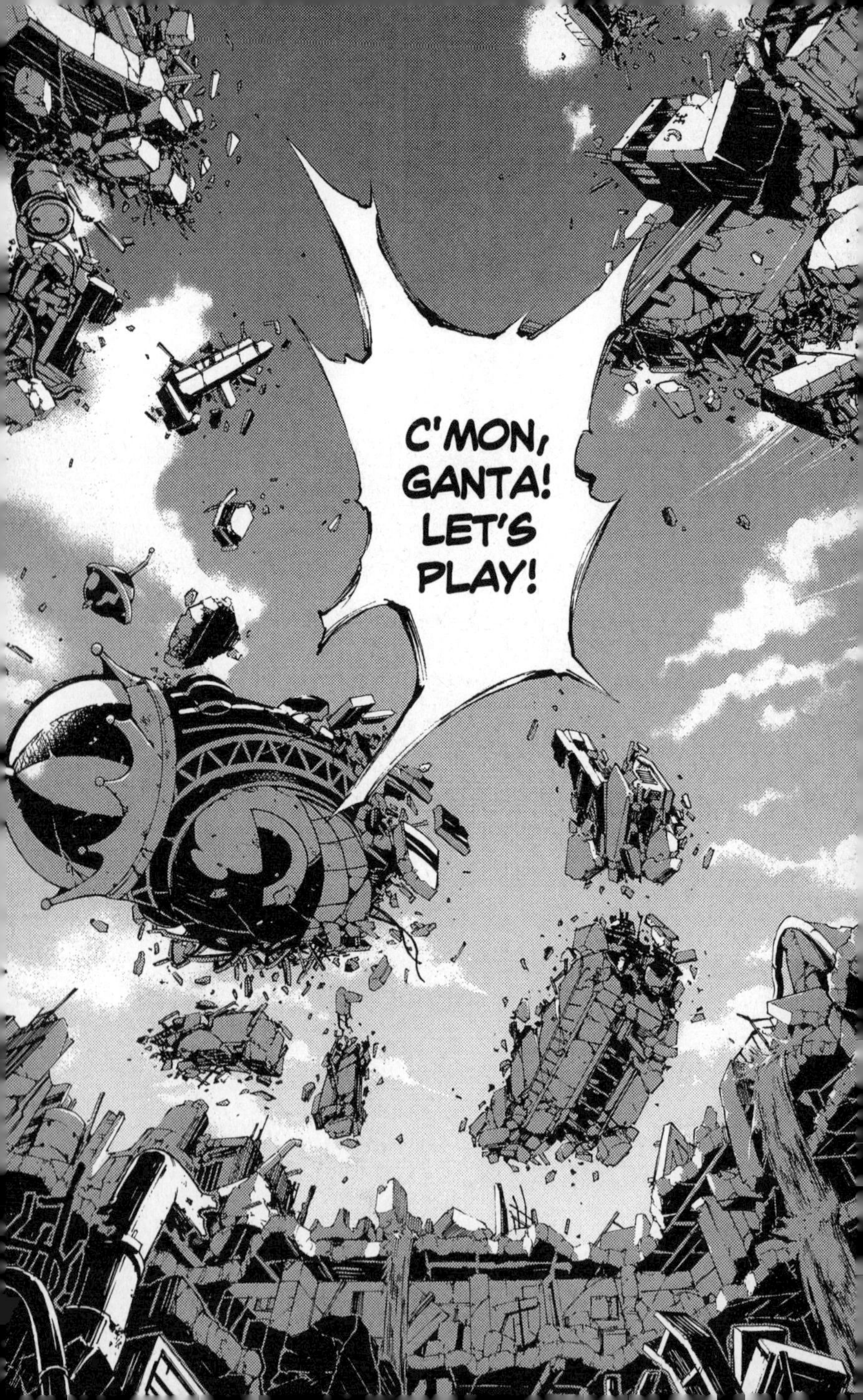
C'MON, GANTA! LET'S PLAY!

DEADMAN
WONDER
LAND

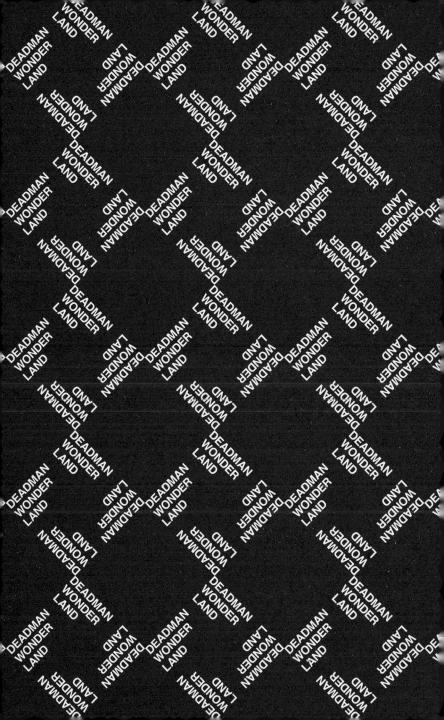

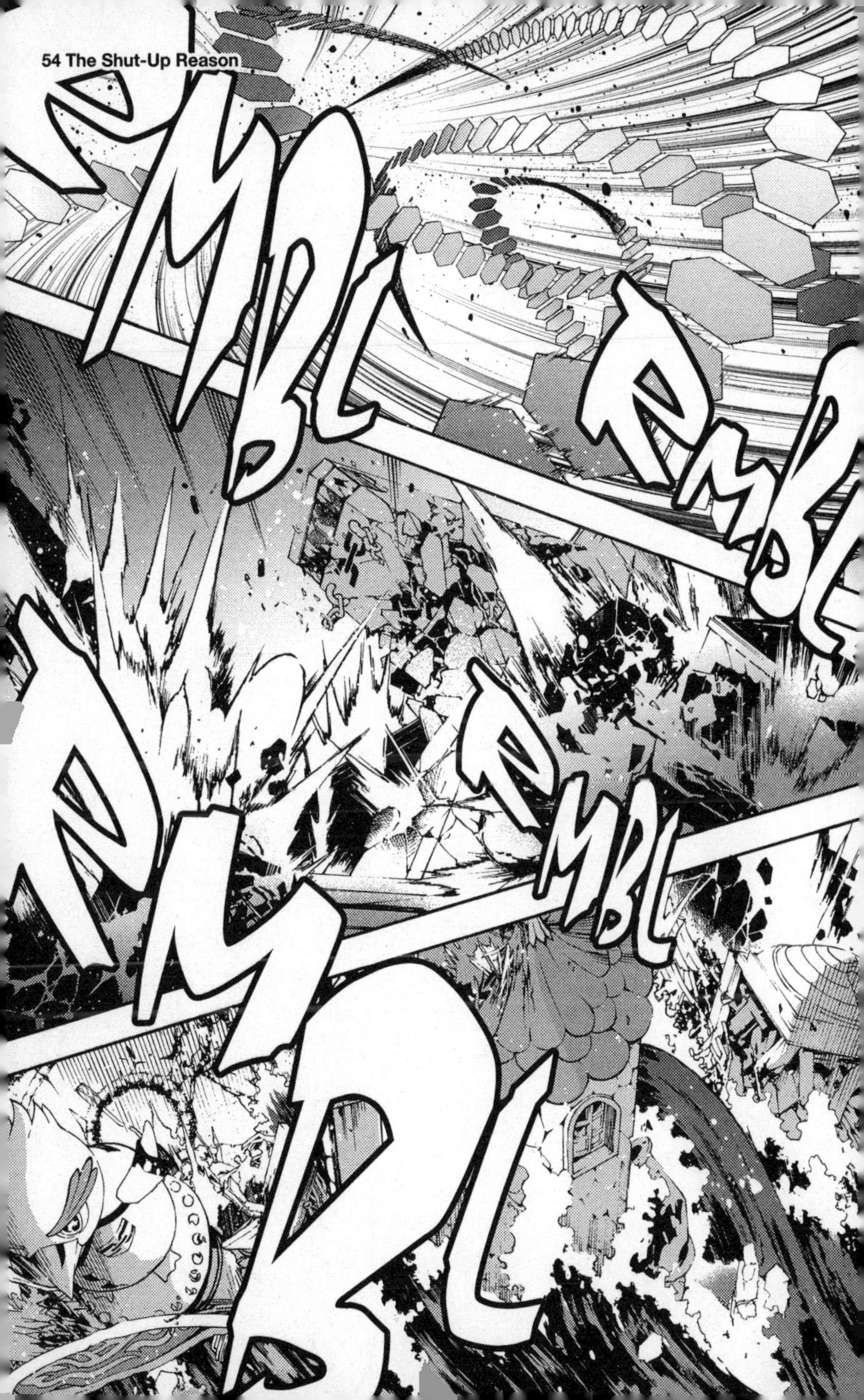

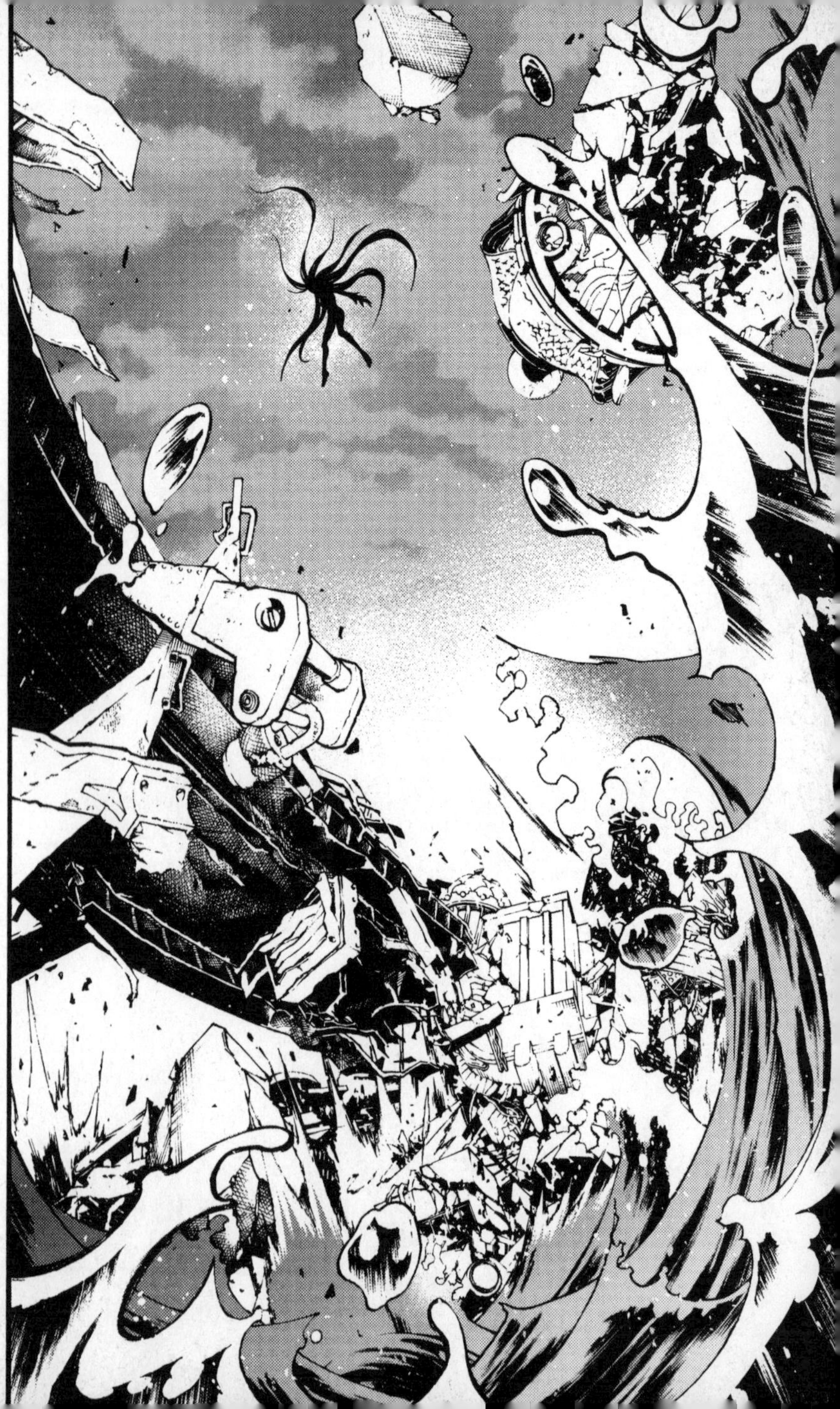

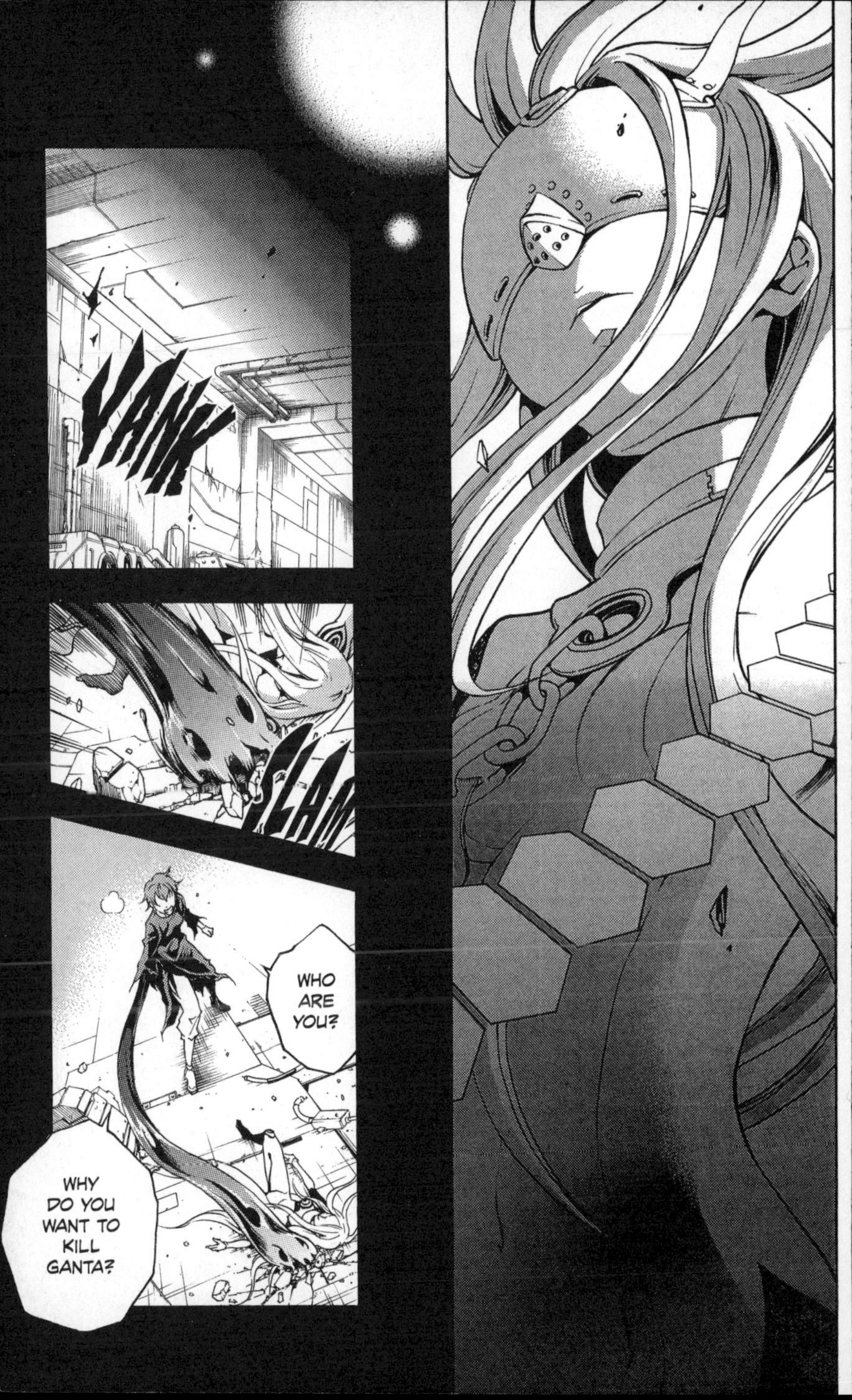
YANK
SLAM
WHO ARE YOU?
WHY DO YOU WANT TO KILL GANTA?

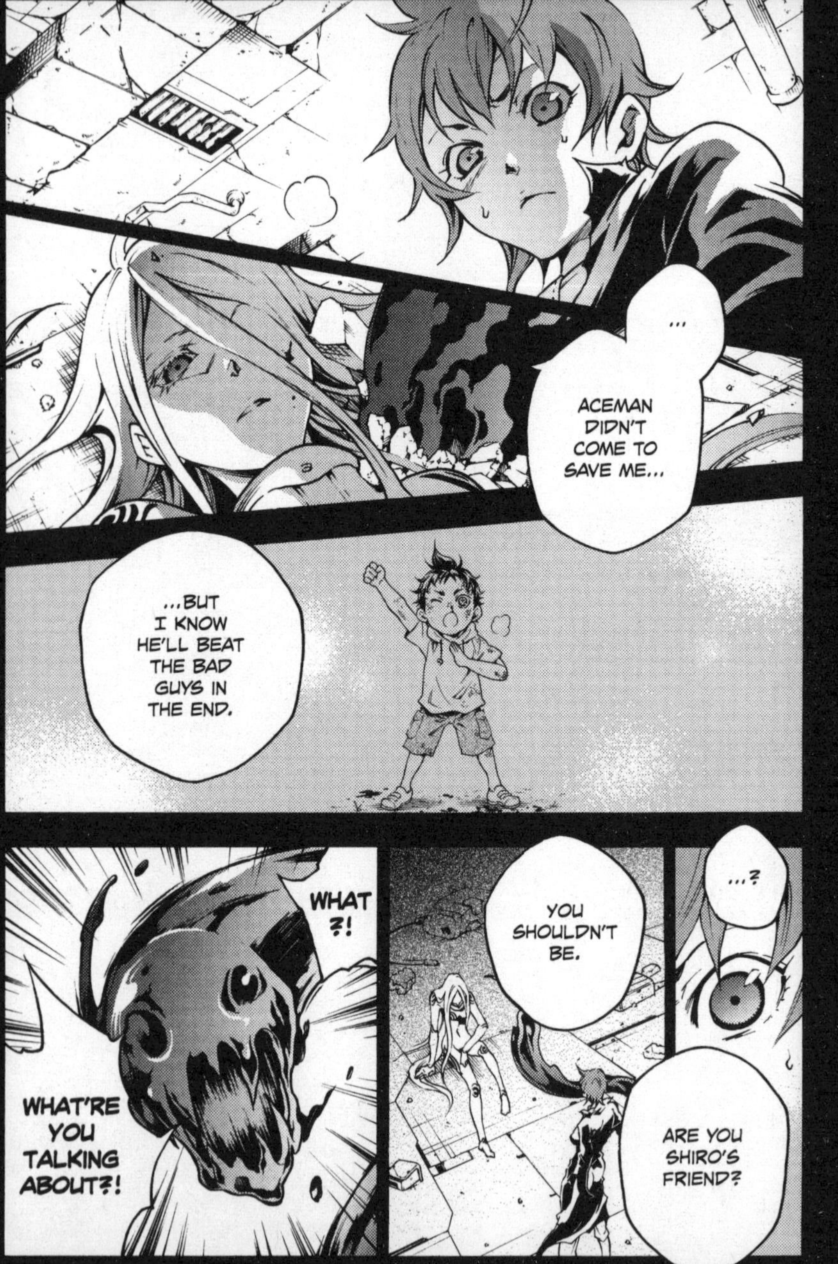
...
ACEMAN DIDN'T COME TO SAVE ME...
...BUT I KNOW HE'LL BEAT THE BAD GUYS IN THE END.
...?
ARE YOU SHIRO'S FRIEND?
YOU SHOULDN'T BE.
WHAT?!
WHAT'RE YOU TALKING ABOUT?!

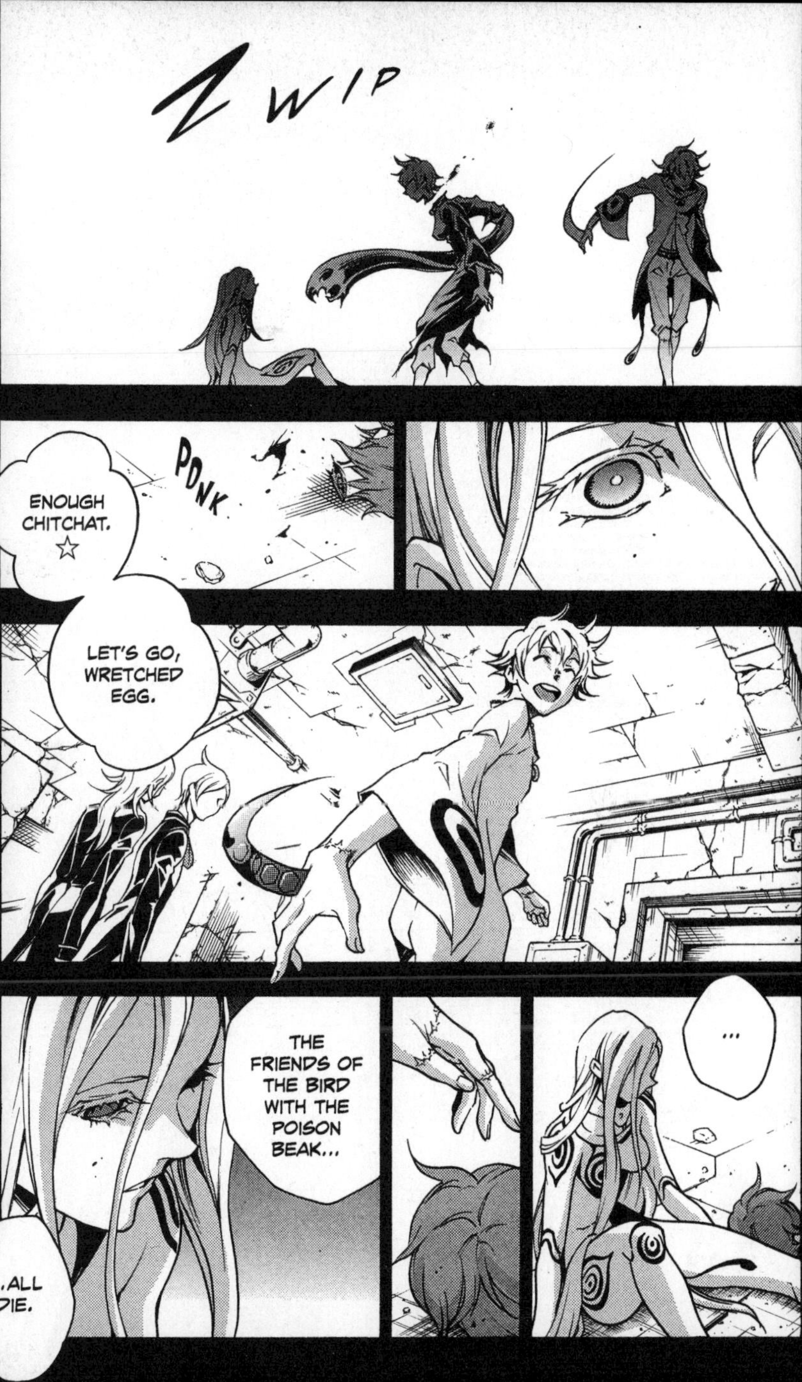
ZWIP
PONK
ENOUGH CHITCHAT. ☆
LET'S GO, WRETCHED EGG.
...
THE FRIENDS OF THE BIRD WITH THE POISON BEAK...
...ALL DIE.

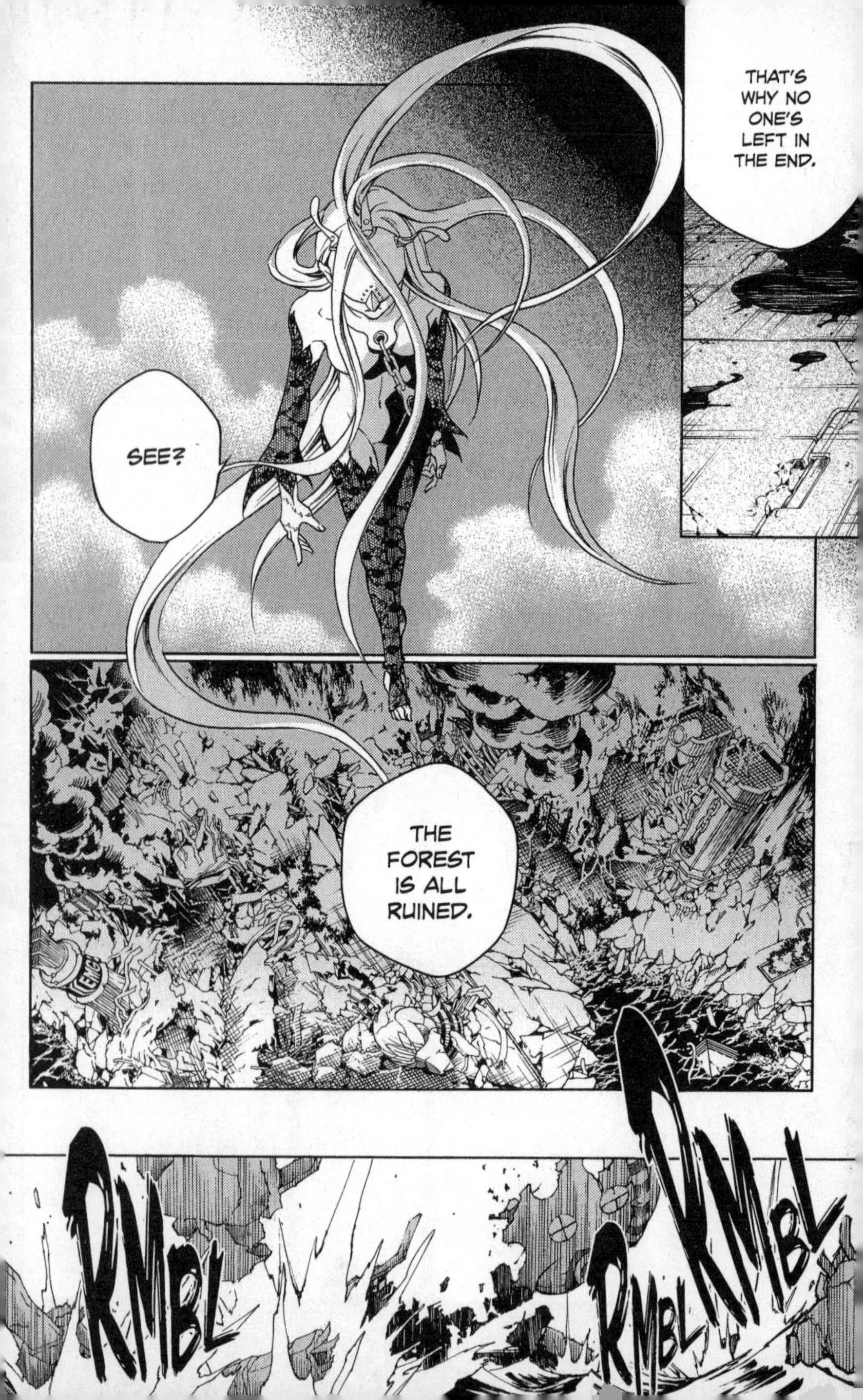
THAT'S WHY NO ONE'S LEFT IN THE END.
SEE?
THE FOREST IS ALL RUINED.
RMBL RMBL
RMBL
RMBL

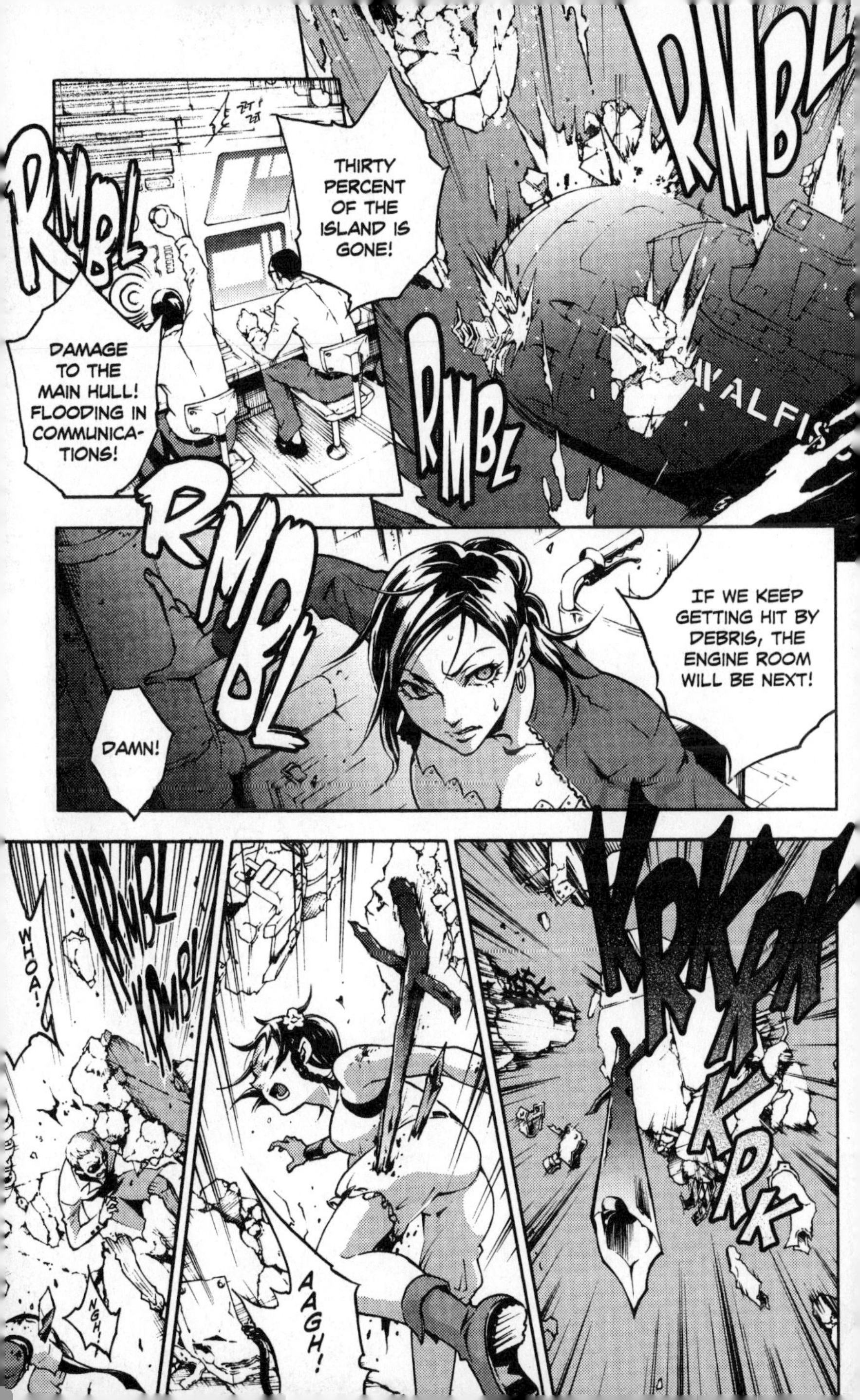

RMBL
THIRTY PERCENT OF THE ISLAND IS GONE!
RMBL
DAMAGE TO THE MAIN HULL! FLOODING IN COMMUNICA-TIONS!
RMBL
IF WE KEEP GETTING HIT BY DEBRIS, THE ENGINE ROOM WILL BE NEXT!
RMMBL
DAMN!
AAGH!
KRMBL
KRMBL
WHOA!
NGH!

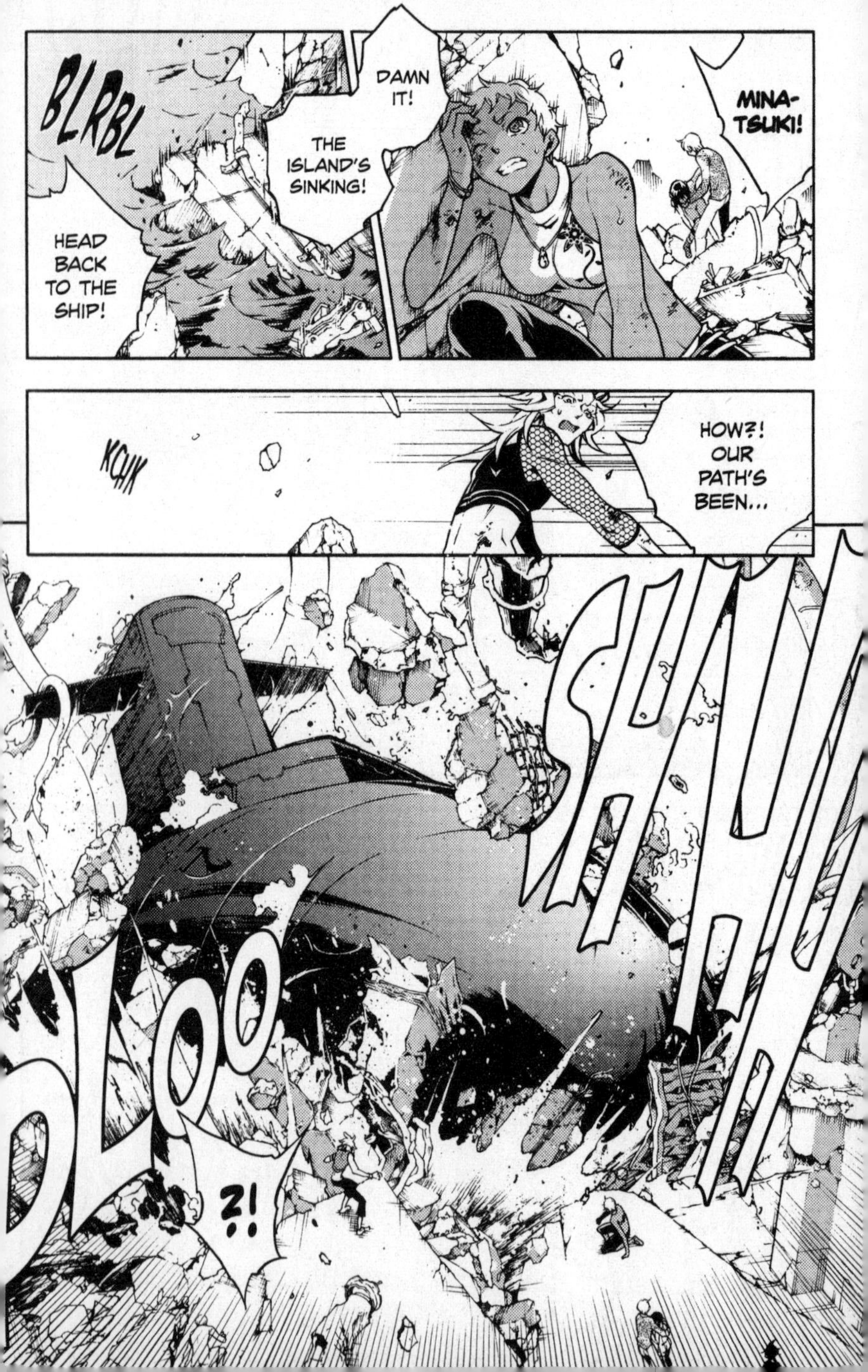
MINA-TSUKI!
DAMN IT!
THE ISLAND'S SINKING!
BLRBL
HEAD BACK TO THE SHIP!
HOW?! OUR PATH'S BEEN...
KCHK
?!

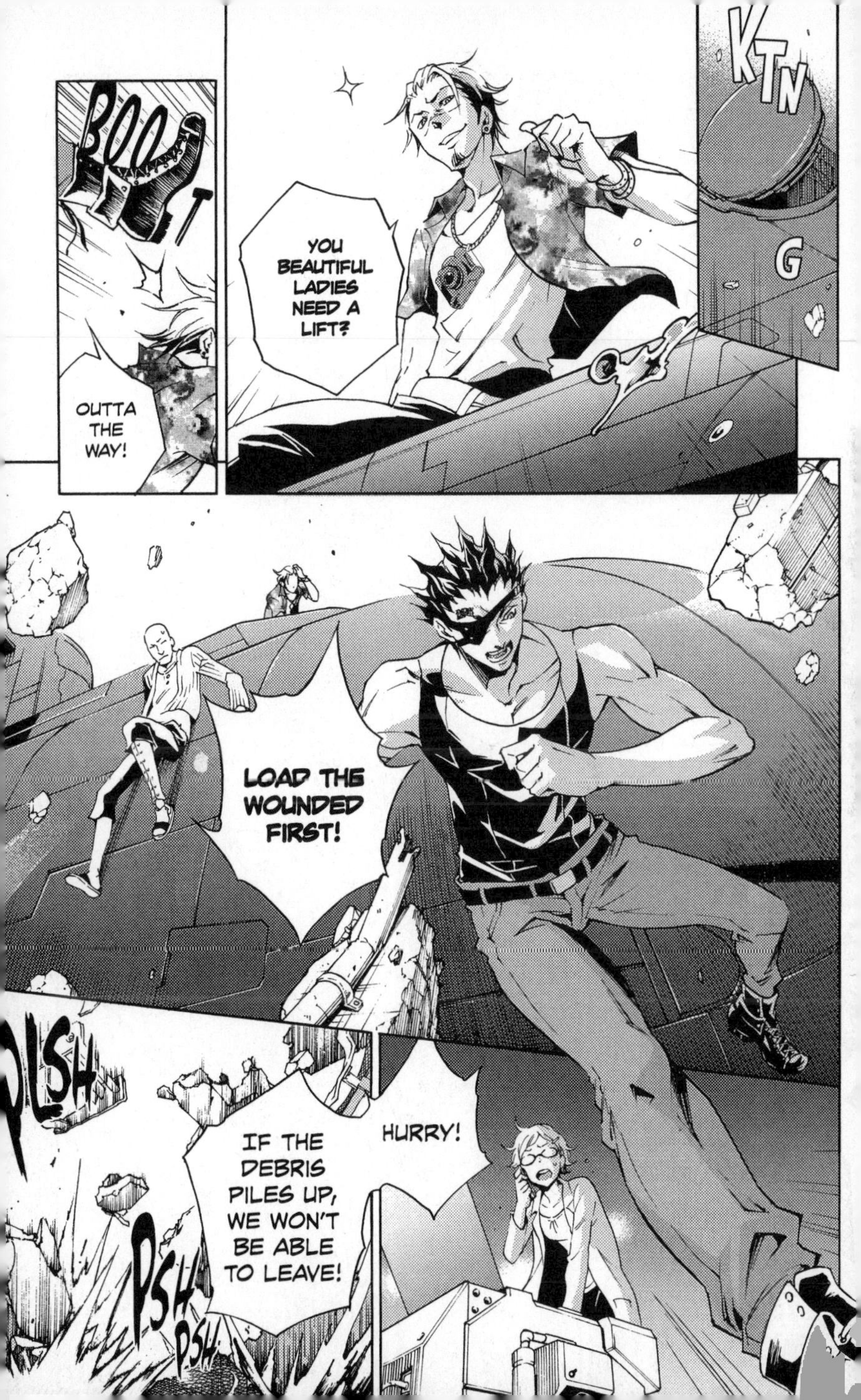
KTN
G
YOU BEAUTIFUL LADIES NEED A LIFT?
BOOT
OUTTA THE WAY!
LOAD THE WOUNDED FIRST!
HURRY!
IF THE DEBRIS PILES UP, WE WON'T BE ABLE TO LEAVE!
PLSH
PSH
PSH

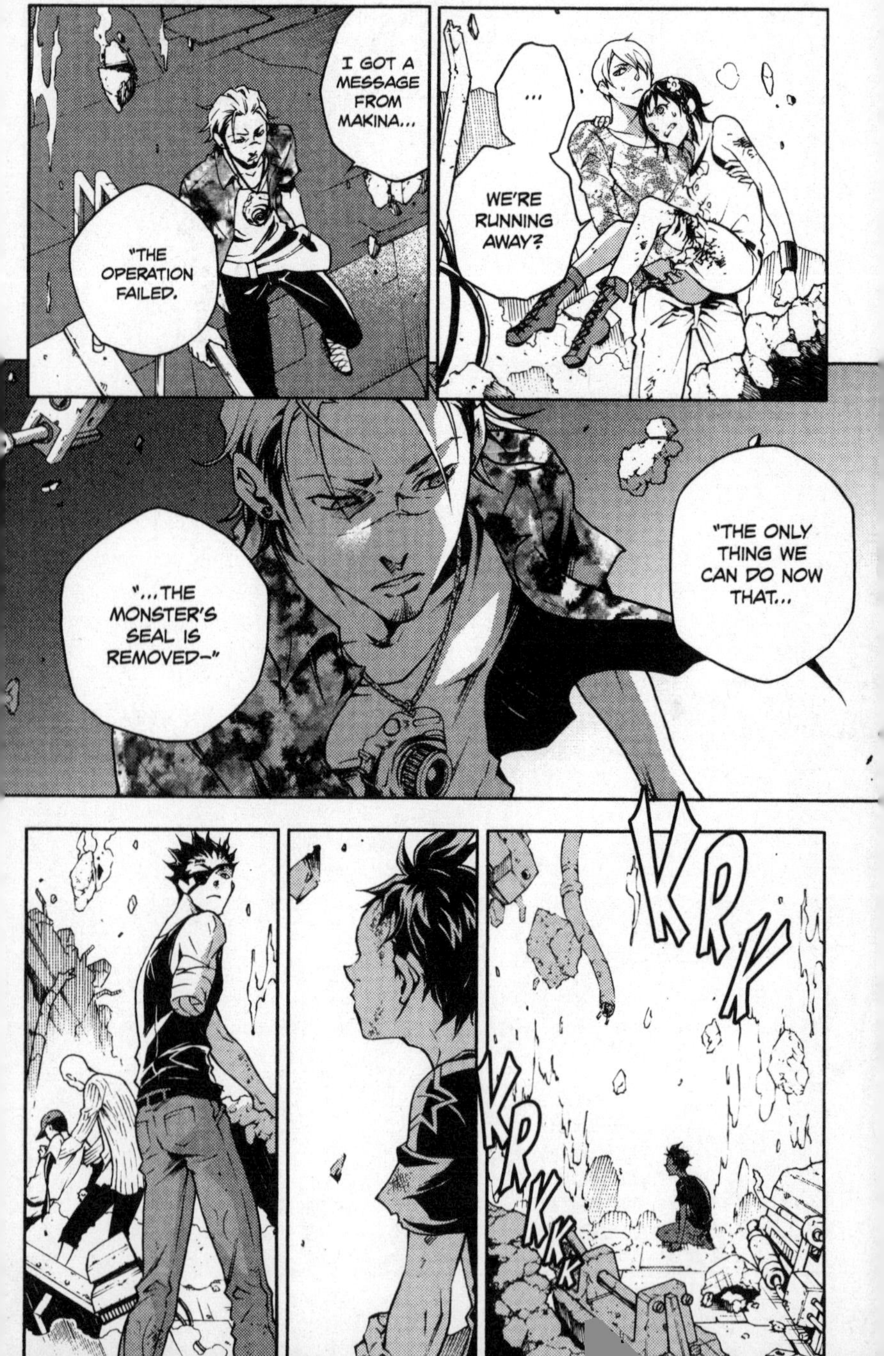
...
WE'RE RUNNING AWAY?
I GOT A MESSAGE FROM MAKINA...
"THE OPERATION FAILED.
"THE ONLY THING WE CAN DO NOW THAT...
"...THE MONSTER'S SEAL IS REMOVED–"
KRK
KRKKK

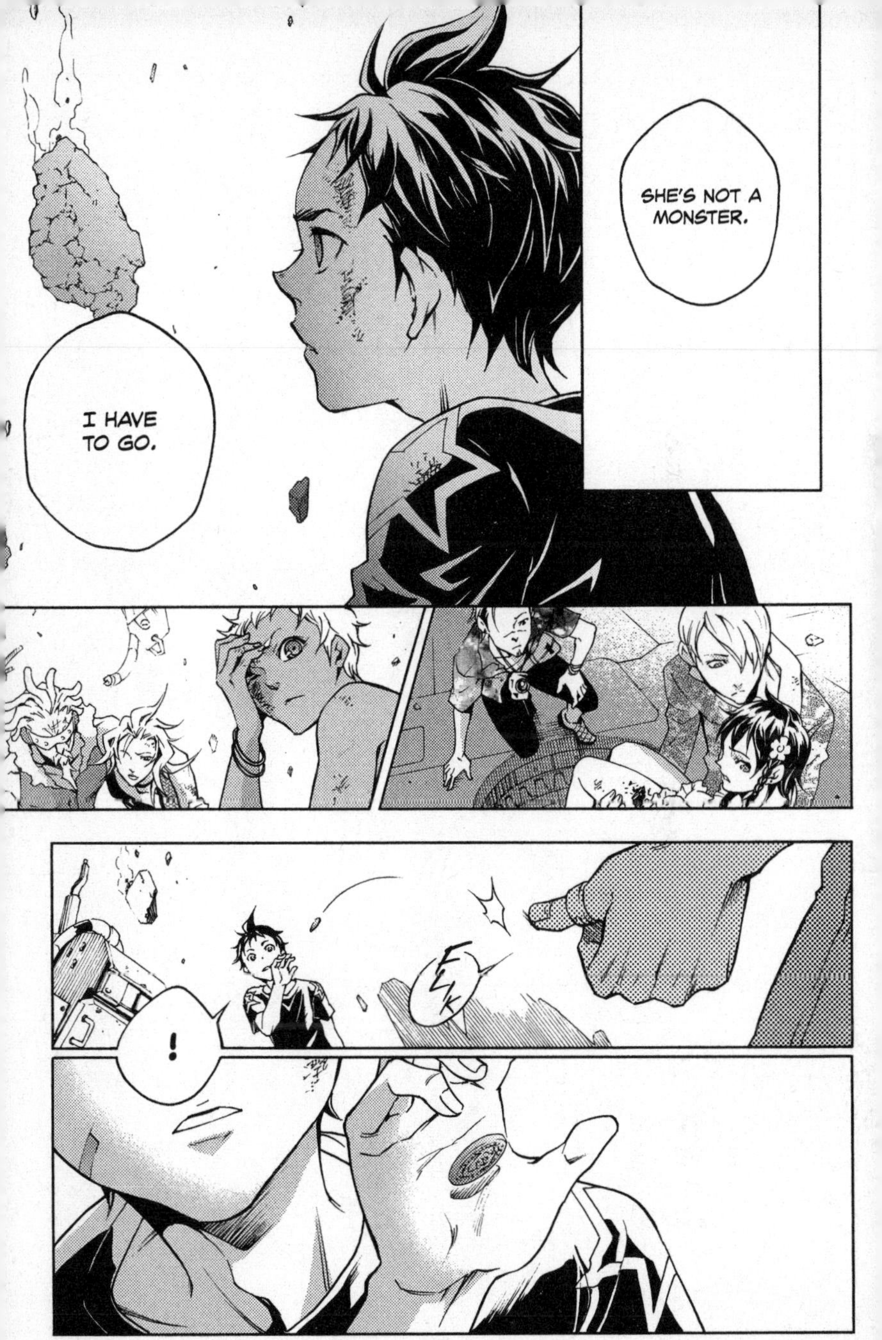
SHE'S NOT A MONSTER.
I HAVE TO GO.
FLIK
!

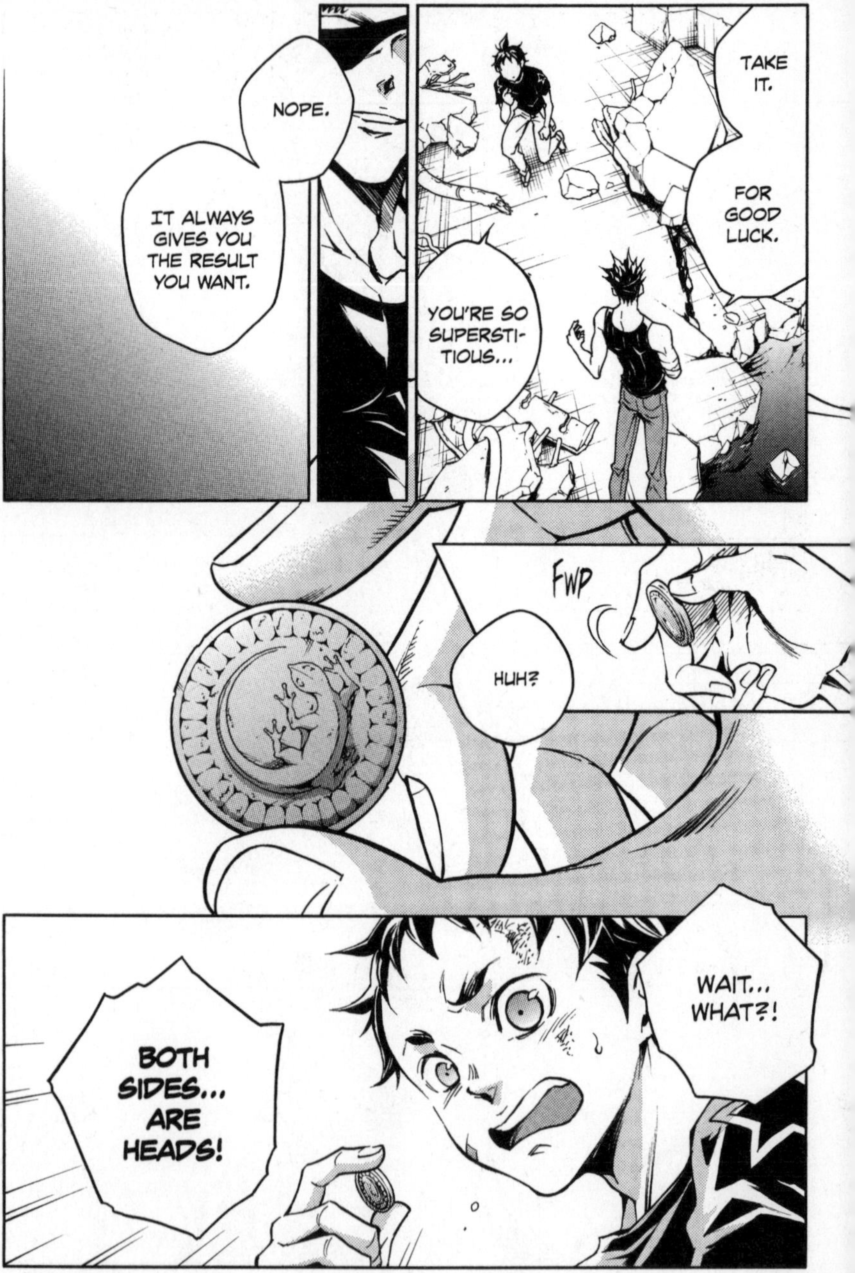
TAKE IT.
FOR GOOD LUCK.
YOU'RE SO SUPERSTITIOUS...
NOPE.
IT ALWAYS GIVES YOU THE RESULT YOU WANT.
FWP
HUH?
WAIT... WHAT?!
BOTH SIDES... ARE HEADS!

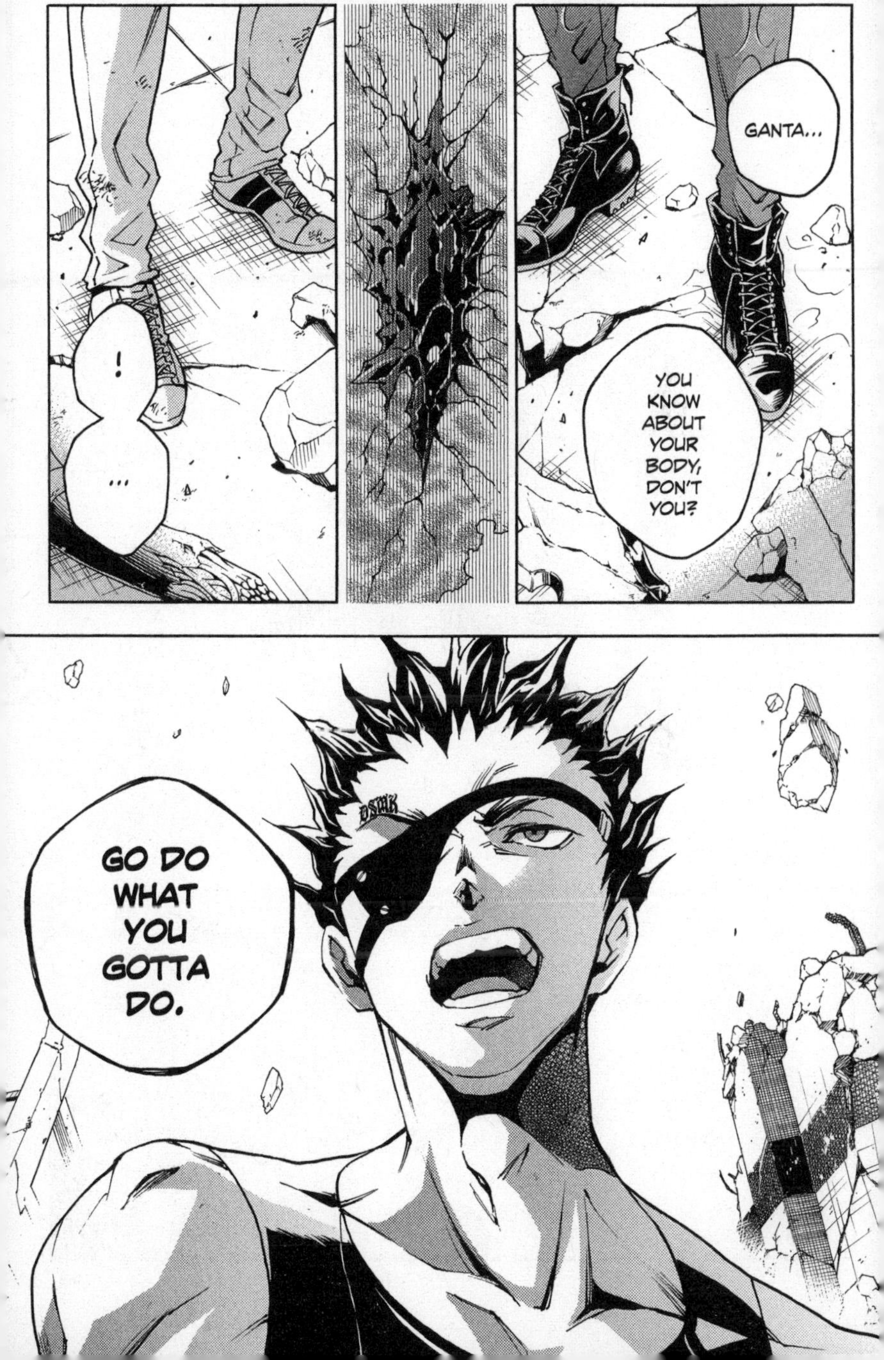
GANTA...
YOU KNOW ABOUT YOUR BODY, DON'T YOU?
!
...
GO DO WHAT YOU GOTTA DO.

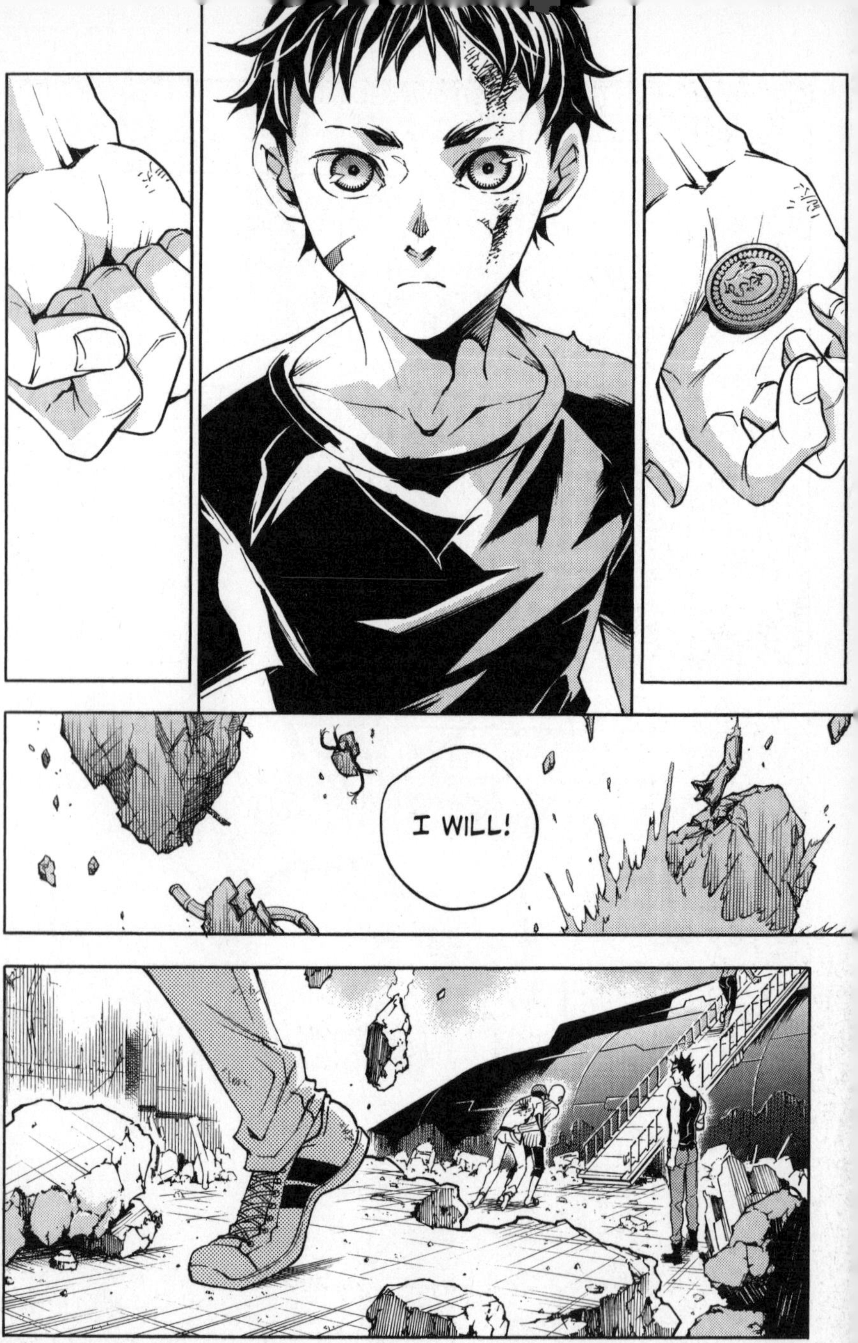
I WILL!

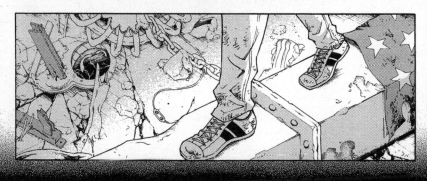

SHIRO...

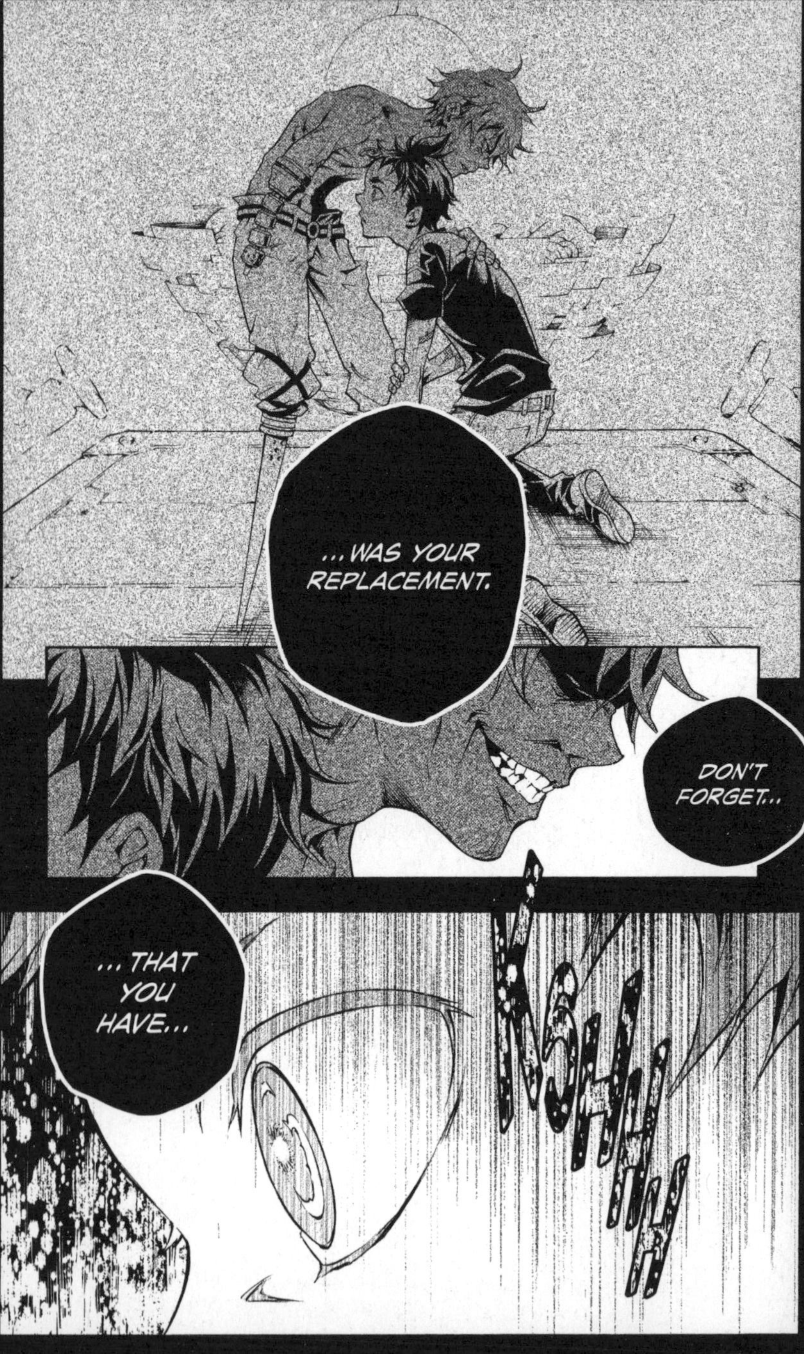
...WAS YOUR REPLACEMENT.
DON'T FORGET...
...THAT YOU HAVE...

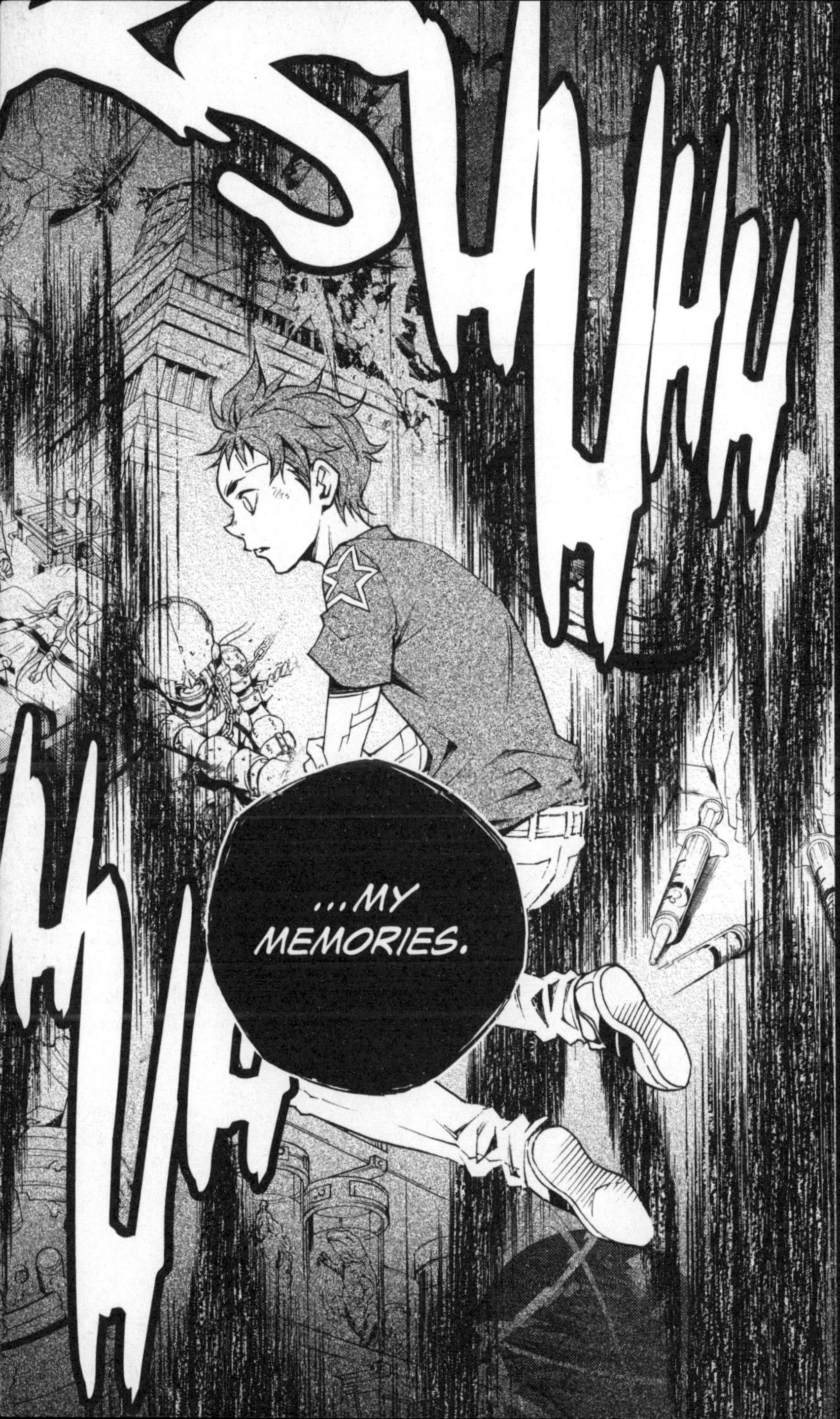
...MY MEMORIES.

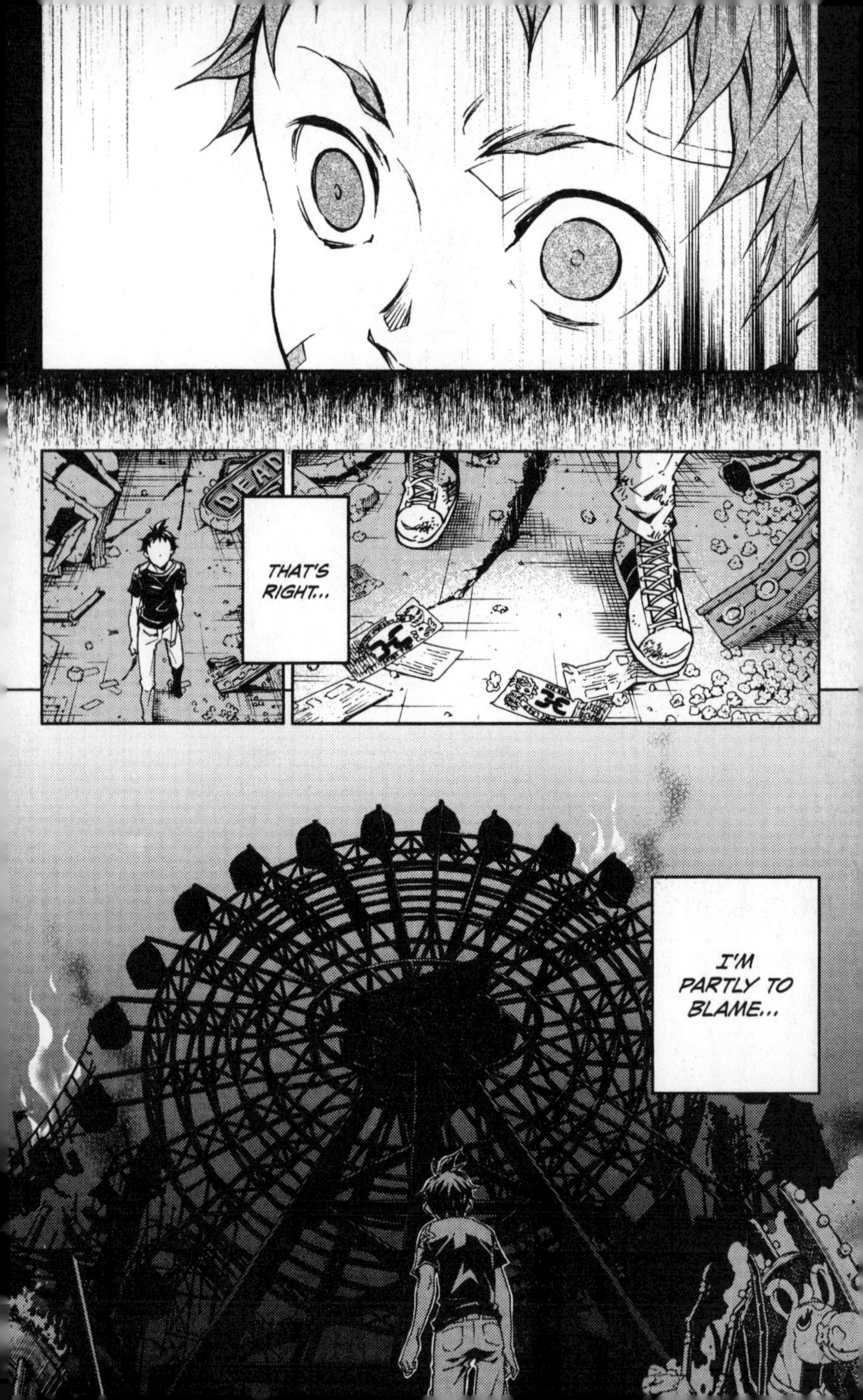
DEAD
THAT'S RIGHT...
I'M PARTLY TO BLAME...

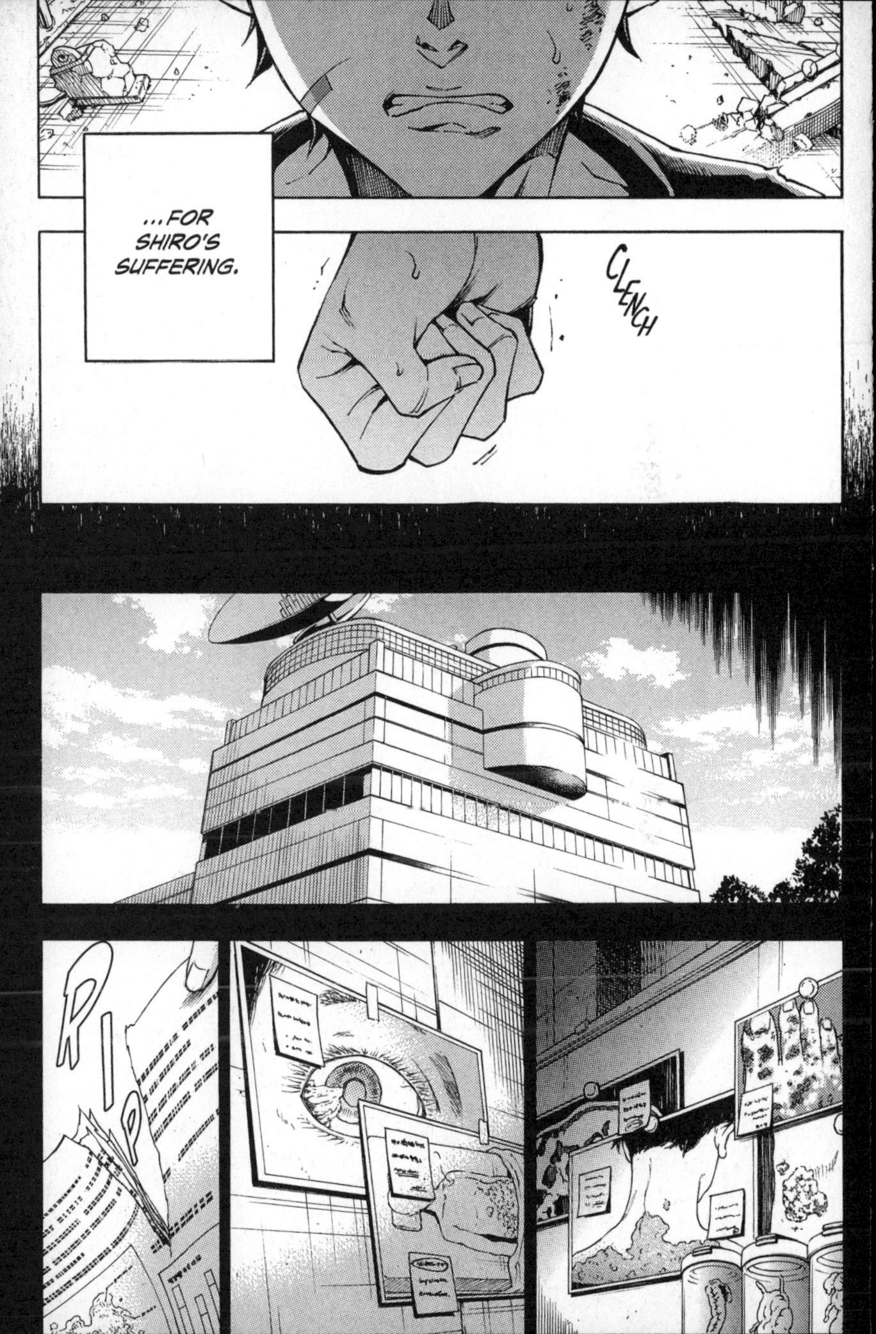
...FOR SHIRO'S SUFFERING.
CLENCH
RIP

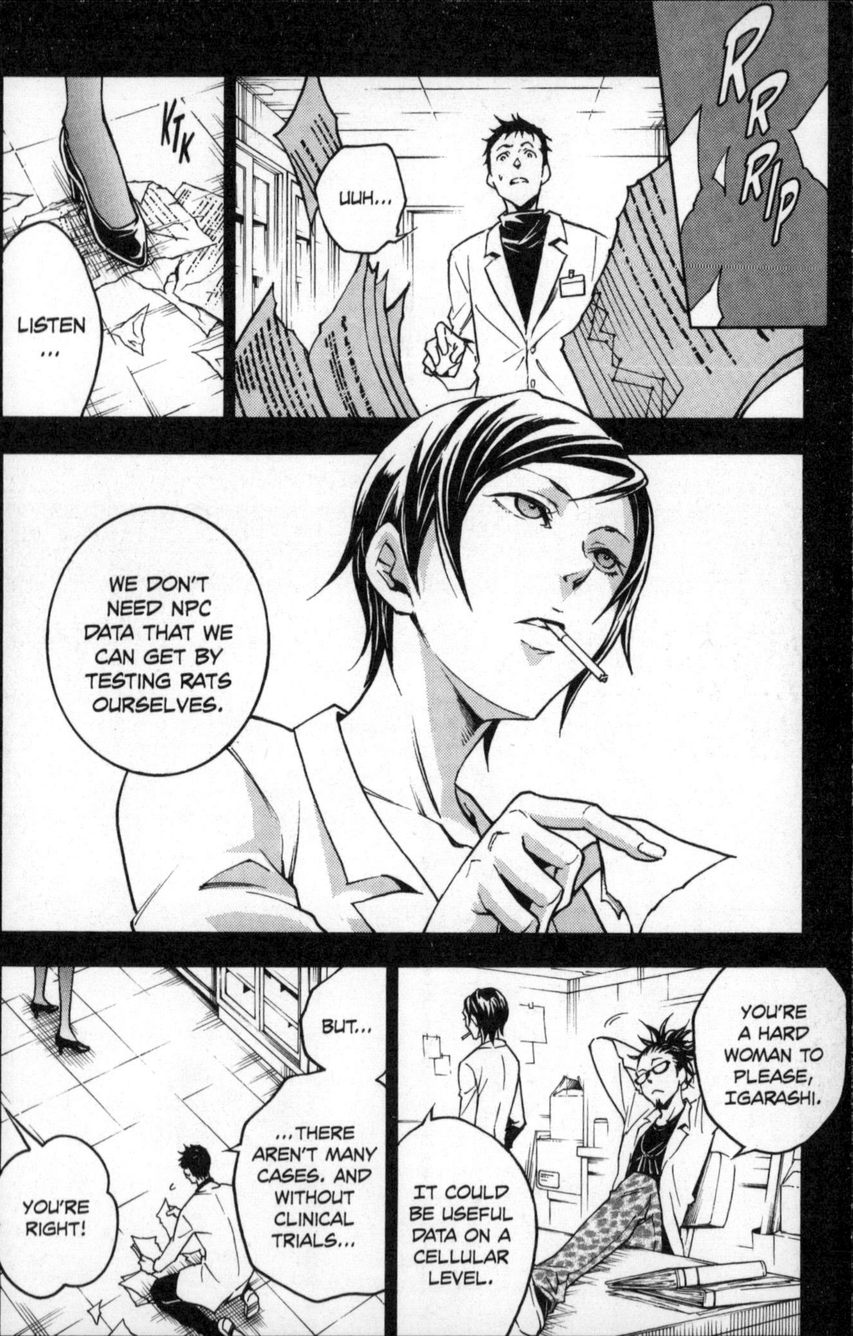
RRRIP
UUH...
KTK
LISTEN...
WE DON'T NEED NPC DATA THAT WE CAN GET BY TESTING RATS OURSELVES.
YOU'RE A HARD WOMAN TO PLEASE, IGARASHI.
IT COULD BE USEFUL DATA ON A CELLULAR LEVEL.
BUT...
...THERE AREN'T MANY CASES. AND WITHOUT CLINICAL TRIALS...
YOU'RE RIGHT!

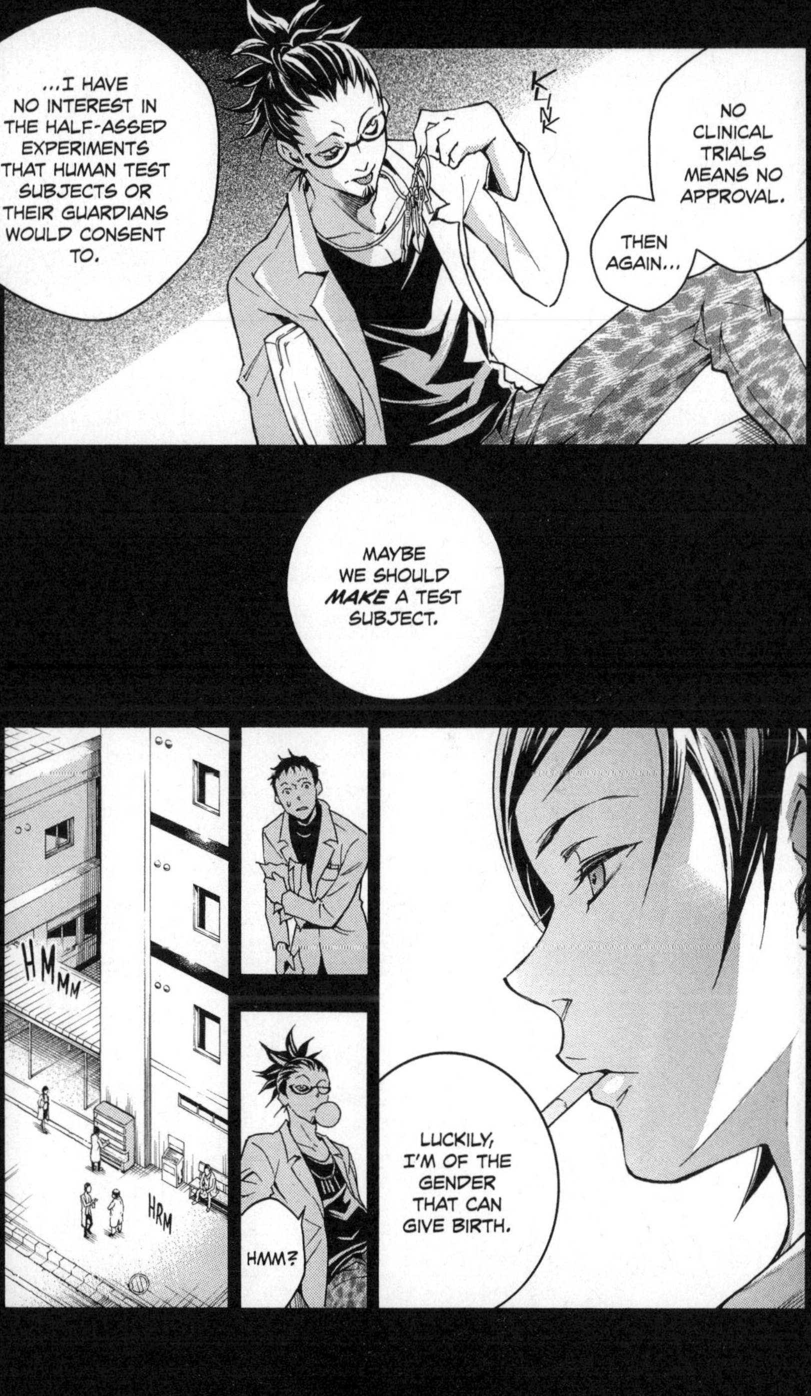
NO CLINICAL TRIALS MEANS NO APPROVAL.
THEN AGAIN...
KLINK
...I HAVE NO INTEREST IN THE HALF-ASSED EXPERIMENTS THAT HUMAN TEST SUBJECTS OR THEIR GUARDIANS WOULD CONSENT TO.
MAYBE WE SHOULD *MAKE* A TEST SUBJECT.
LUCKILY, I'M OF THE GENDER THAT CAN GIVE BIRTH.
HMM?
HMMM
HRM

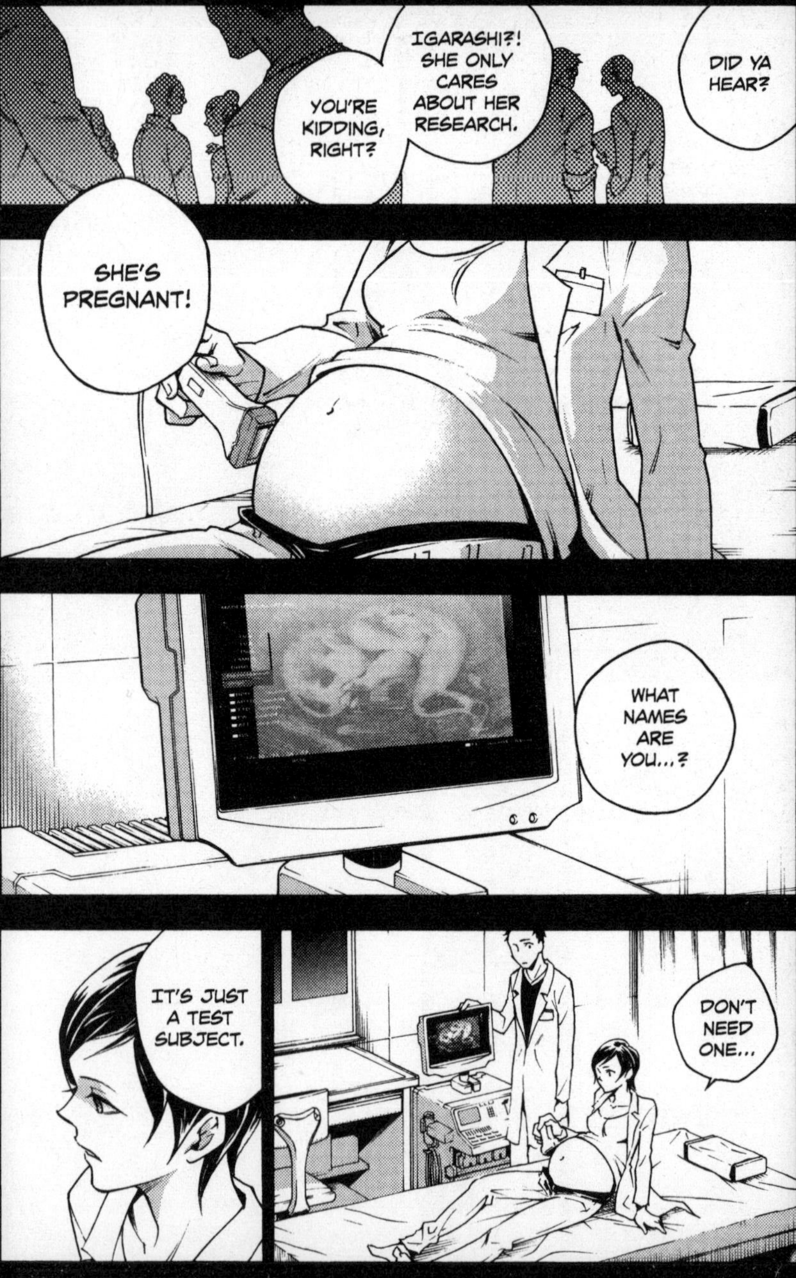
DID YA HEAR?
IGARASHI?! SHE ONLY CARES ABOUT HER RESEARCH.
YOU'RE KIDDING, RIGHT?
SHE'S PREGNANT!
WHAT NAMES ARE YOU...?
DON'T NEED ONE...
IT'S JUST A TEST SUBJECT.

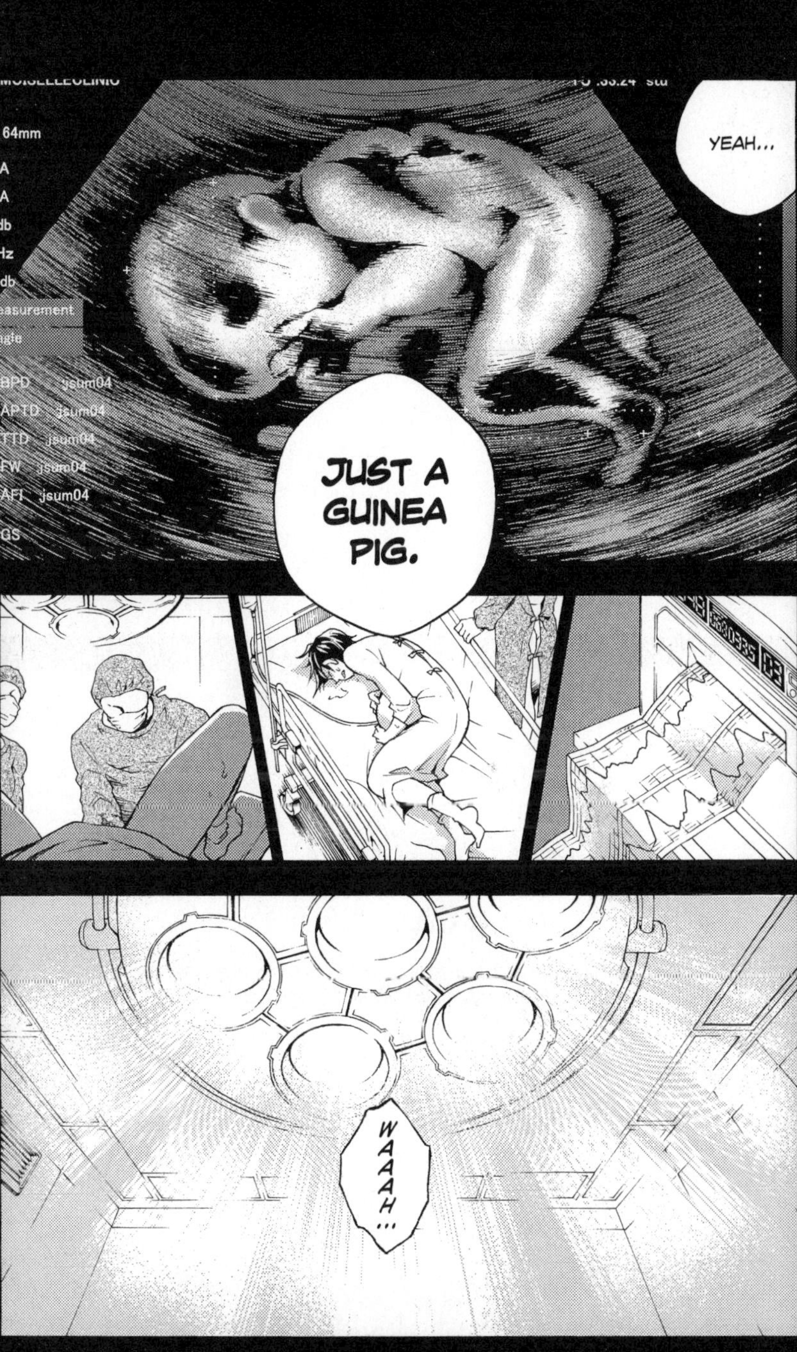
YEAH...
JUST A GUINEA PIG.
WAAAH...

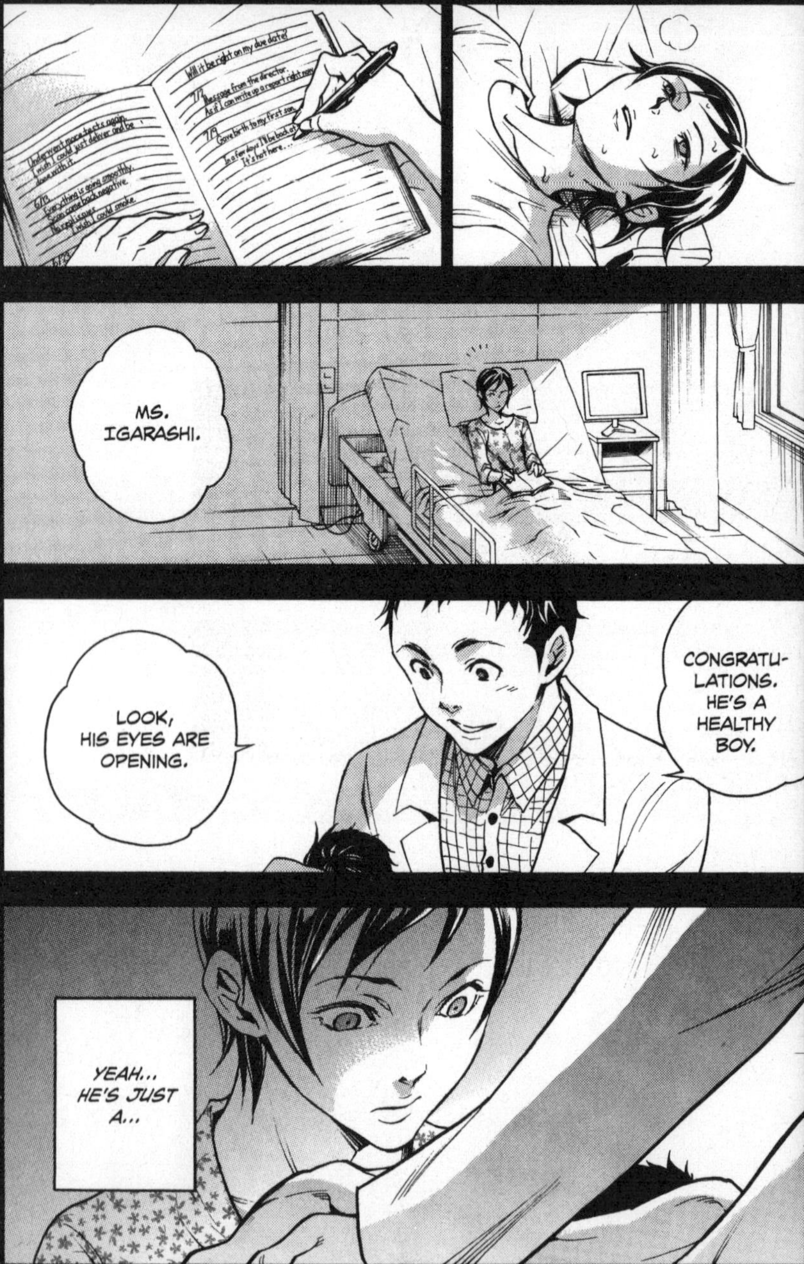
Underwent more tests again.
I wish I could just deliver and be done with it.
6/13
Everything is going smoothly.
Scan came back negative.
No real issues.
I wish I could smoke.
Will it be right on my due date?
7/7
Message from the director.
As if I can write up a report right now.
7/9
Gave birth to my first son. I'll be back at
In a few days
It's hot here...
MS. IGARASHI.
CONGRATULATIONS. HE'S A HEALTHY BOY.
LOOK, HIS EYES ARE OPENING.
YEAH... HE'S JUST A...

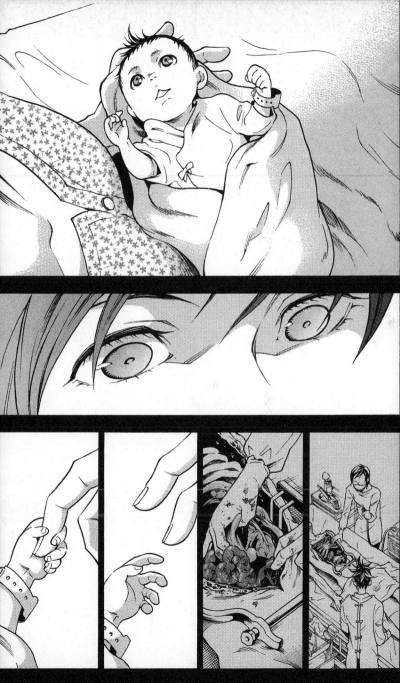

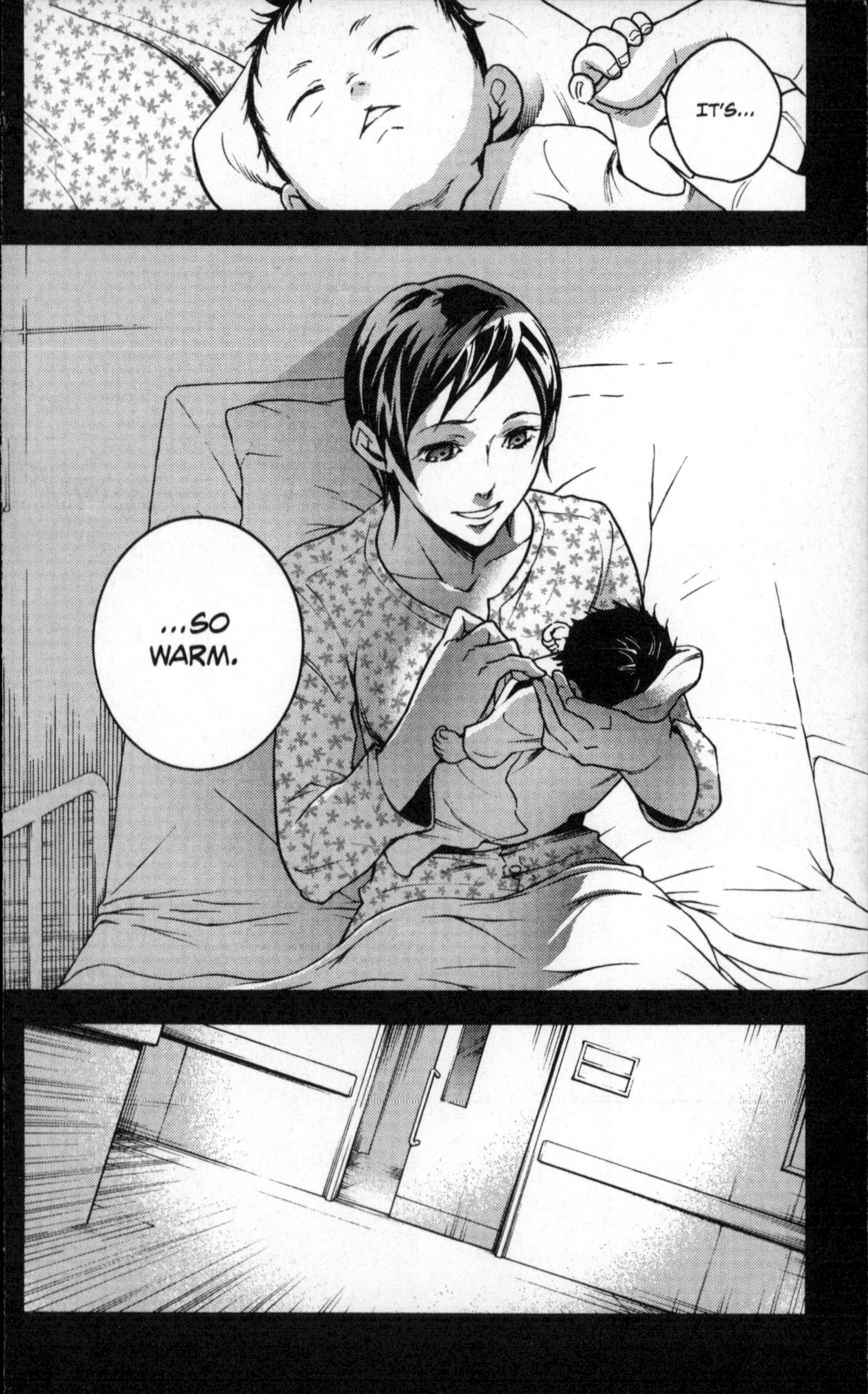
IT'S...
...SO WARM.

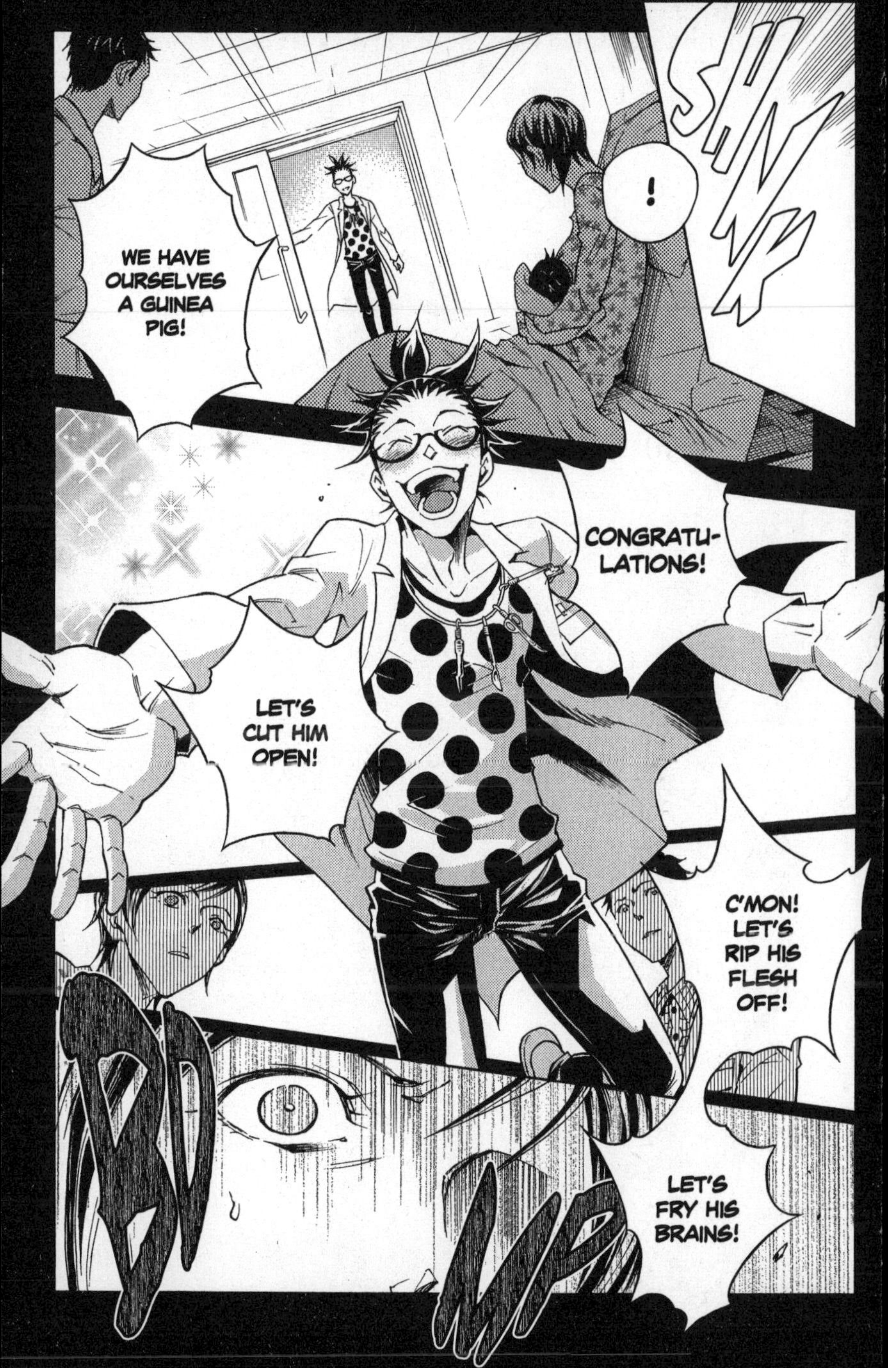
!
WE HAVE OURSELVES A GUINEA PIG!
CONGRATU-LATIONS!
LET'S CUT HIM OPEN!
C'MON! LET'S RIP HIS FLESH OFF!
LET'S FRY HIS BRAINS!

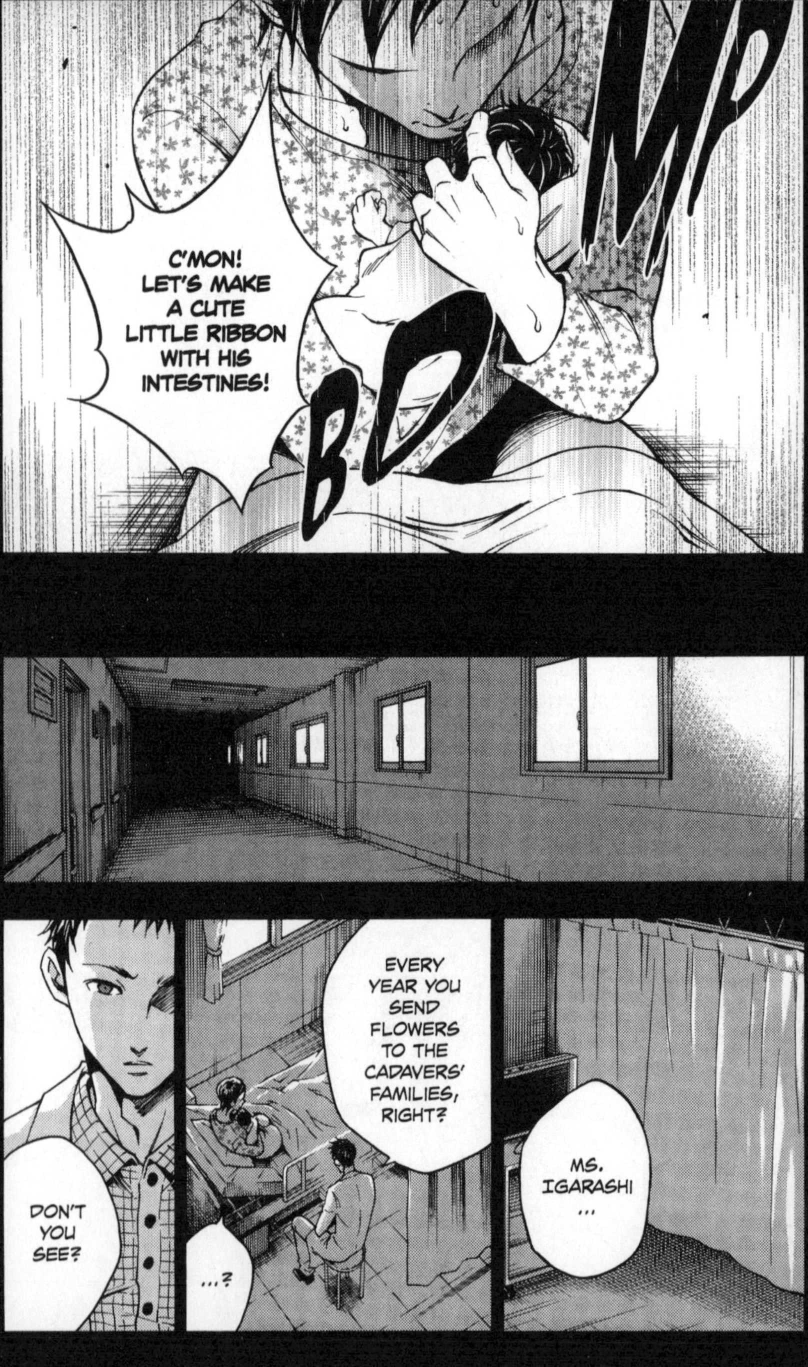
C'MON! LET'S MAKE A CUTE LITTLE RIBBON WITH HIS INTESTINES!
BDMP
MS. IGARASHI ...
EVERY YEAR YOU SEND FLOWERS TO THE CADAVERS' FAMILIES, RIGHT?
...?
DON'T YOU SEE?

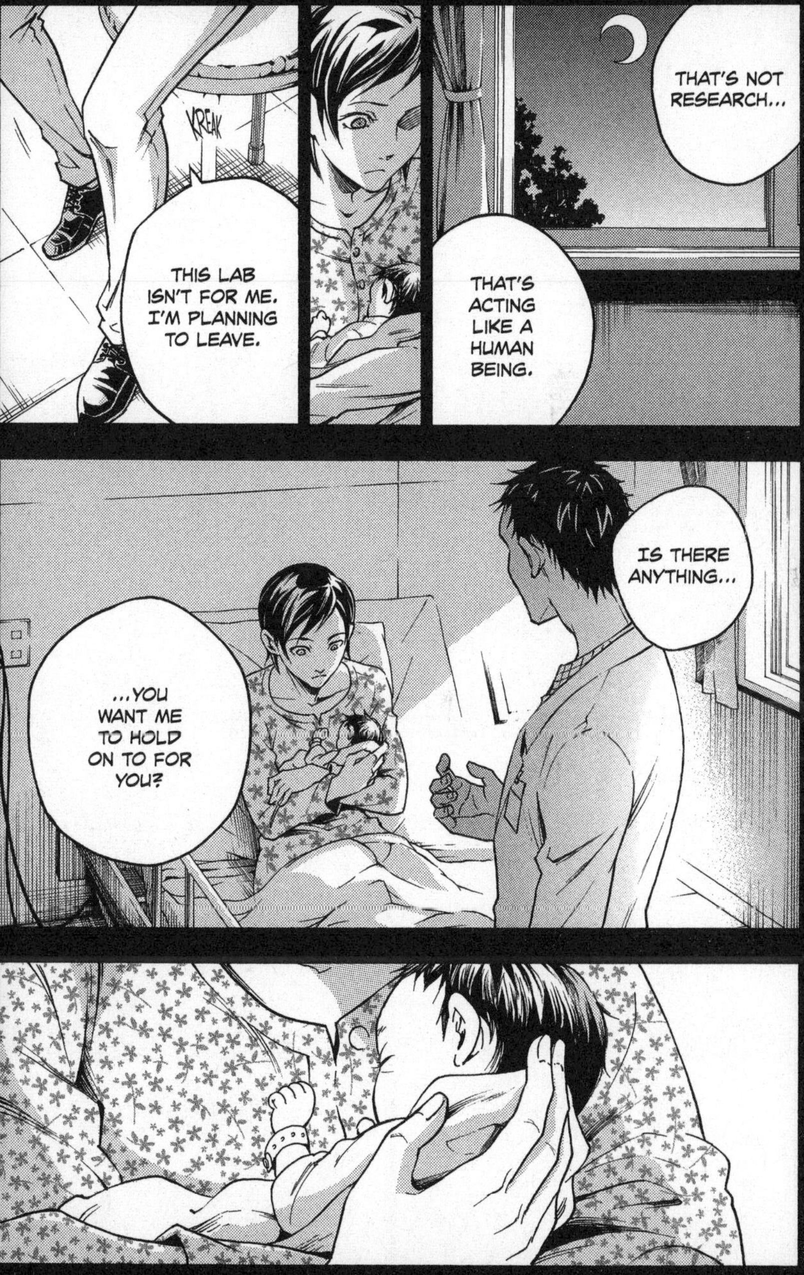
THAT'S NOT RESEARCH...
THAT'S ACTING LIKE A HUMAN BEING.
KREAK
THIS LAB ISN'T FOR ME. I'M PLANNING TO LEAVE.
IS THERE ANYTHING...
...YOU WANT ME TO HOLD ON TO FOR YOU?

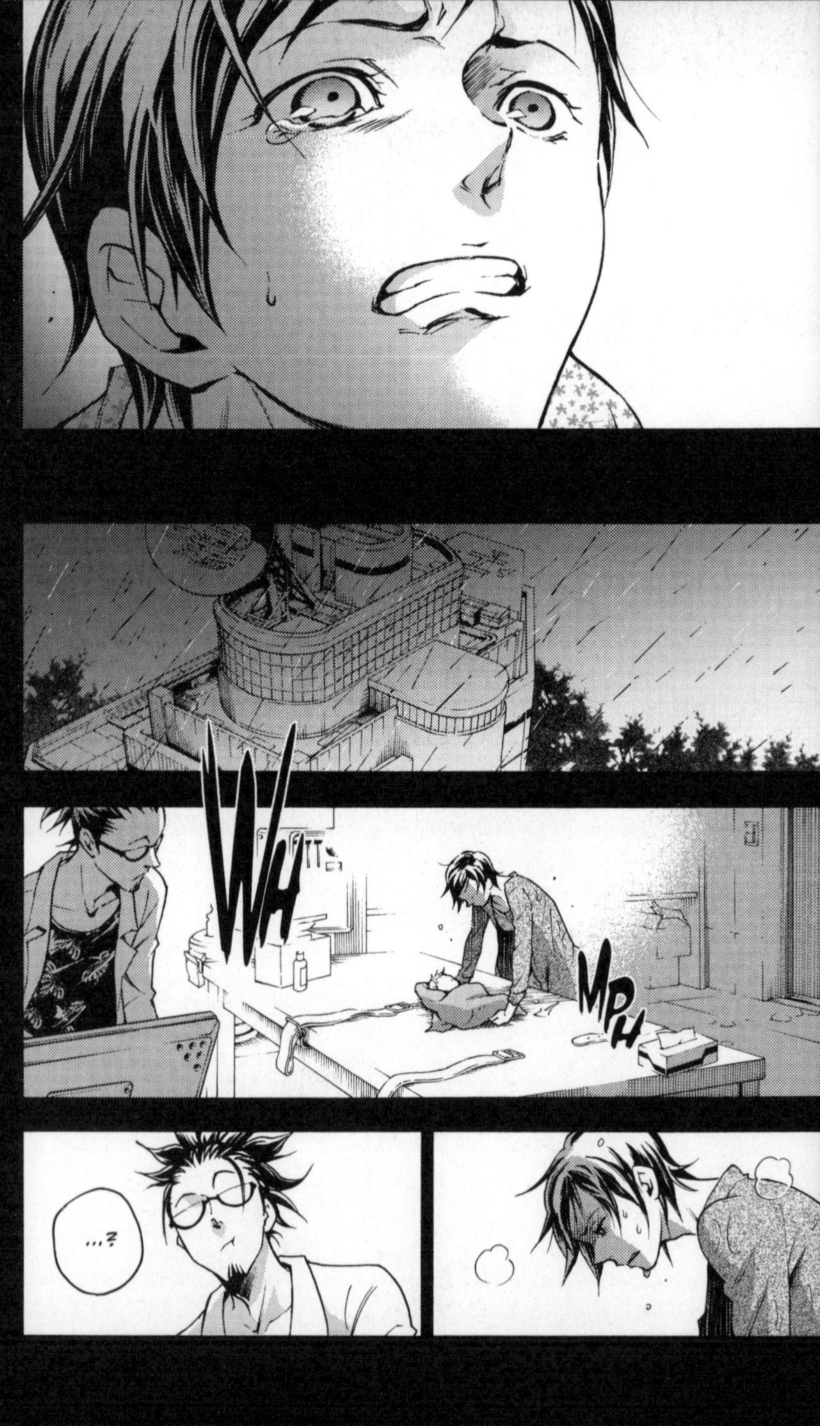
WH
MPH
...?

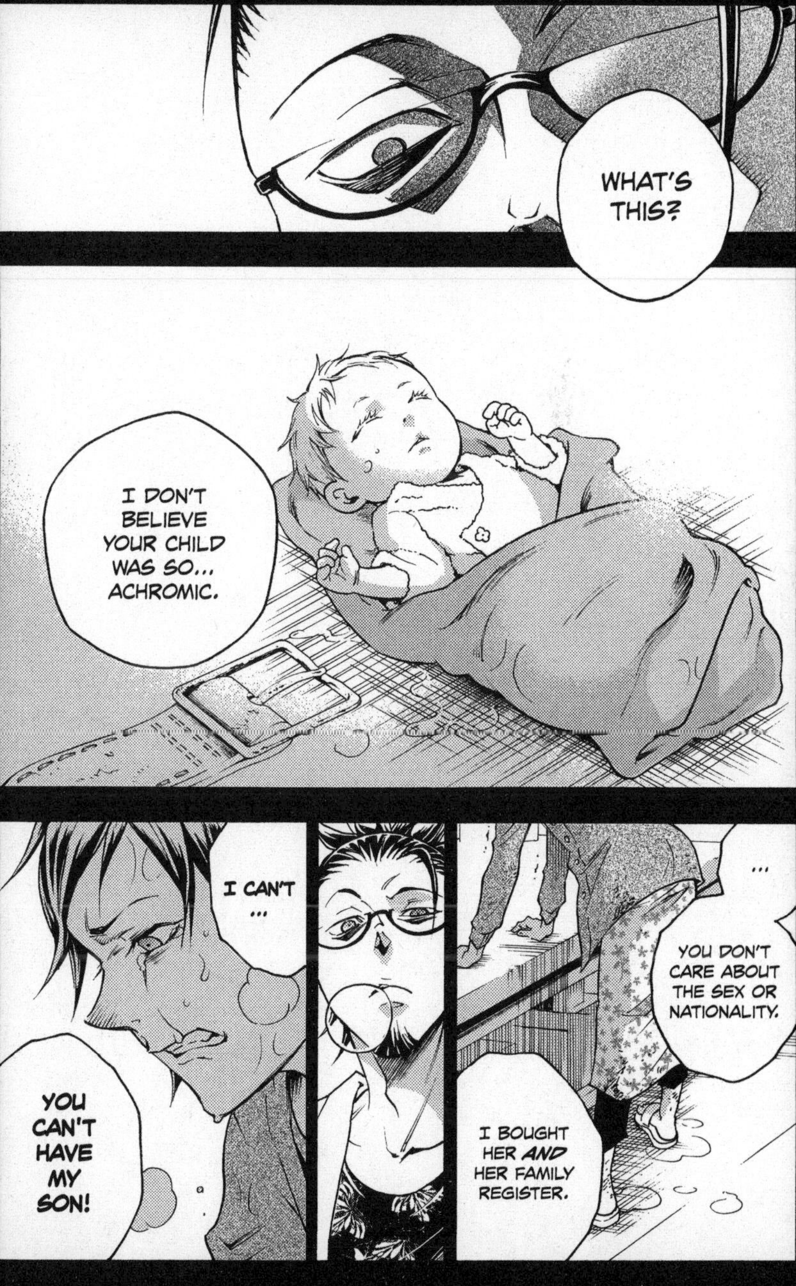
WHAT'S THIS?
I DON'T BELIEVE YOUR CHILD WAS SO... ACHROMIC.
...
YOU DON'T CARE ABOUT THE SEX OR NATIONALITY.
I BOUGHT HER *AND* HER FAMILY REGISTER.
I CAN'T ...
YOU CAN'T HAVE MY SON!

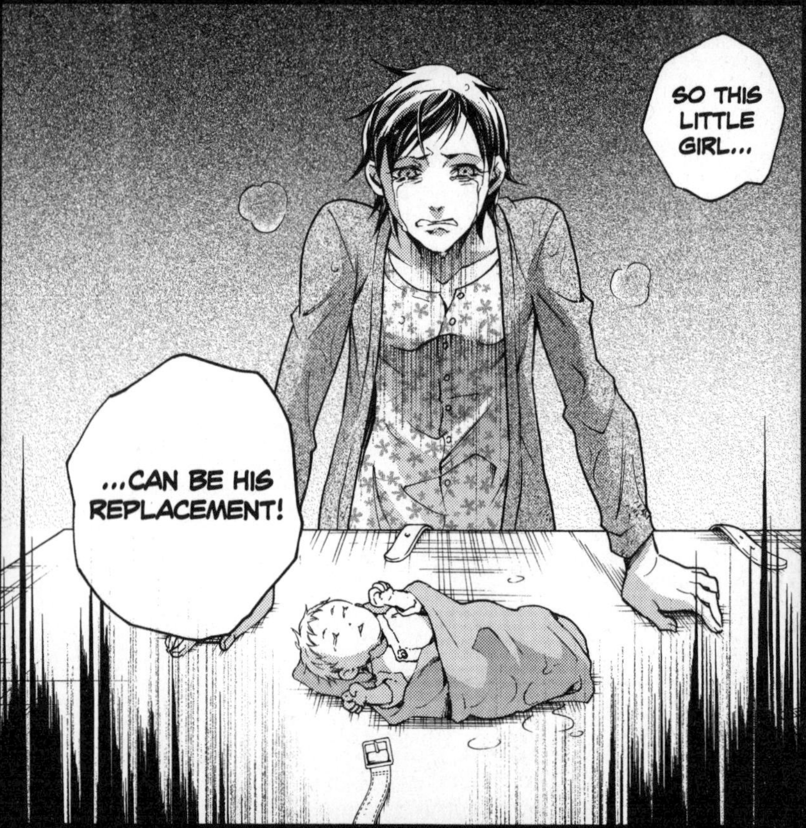
SO THIS LITTLE GIRL...
...CAN BE HIS REPLACEMENT!

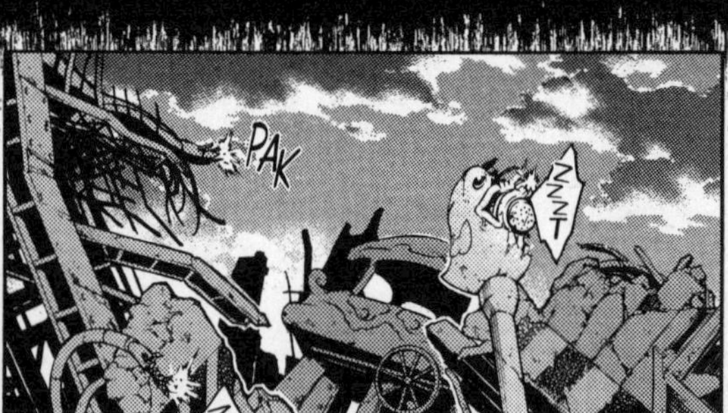
PAK
ZZZT
ZZZT

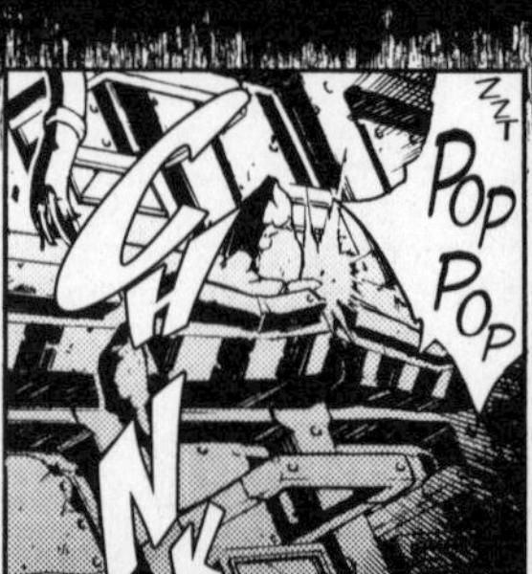
ZZZT
POP POP POP
CHNK

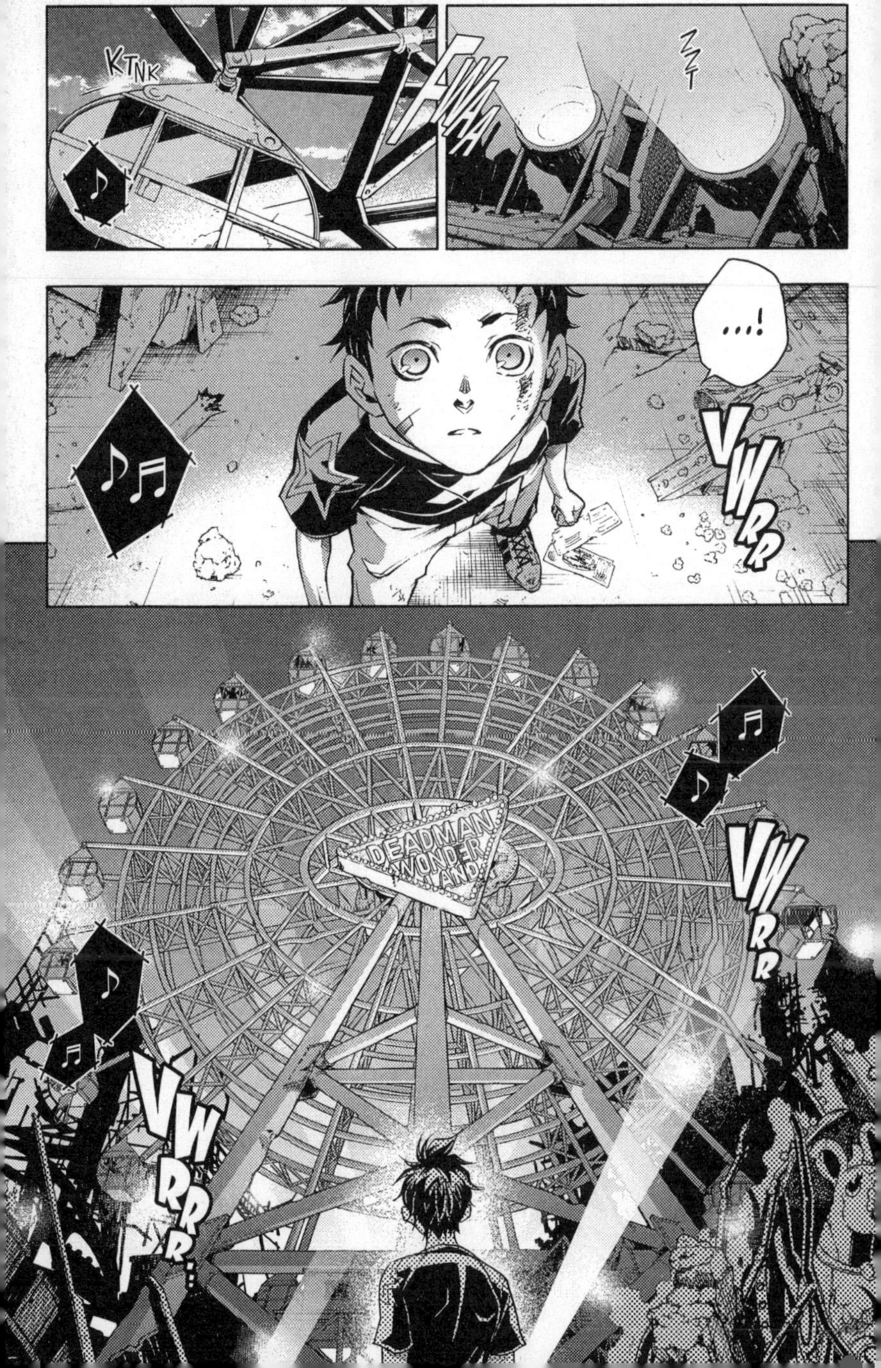
ZZT
FWAA
KTNK
...!
VWRR
VWRR
DEADMAN WONDERLAND
VWRRR...

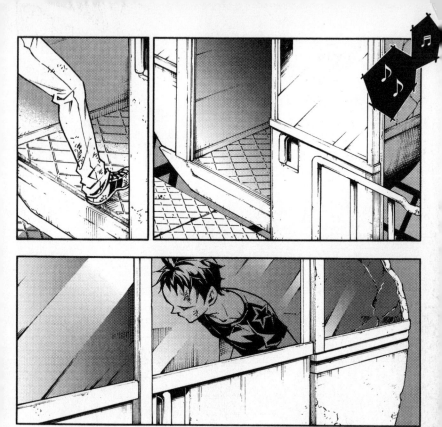

WE
SAID...

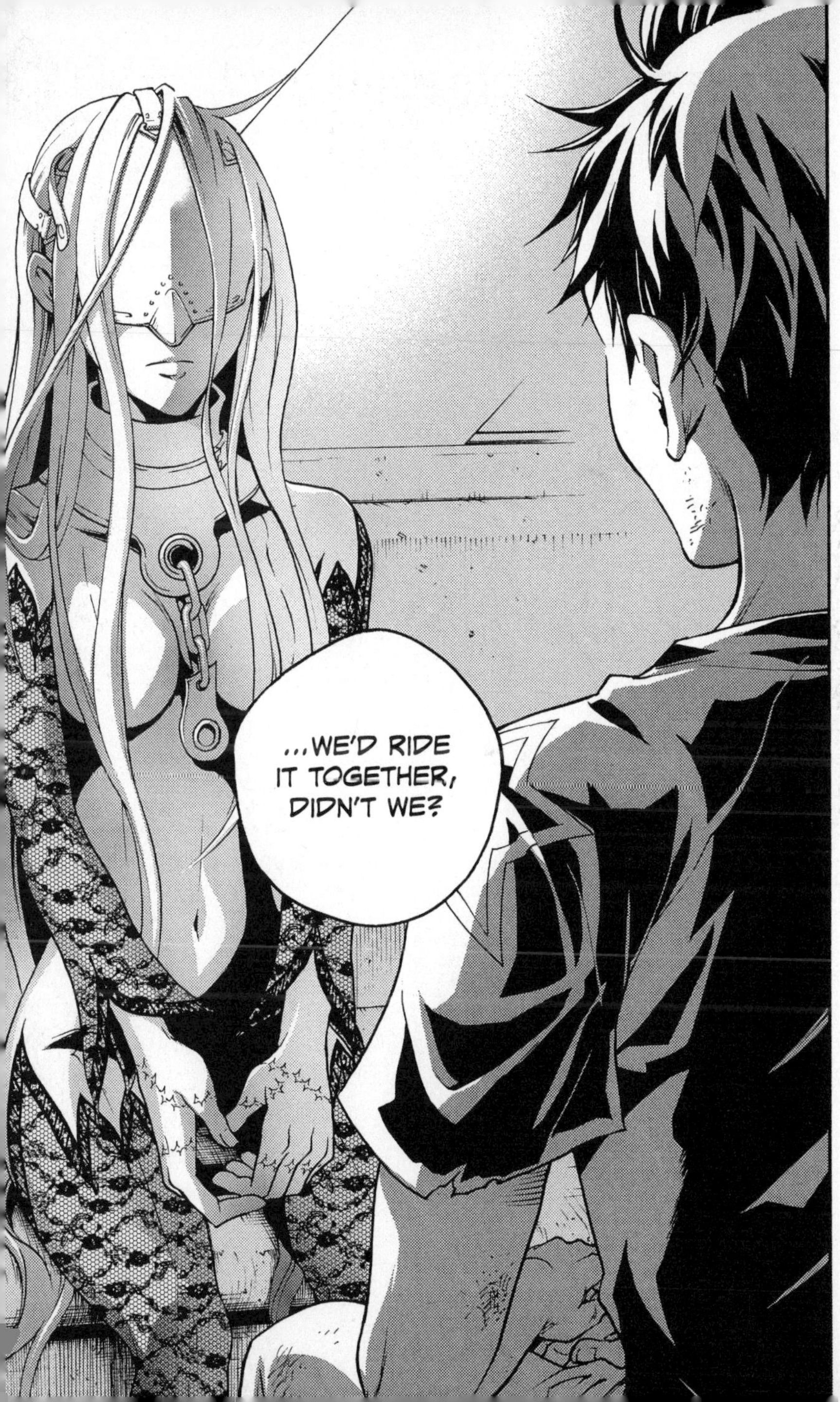
...WE'D RIDE IT TOGETHER, DIDN'T WE?

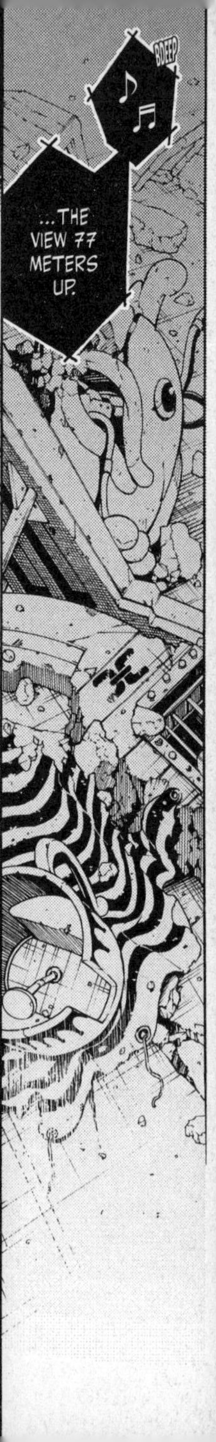
BOEEP
♪ ♬
...THE VIEW 77 METERS UP.

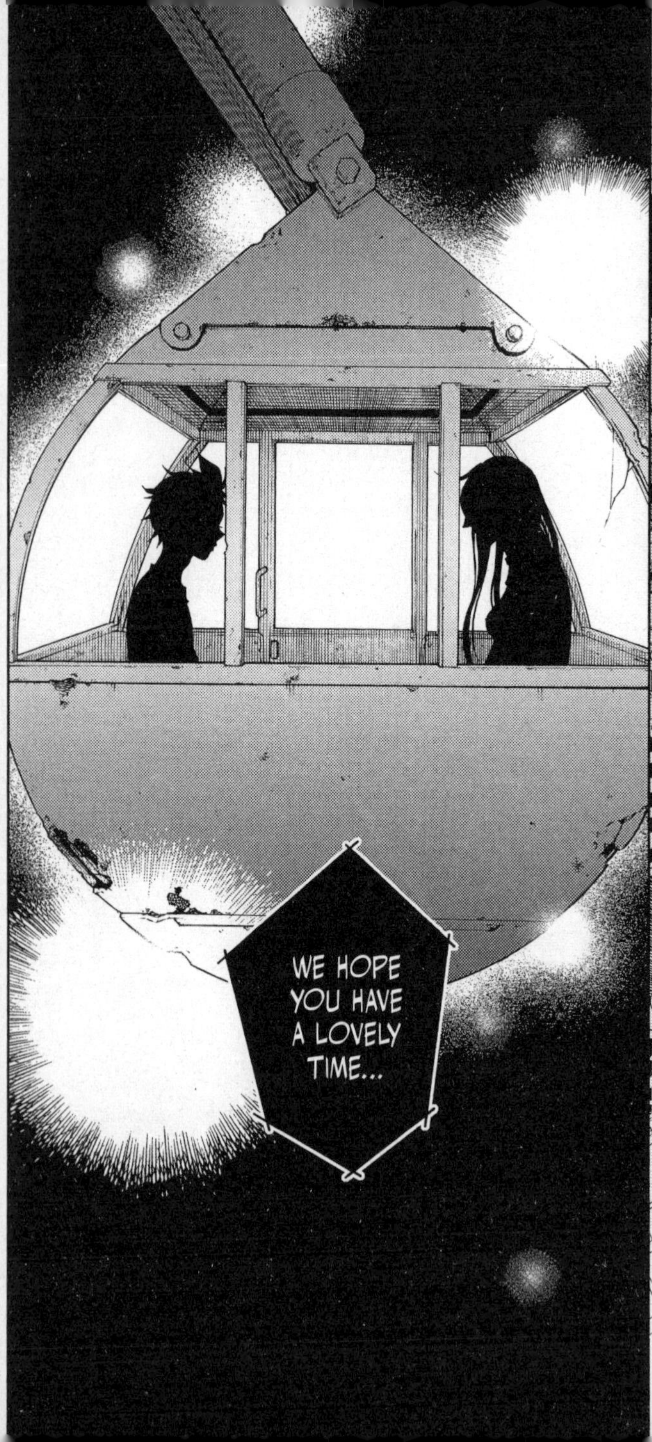
WE HOPE YOU HAVE A LOVELY TIME...

DEADMAN WONDER LAND

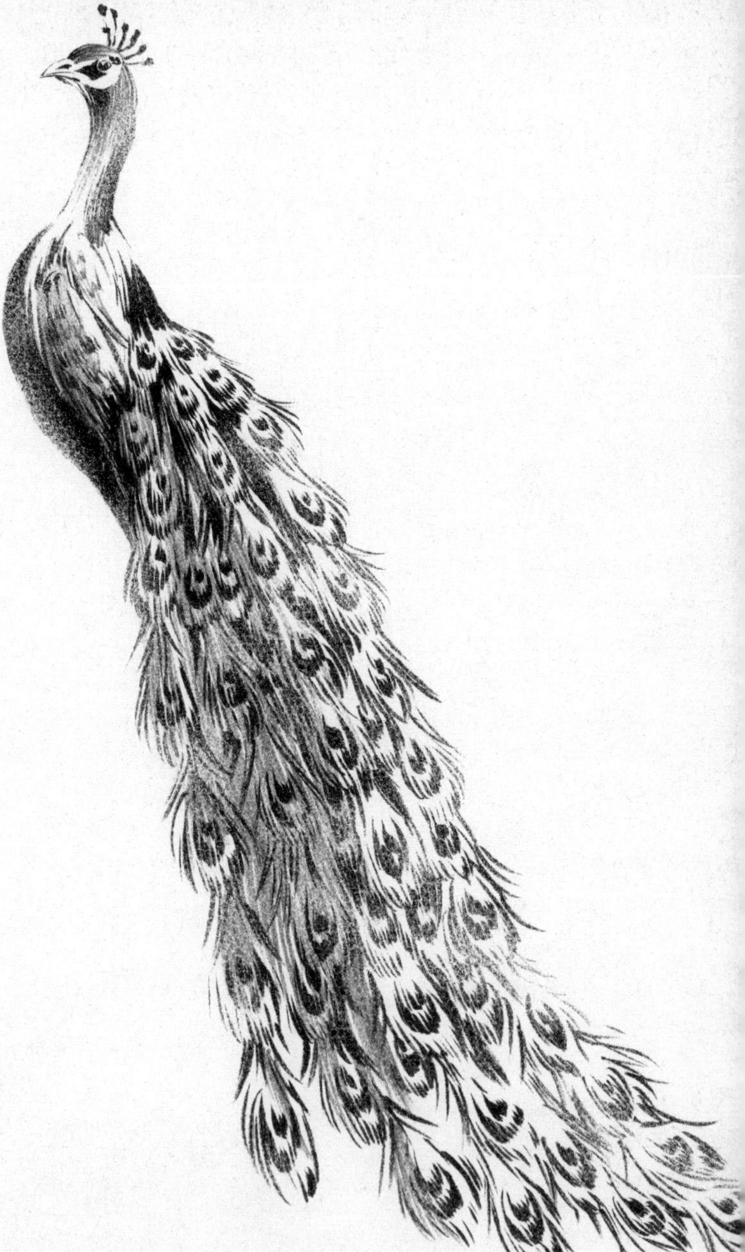

55 A Foolish Wish

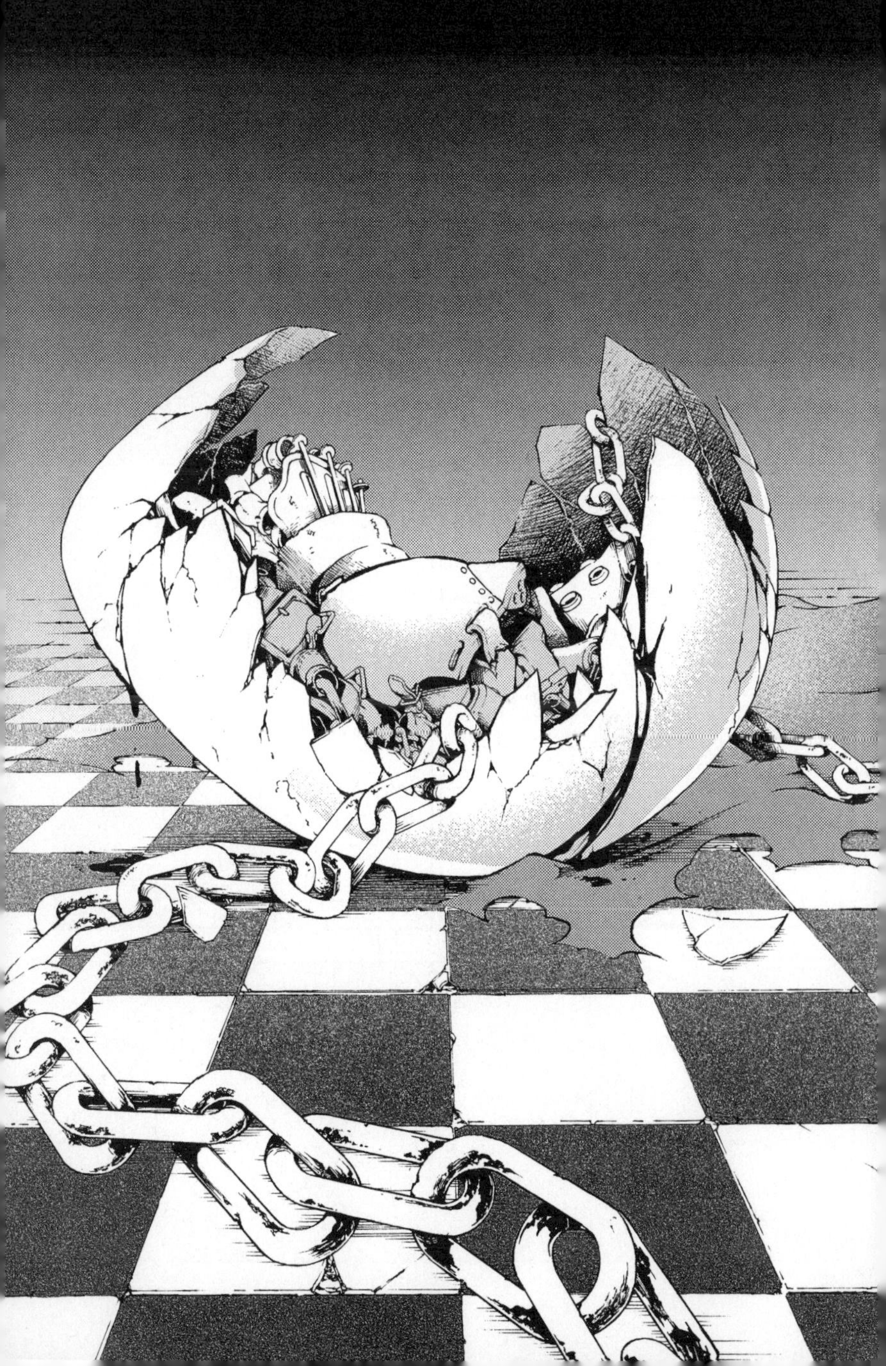

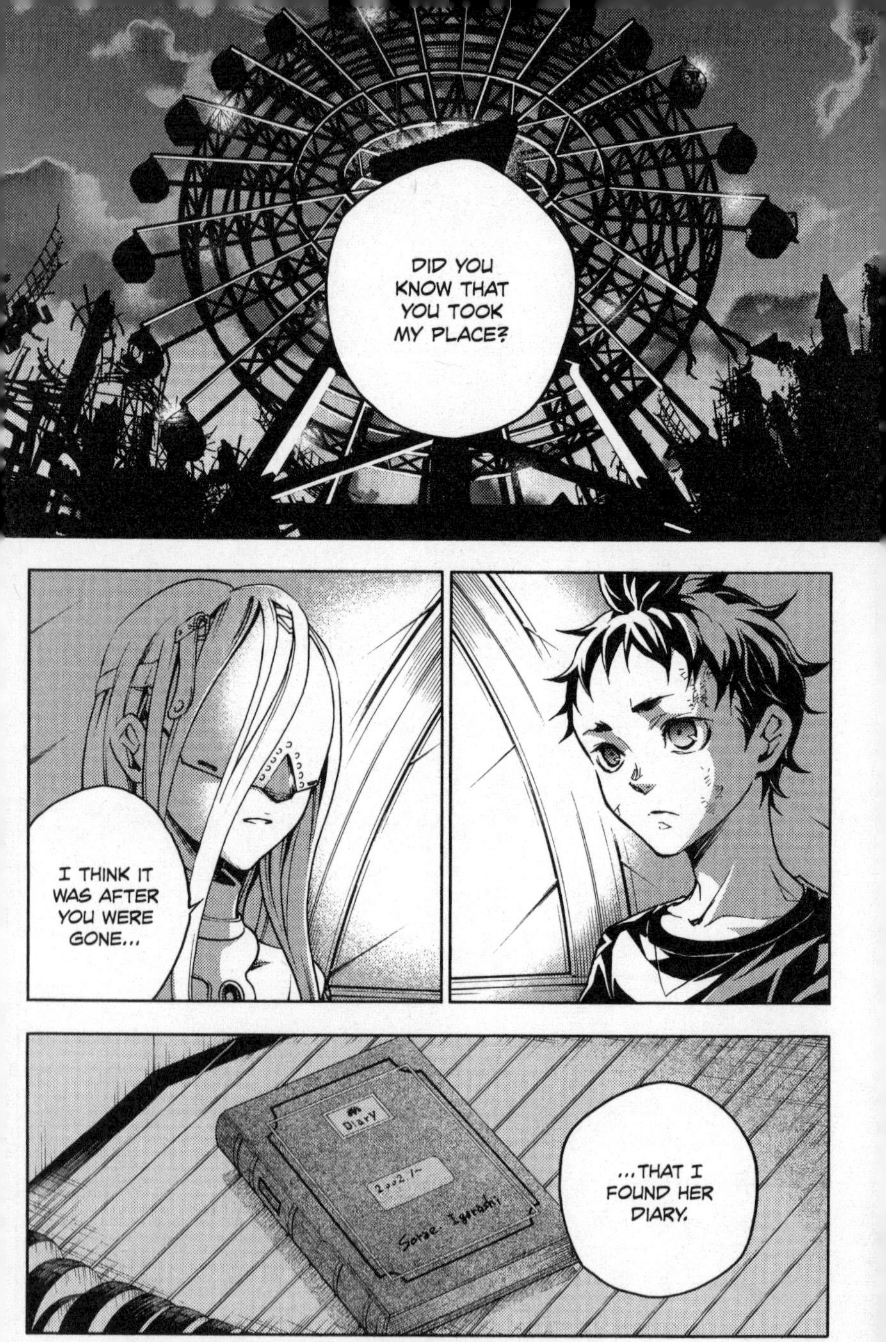
DID YOU KNOW THAT YOU TOOK MY PLACE?
I THINK IT WAS AFTER YOU WERE GONE...
...THAT I FOUND HER DIARY.
Diary

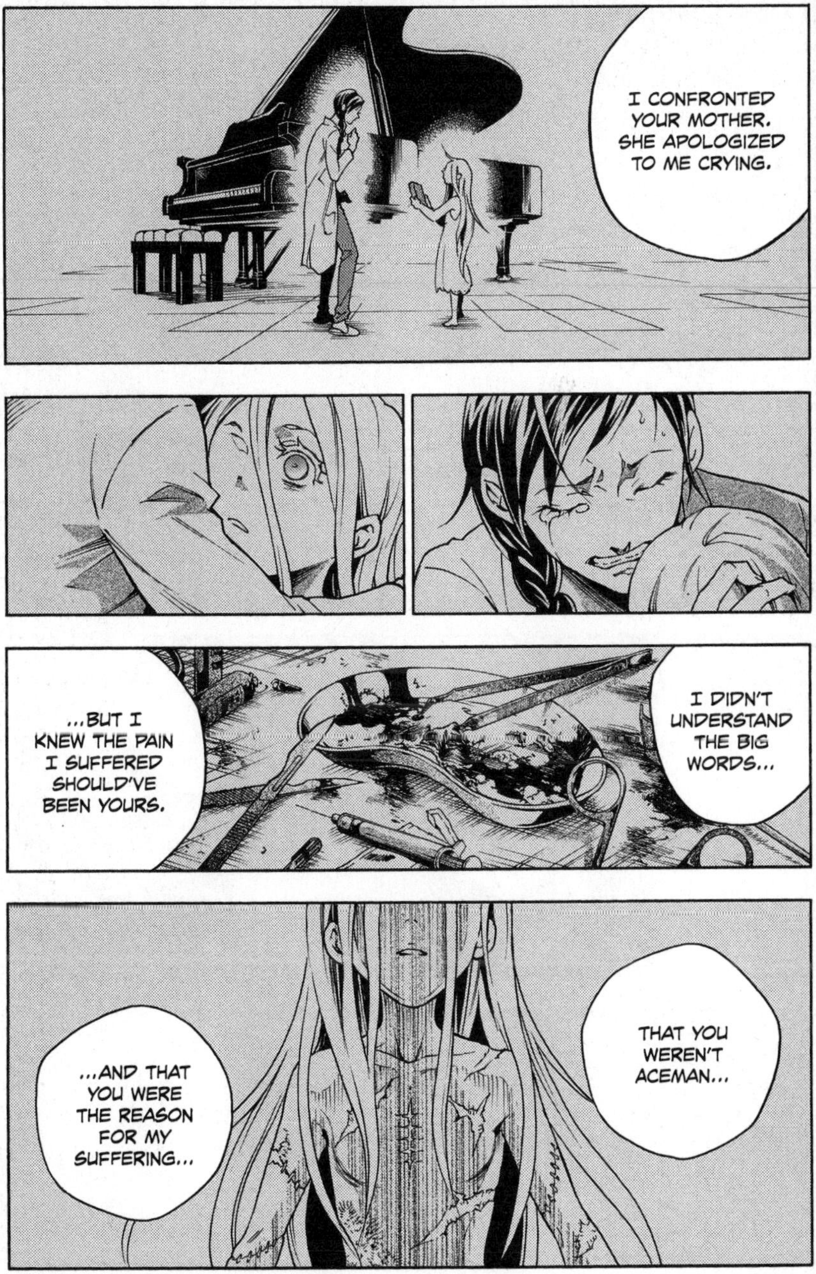
I CONFRONTED YOUR MOTHER. SHE APOLOGIZED TO ME CRYING.
I DIDN'T UNDERSTAND THE BIG WORDS...
...BUT I KNEW THE PAIN I SUFFERED SHOULD'VE BEEN YOURS.
THAT YOU WEREN'T ACEMAN...
...AND THAT YOU WERE THE REASON FOR MY SUFFERING...

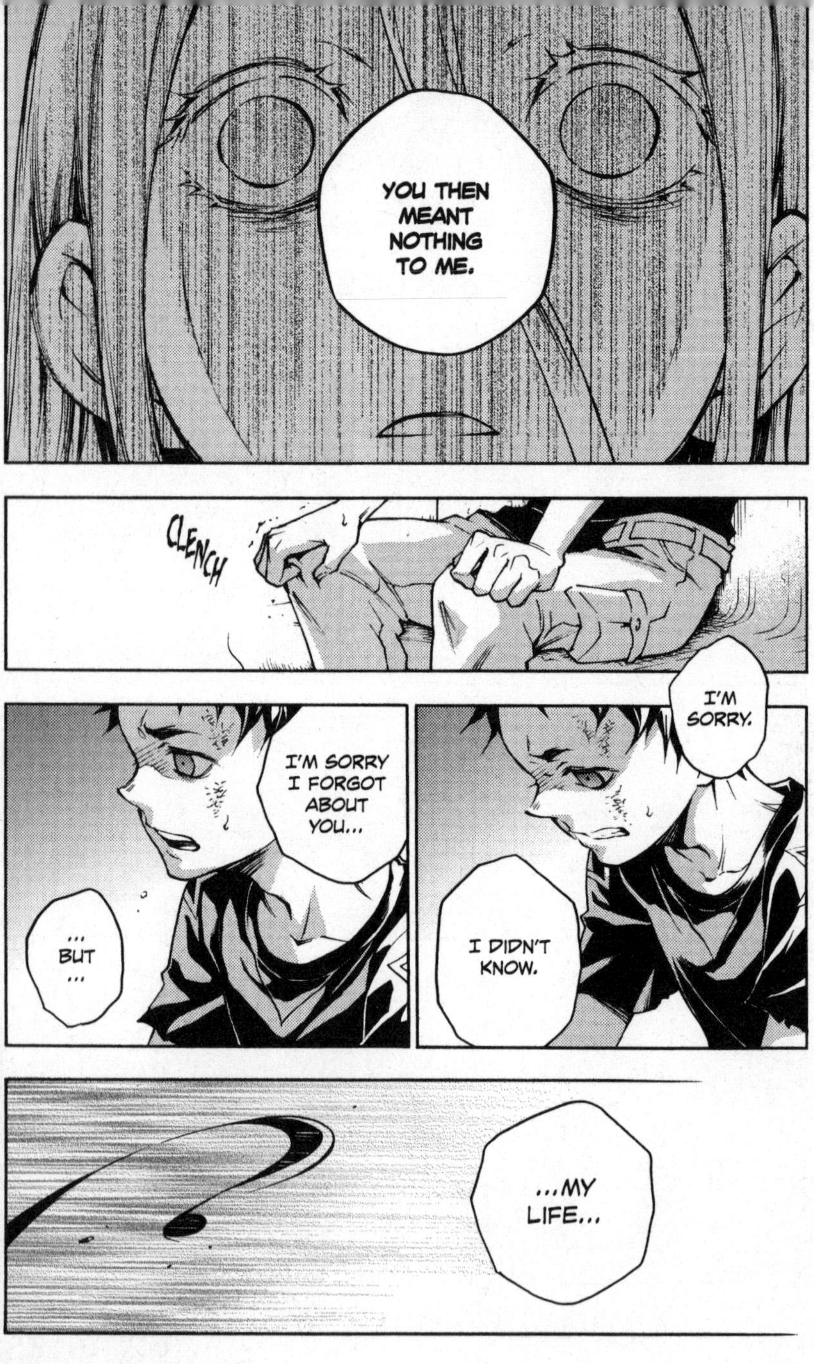
YOU THEN MEANT NOTHING TO ME.
CLENCH
I'M SORRY.
I DIDN'T KNOW.
I'M SORRY I FORGOT ABOUT YOU...
...BUT...
...MY LIFE...

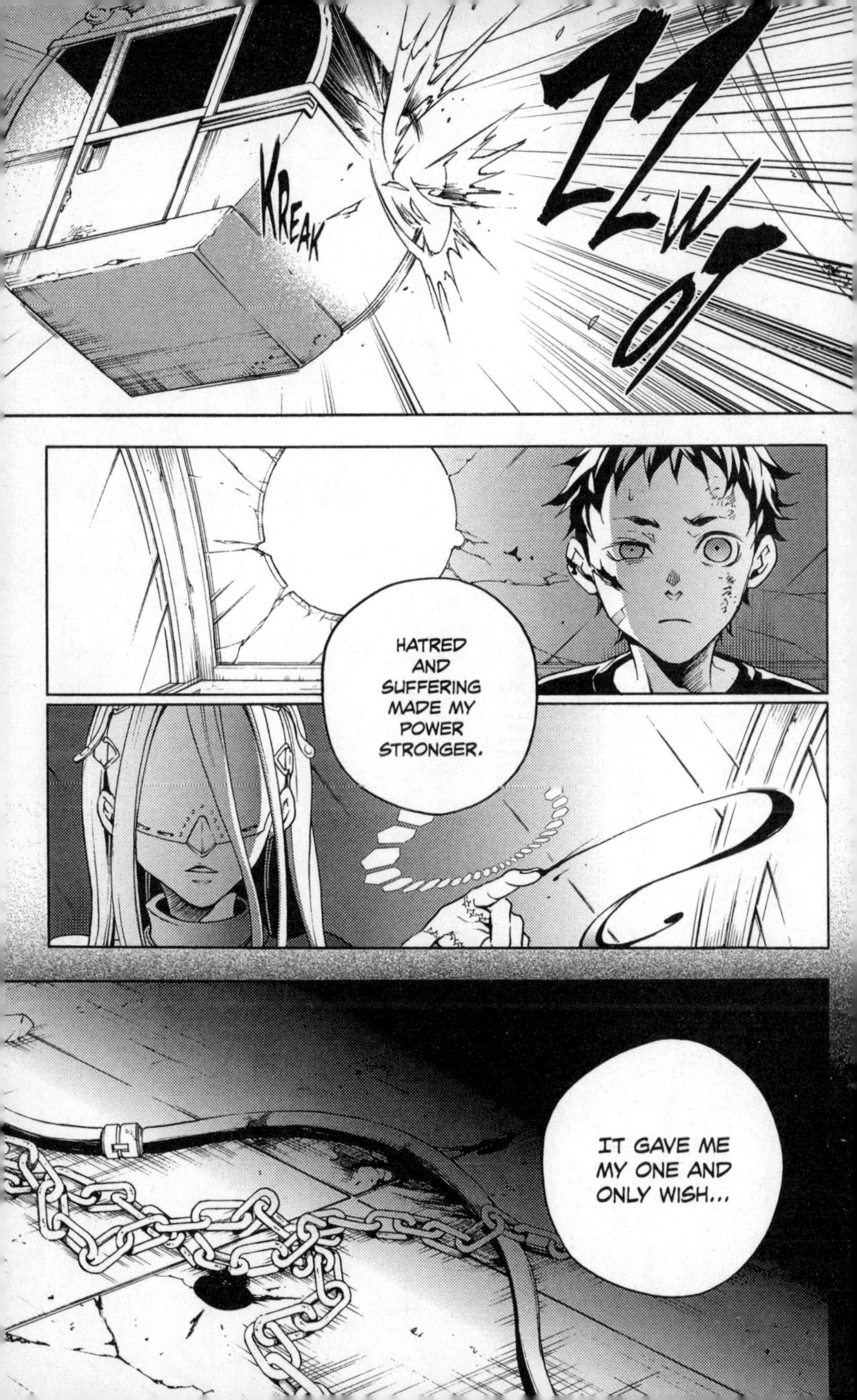
KREAK
HATRED AND SUFFERING MADE MY POWER STRONGER.
IT GAVE ME MY ONE AND ONLY WISH...

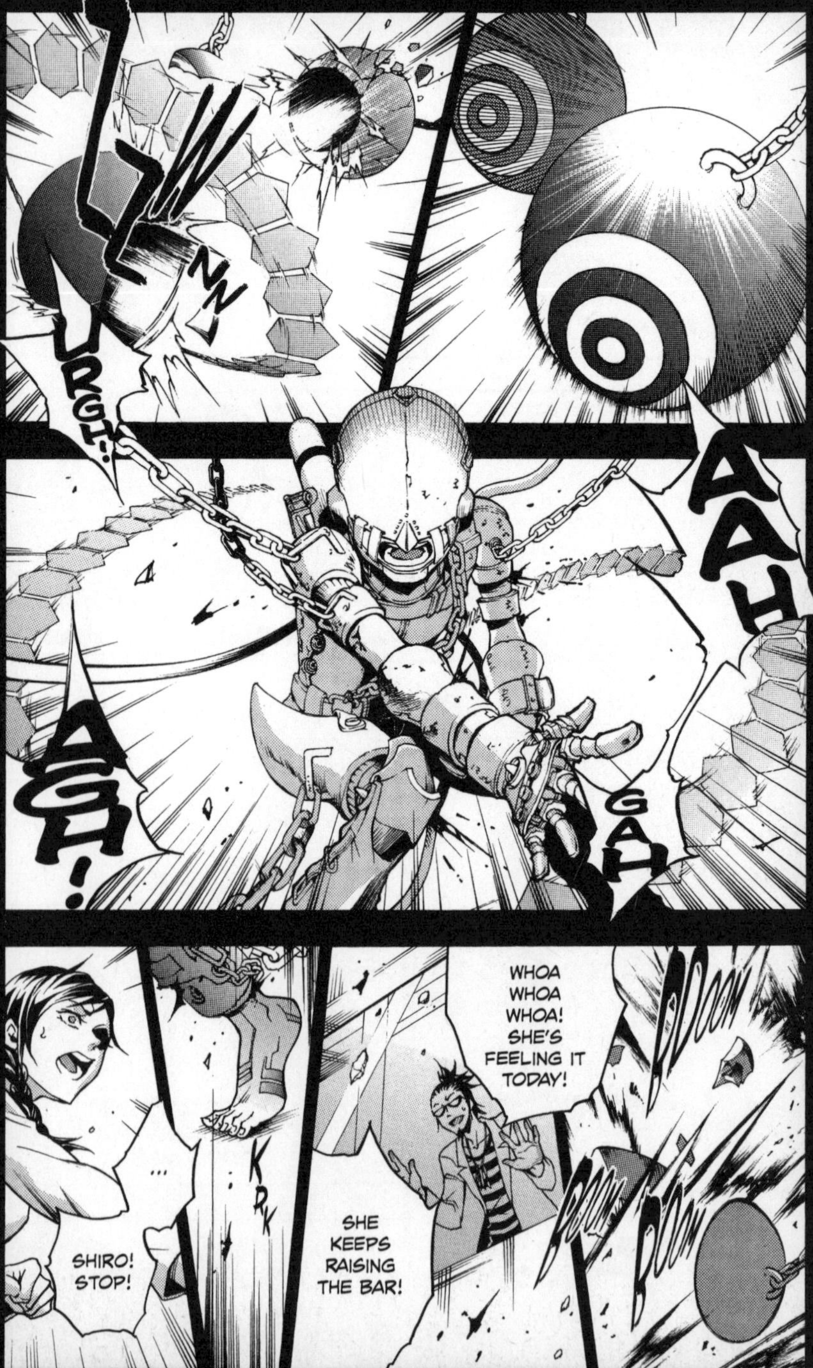
URGH!!
AAH
GAH
AGH!!
WHOA WHOA WHOA! SHE'S FEELING IT TODAY!
SHE KEEPS RAISING THE BAR!
KRK
...
SHIRO! STOP!

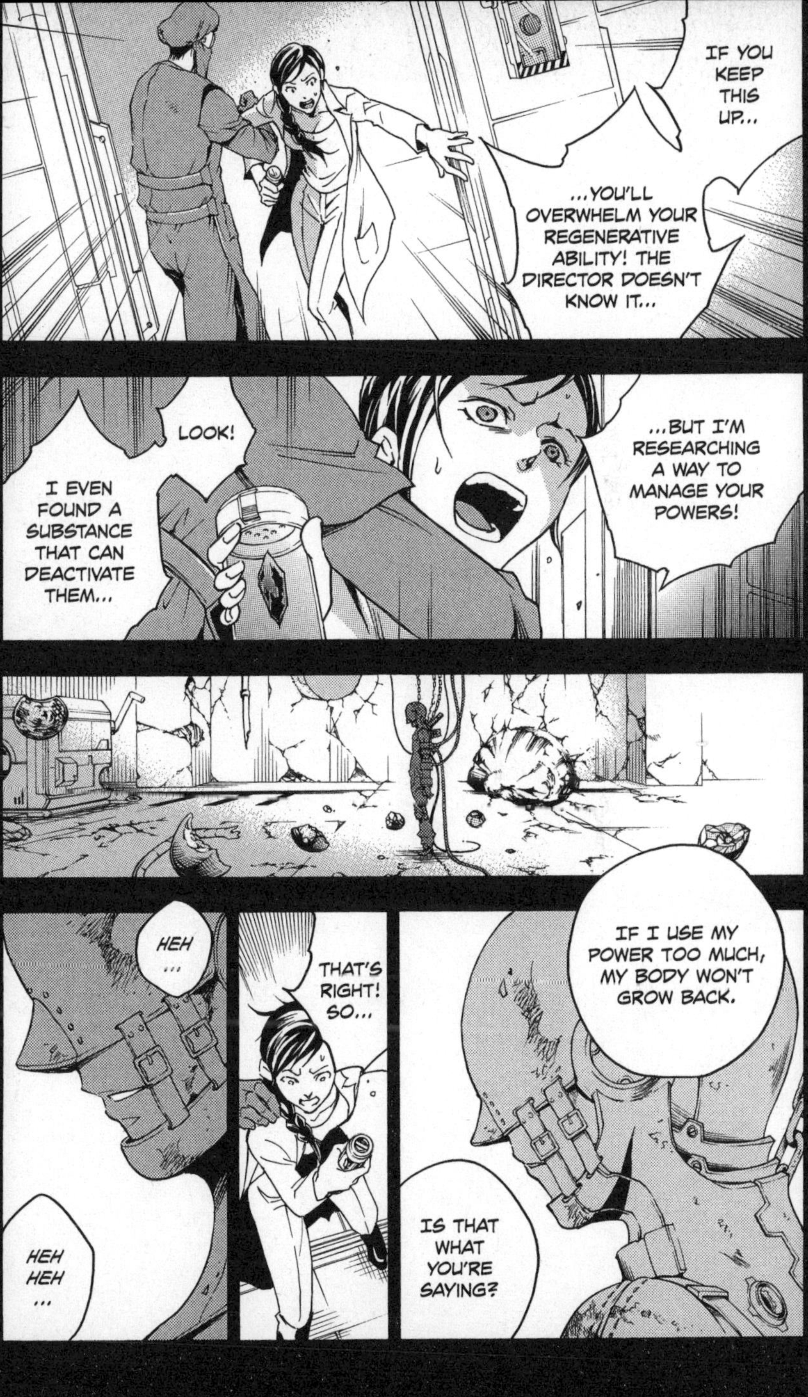
IF YOU KEEP THIS UP...
...YOU'LL OVERWHELM YOUR REGENERATIVE ABILITY! THE DIRECTOR DOESN'T KNOW IT...
...BUT I'M RESEARCHING A WAY TO MANAGE YOUR POWERS!
LOOK!
I EVEN FOUND A SUBSTANCE THAT CAN DEACTIVATE THEM...
IF I USE MY POWER TOO MUCH, MY BODY WON'T GROW BACK.
IS THAT WHAT YOU'RE SAYING?
THAT'S RIGHT! SO...
HEH ...
HEH HEH ...

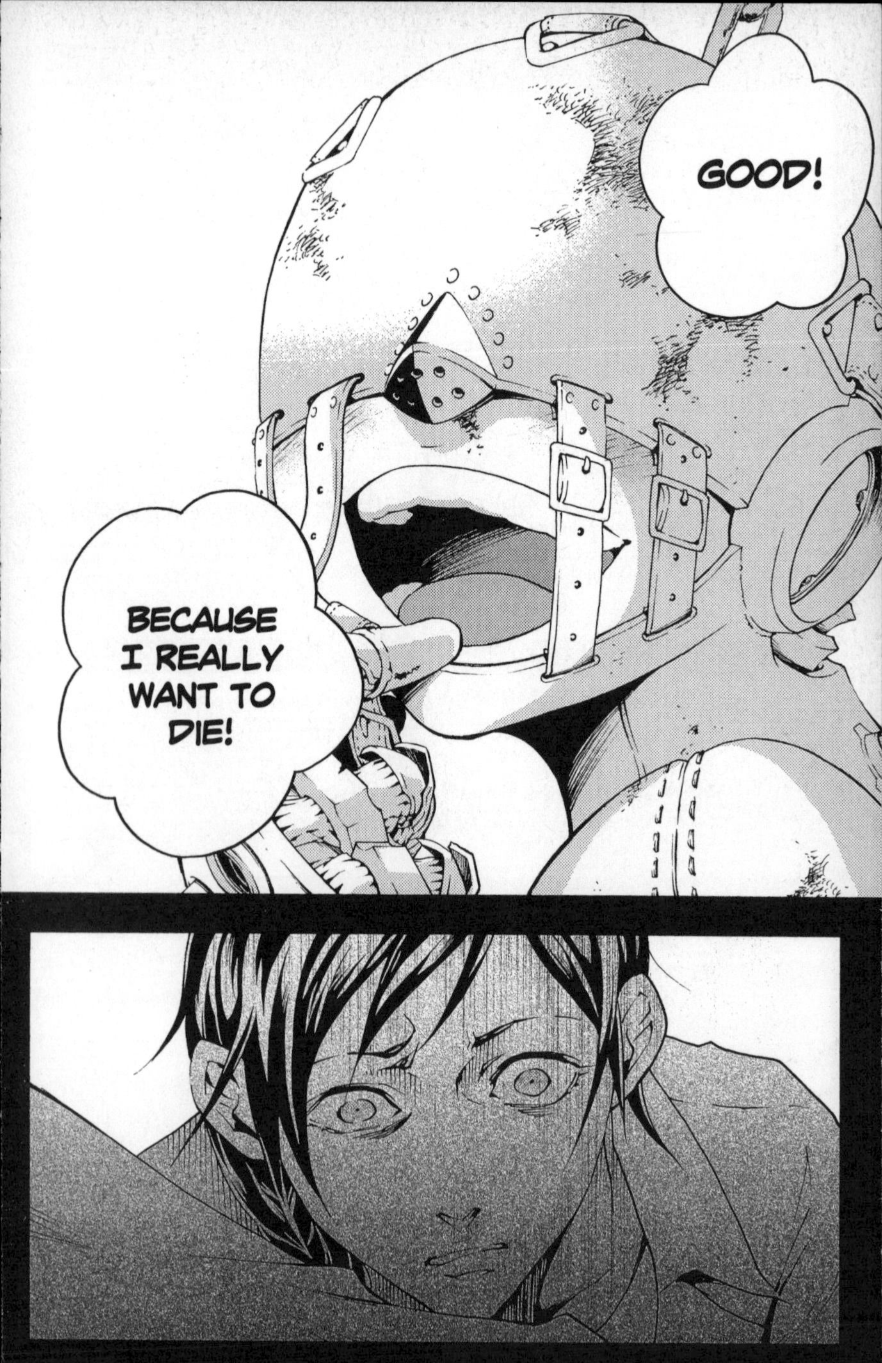
GOOD!
BECAUSE I REALLY WANT TO DIE!

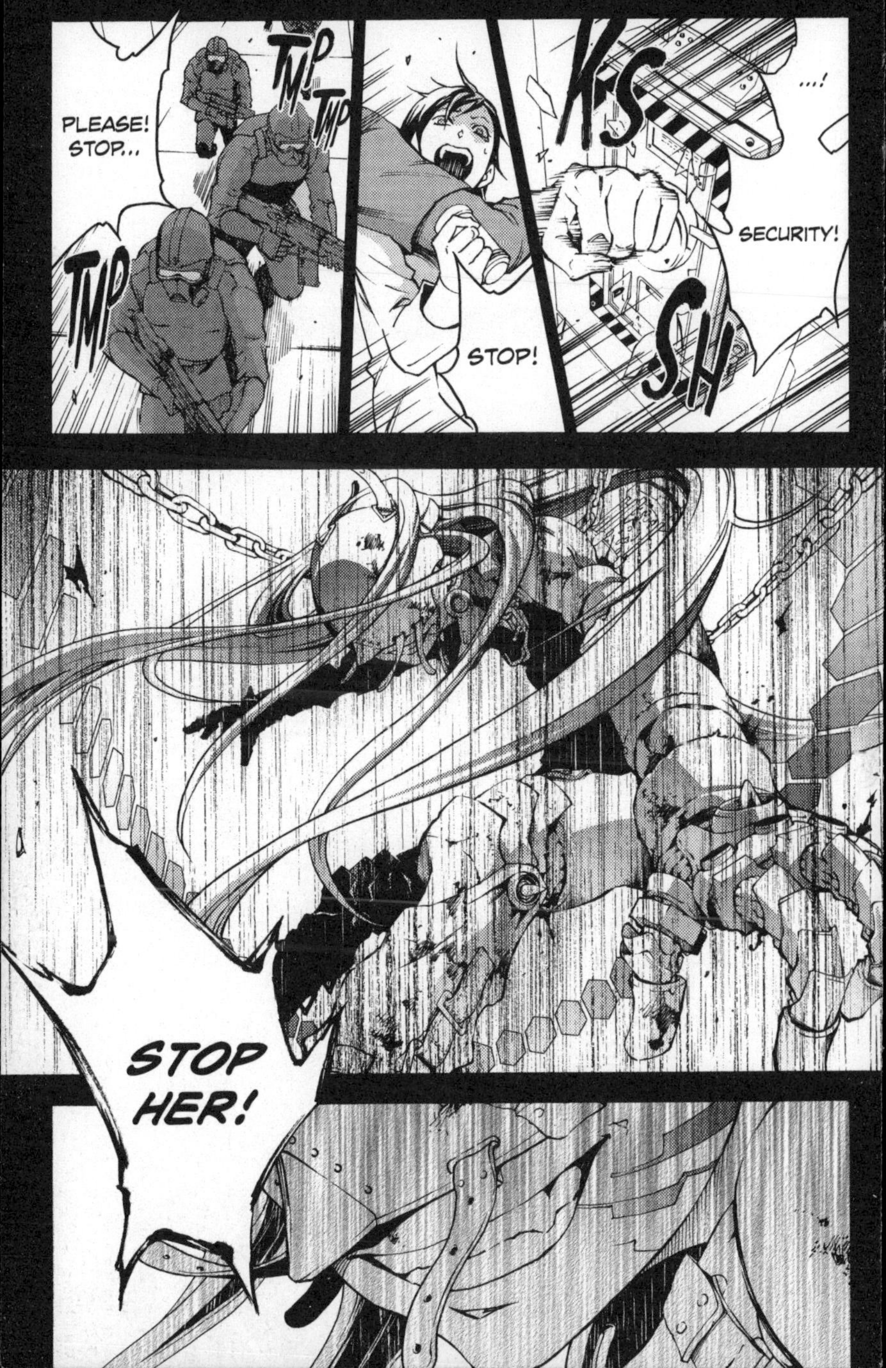
...!
K-S
SECURITY!
SH
STOP!
PLEASE! STOP...
TMP
TMP
TMP
TMP
STOP HER!

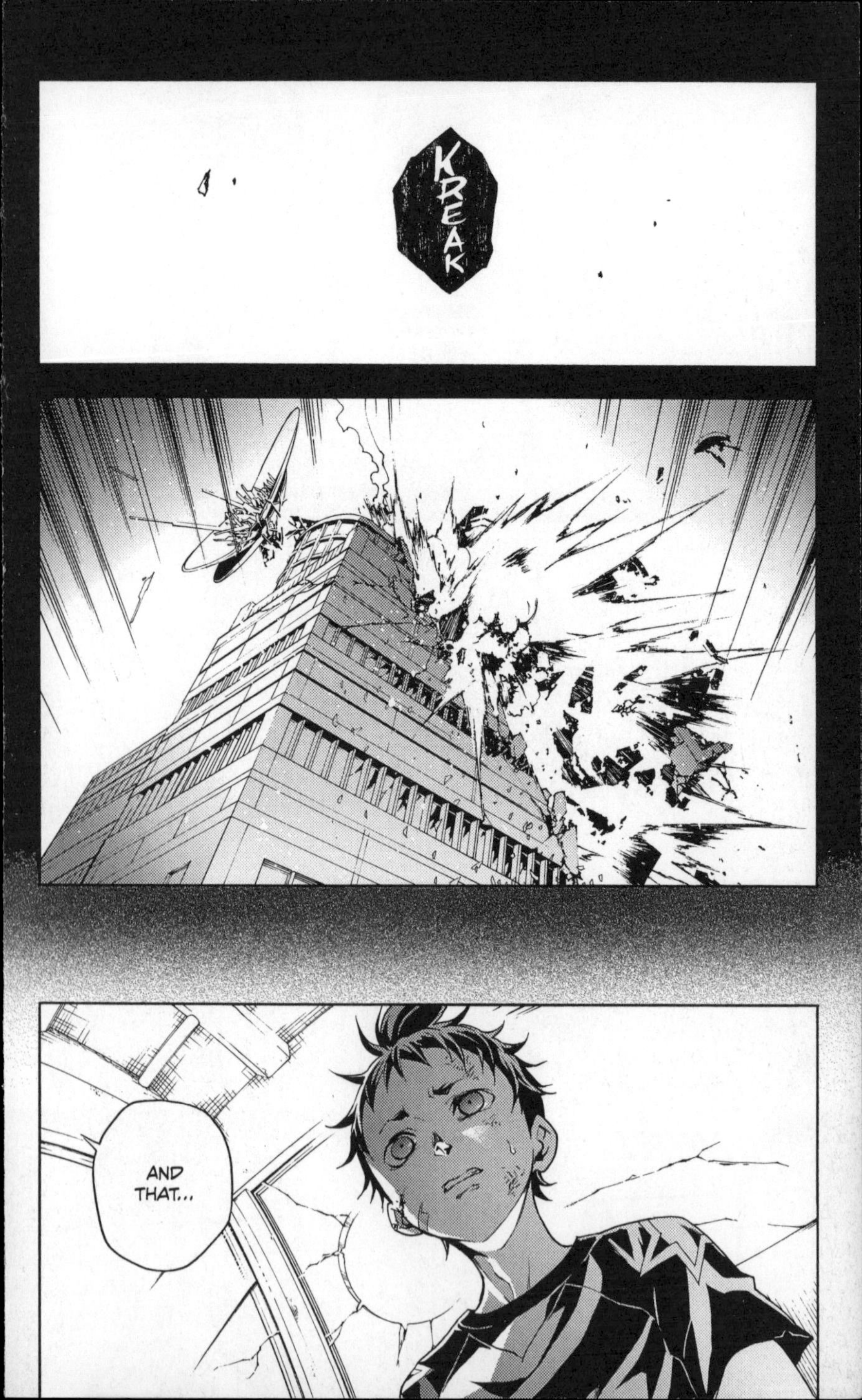
KREAK
AND THAT...

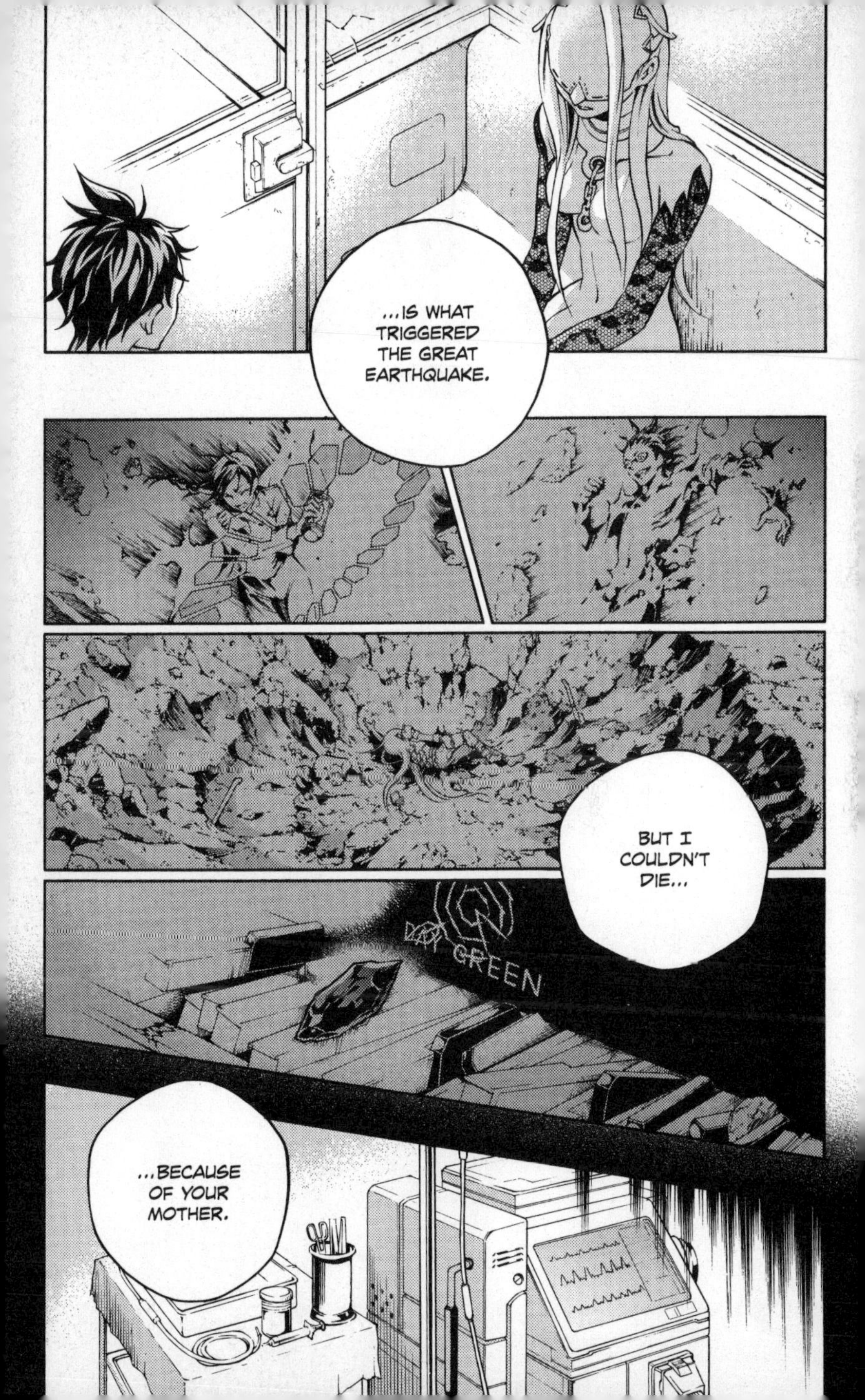
...IS WHAT TRIGGERED THE GREAT EARTHQUAKE.
BUT I COULDN'T DIE...
GREEN
...BECAUSE OF YOUR MOTHER.

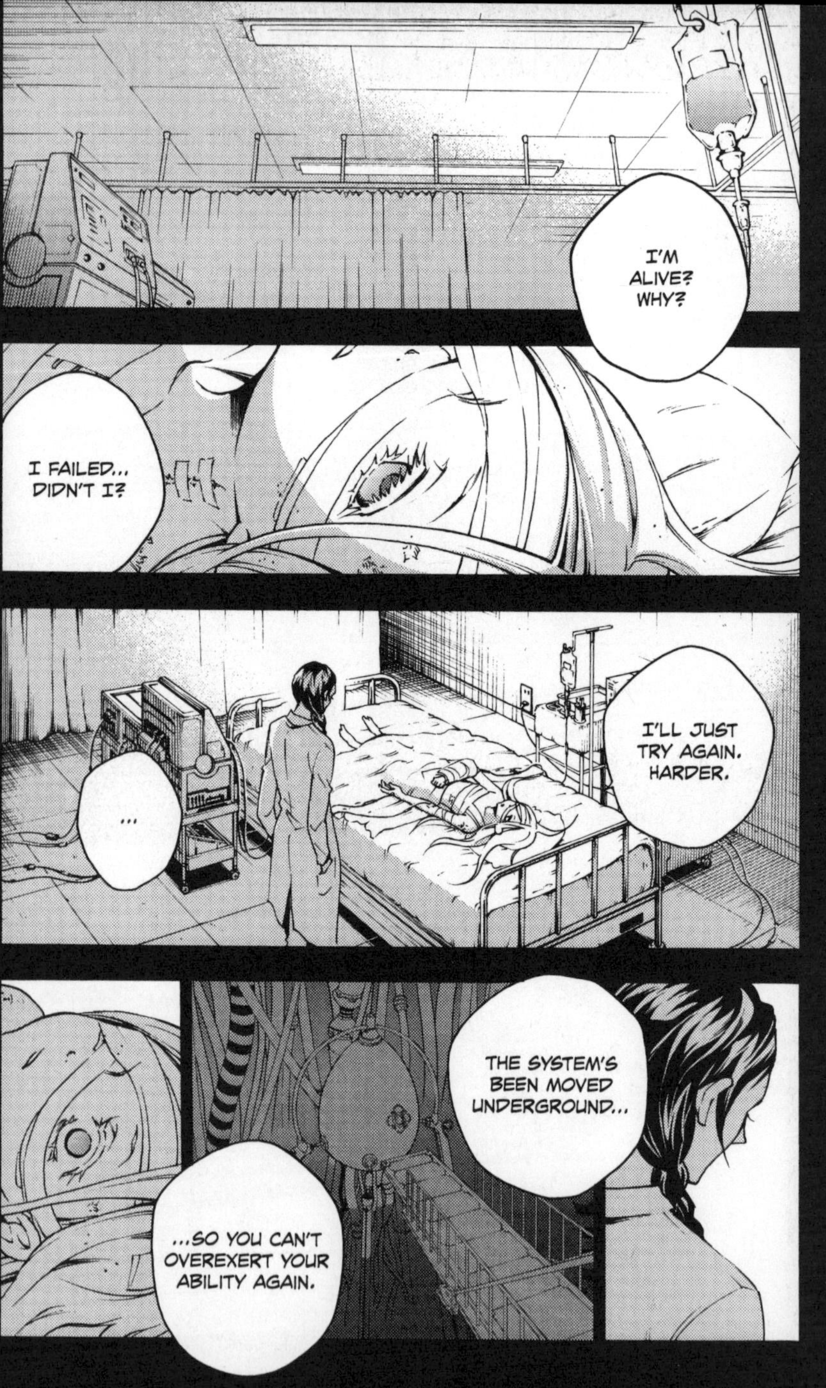
I'M ALIVE? WHY?
I FAILED... DIDN'T I?
I'LL JUST TRY AGAIN. HARDER.
...
THE SYSTEM'S BEEN MOVED UNDERGROUND...
...SO YOU CAN'T OVEREXERT YOUR ABILITY AGAIN.

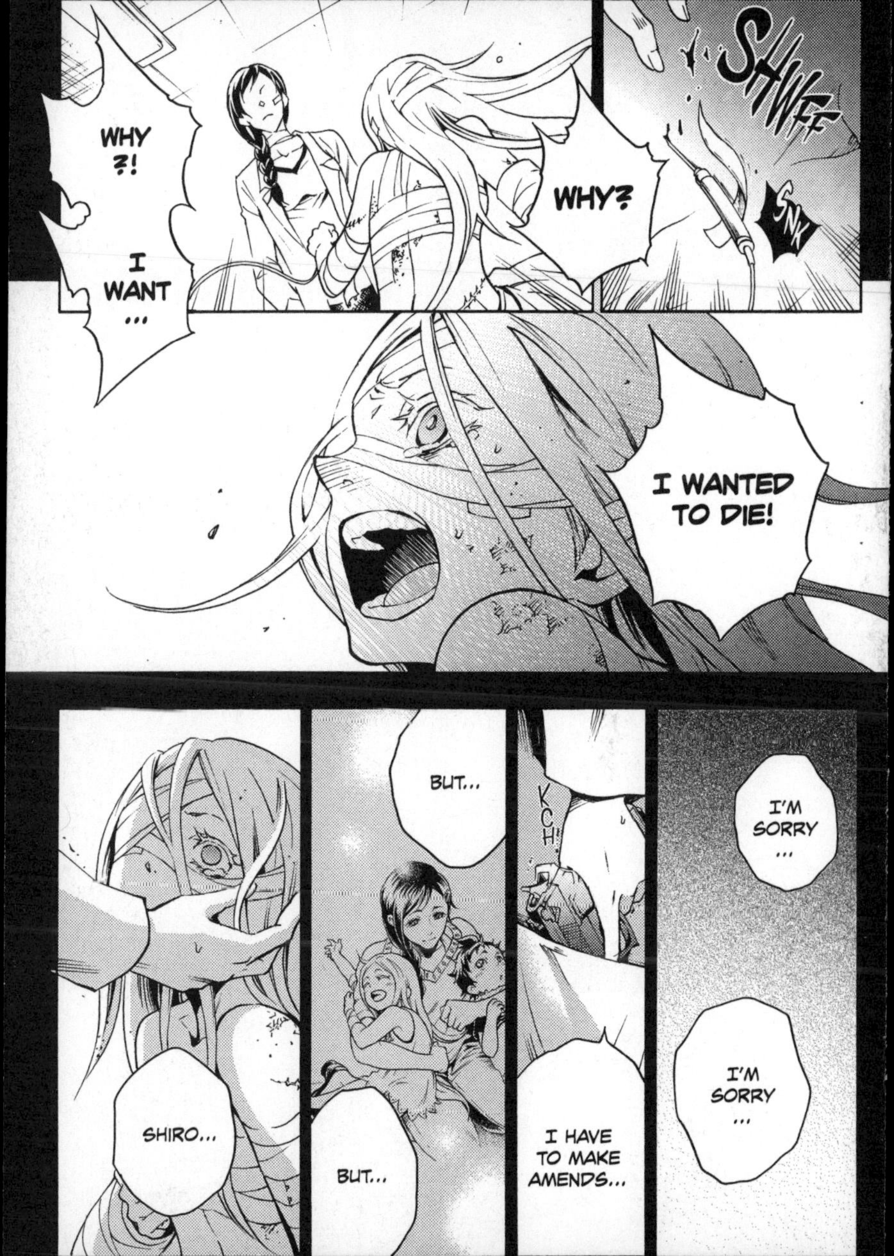
SHWFF
SNK
WHY?
WHY ?!
I WANT ...
I WANTED TO DIE!
I'M SORRY ...
I'M SORRY ...
KCH
I HAVE TO MAKE AMENDS...
BUT...
BUT...
SHIRO...

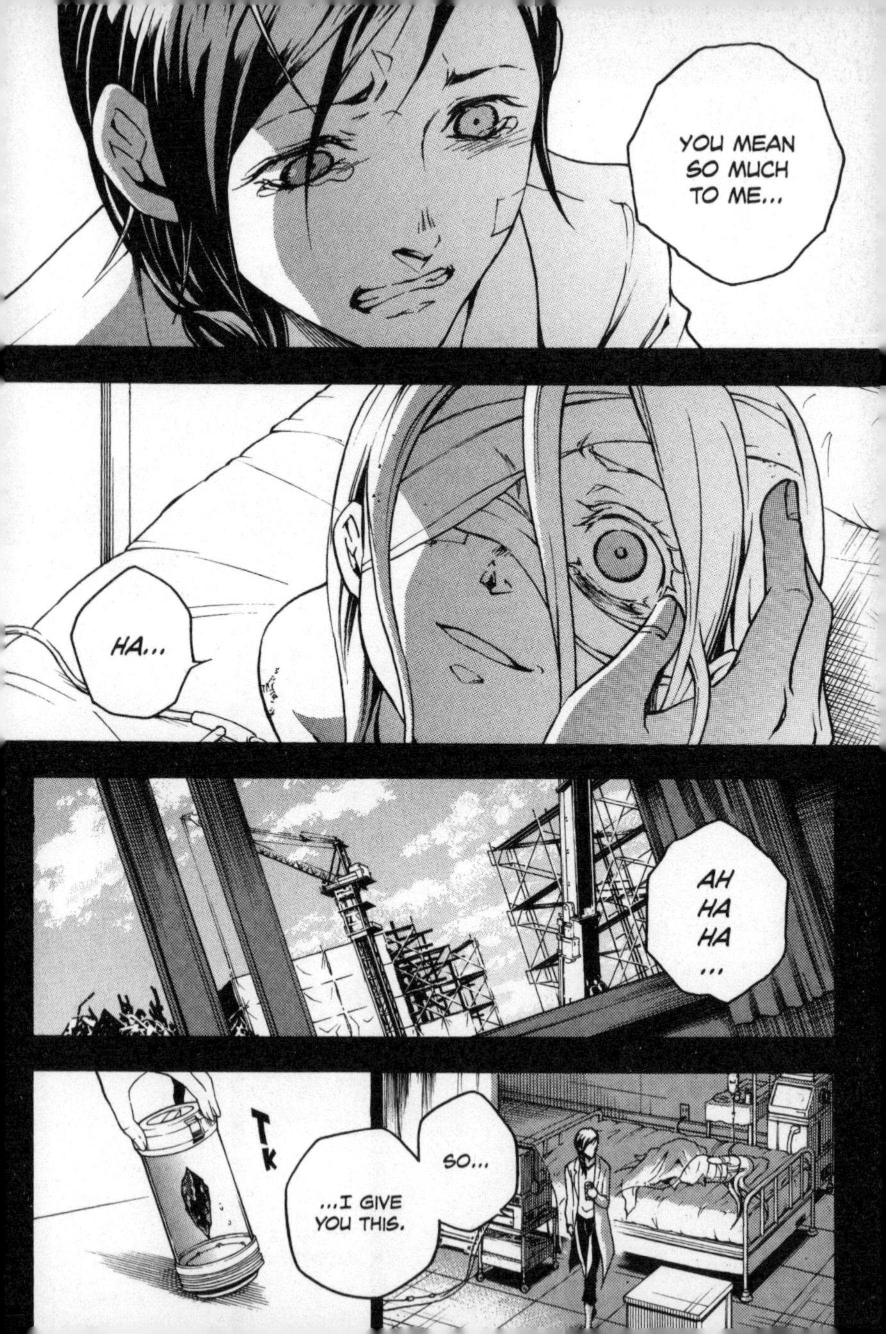
YOU MEAN SO MUCH TO ME...
HA...
AH HA HA ...
SO...
...I GIVE YOU THIS.
TK

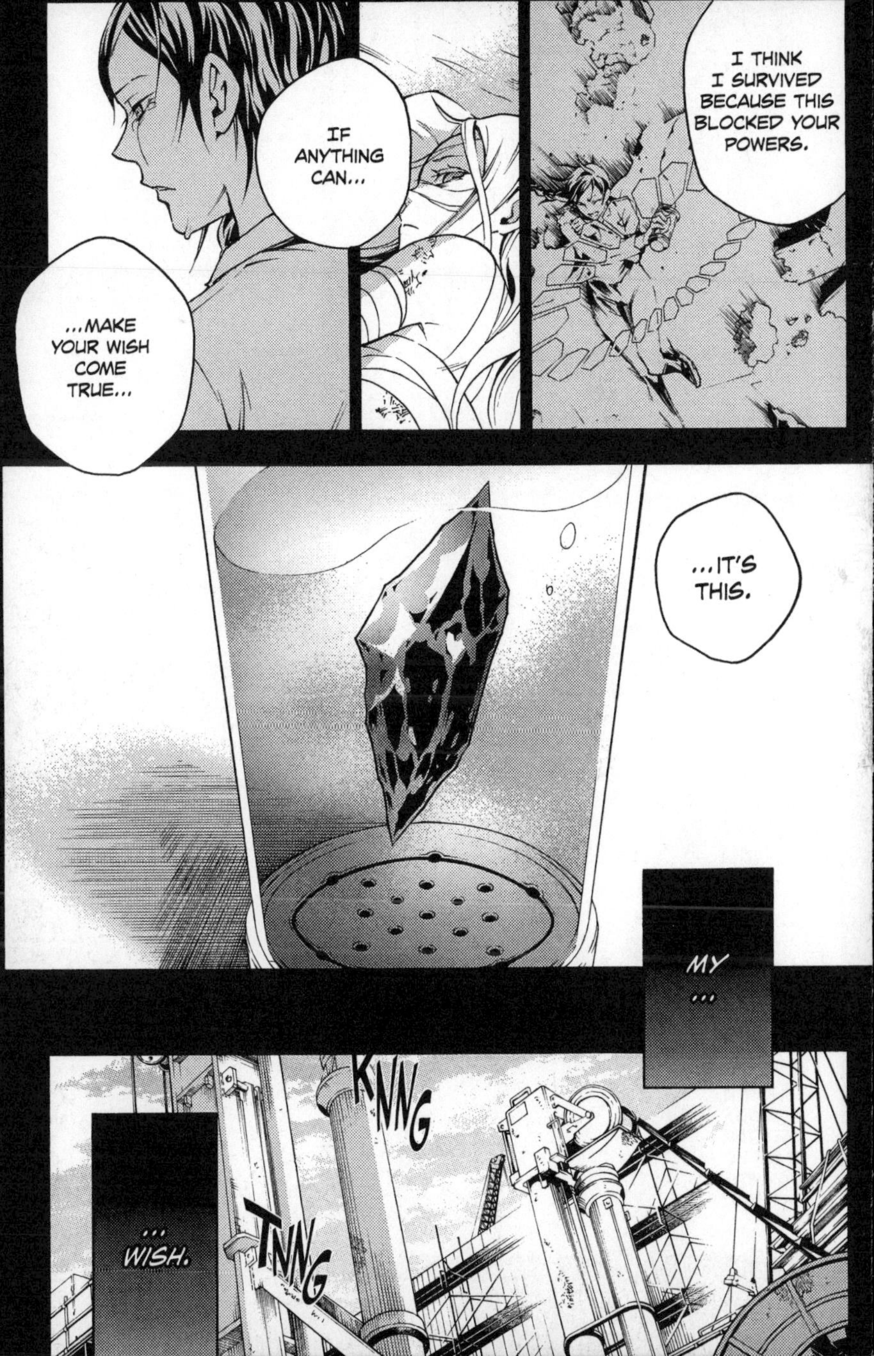
I THINK I SURVIVED BECAUSE THIS BLOCKED YOUR POWERS.
IF ANYTHING CAN...
...MAKE YOUR WISH COME TRUE...
...IT'S THIS.
MY ...
KNNG
TNNG
... WISH.

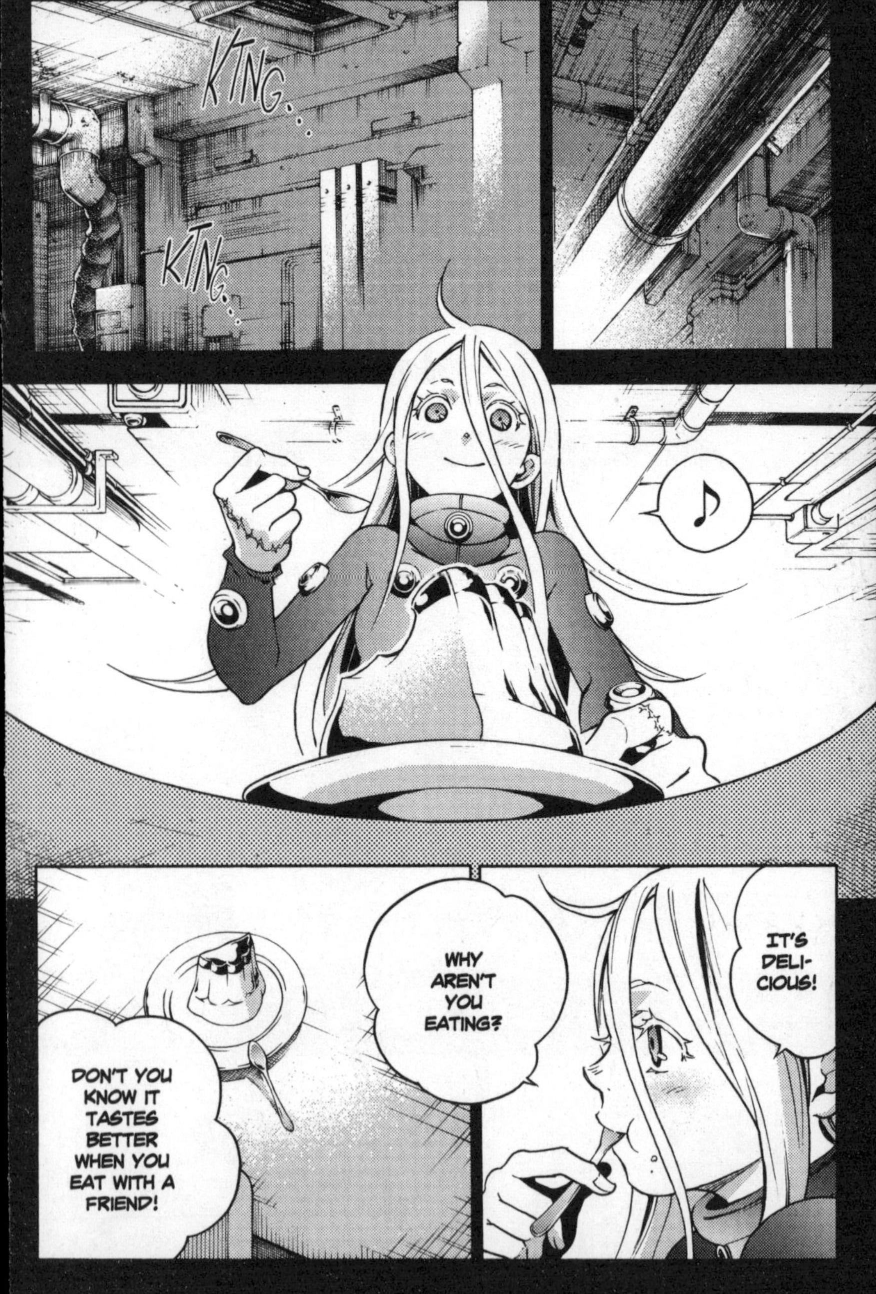
KTING...
KTING...
♪
IT'S DELI-CIOUS!
WHY AREN'T YOU EATING?
DON'T YOU KNOW IT TASTES BETTER WHEN YOU EAT WITH A FRIEND!

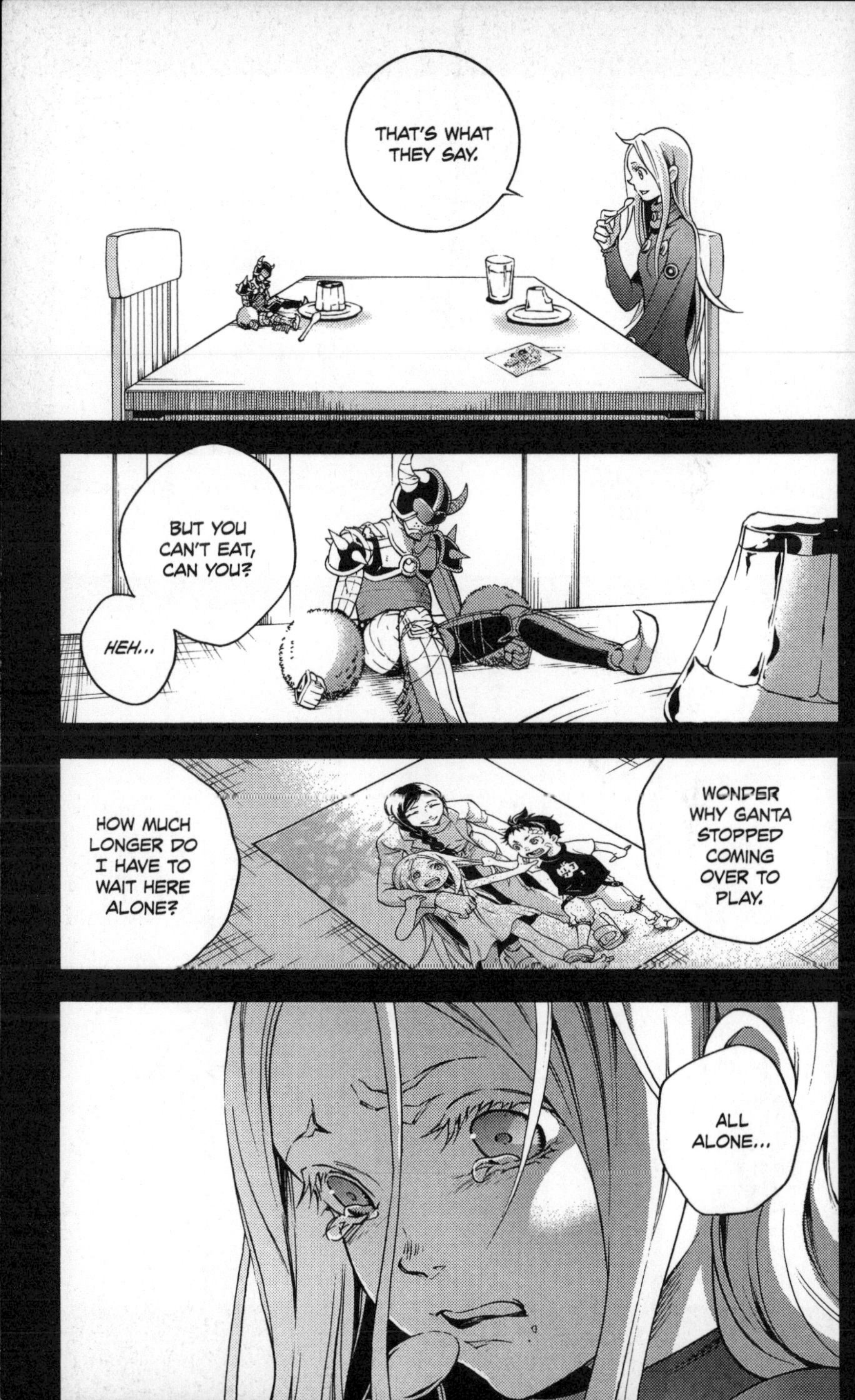
THAT'S WHAT THEY SAY.
BUT YOU CAN'T EAT, CAN YOU?
HEH...
WONDER WHY GANTA STOPPED COMING OVER TO PLAY.
HOW MUCH LONGER DO I HAVE TO WAIT HERE ALONE?
ALL ALONE...

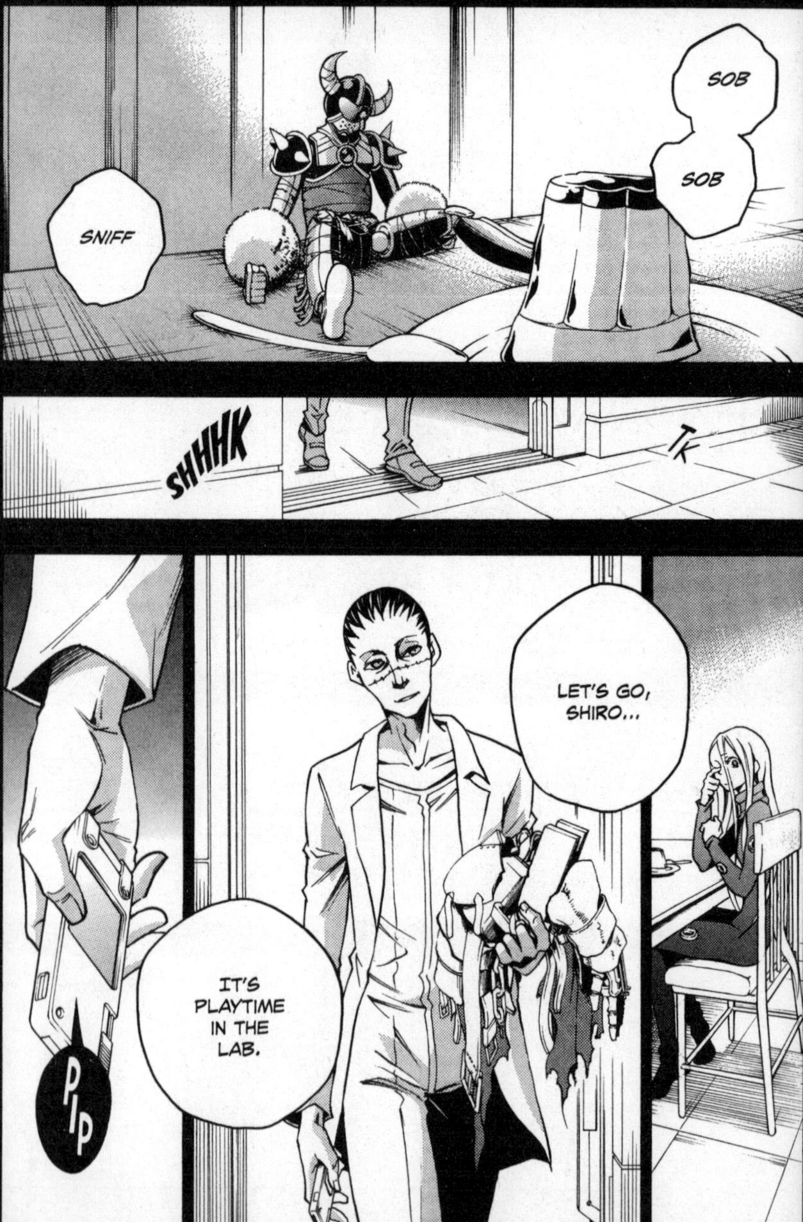
SOB
SOB
SNIFF
TK
SHHHK
LET'S GO, SHIRO...
IT'S PLAYTIME IN THE LAB.
PIP

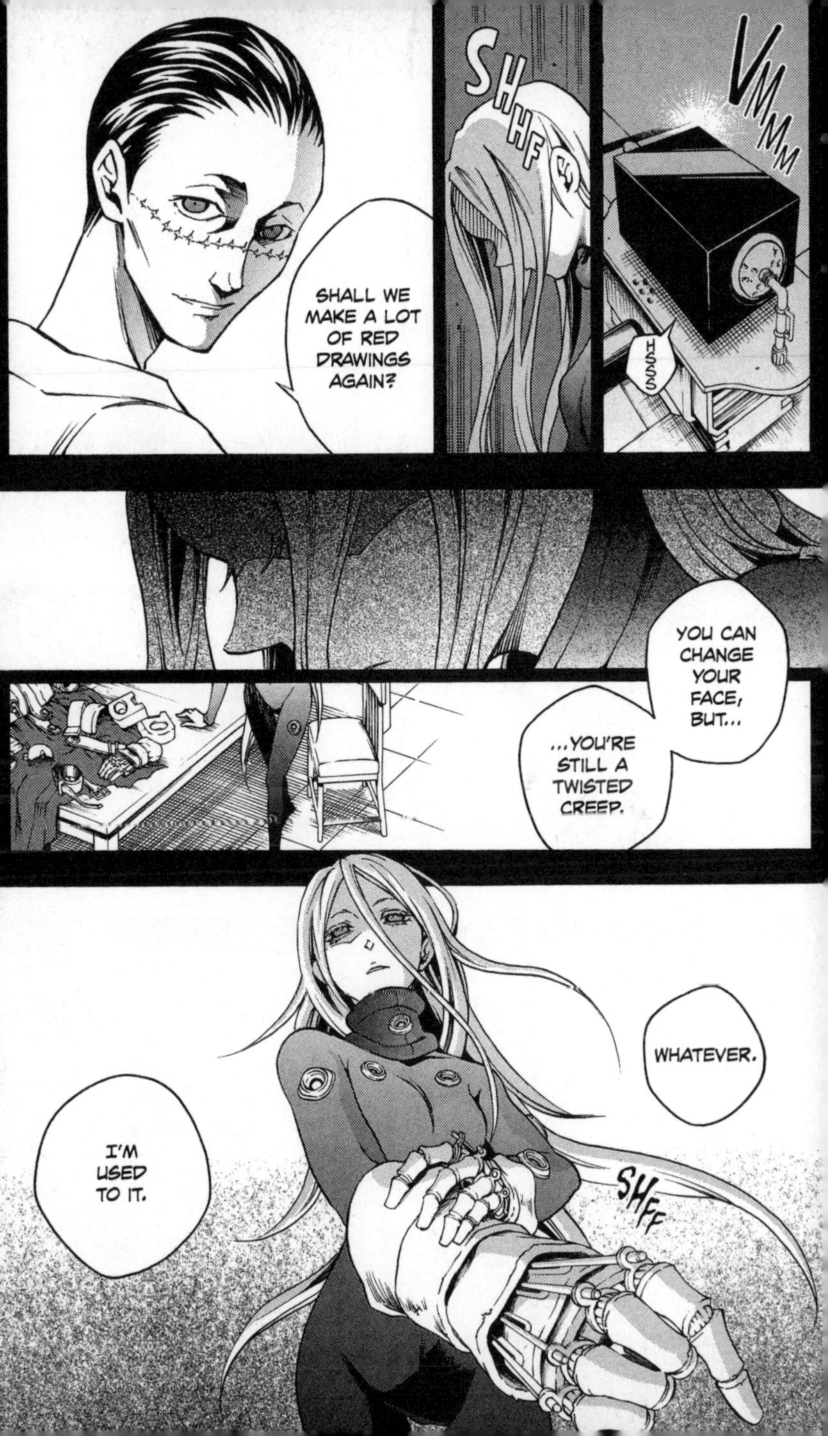
VMMM
HSSS
SHHF
SHALL WE MAKE A LOT OF RED DRAWINGS AGAIN?
YOU CAN CHANGE YOUR FACE, BUT...
...YOU'RE STILL A TWISTED CREEP.
WHATEVER.
SHFF
I'M USED TO IT.

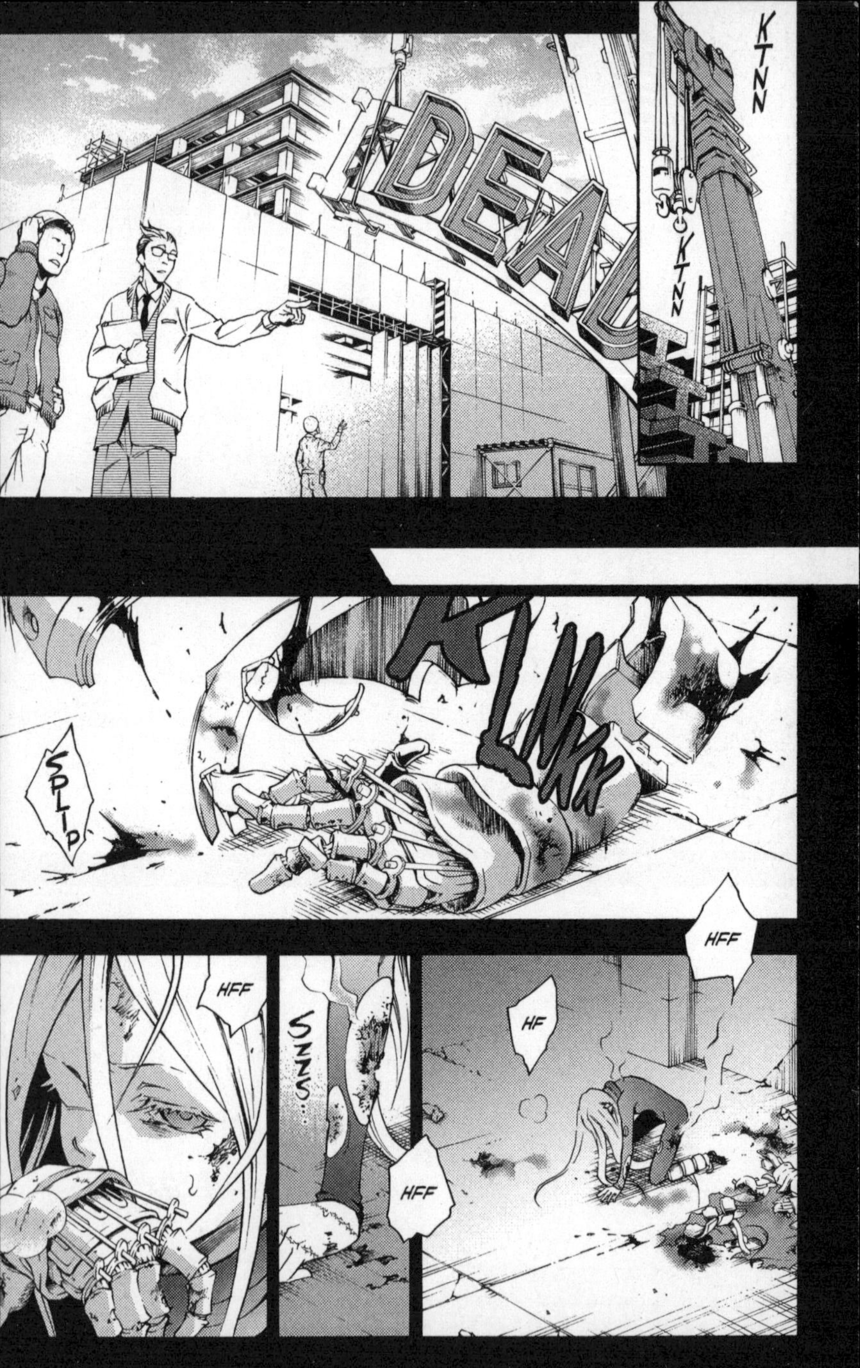
KTNN
KTNN
KLINKK
SPLIP
HFF
HF
SZZS...
HFF
HFF

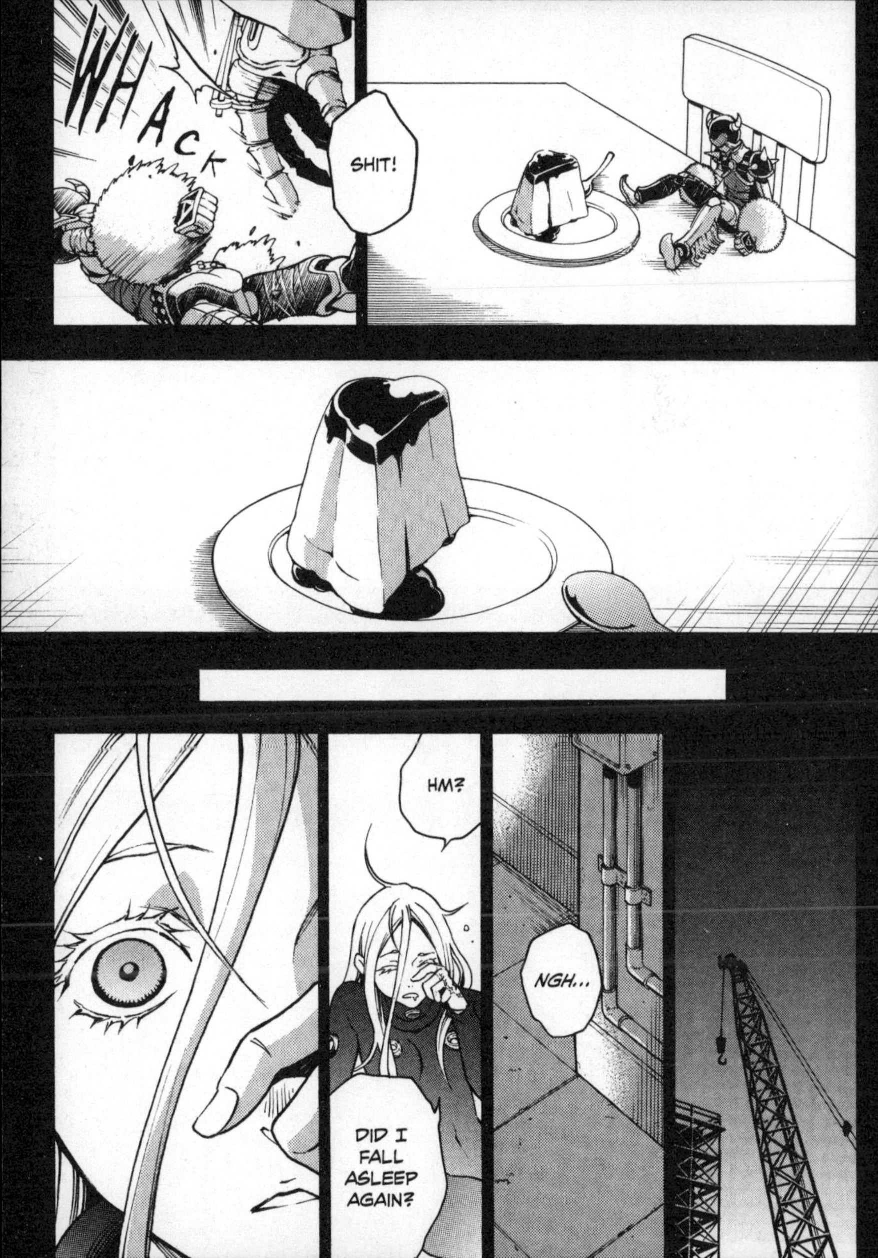
SHIT!
WHACK
NGH...
HM?
DID I FALL ASLEEP AGAIN?

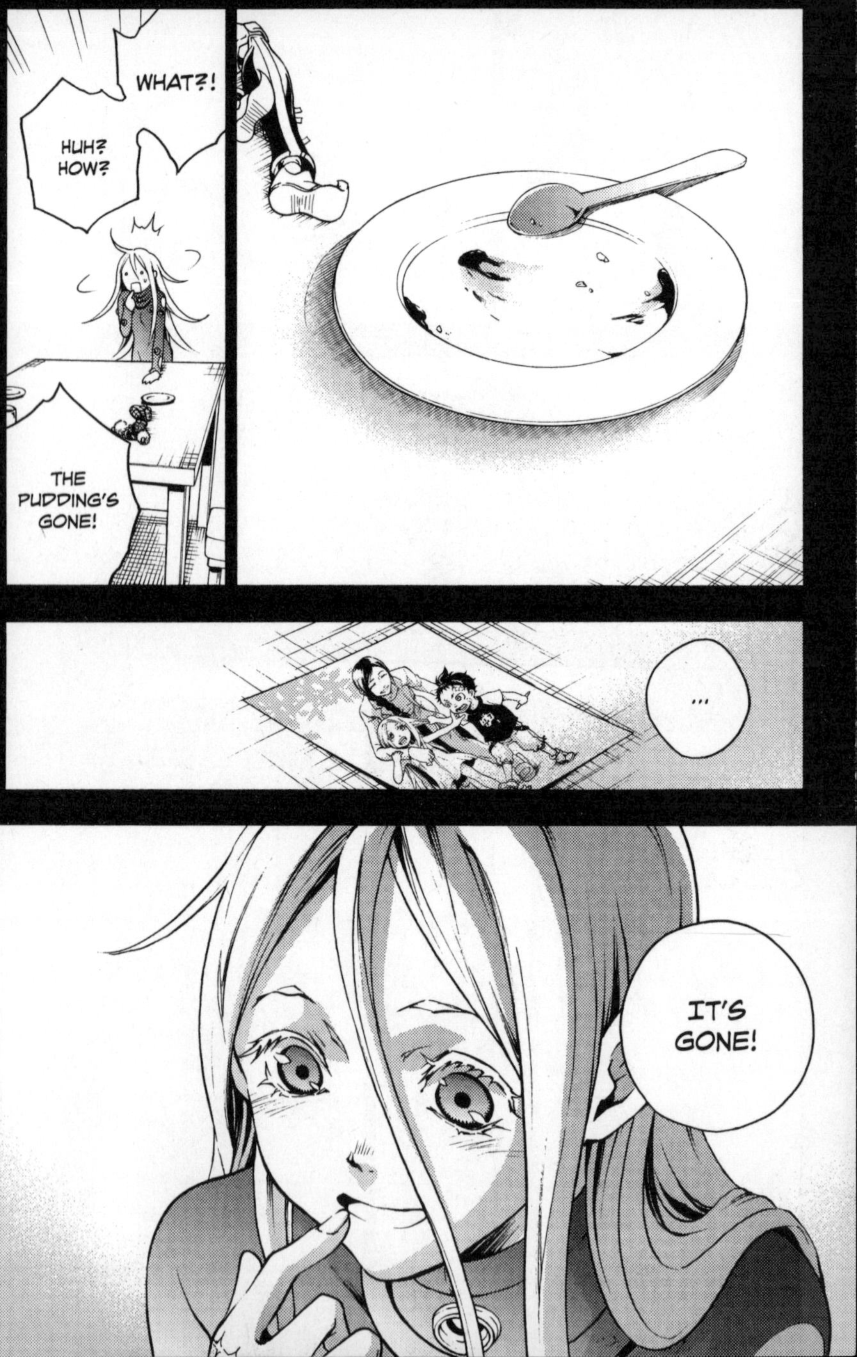
WHAT?!
HUH? HOW?
THE PUDDING'S GONE!
...
IT'S GONE!

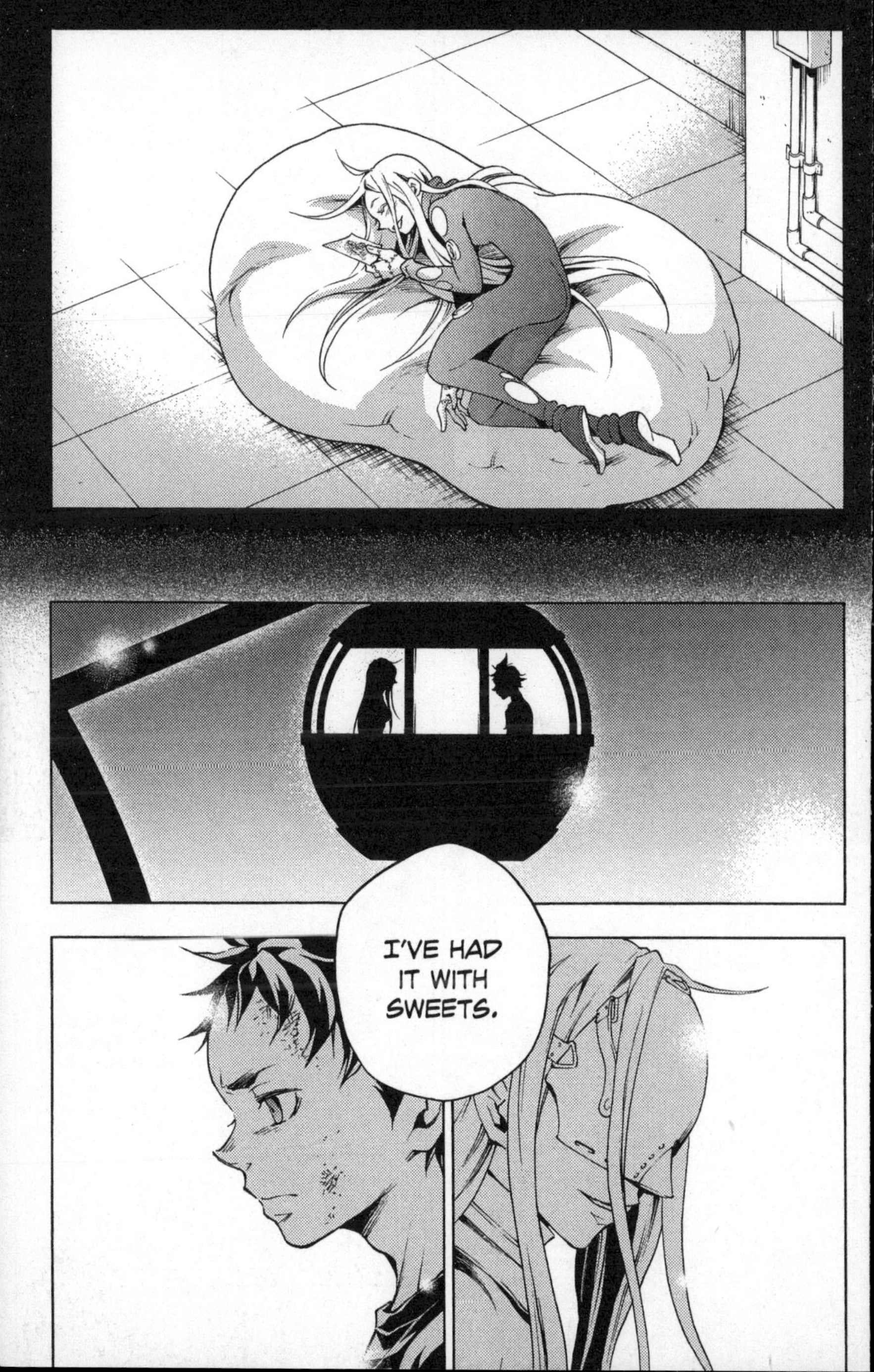
I'VE HAD IT WITH SWEETS.

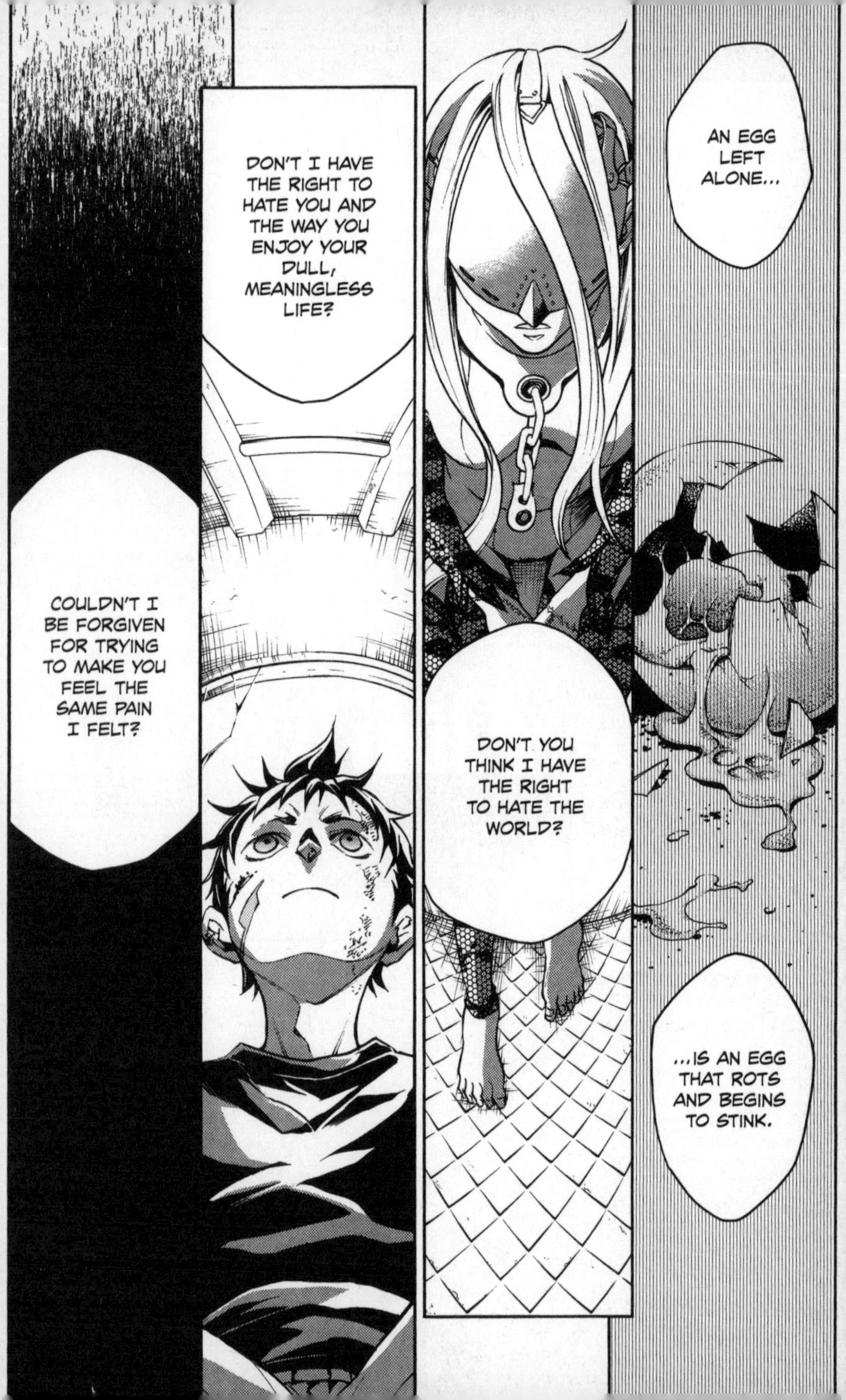
AN EGG LEFT ALONE...
...IS AN EGG THAT ROTS AND BEGINS TO STINK.
DON'T YOU THINK I HAVE THE RIGHT TO HATE THE WORLD?
DON'T I HAVE THE RIGHT TO HATE YOU AND THE WAY YOU ENJOY YOUR DULL, MEANINGLESS LIFE?
COULDN'T I BE FORGIVEN FOR TRYING TO MAKE YOU FEEL THE SAME PAIN I FELT?

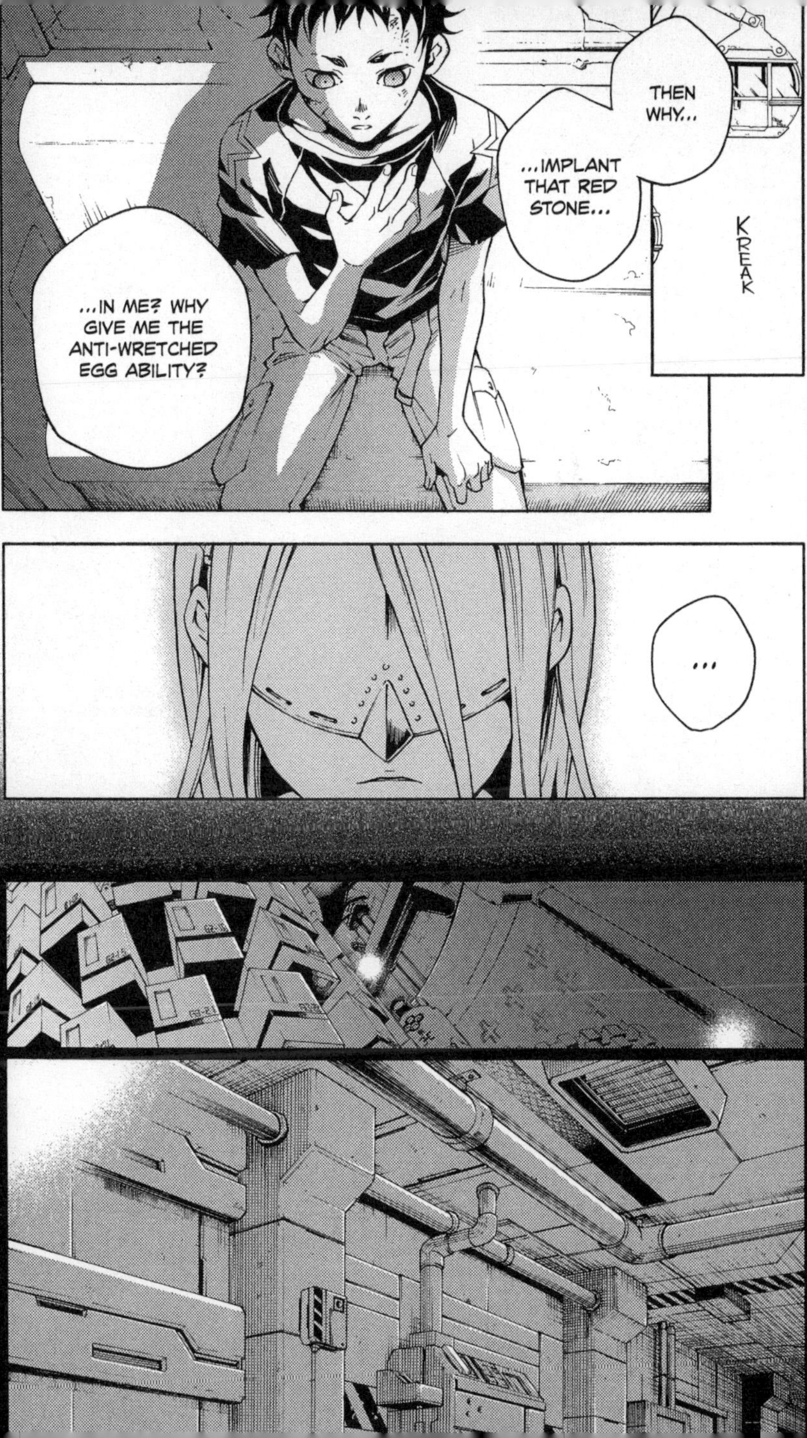
THEN WHY...
...IMPLANT THAT RED STONE...
KREAK
...IN ME? WHY GIVE ME THE ANTI-WRETCHED EGG ABILITY?
...

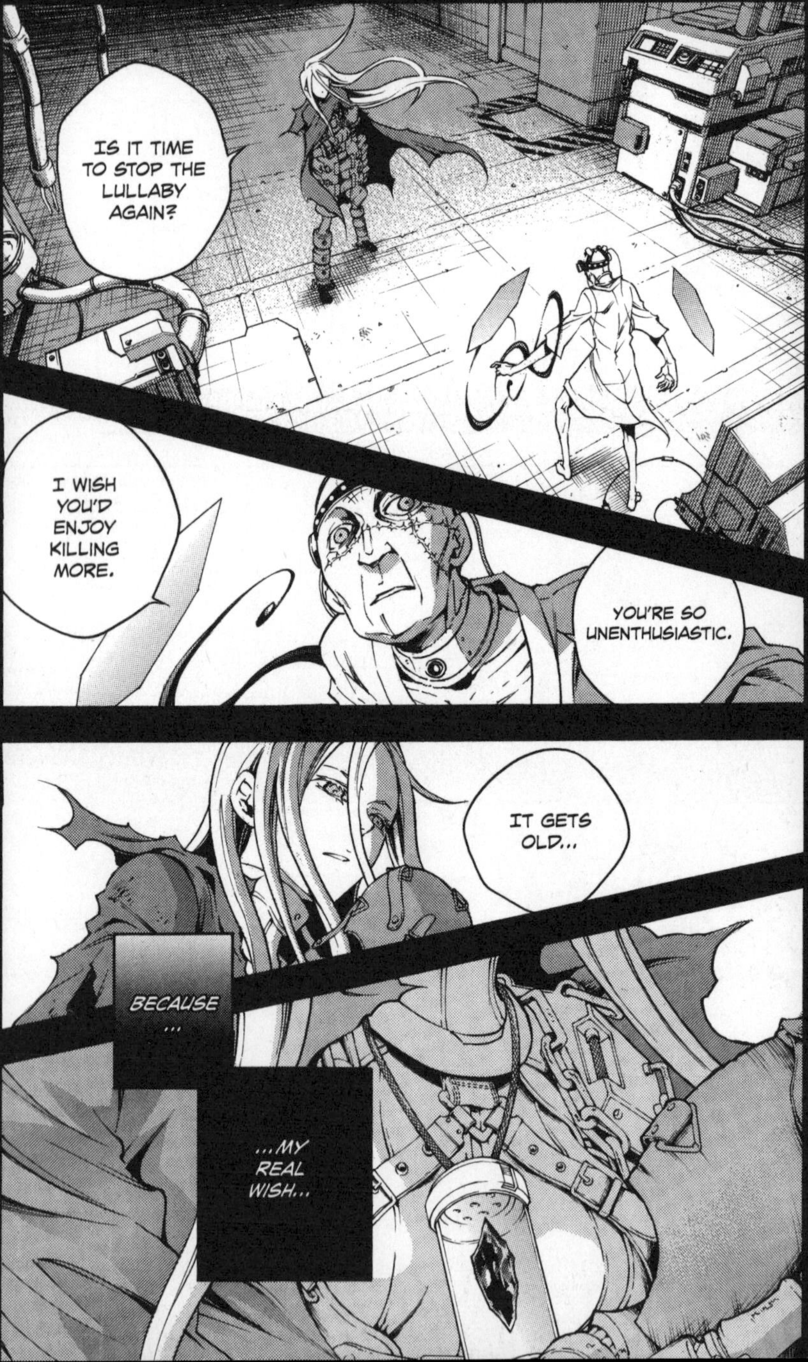
IS IT TIME TO STOP THE LULLABY AGAIN?
I WISH YOU'D ENJOY KILLING MORE.
YOU'RE SO UNENTHUSIASTIC.
IT GETS OLD...
BECAUSE ...
...MY REAL WISH...

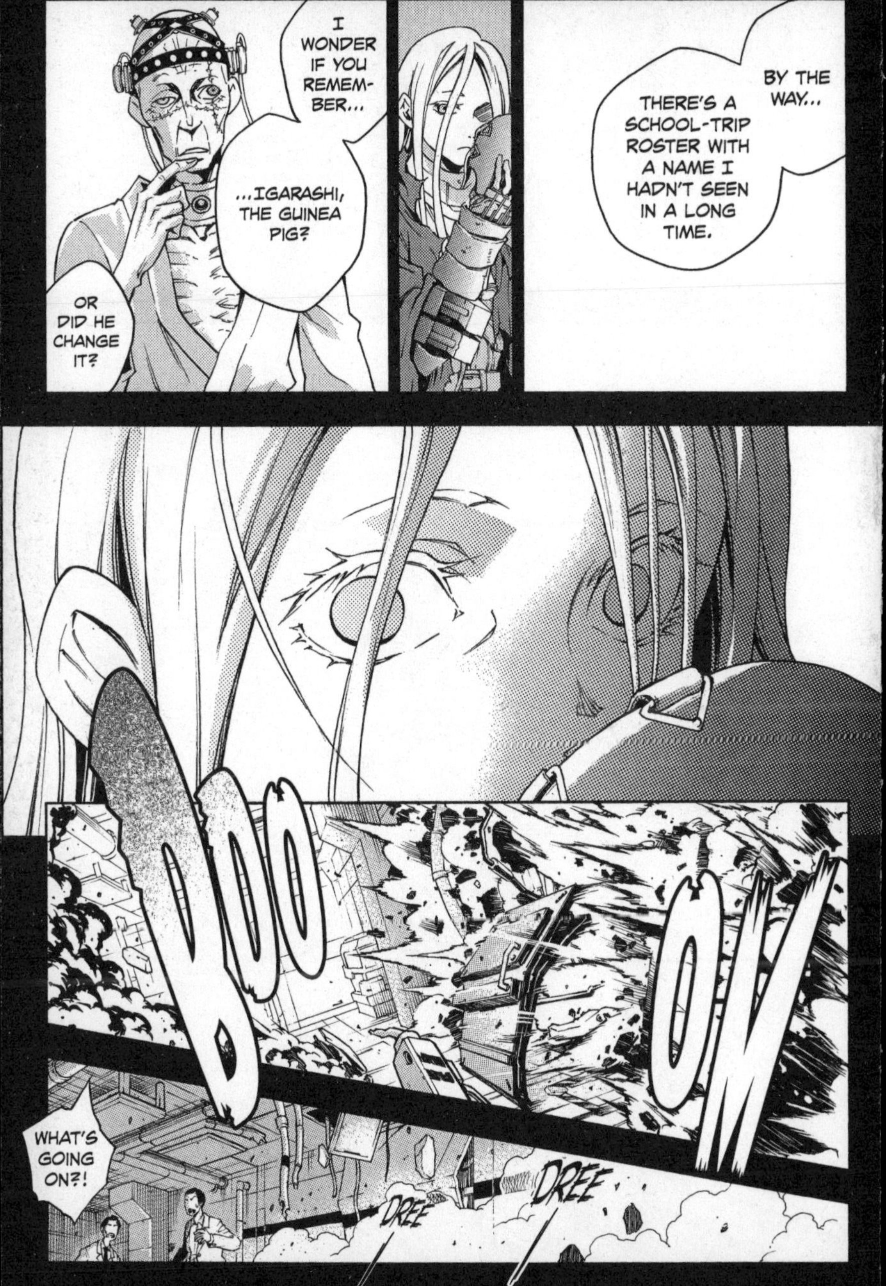
BY THE WAY...
THERE'S A SCHOOL-TRIP ROSTER WITH A NAME I HADN'T SEEN IN A LONG TIME.
I WONDER IF YOU REMEMBER...
...IGARASHI, THE GUINEA PIG?
OR DID HE CHANGE IT?
WHAT'S GOING ON?!
DREE
DREE

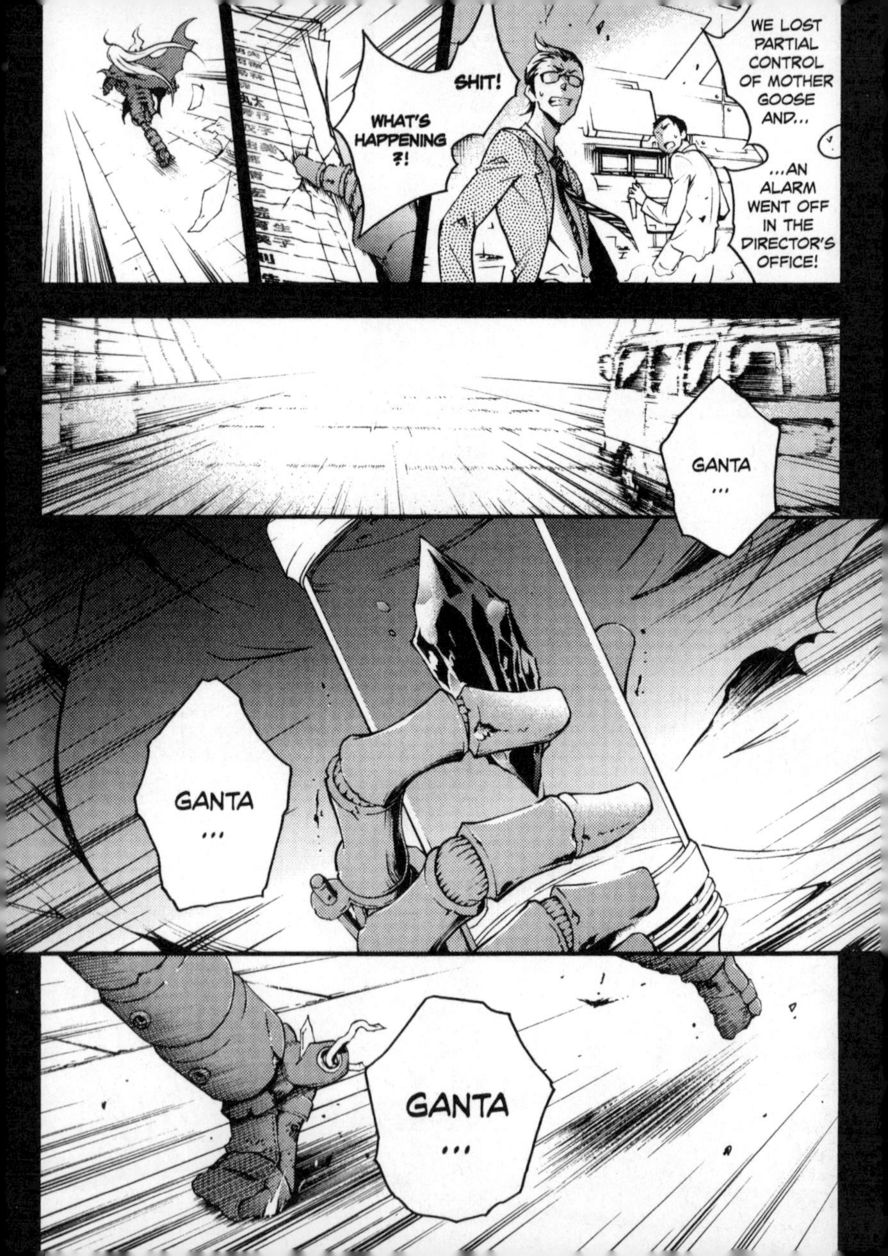
WE LOST PARTIAL CONTROL OF MOTHER GOOSE AND...
...AN ALARM WENT OFF IN THE DIRECTOR'S OFFICE!
SHIT!
WHAT'S HAPPENING ?!
GANTA ...
GANTA ...
GANTA ...

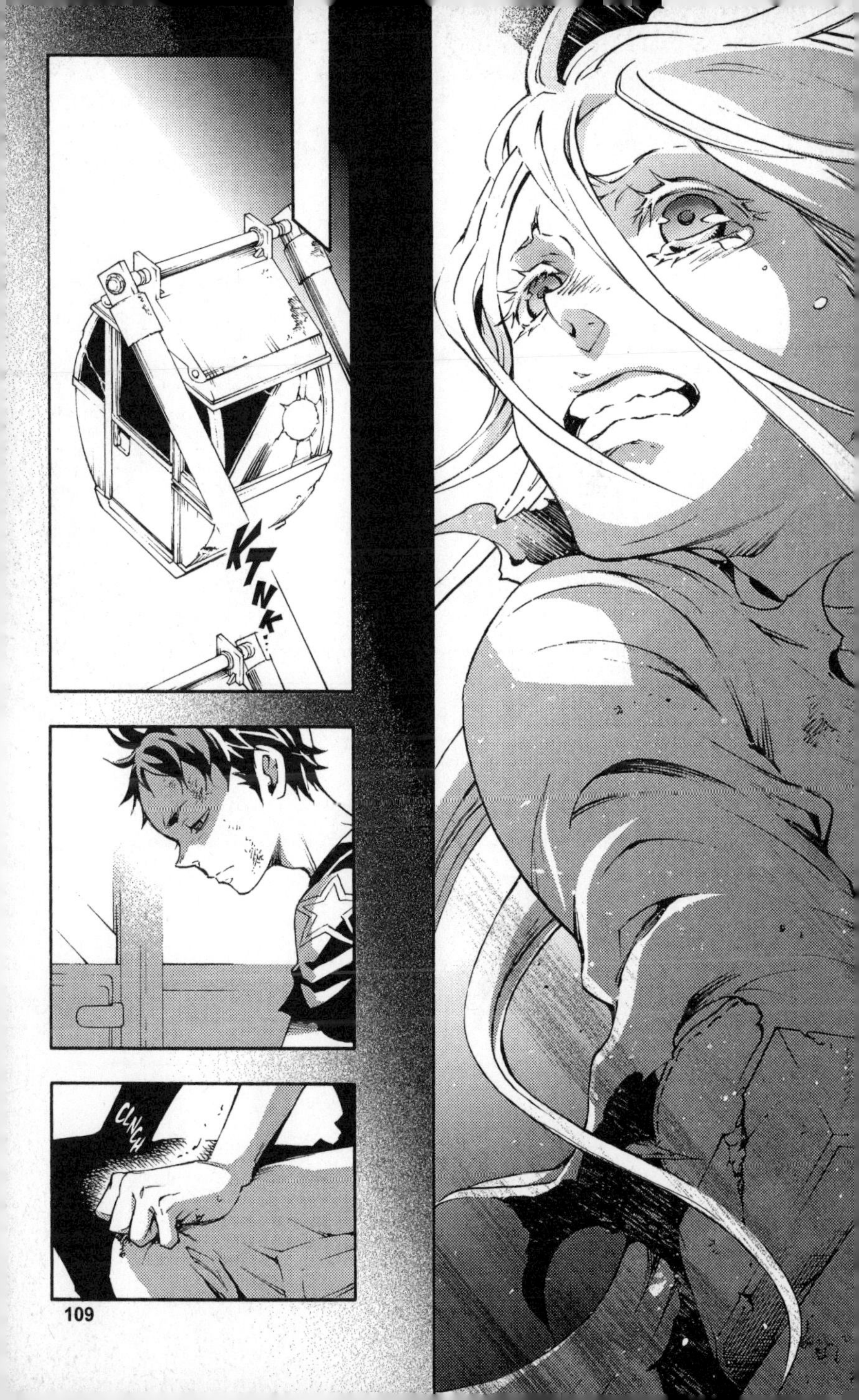
KTNK...
CLNCH

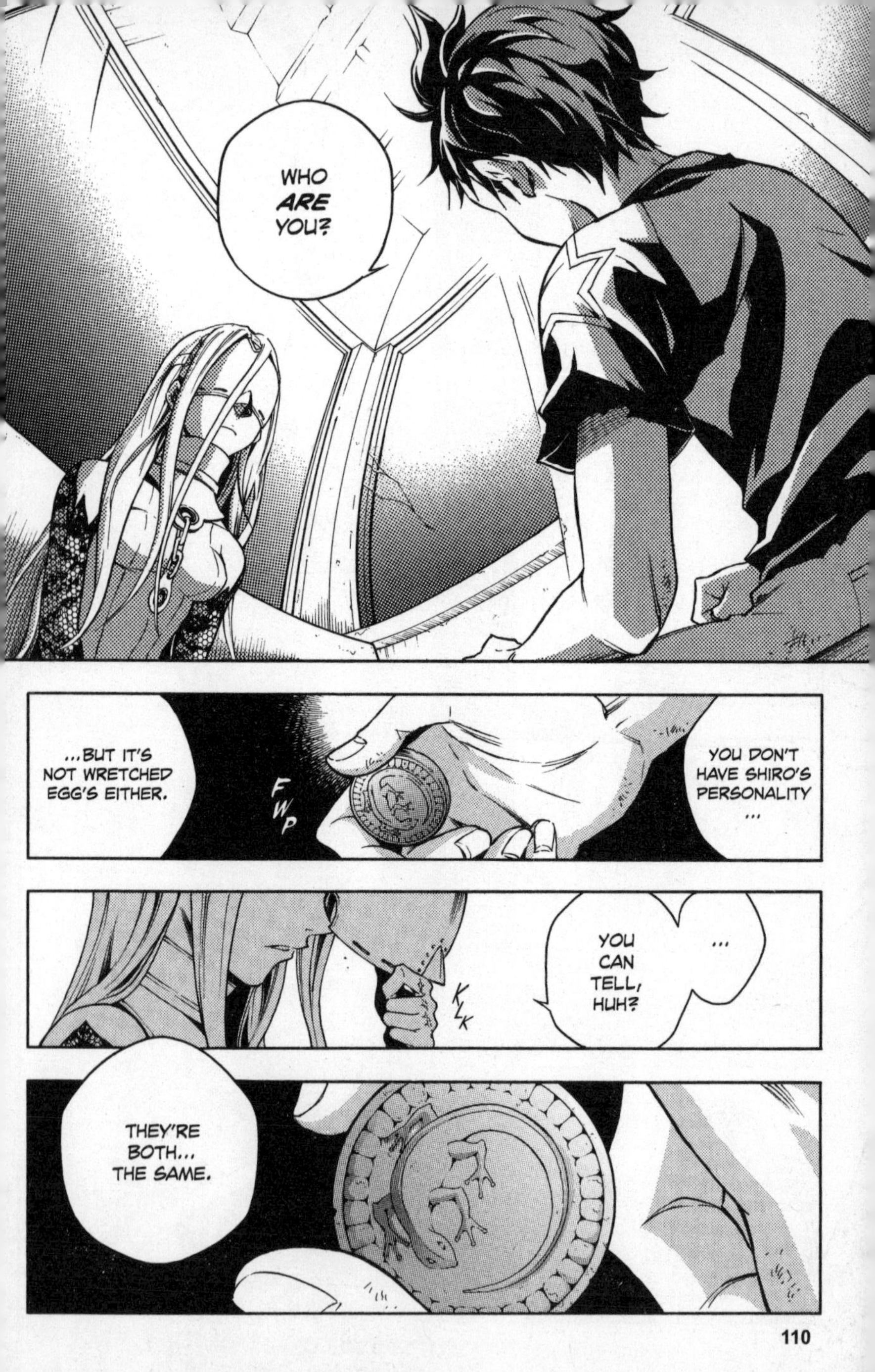
WHO ARE YOU?
YOU DON'T HAVE SHIRO'S PERSONALITY ...
FWP
...BUT IT'S NOT WRETCHED EGG'S EITHER.
...
YOU CAN TELL, HUH?
KLK
THEY'RE BOTH... THE SAME.

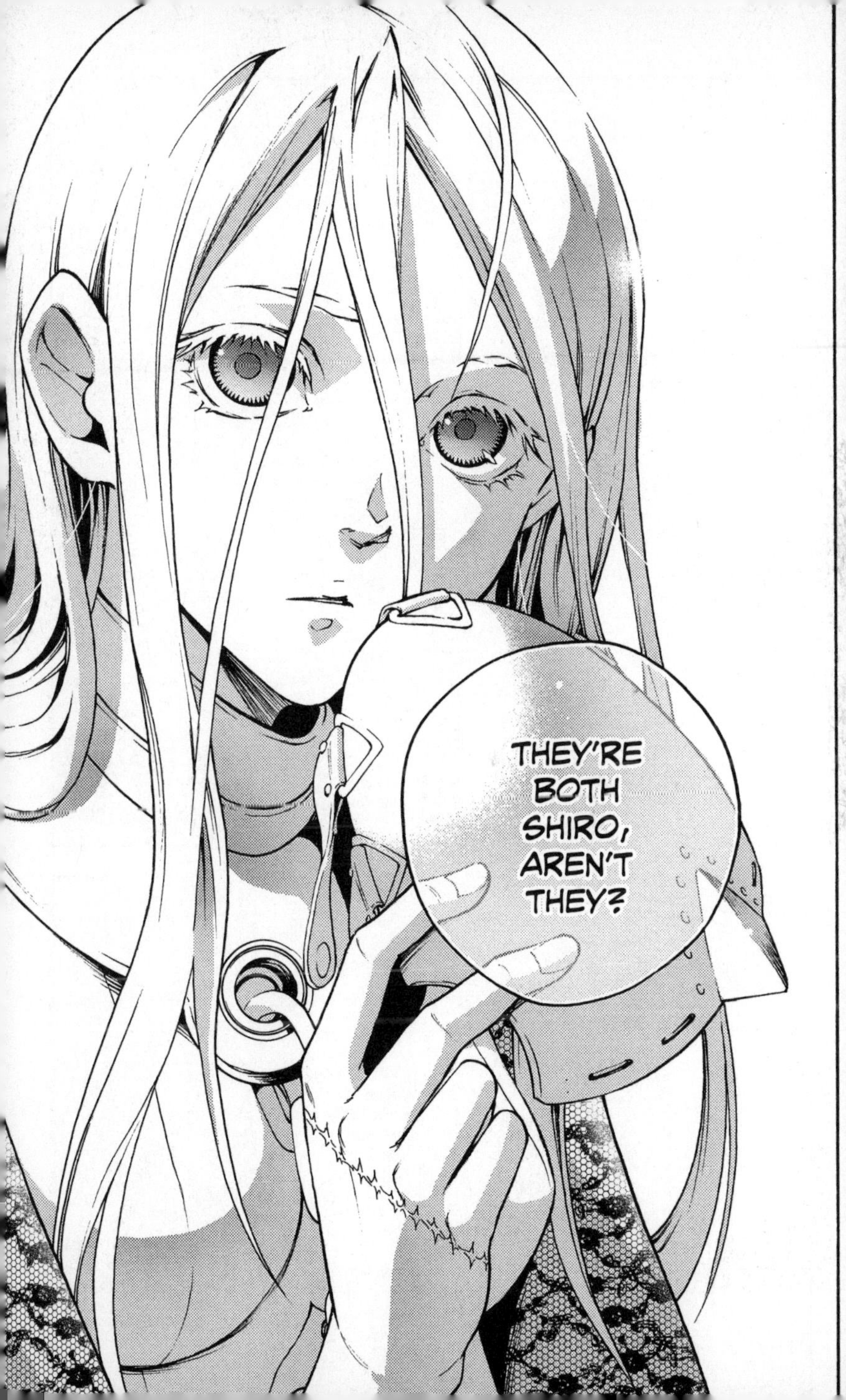
THEY'RE BOTH SHIRO, AREN'T THEY?

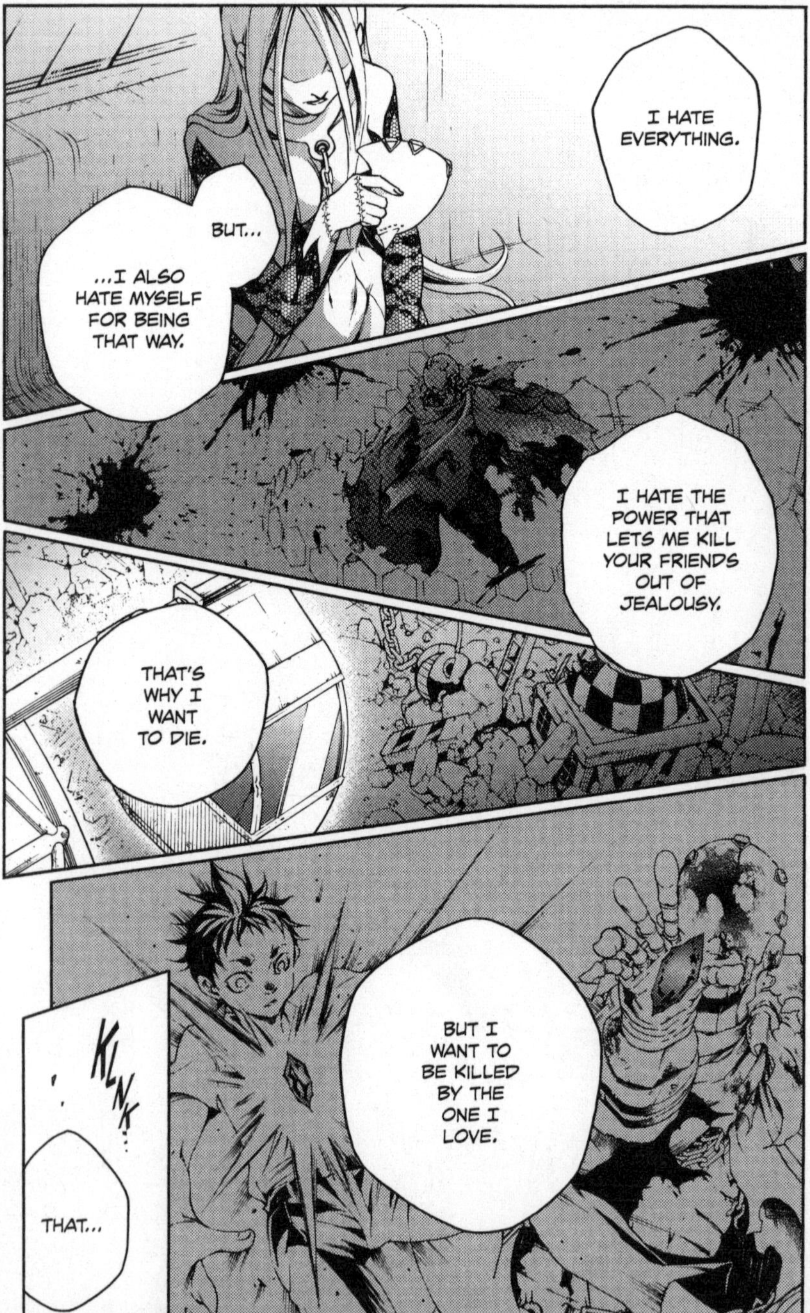
I HATE EVERYTHING.
BUT...
...I ALSO HATE MYSELF FOR BEING THAT WAY.
I HATE THE POWER THAT LETS ME KILL YOUR FRIENDS OUT OF JEALOUSY.
THAT'S WHY I WANT TO DIE.
BUT I WANT TO BE KILLED BY THE ONE I LOVE.
KLNK
THAT...

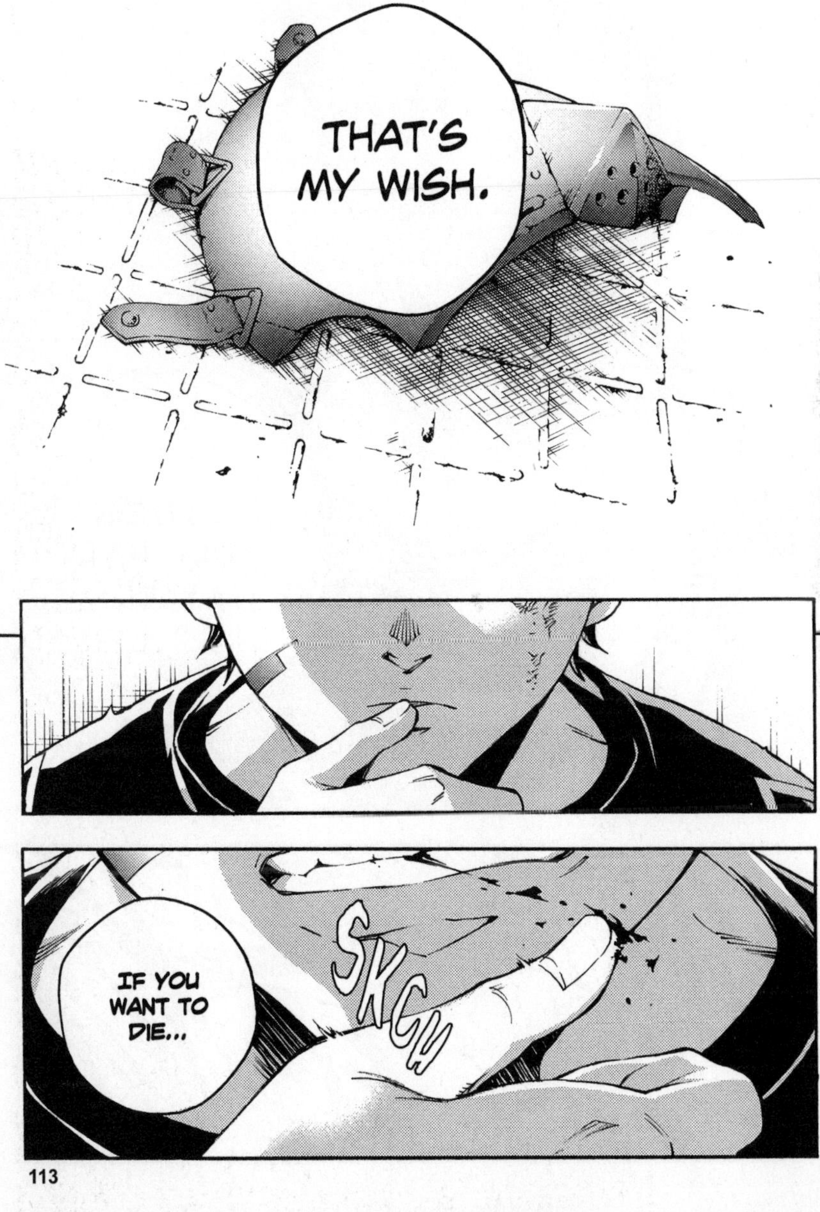
THAT'S MY WISH.
IF YOU WANT TO DIE...
SKCH

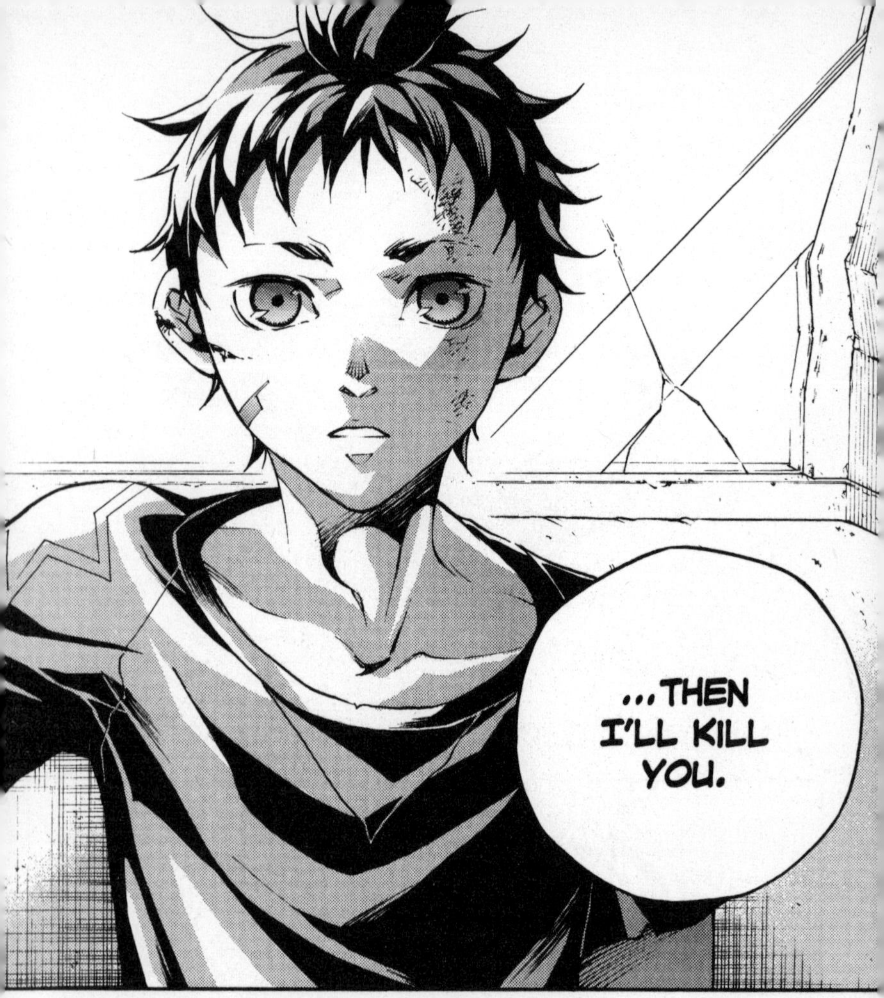
...THEN I'LL KILL YOU.

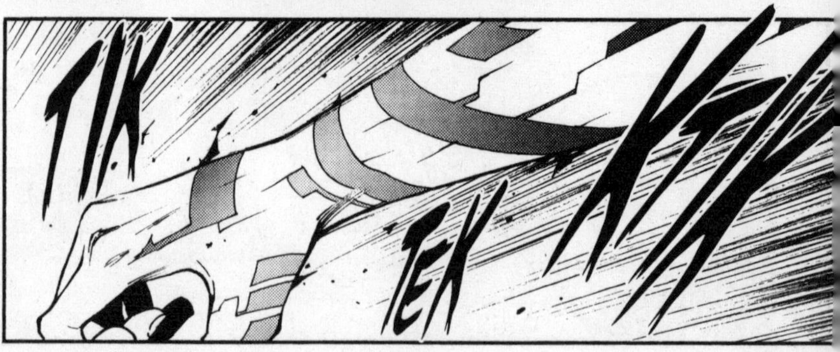
TIK
TEK

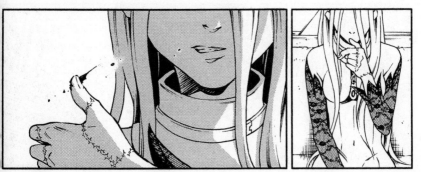

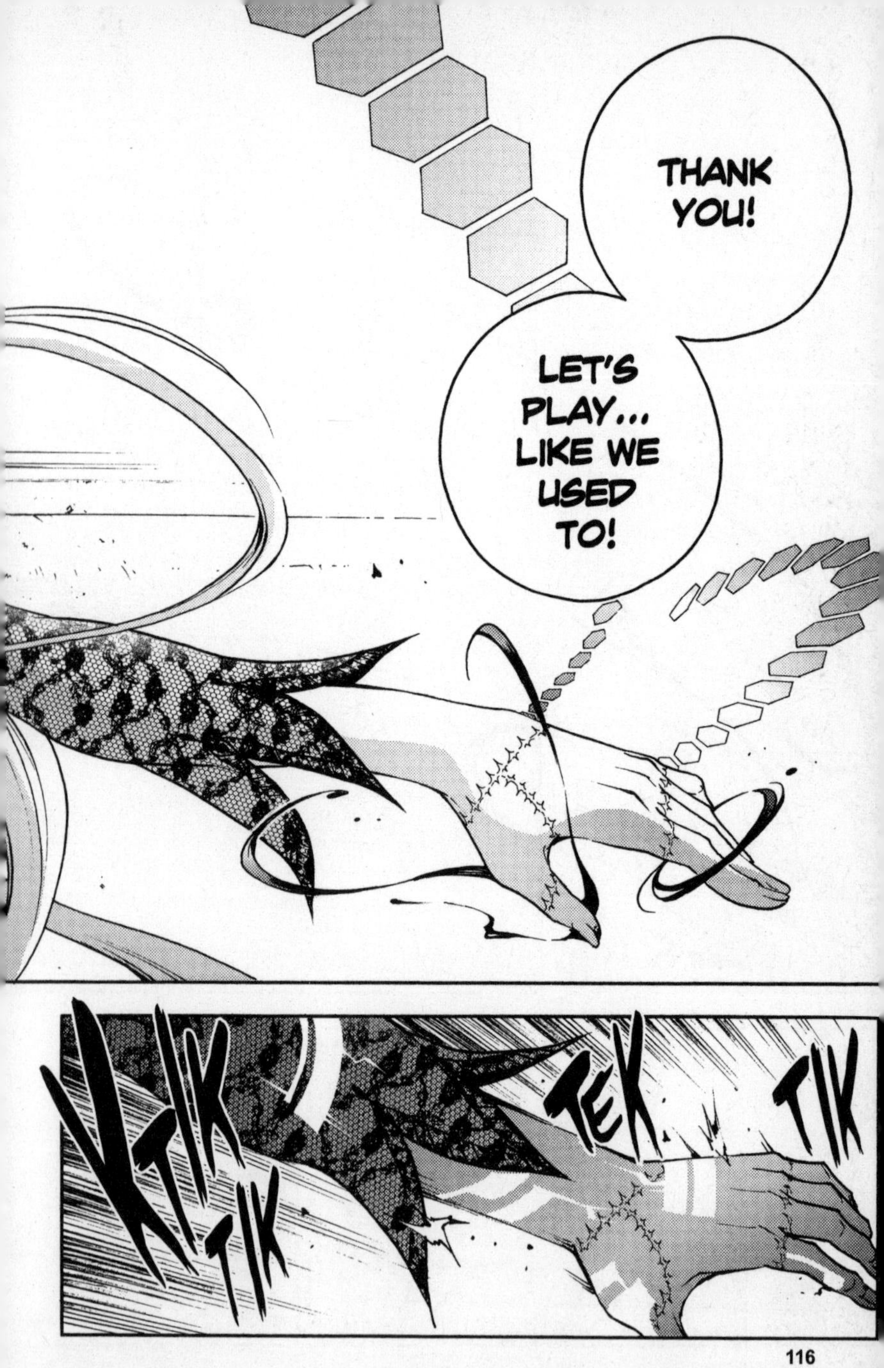
THANK YOU!
LET'S PLAY... LIKE WE USED TO!
TIK
TEK
TIK
TIK

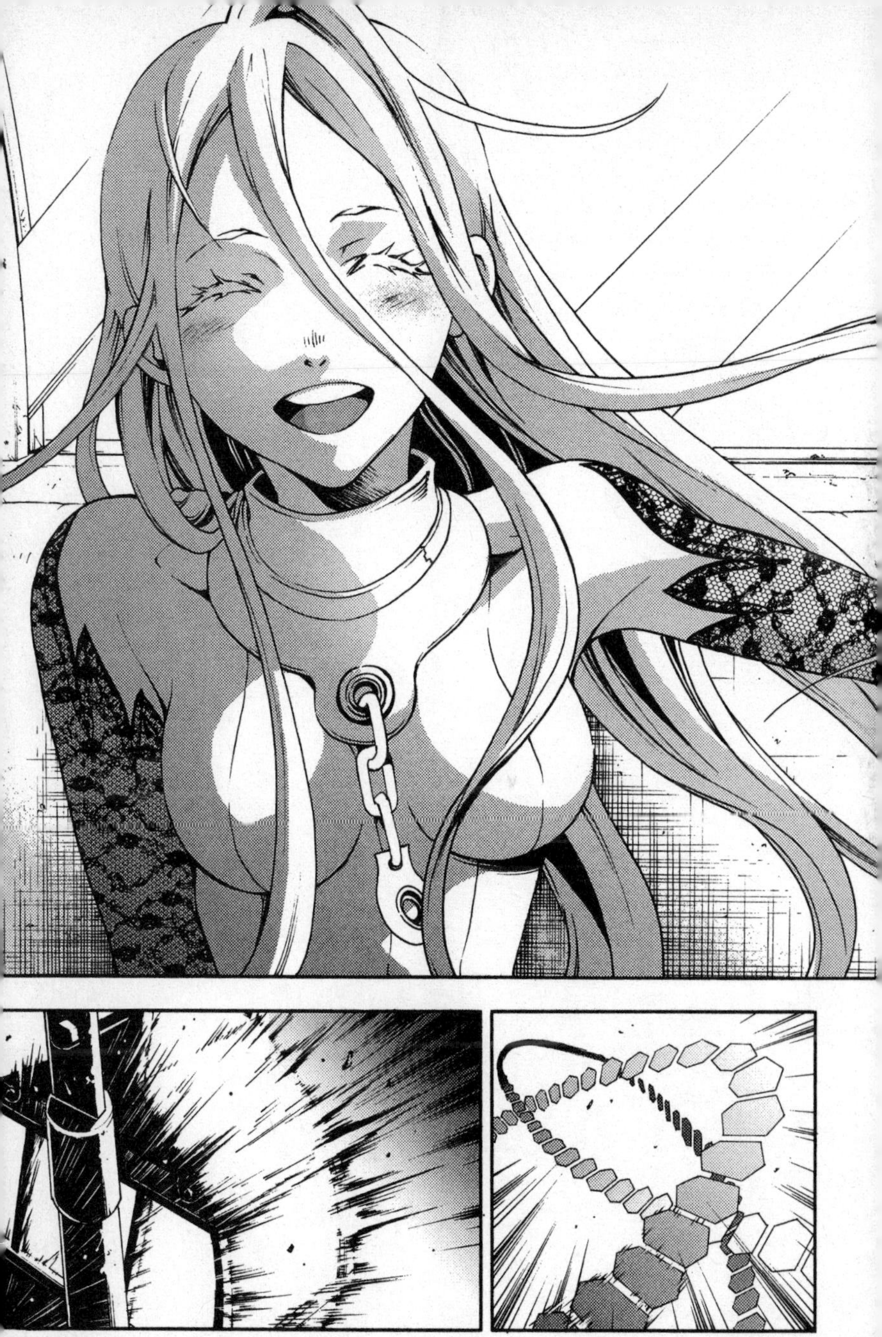

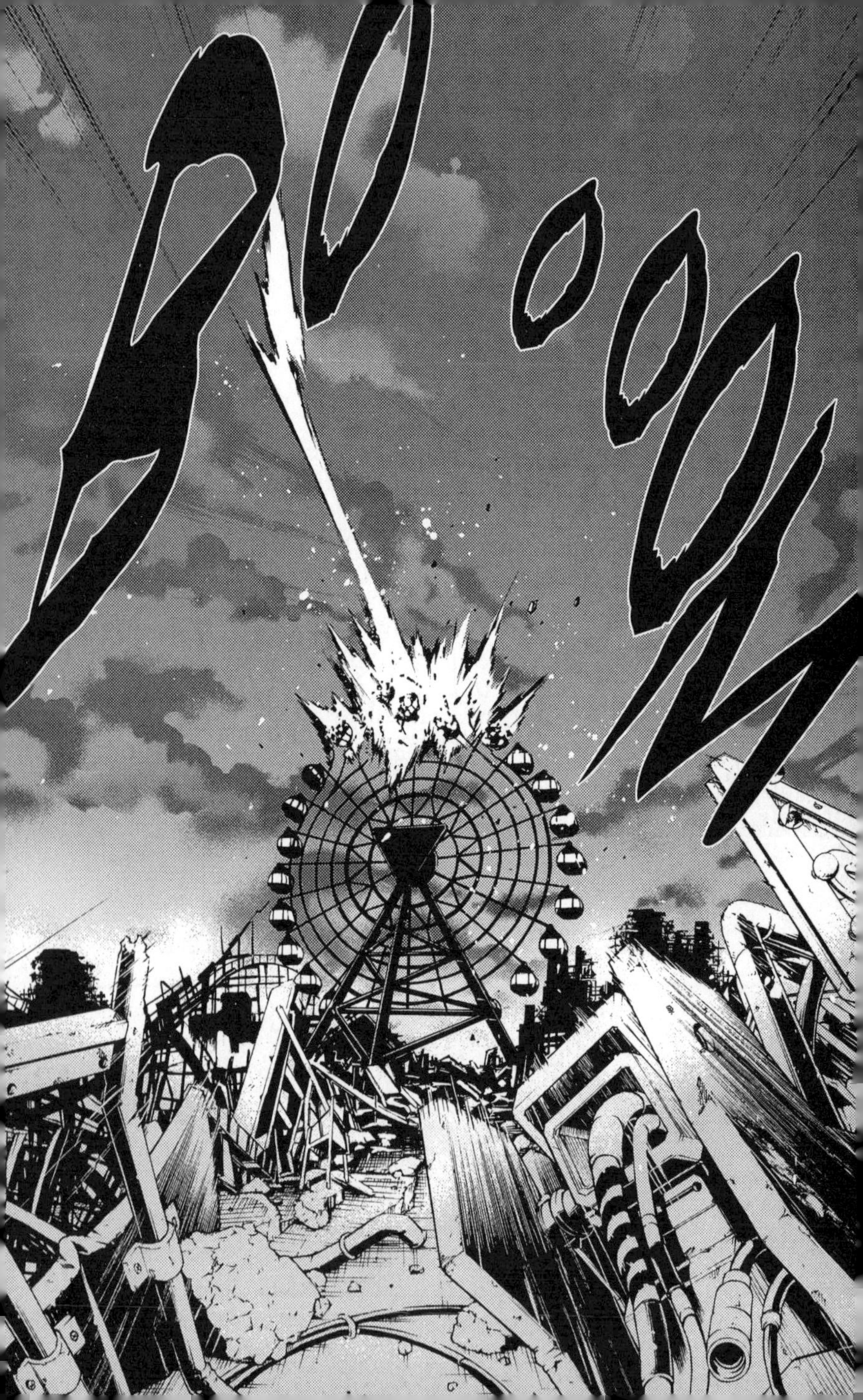
BOOOOM

DEA
WONDE
AND

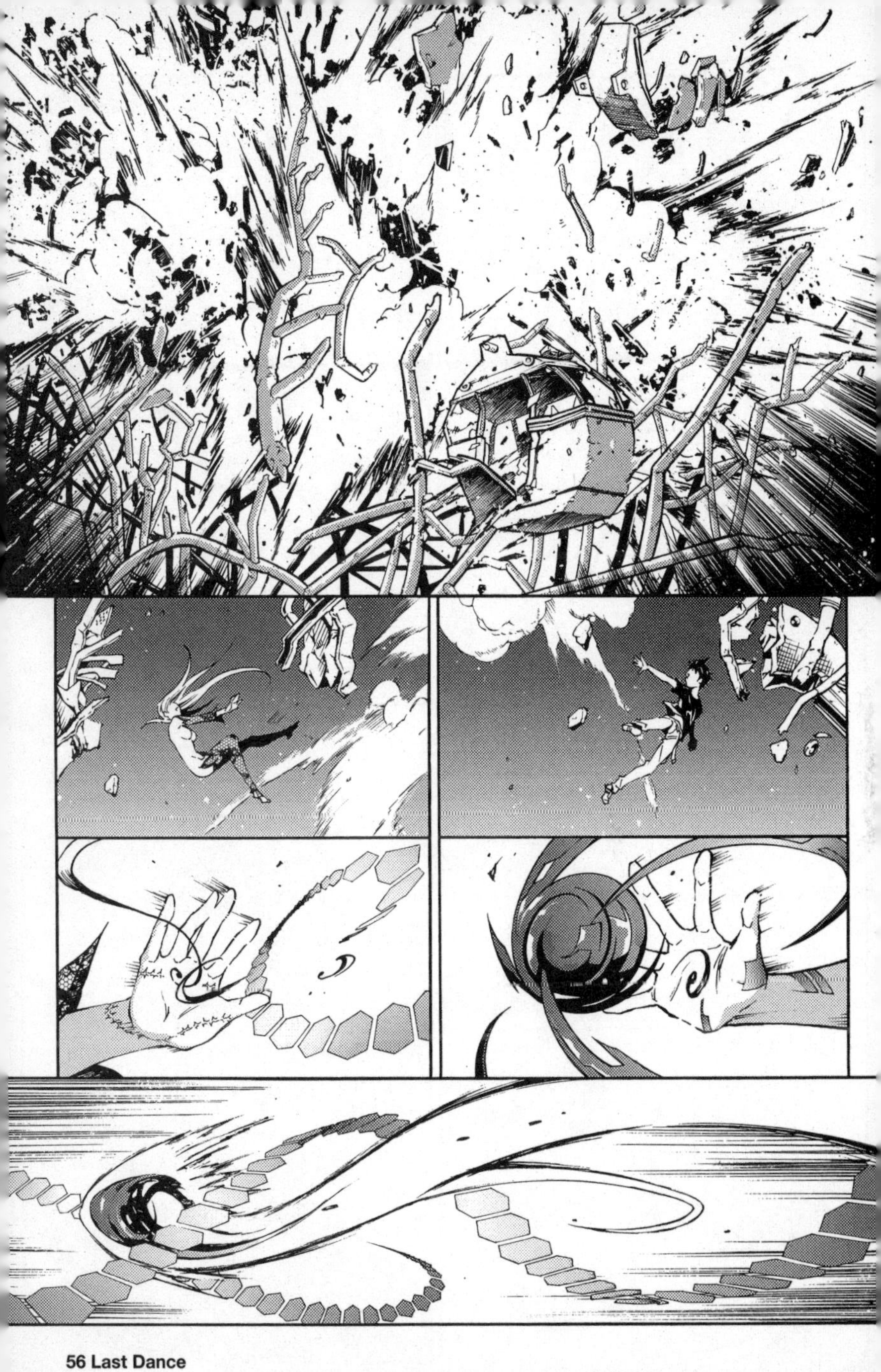

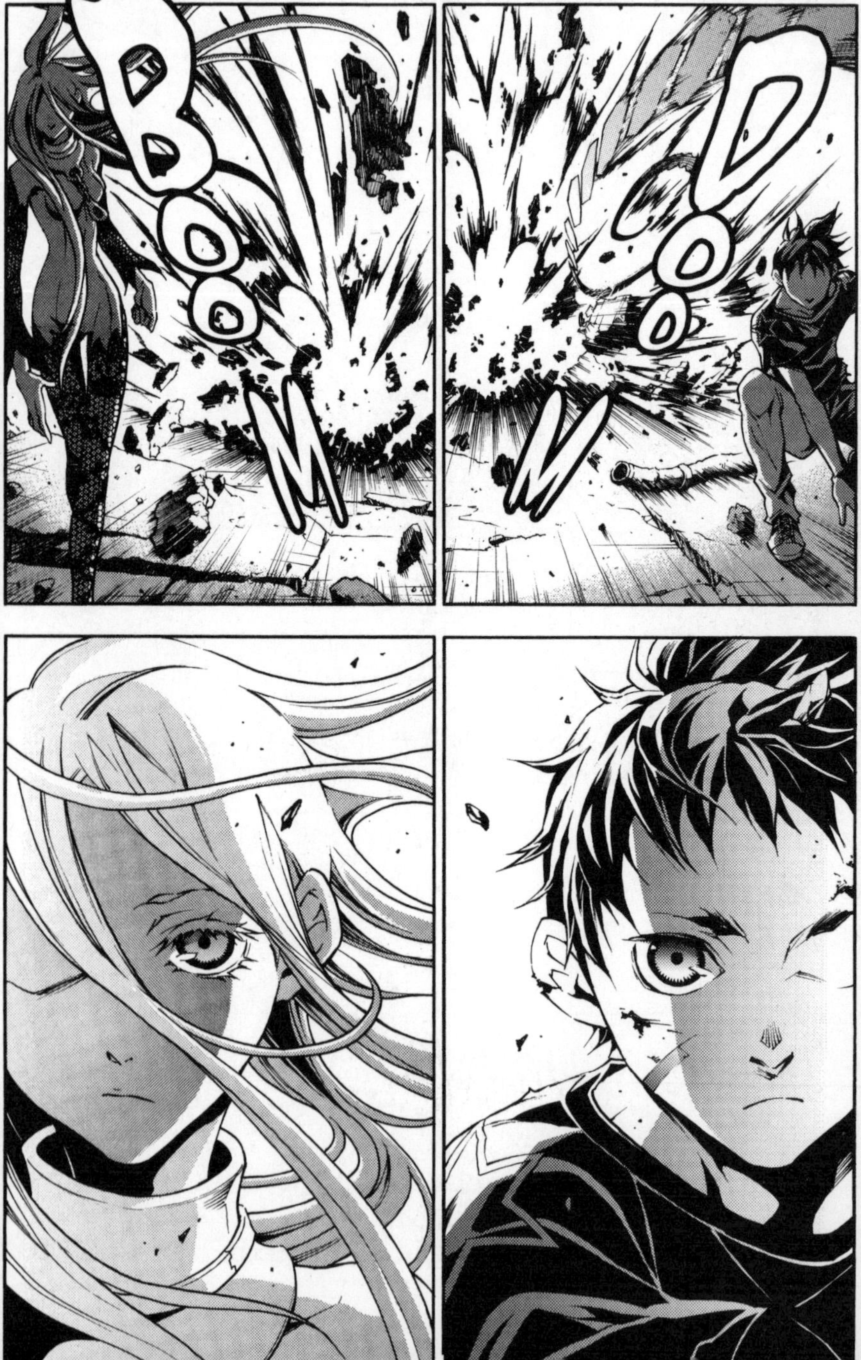
DOOOM
BOOM

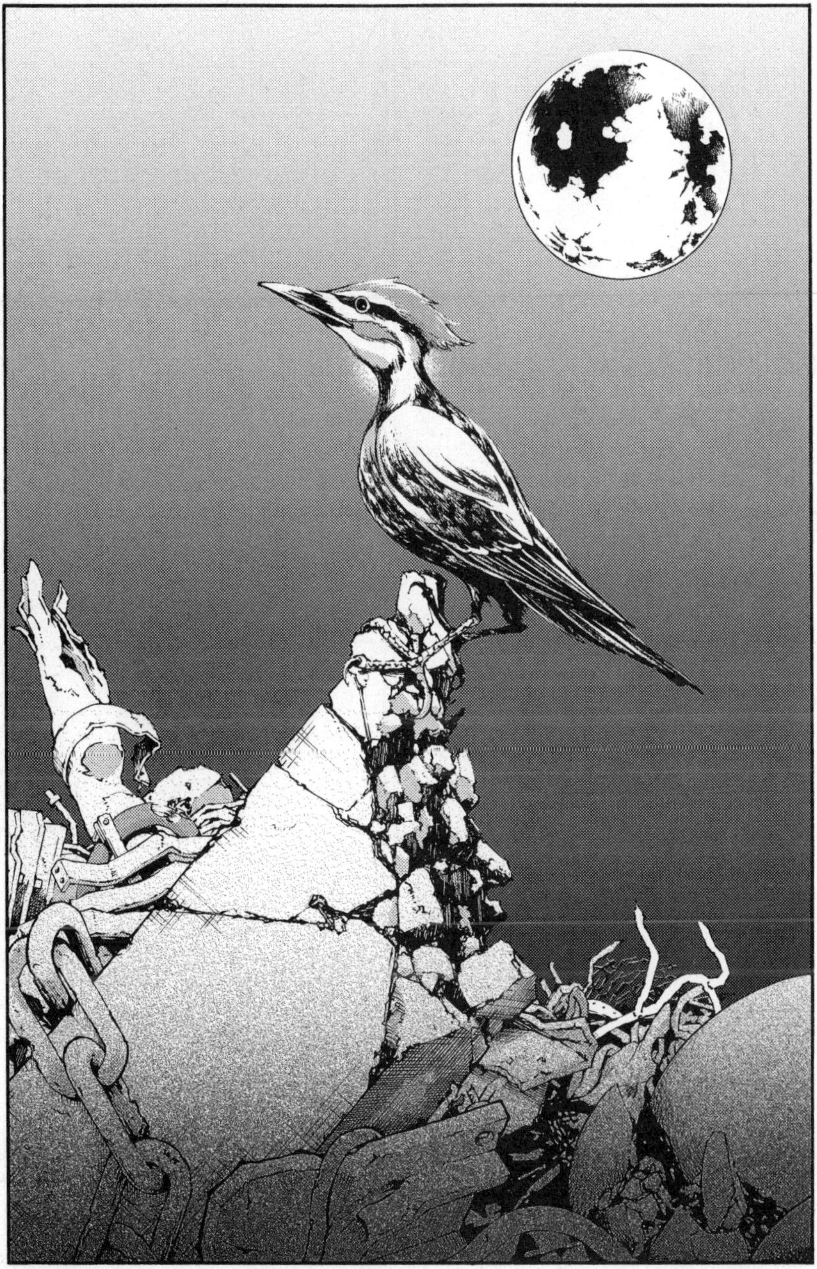

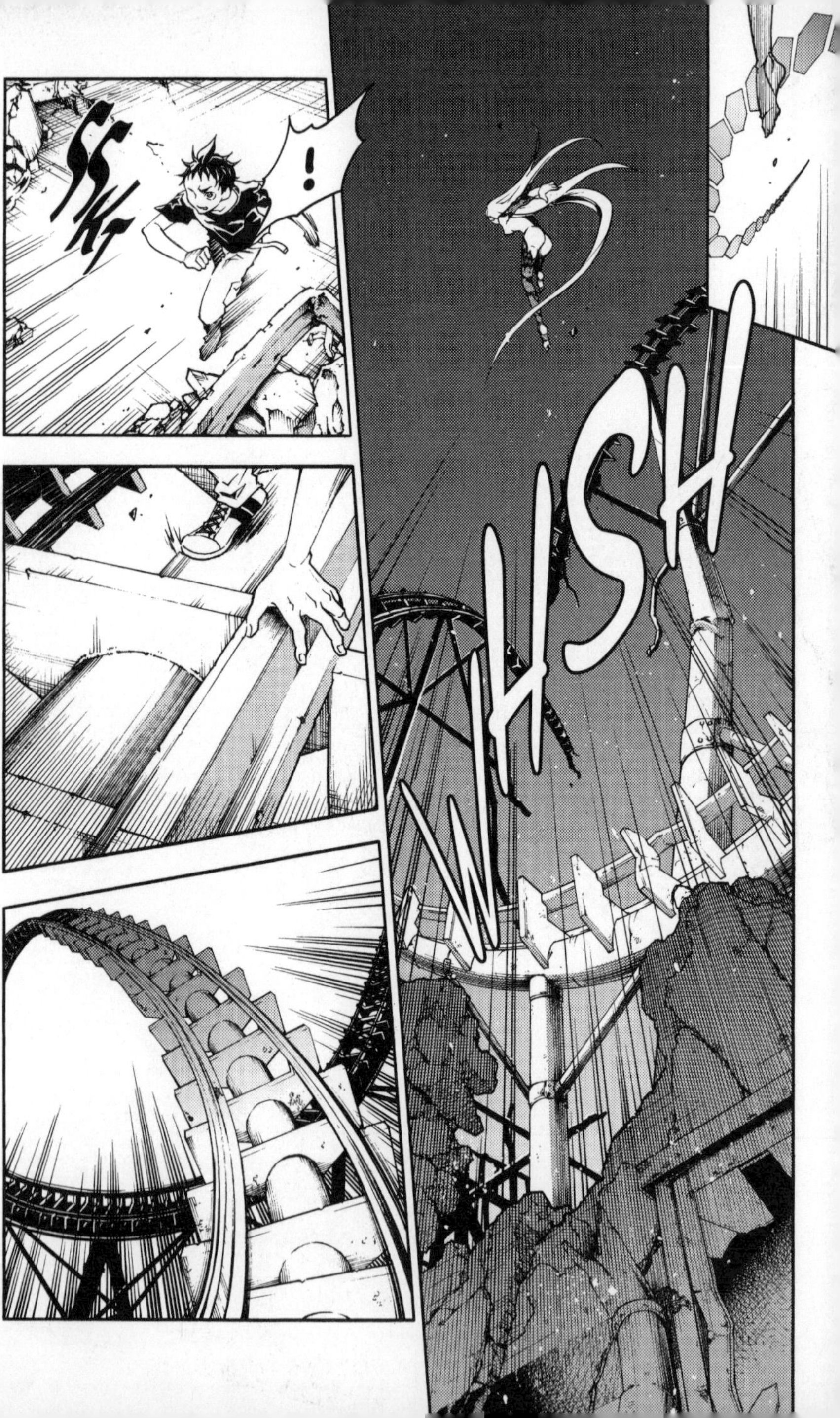
WHSH
!
SSKT

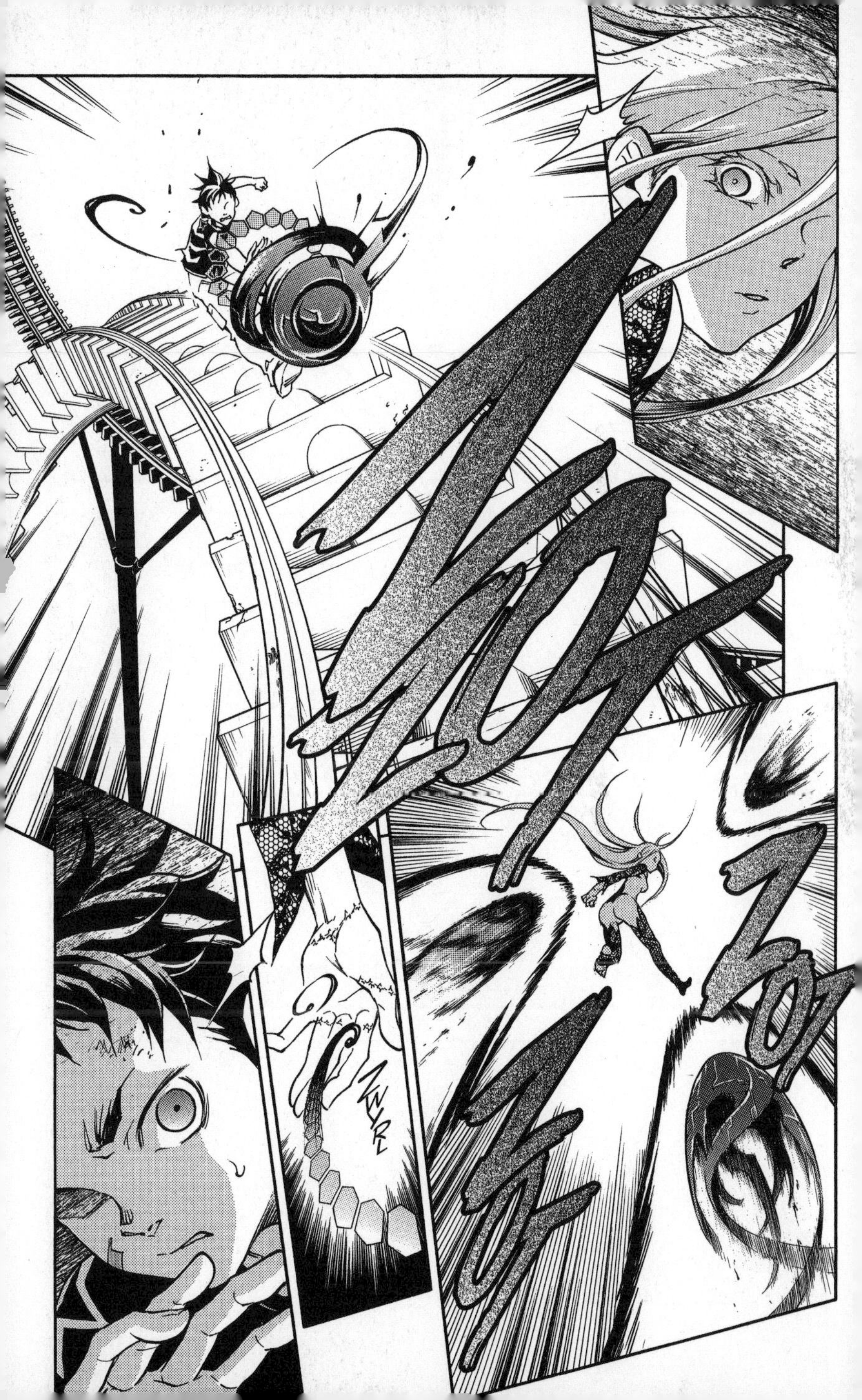

WHRL

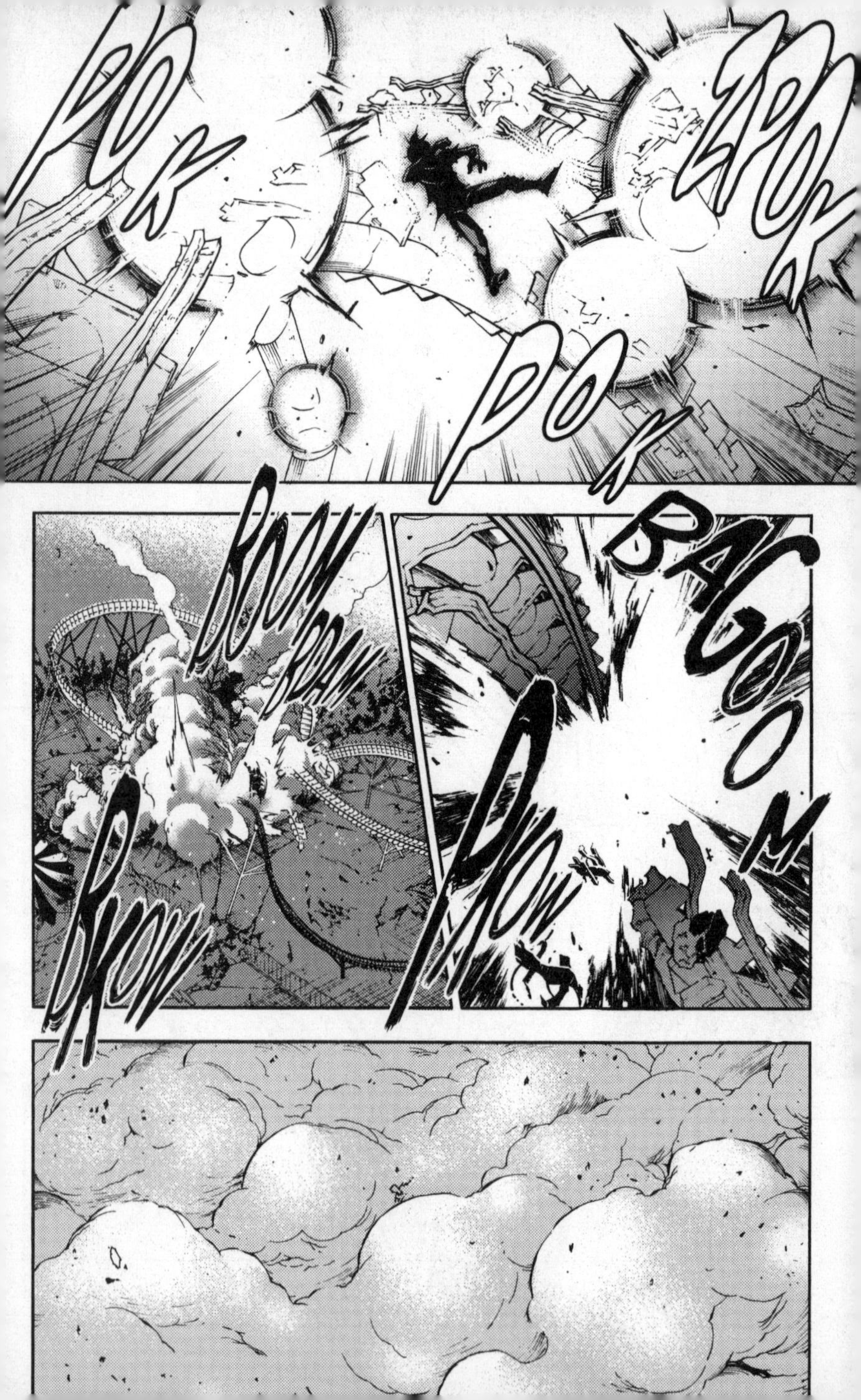
POK
POK
BAGOOM

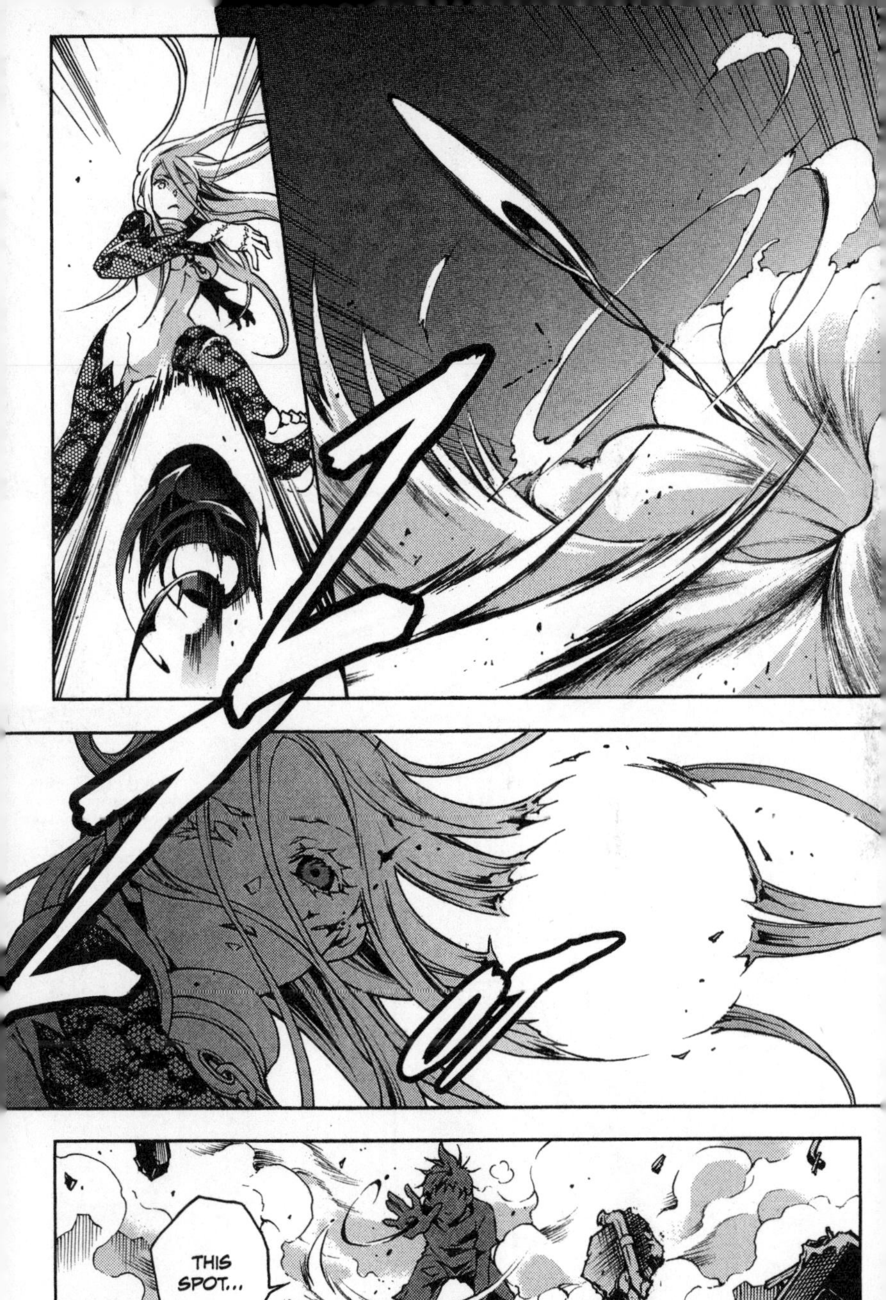
THIS SPOT...

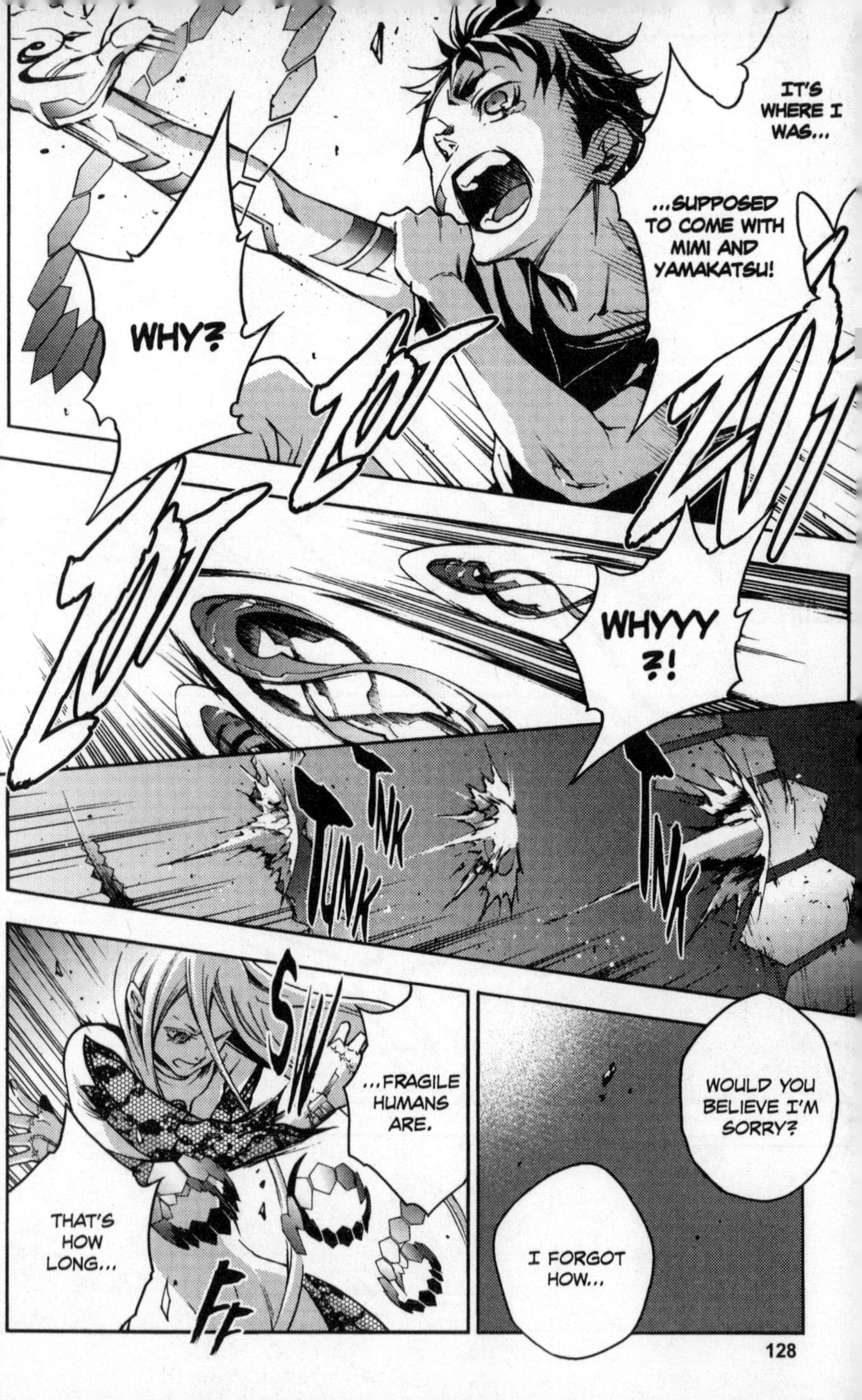
IT'S WHERE I WAS...
...SUPPOSED TO COME WITH MIMI AND YAMAKATSU!
WHY?
WHYYY ?!
TINK
TUNK
TINK
WOULD YOU BELIEVE I'M SORRY?
I FORGOT HOW...
...FRAGILE HUMANS ARE.
THAT'S HOW LONG...

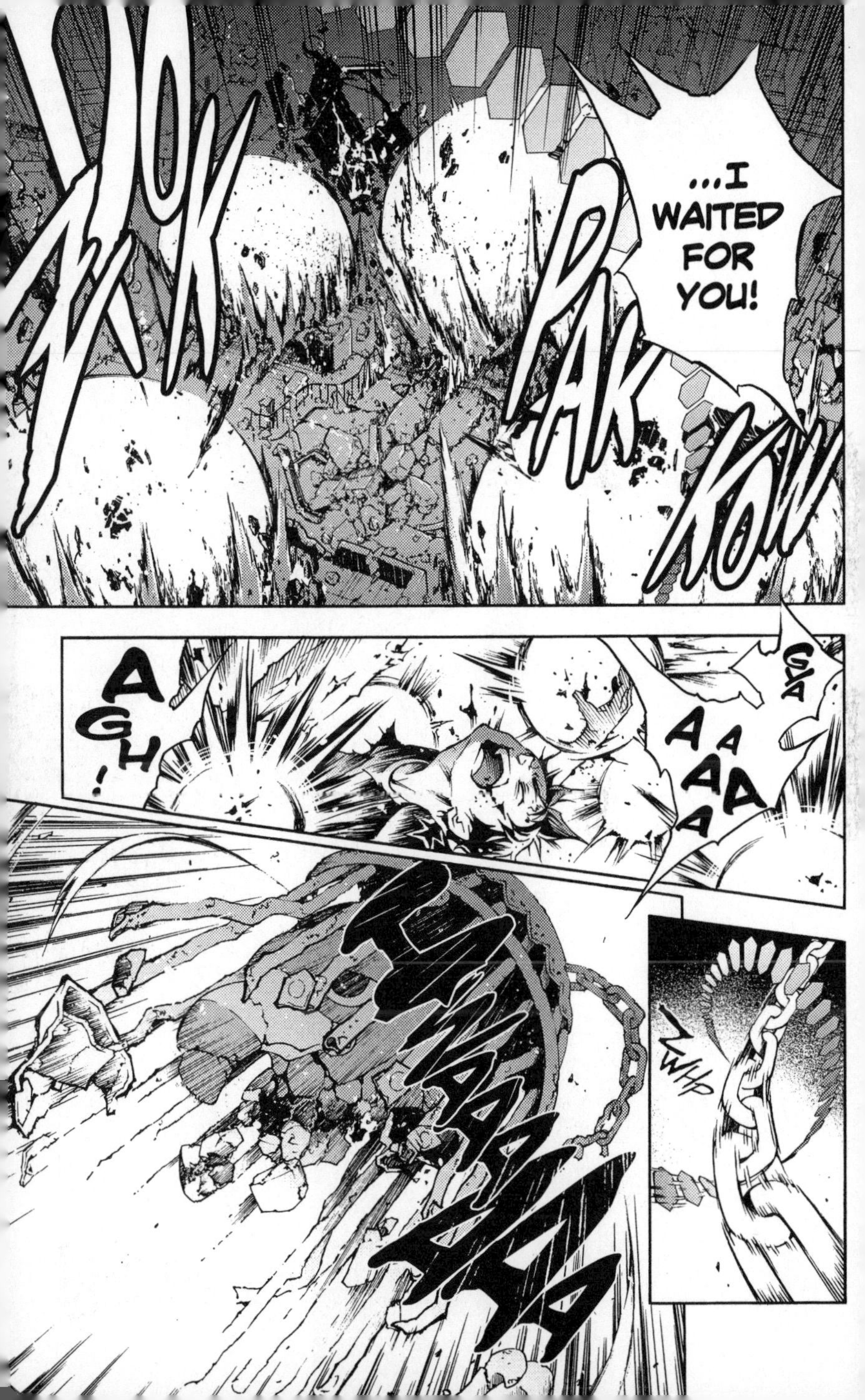
...I WAITED FOR YOU!
GYAAAAAA
AGH!
ZWHIP

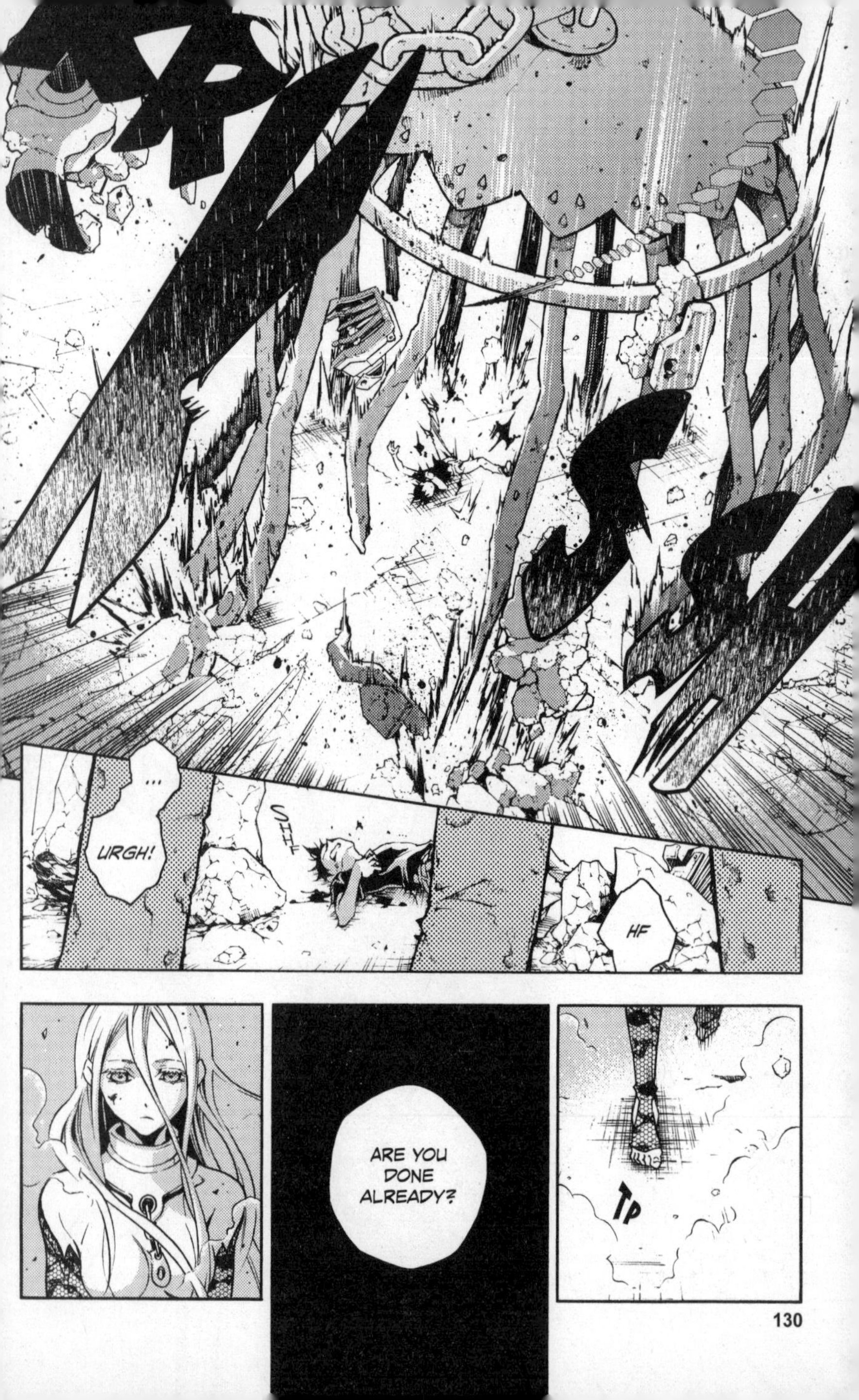
HF
SHHF
...
URGH!
TP
ARE YOU DONE ALREADY?

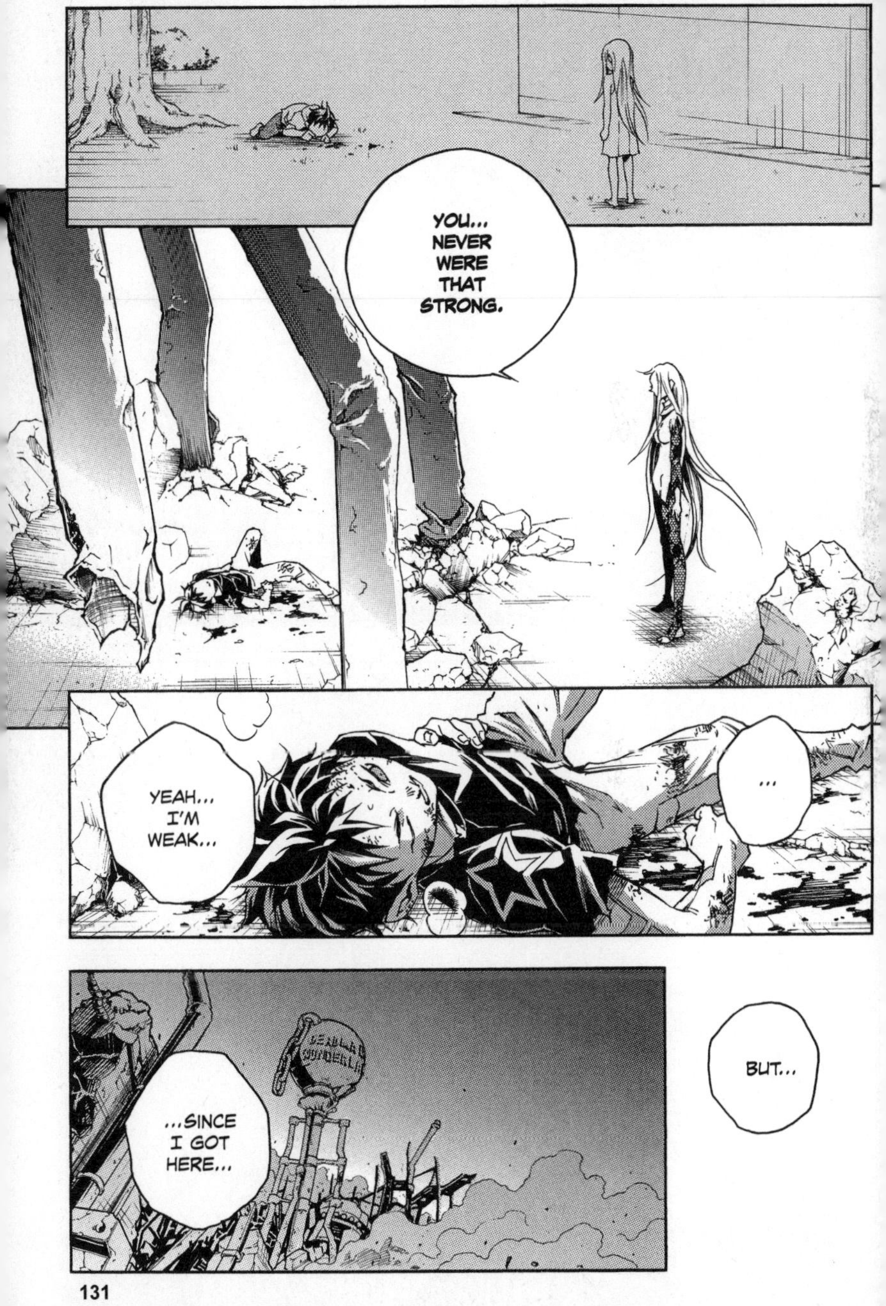
YOU... NEVER WERE THAT STRONG.
...
YEAH... I'M WEAK...
BUT...
...SINCE I GOT HERE...

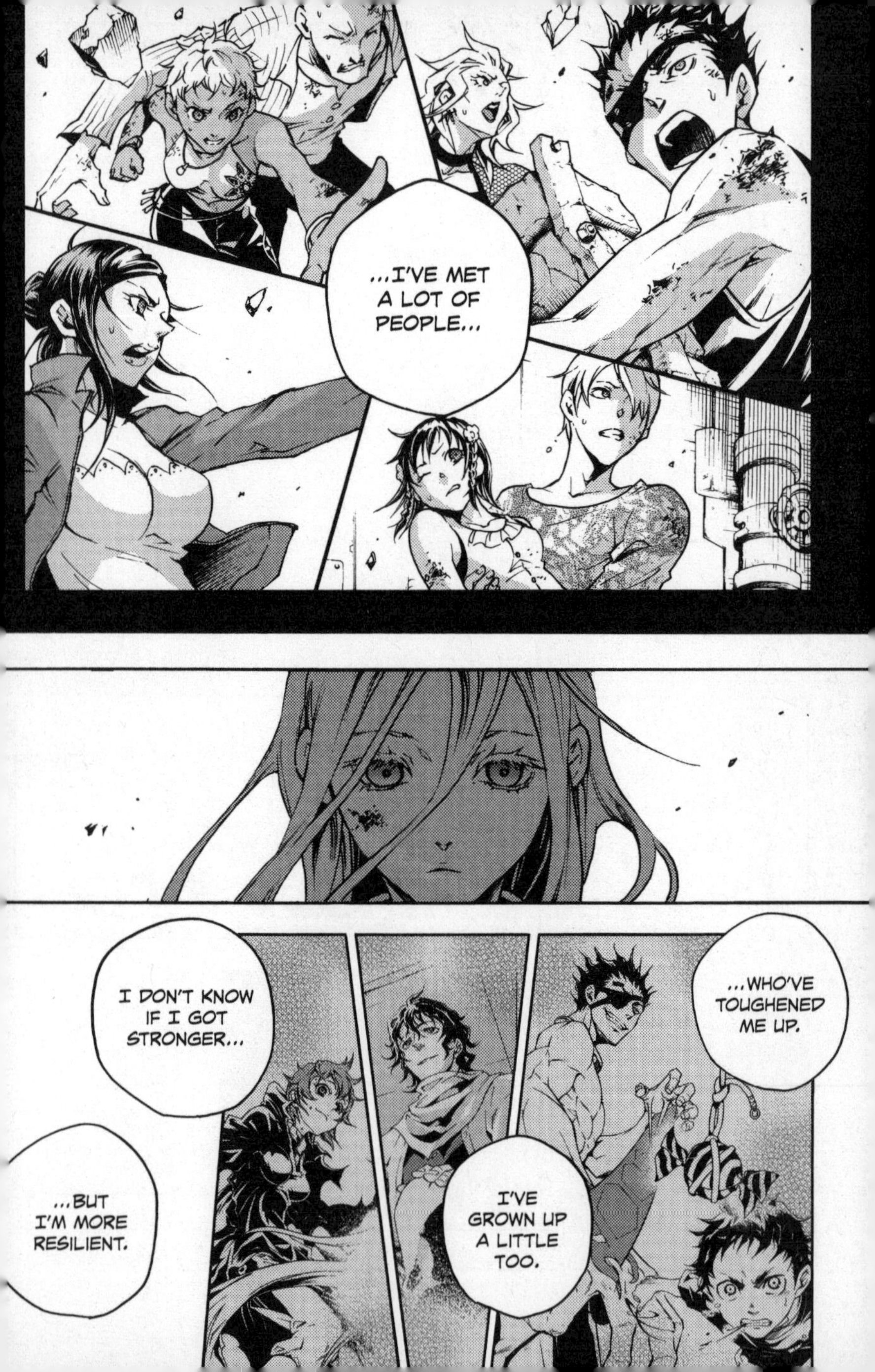
...I'VE MET A LOT OF PEOPLE...
...WHO'VE TOUGHENED ME UP.
I DON'T KNOW IF I GOT STRONGER...
...BUT I'M MORE RESILIENT.
I'VE GROWN UP A LITTLE TOO.

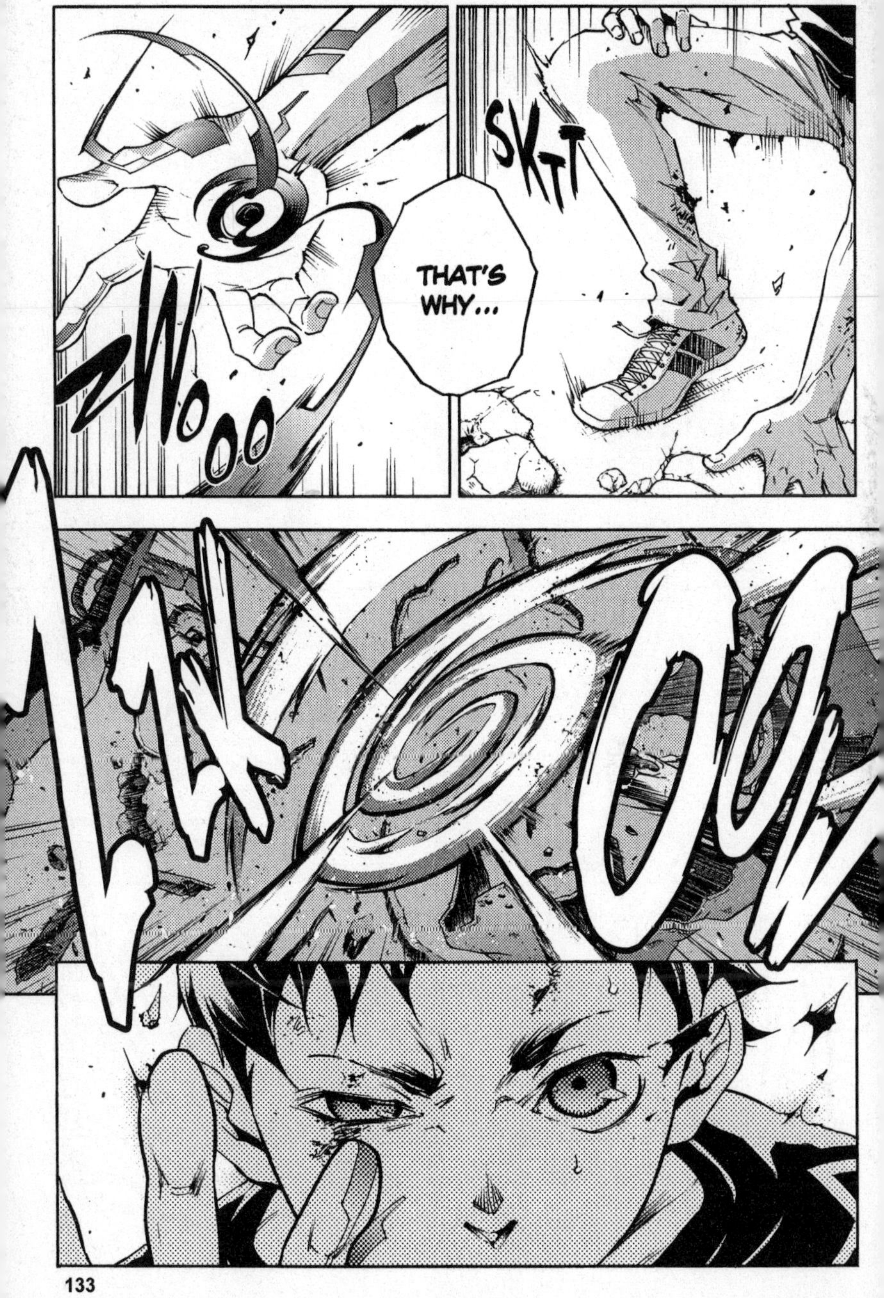
SKTT
THAT'S WHY...
ZWOOO

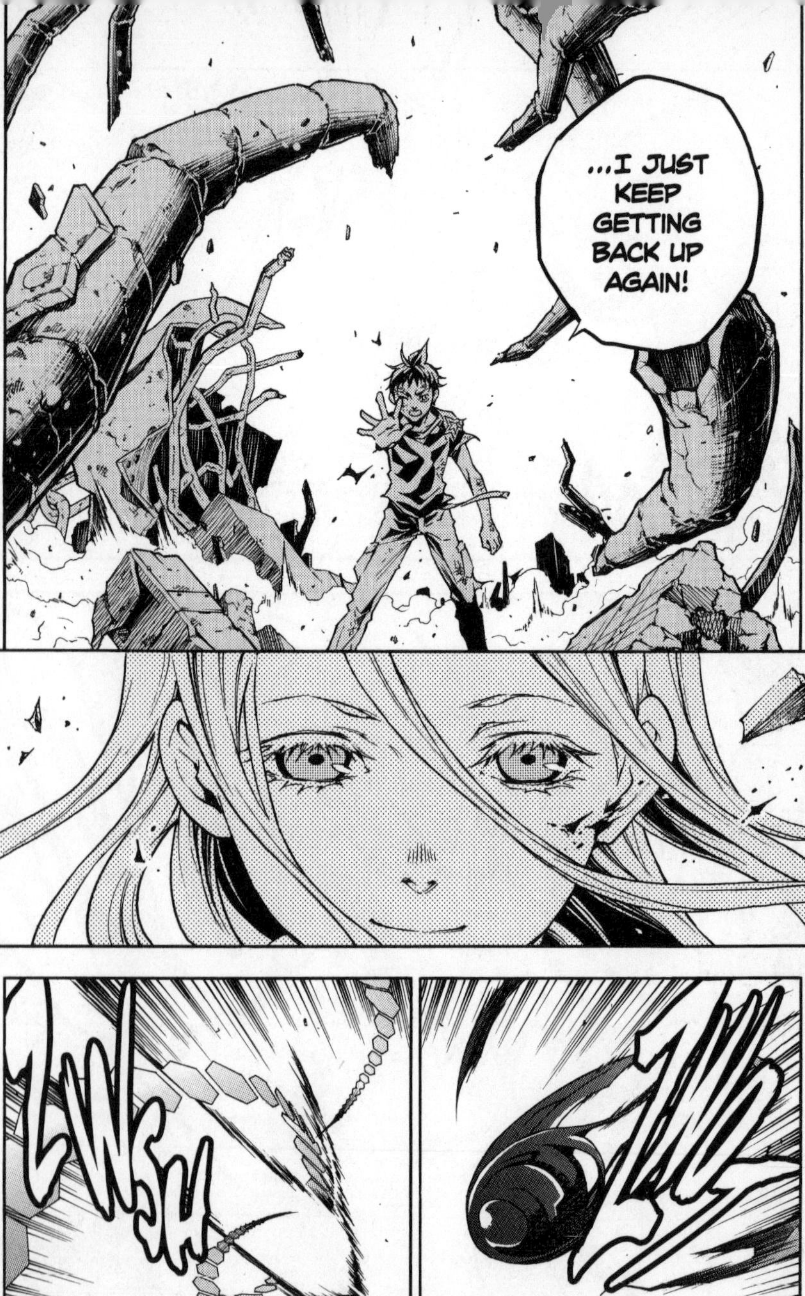
...I JUST KEEP GETTING BACK UP AGAIN!

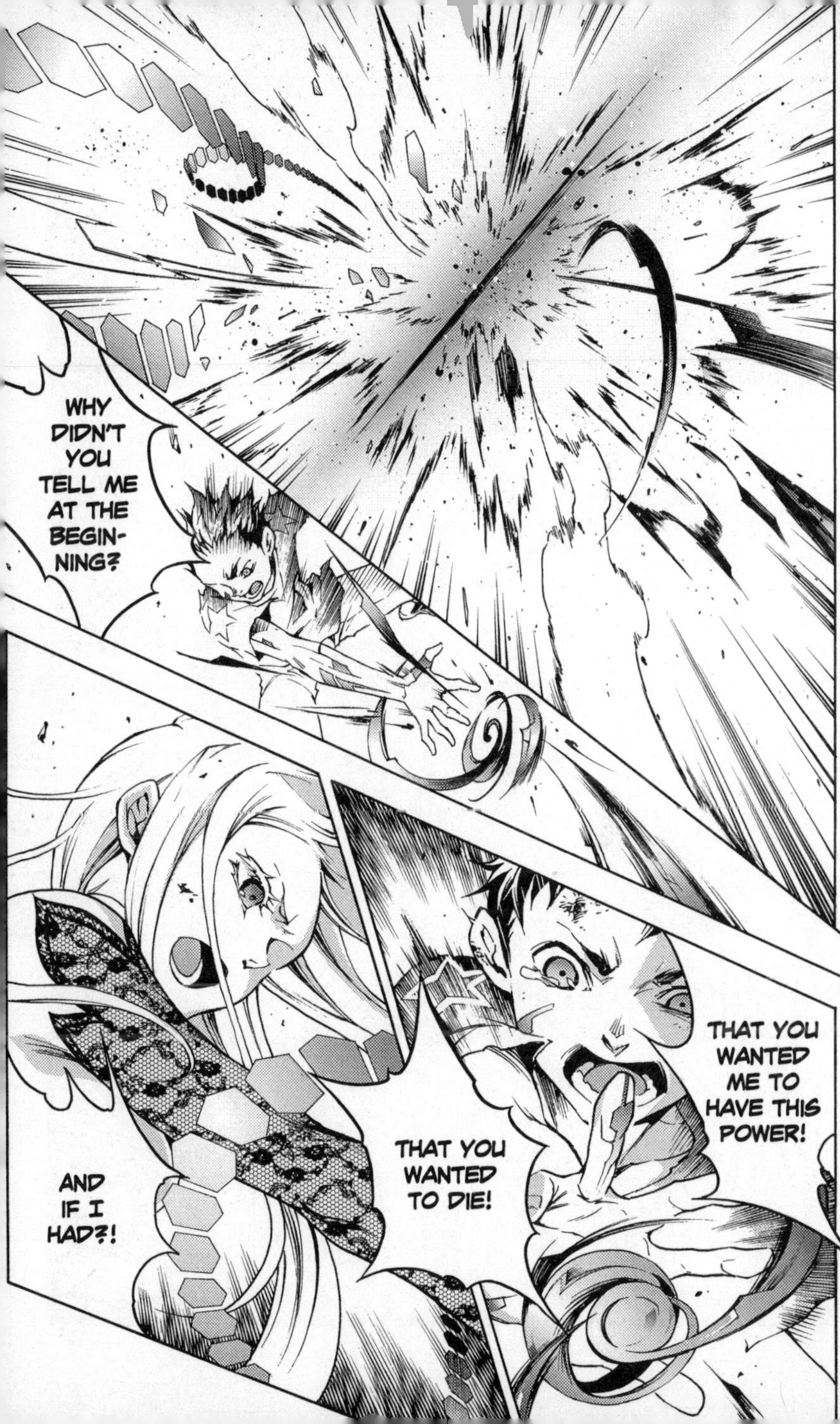
WHY DIDN'T YOU TELL ME AT THE BEGIN-NING?
THAT YOU WANTED ME TO HAVE THIS POWER!
THAT YOU WANTED TO DIE!
AND IF I HAD?!

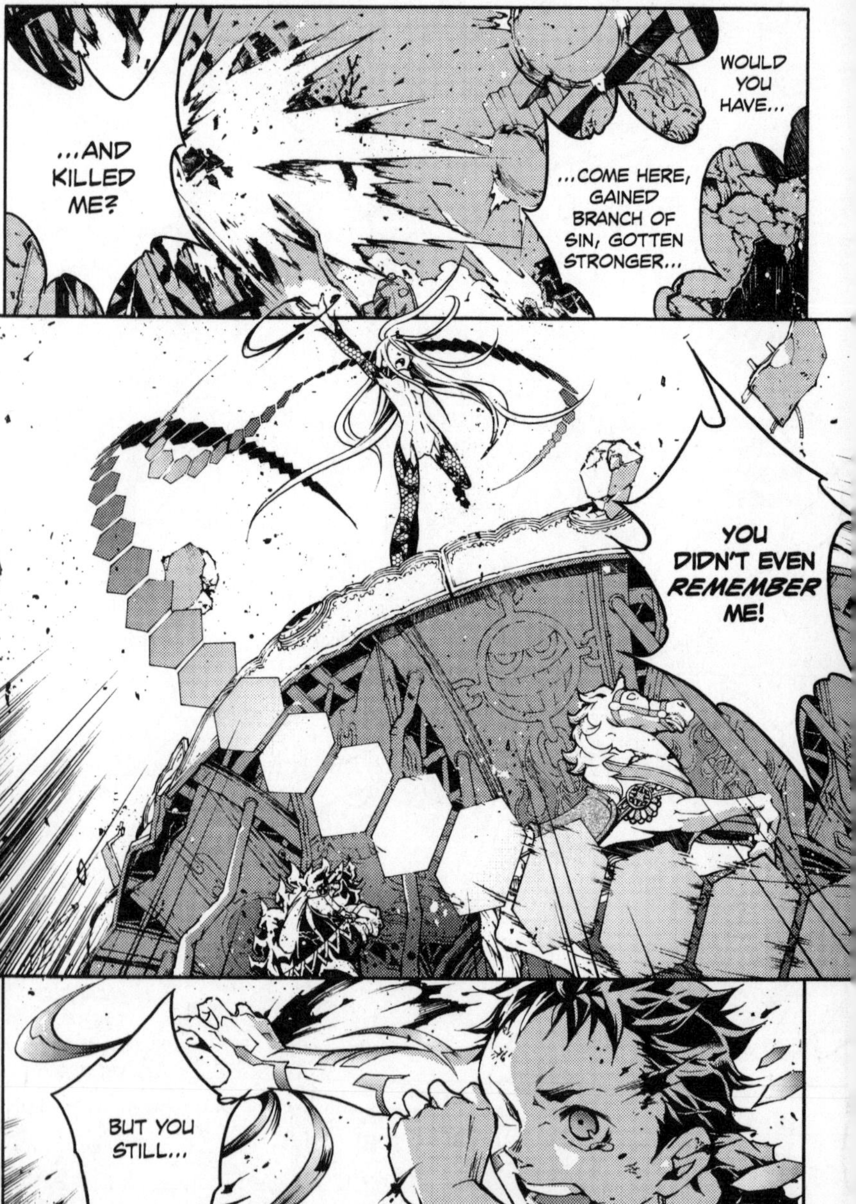
WOULD YOU HAVE...
...COME HERE, GAINED BRANCH OF SIN, GOTTEN STRONGER...
...AND KILLED ME?
YOU DIDN'T EVEN *REMEMBER* ME!
BUT YOU STILL...

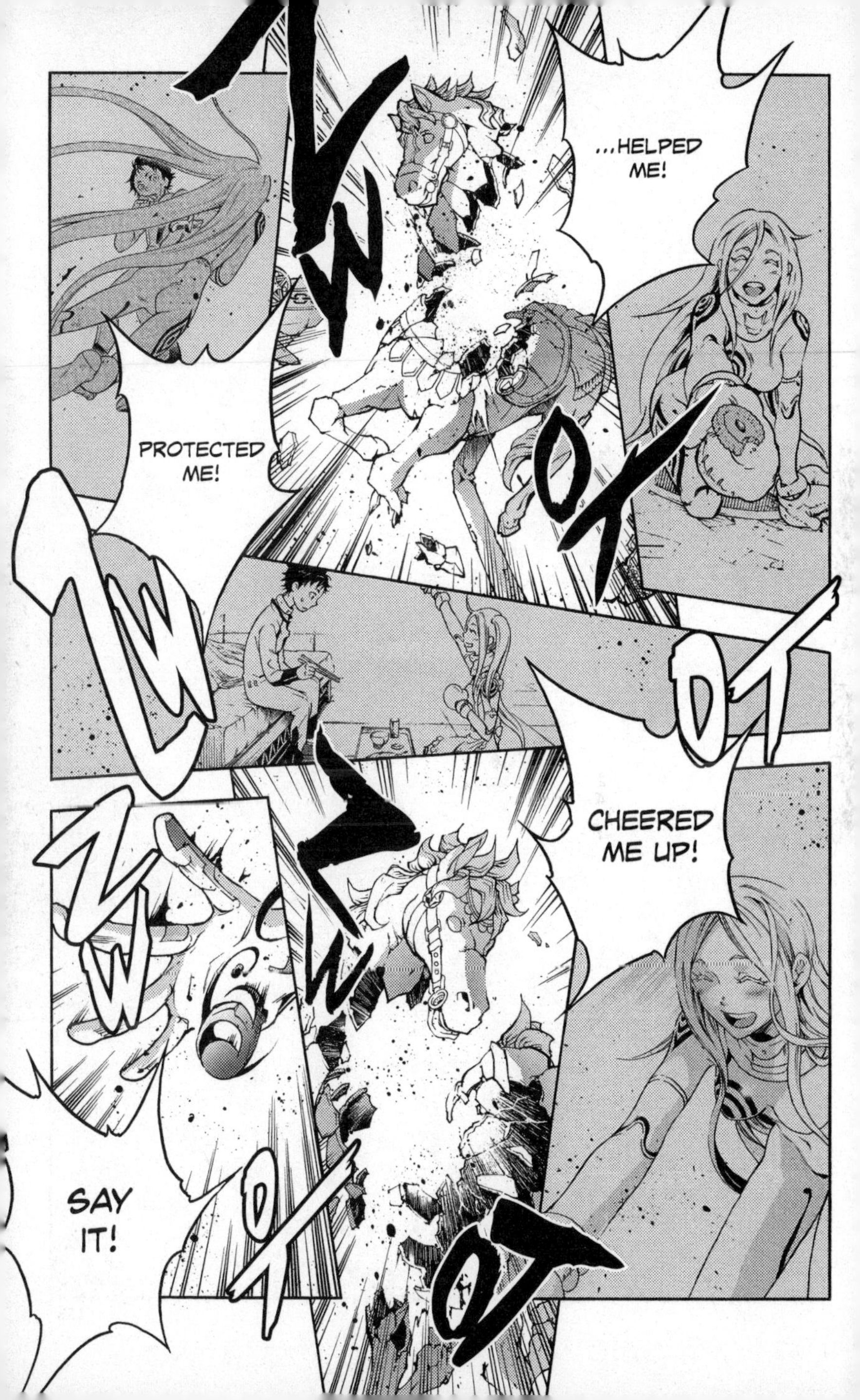
...HELPED ME!
PROTECTED ME!
CHEERED ME UP!
SAY IT!

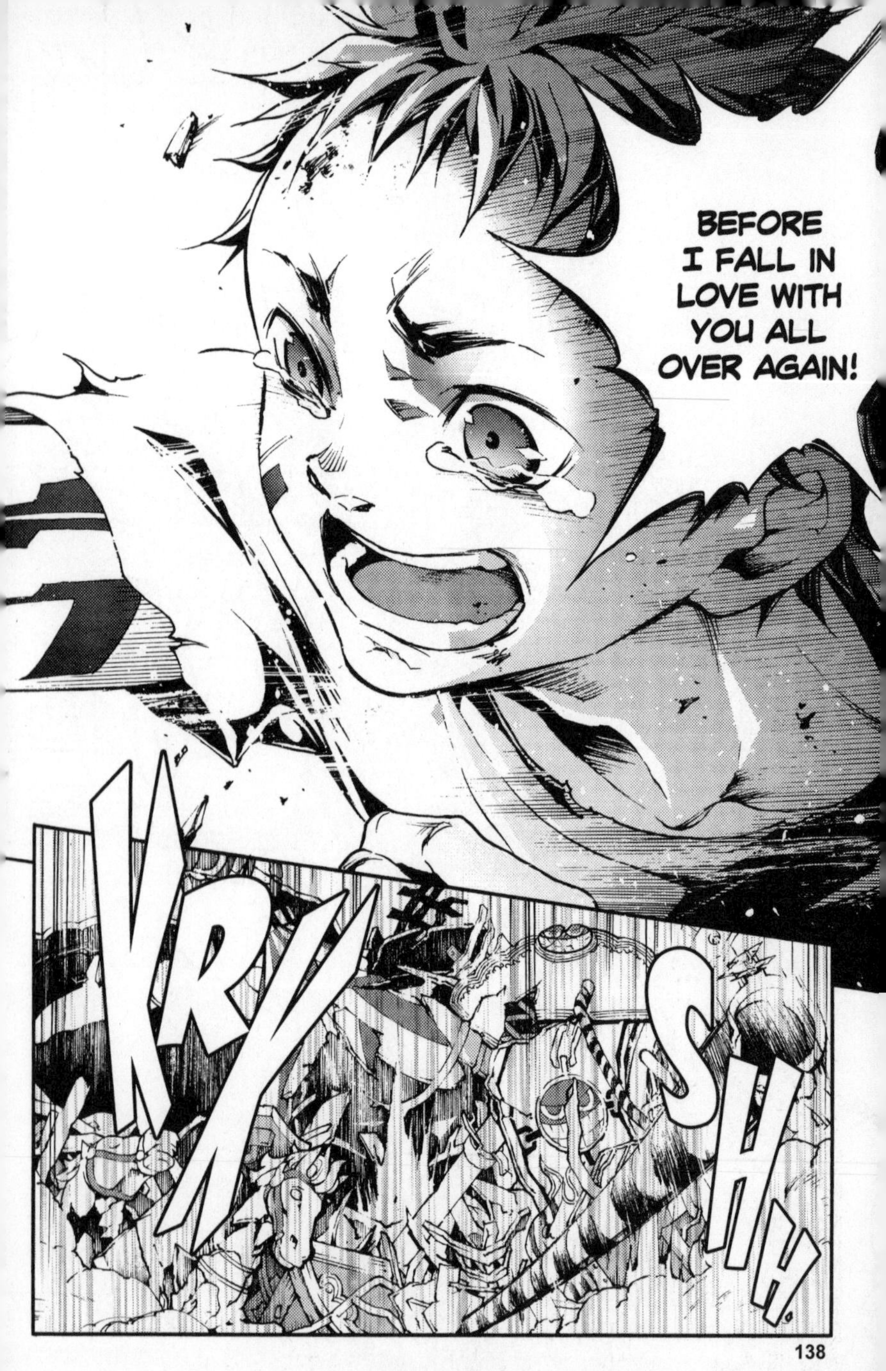
BEFORE I FALL IN LOVE WITH YOU ALL OVER AGAIN!
KRY
SHH

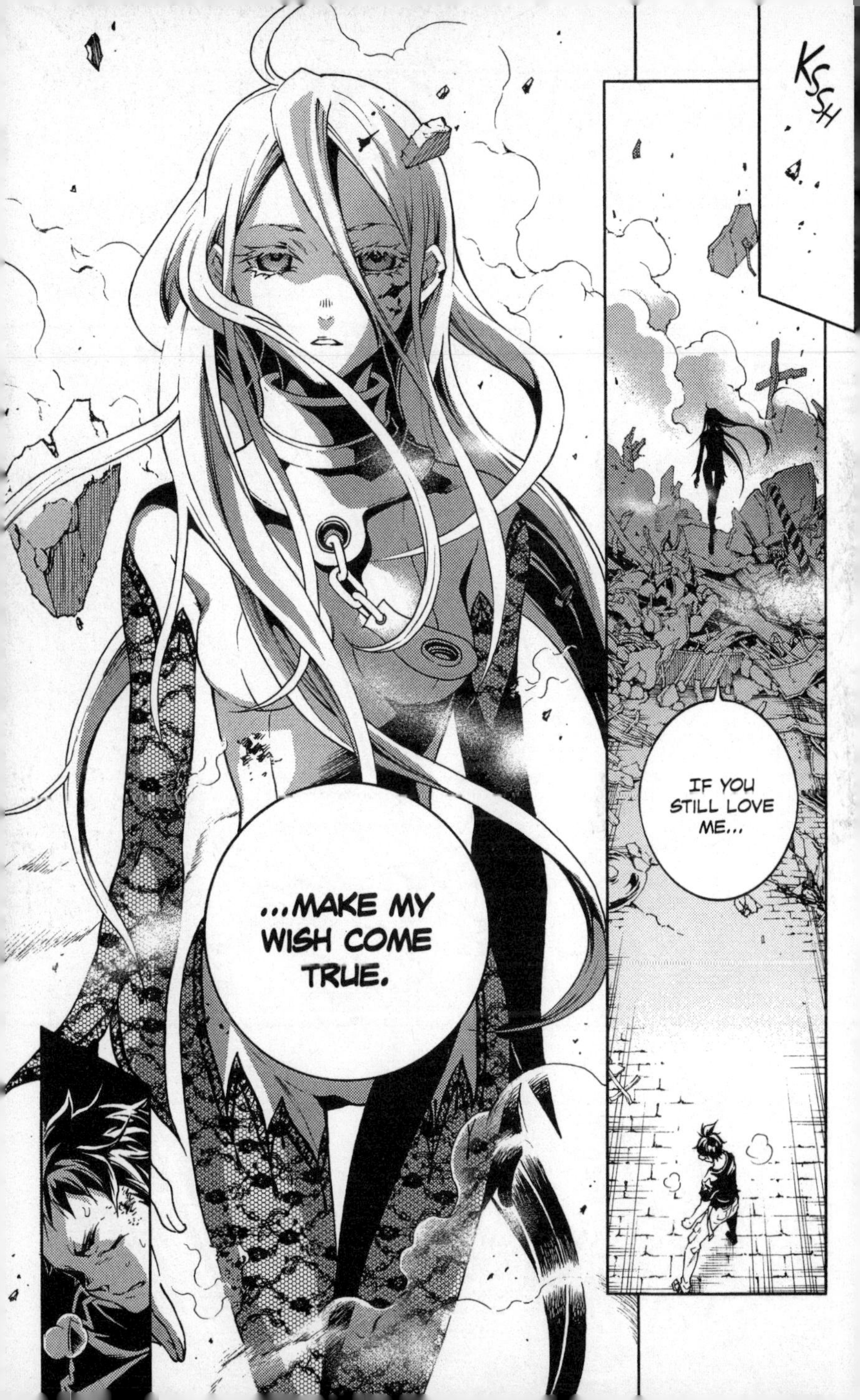
KSSH
IF YOU STILL LOVE ME...
...MAKE MY WISH COME TRUE.

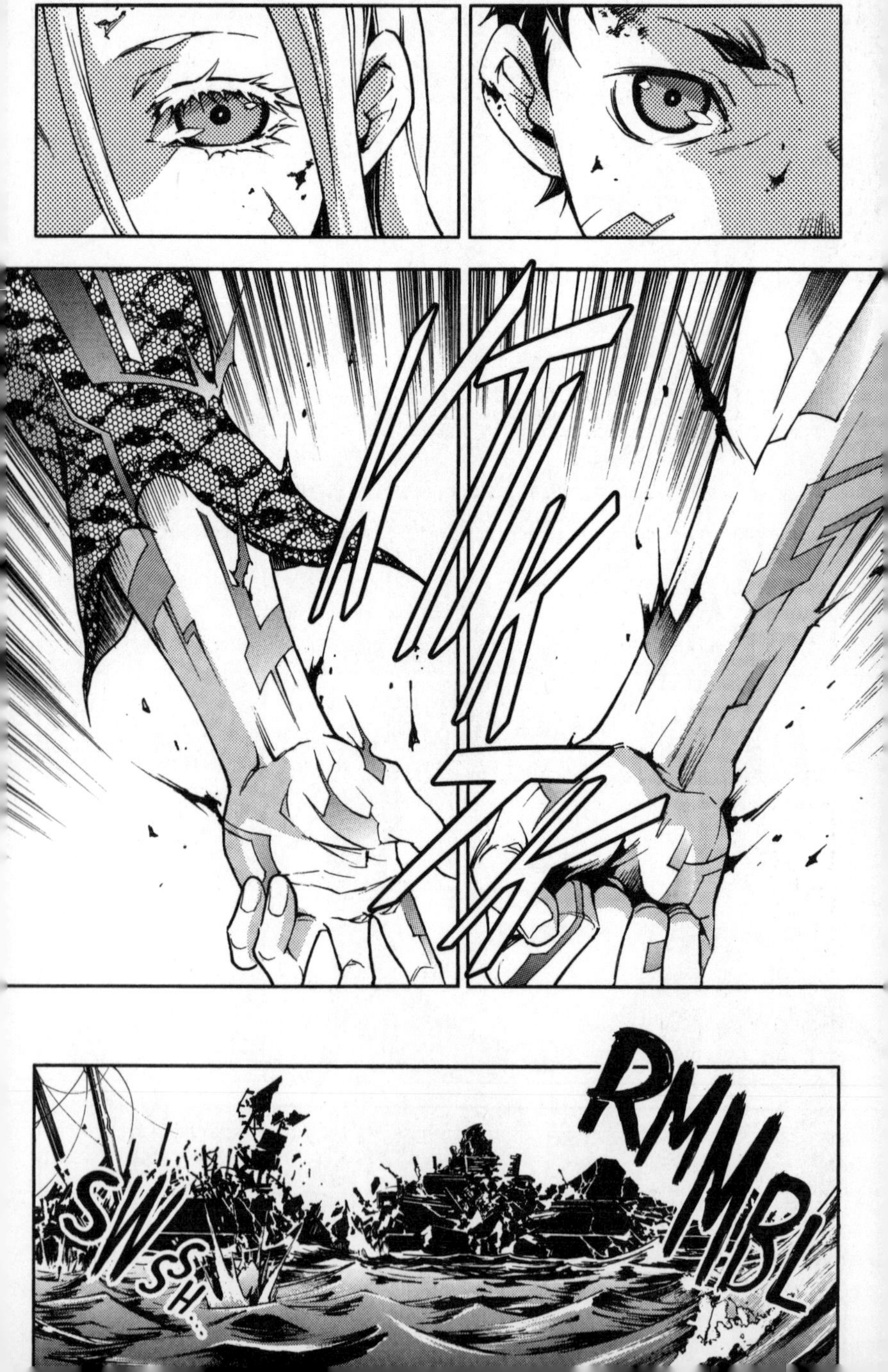
KTK
TK
RMMBL
SWSSH..

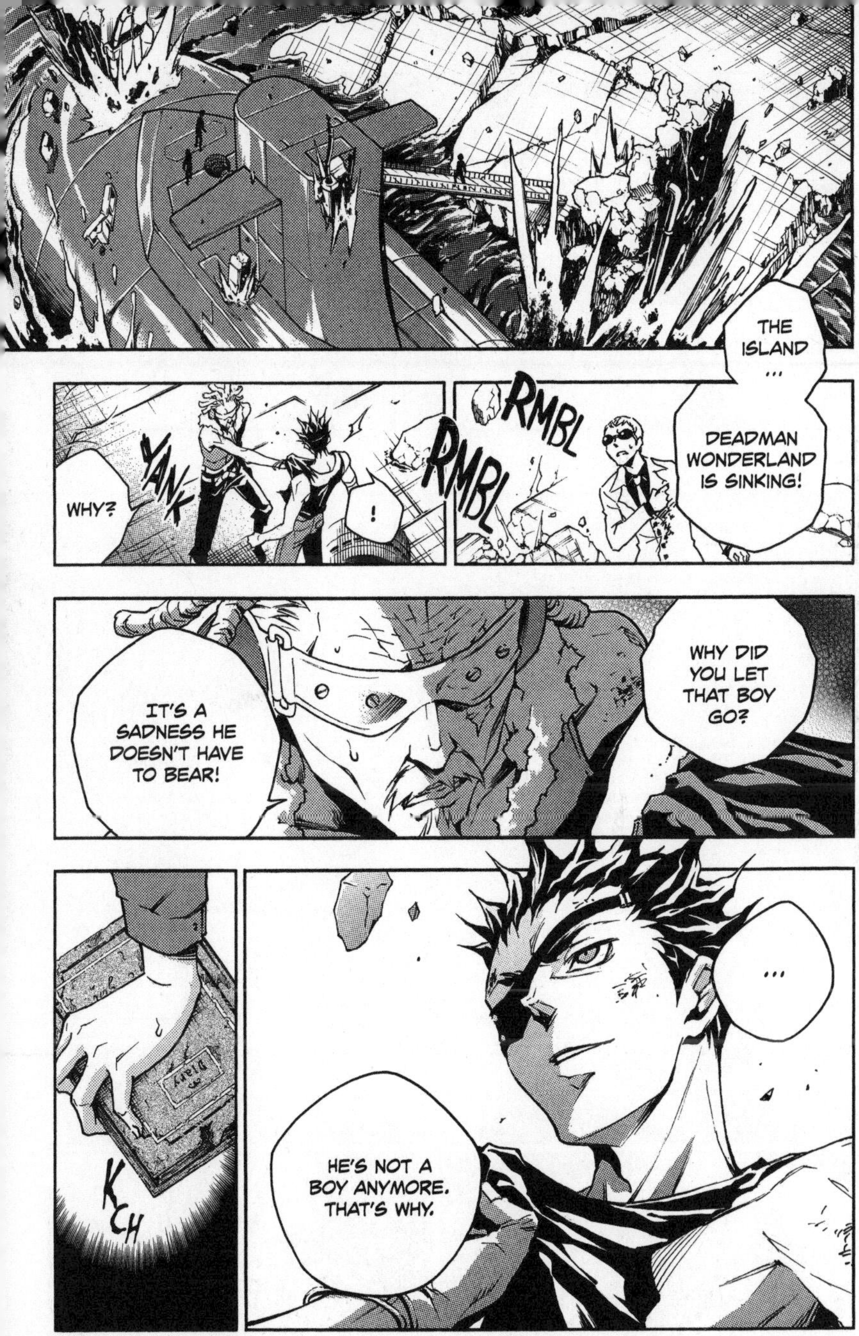
THE ISLAND ...
RMBL
RMBL
DEADMAN WONDERLAND IS SINKING!
!
YANK
WHY?
WHY DID YOU LET THAT BOY GO?
IT'S A SADNESS HE DOESN'T HAVE TO BEAR!
...
HE'S NOT A BOY ANYMORE. THAT'S WHY.
KCH

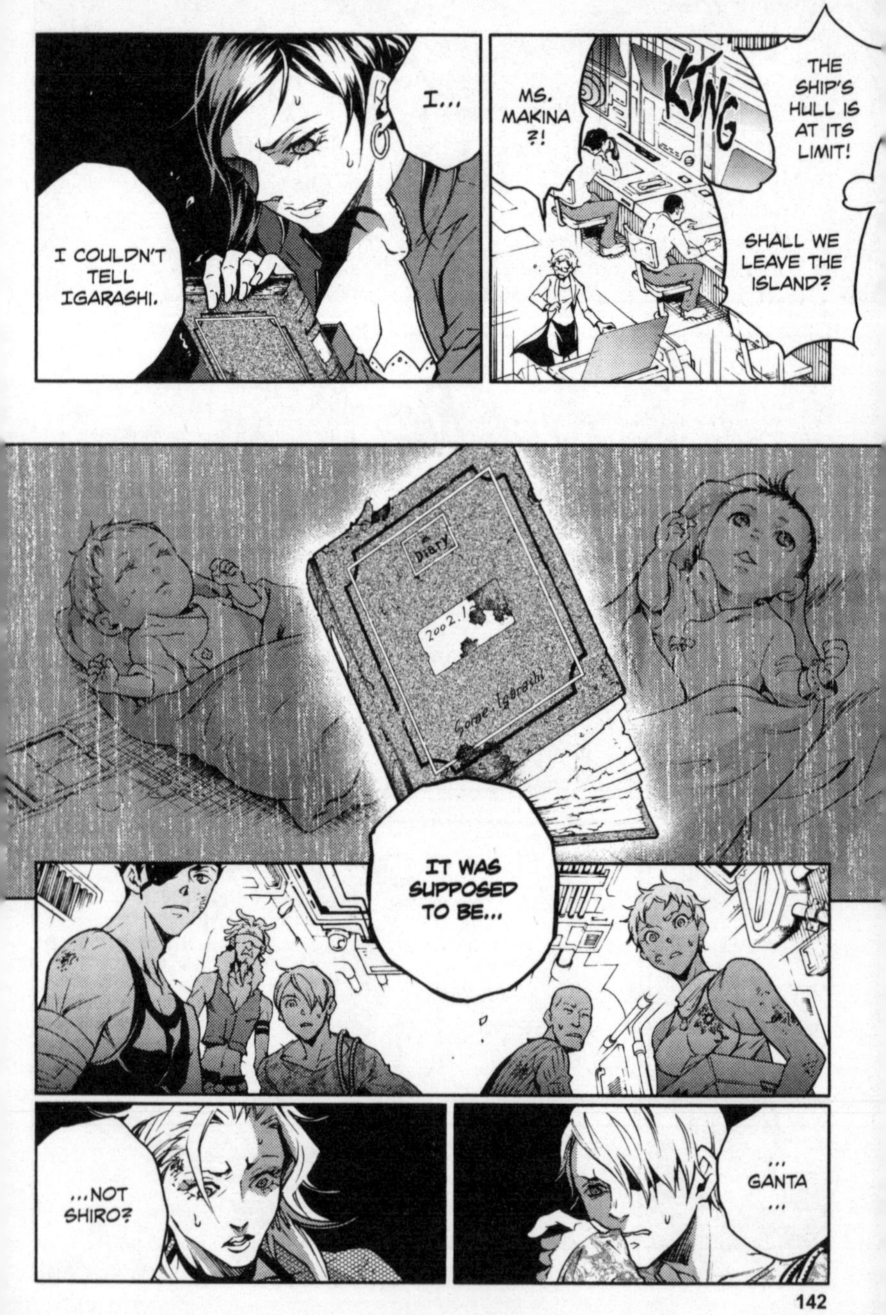
THE SHIP'S HULL IS AT ITS LIMIT!
KTNG
MS. MAKINA ?!
SHALL WE LEAVE THE ISLAND?
I...
I COULDN'T TELL IGARASHI.
Diary
2002.1
Sorae Igarashi
IT WAS SUPPOSED TO BE...
... GANTA ...
...NOT SHIRO?

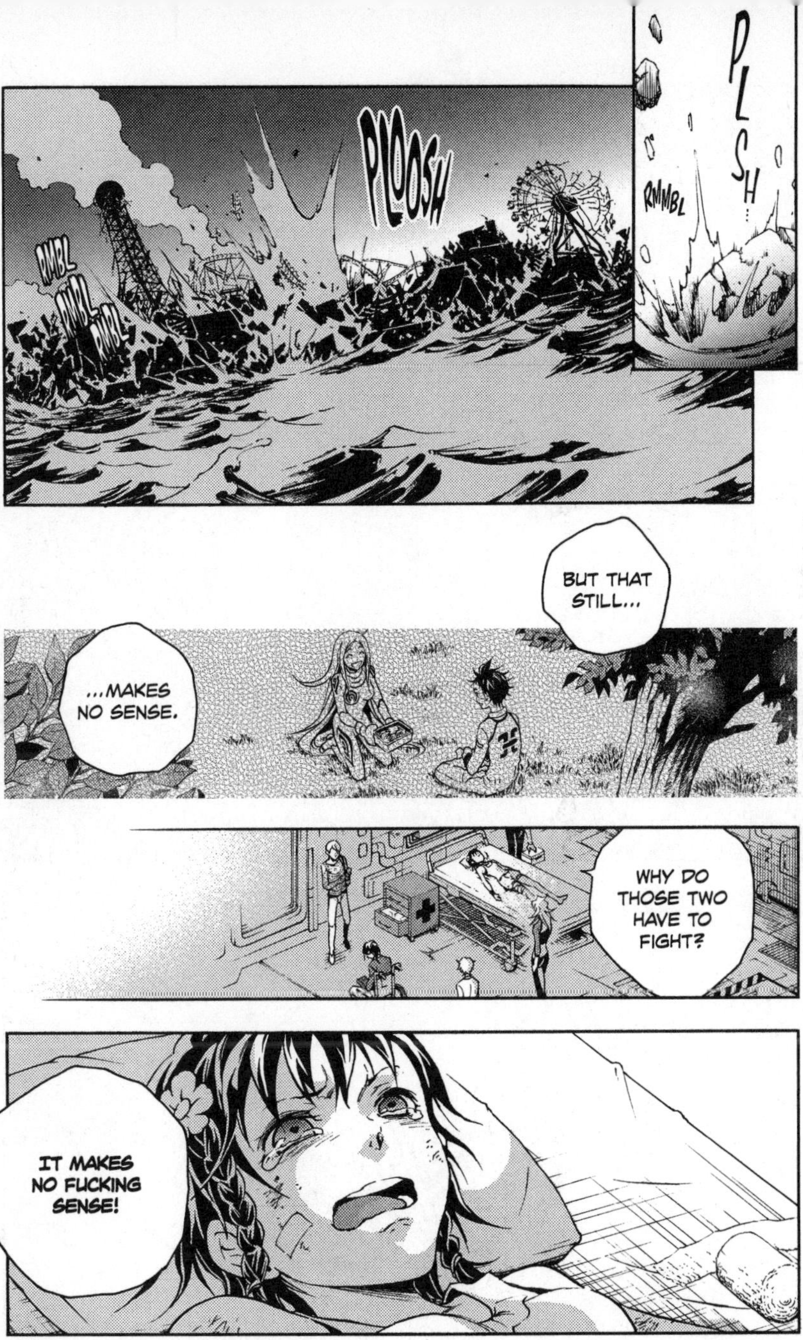
PLSH...
RMMBL
PLOOSH
RMBL
RMBL
RMBL
BUT THAT STILL...
...MAKES NO SENSE.
WHY DO THOSE TWO HAVE TO FIGHT?
IT MAKES NO FUCKING SENSE!

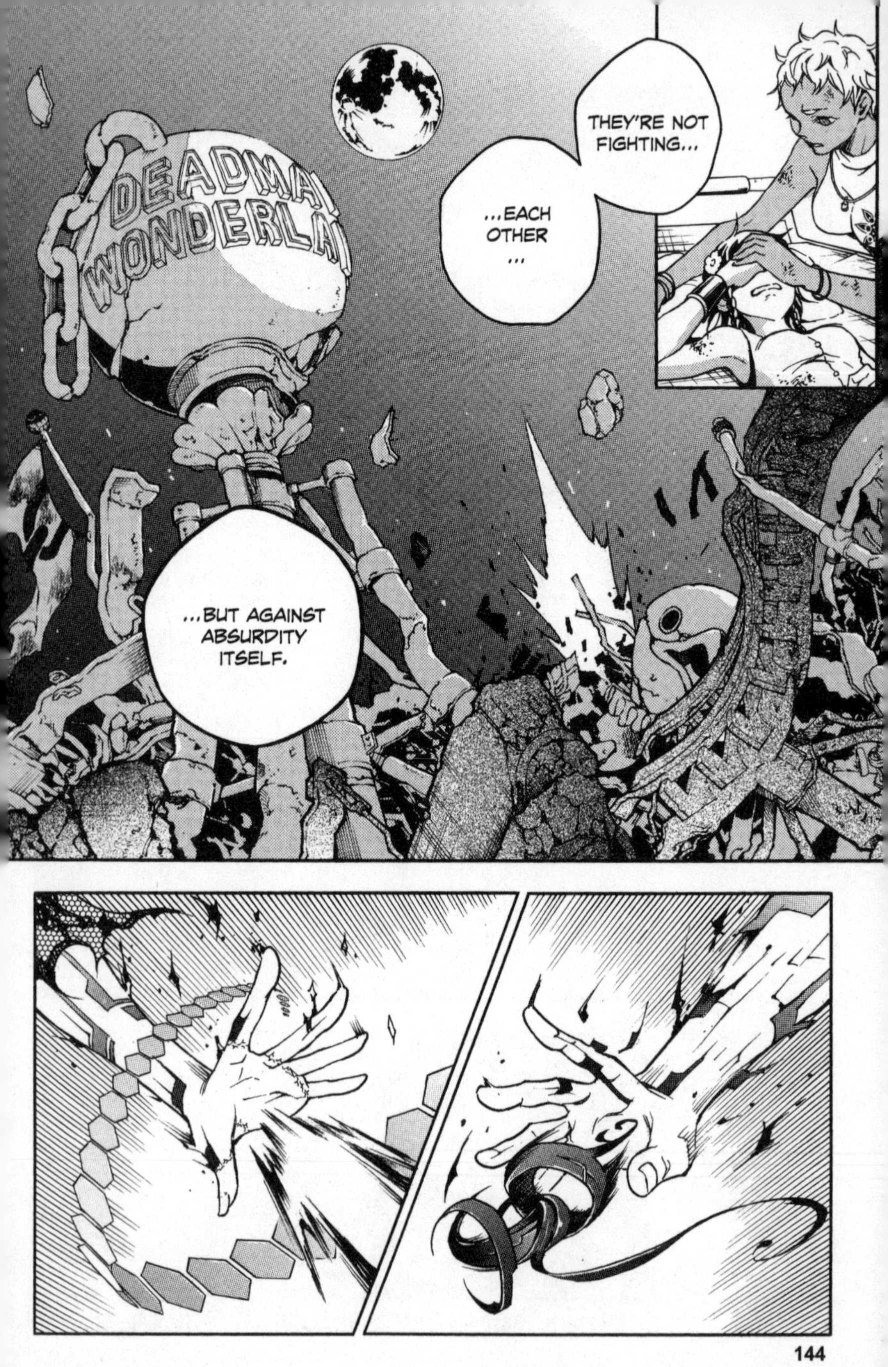
THEY'RE NOT FIGHTING...
...EACH OTHER ...
...BUT AGAINST ABSURDITY ITSELF.

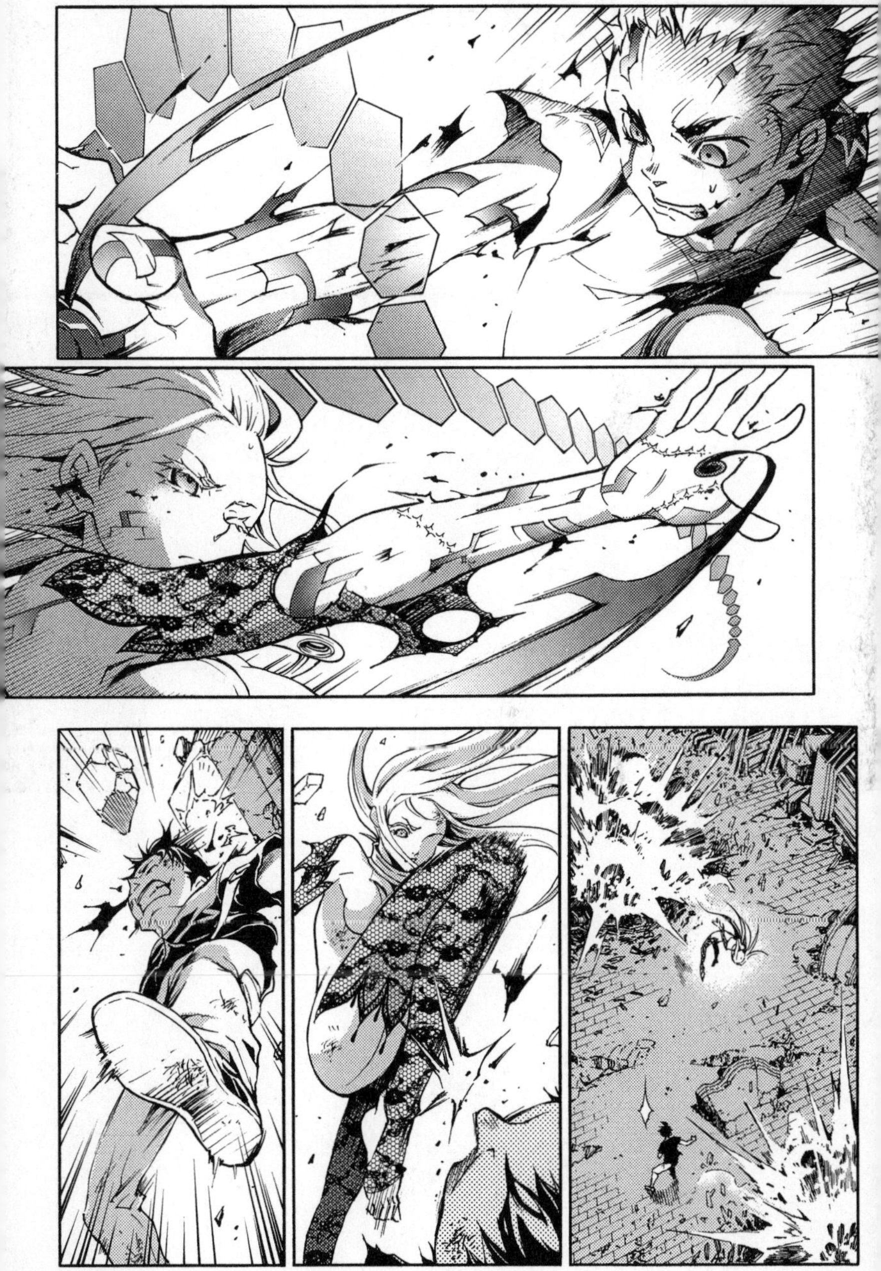

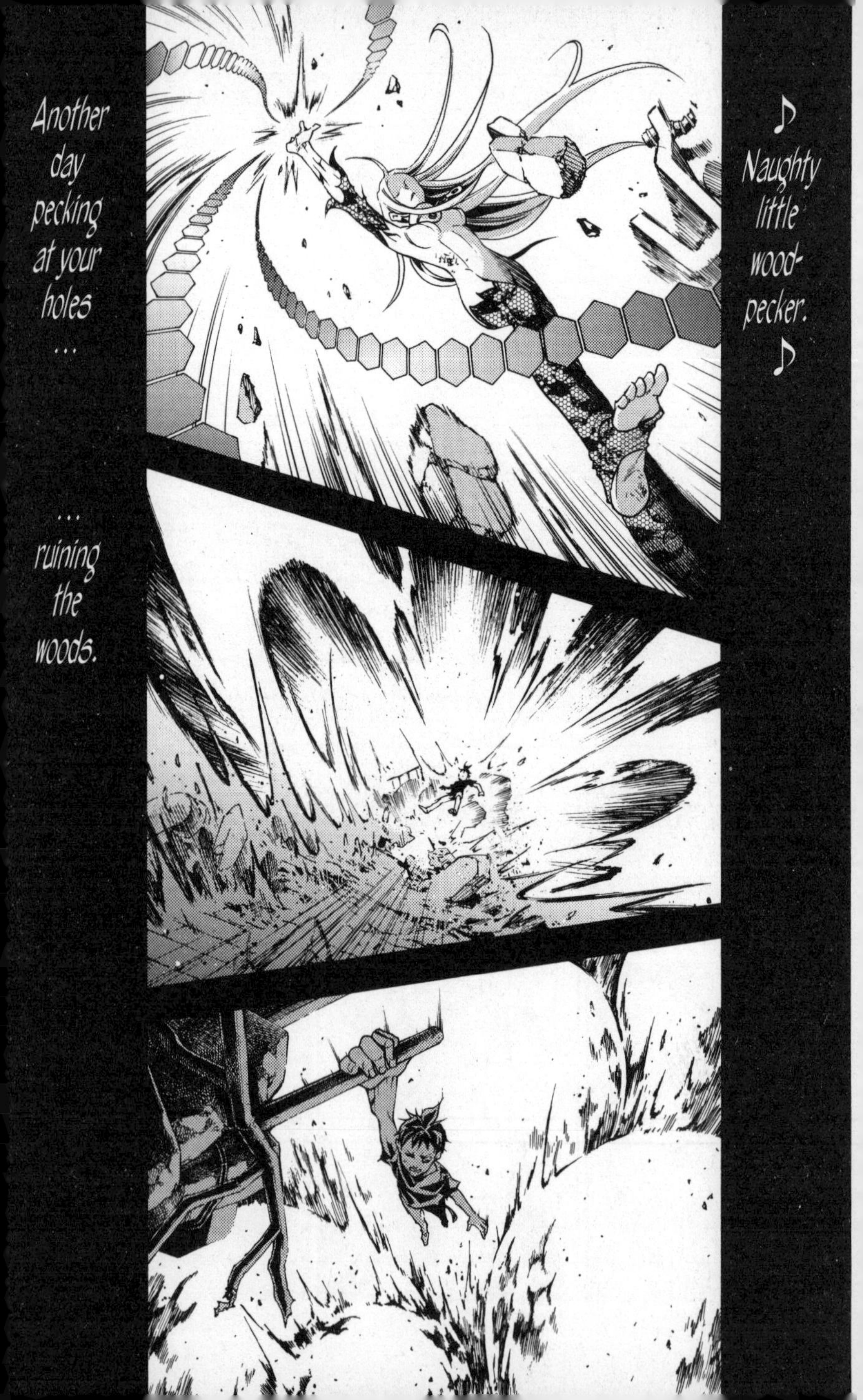
♪ Naughty little wood-pecker. ♪
Another day pecking at your holes ...
... ruining the woods.

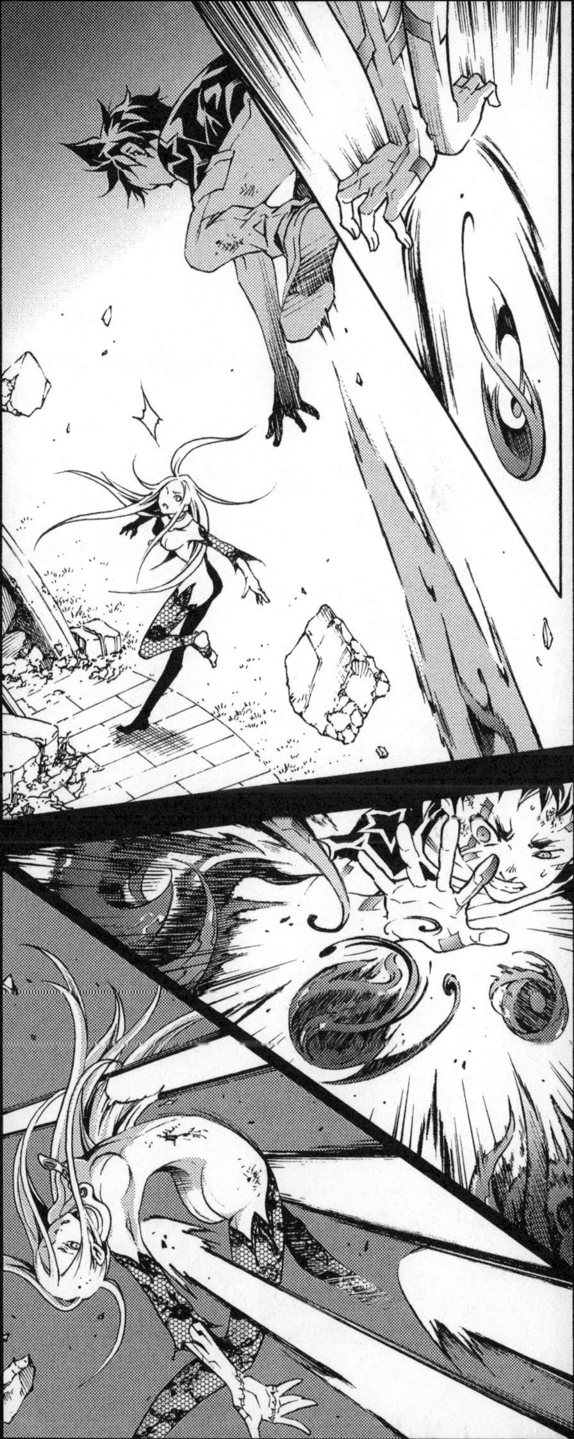

♪ The angry old forest god ...

... changed your beak into a poison knife. ♪

Poor little wood-pecker.

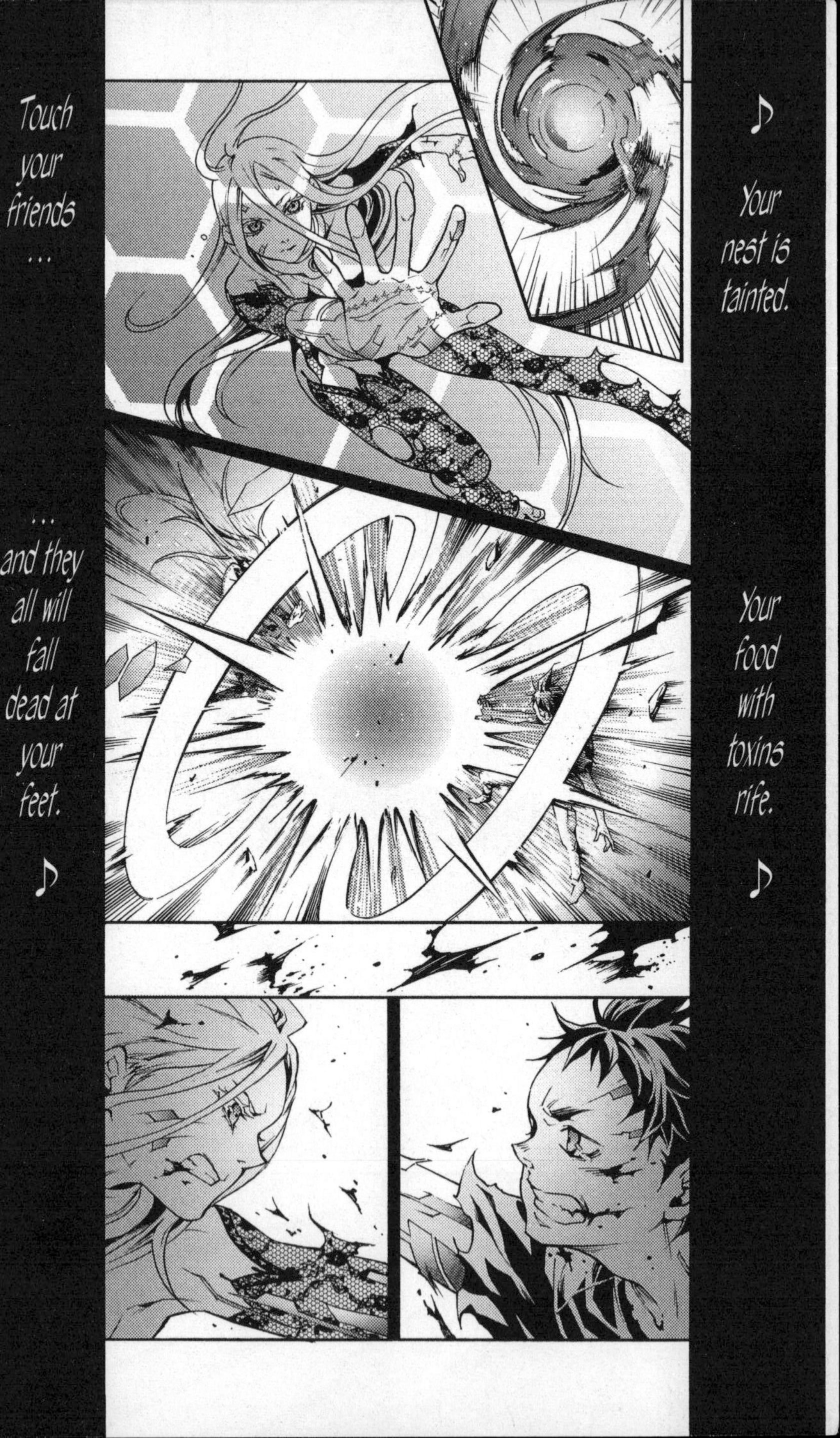
♪
Your nest is tainted.
Your food with toxins rife.
♪
Touch your friends ...
... and they all will fall dead at your feet.
♪

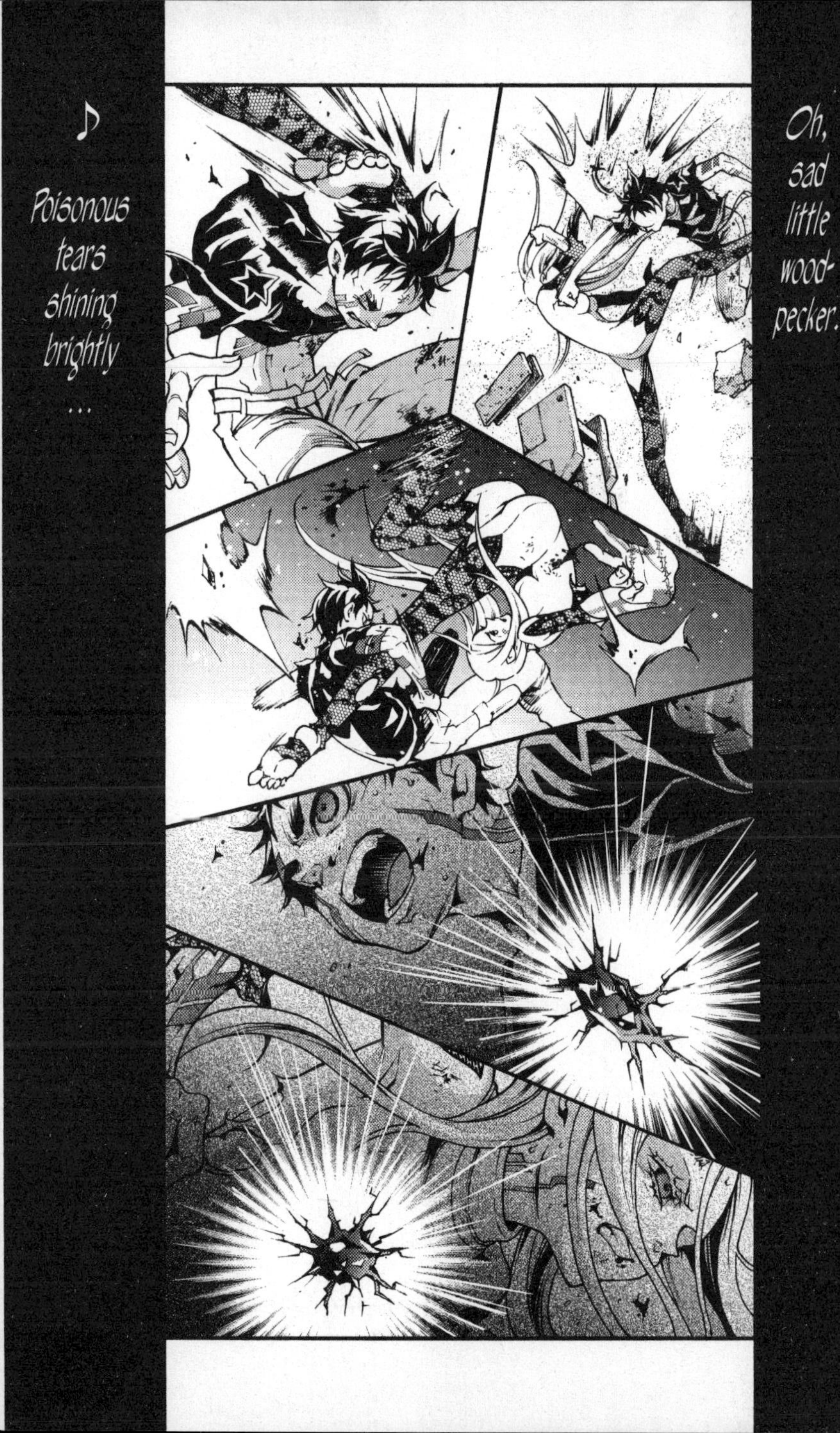
Oh, sad little wood-pecker.
♪ Poisonous tears shining brightly ...

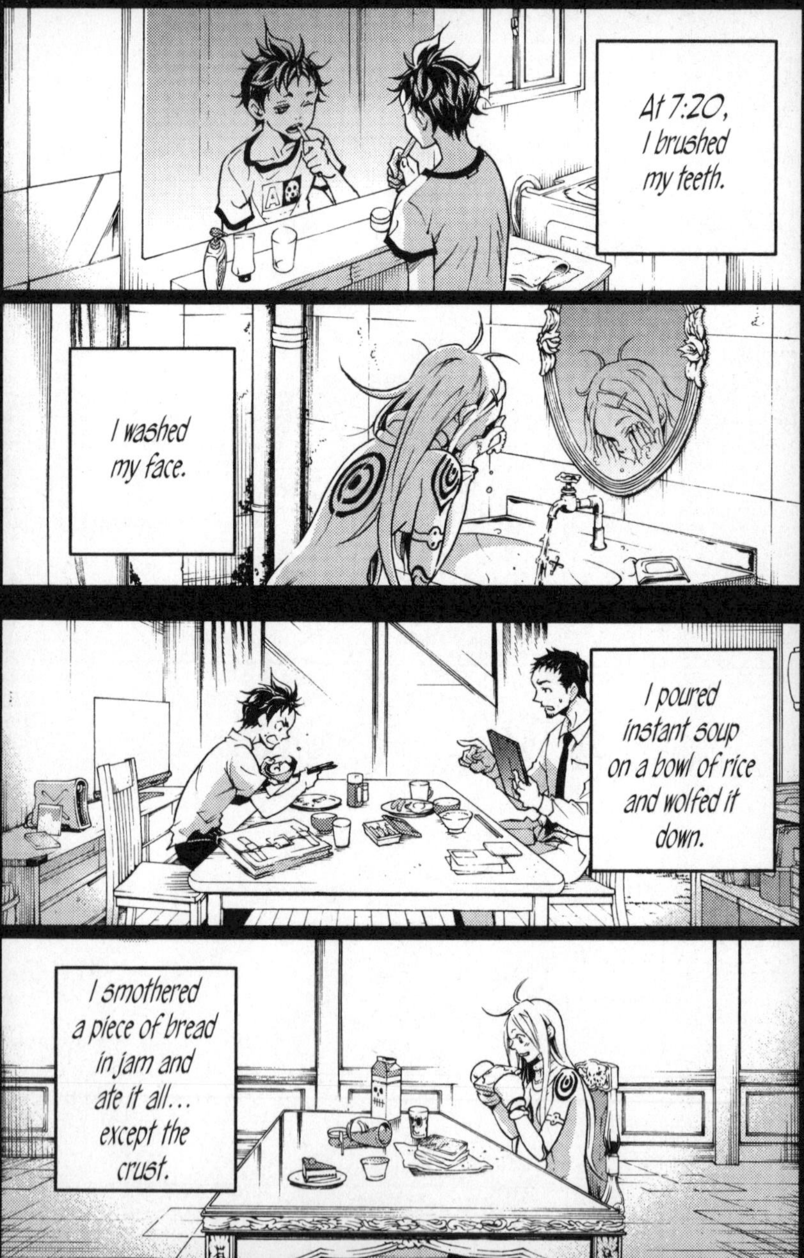
At 7:20, I brushed my teeth.
I washed my face.
I poured instant soup on a bowl of rice and wolfed it down.
I smothered a piece of bread in jam and ate it all... except the crust.

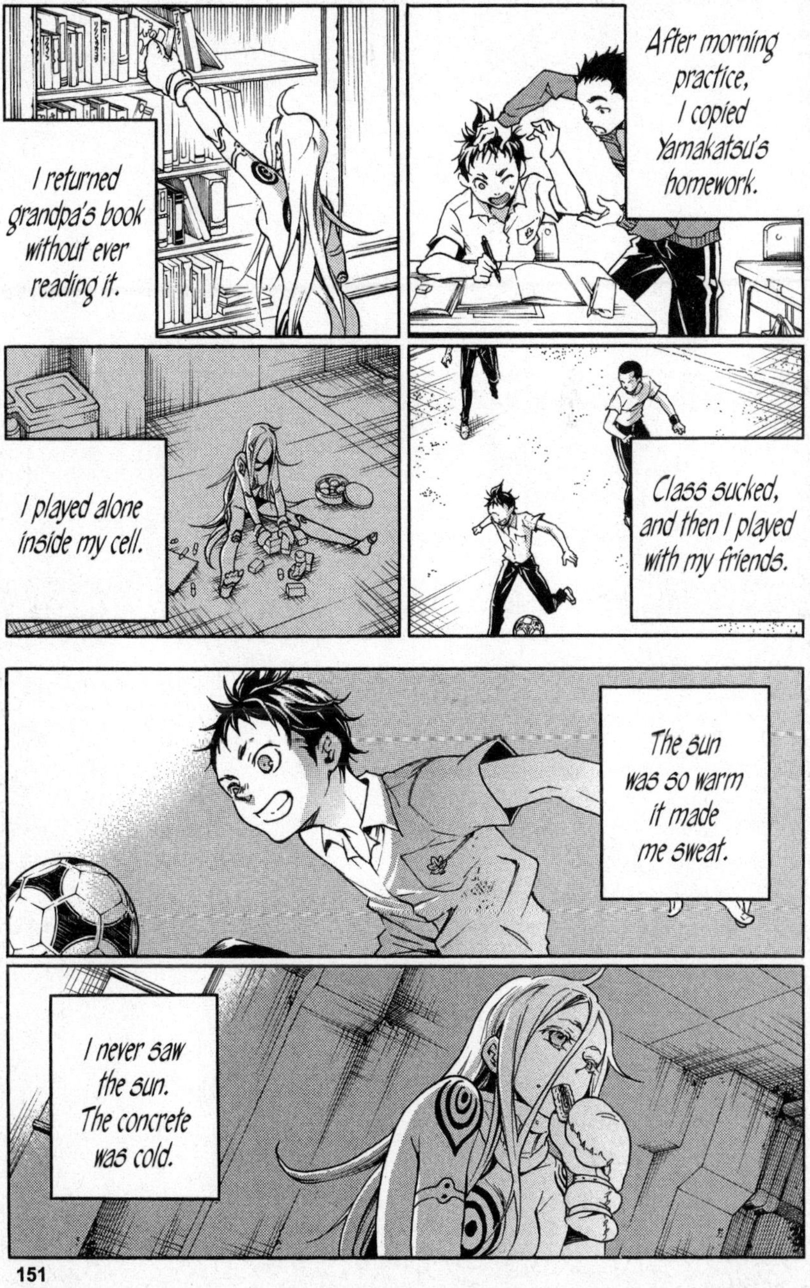
After morning practice, I copied Yamakatsu's homework.
I returned grandpa's book without ever reading it.
Class sucked, and then I played with my friends.
I played alone inside my cell.
The sun was so warm it made me sweat.
I never saw the sun. The concrete was cold.

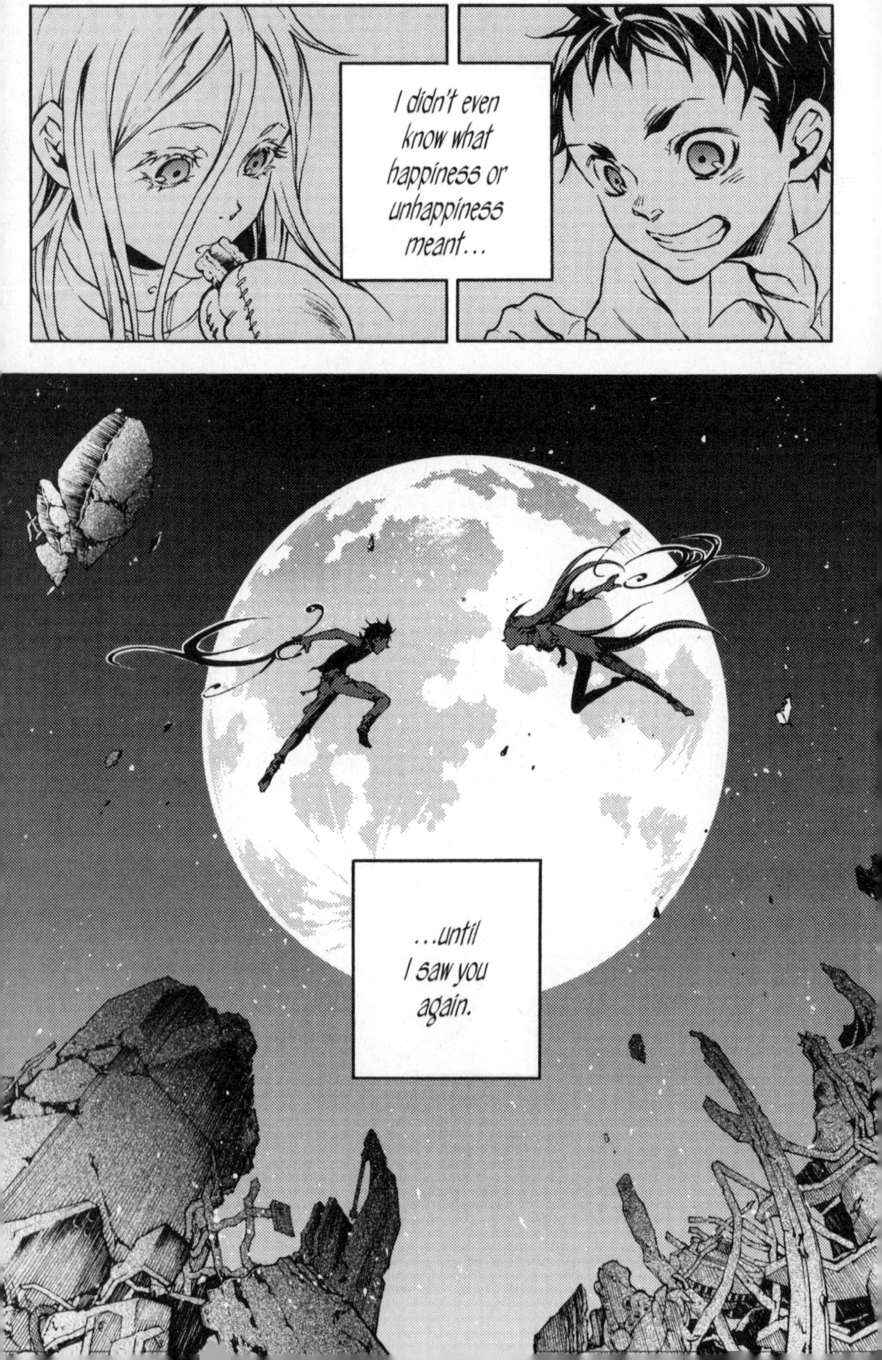
I didn't even know what happiness or unhappiness meant...
...until I saw you again.

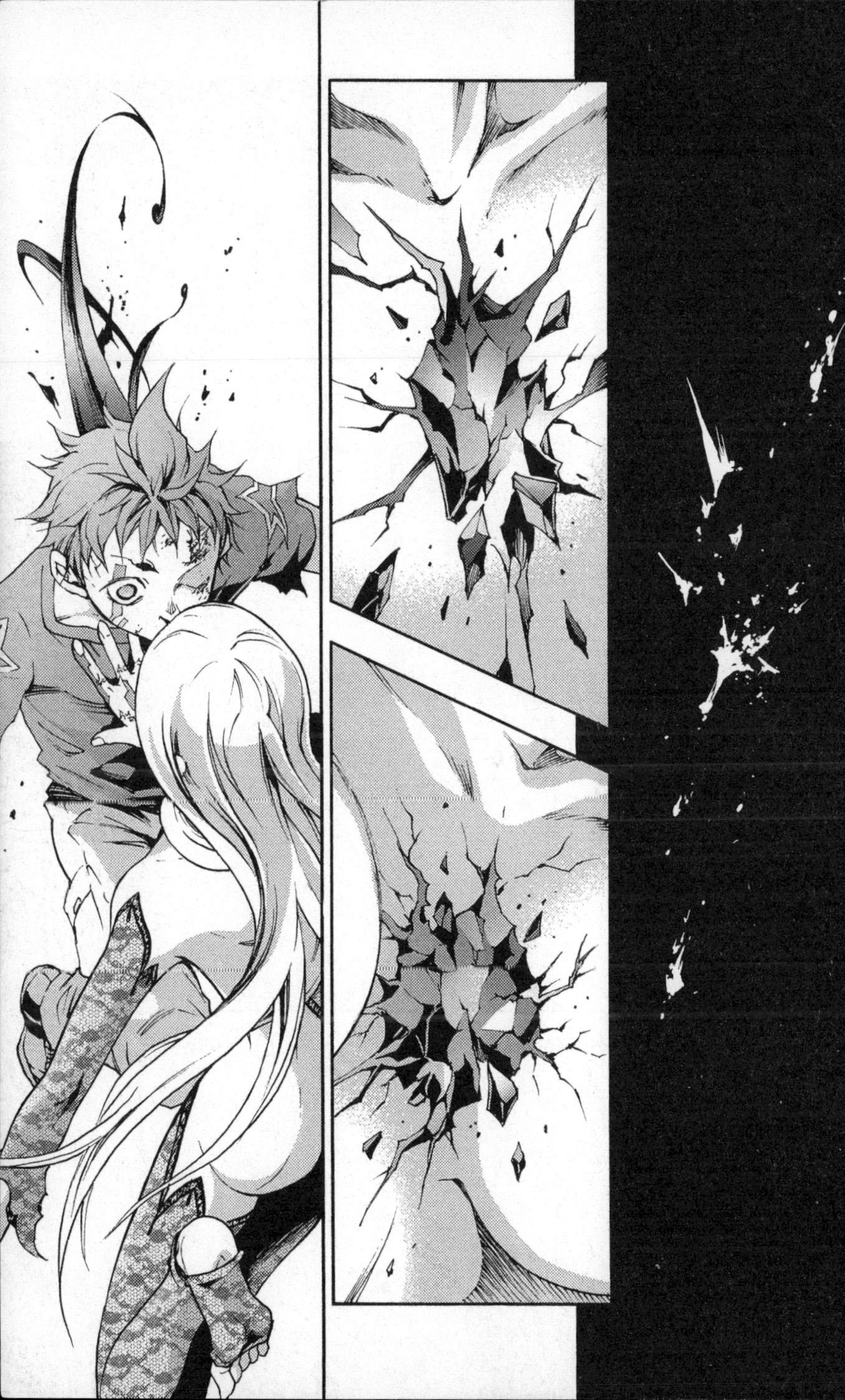

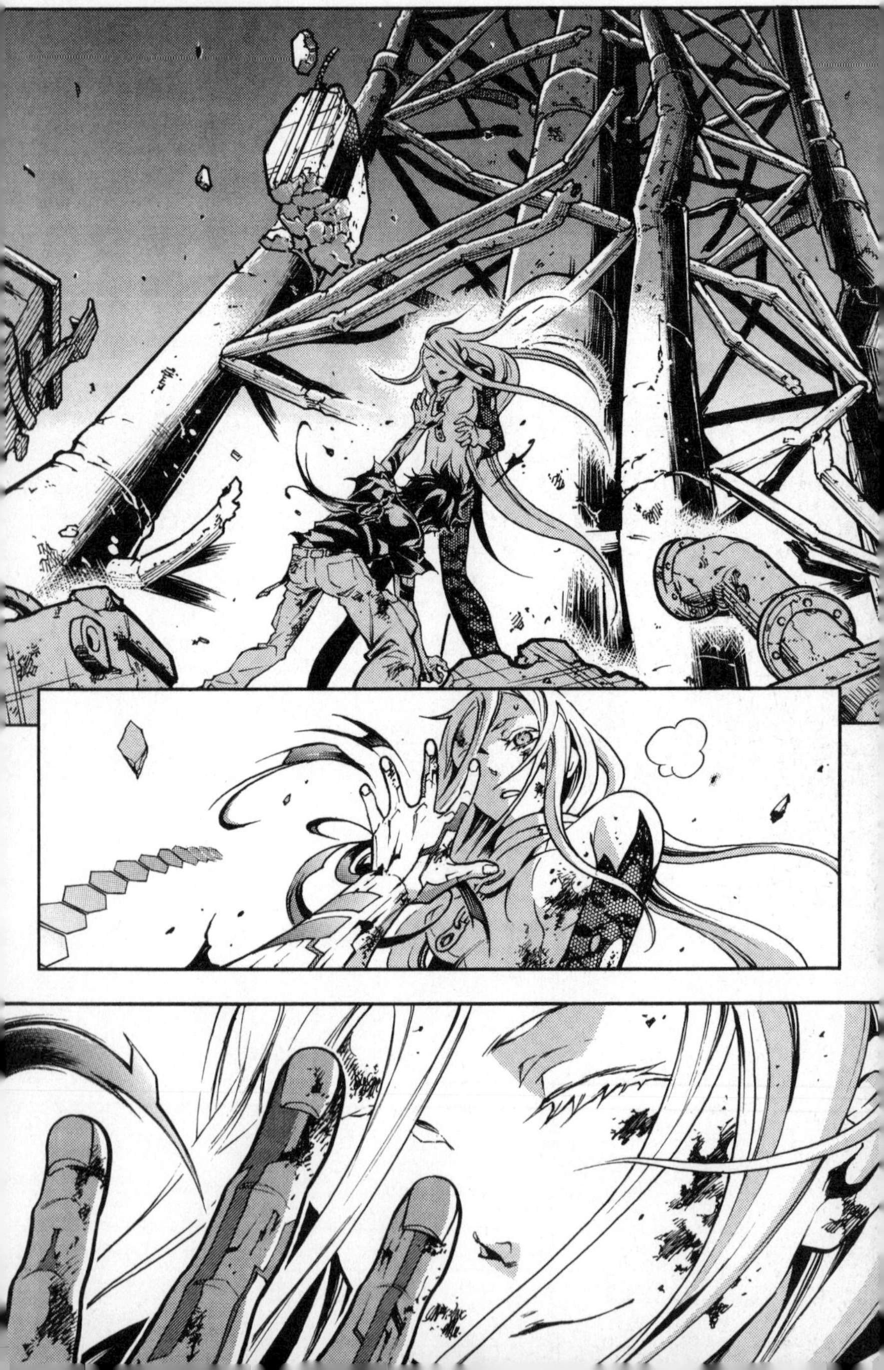

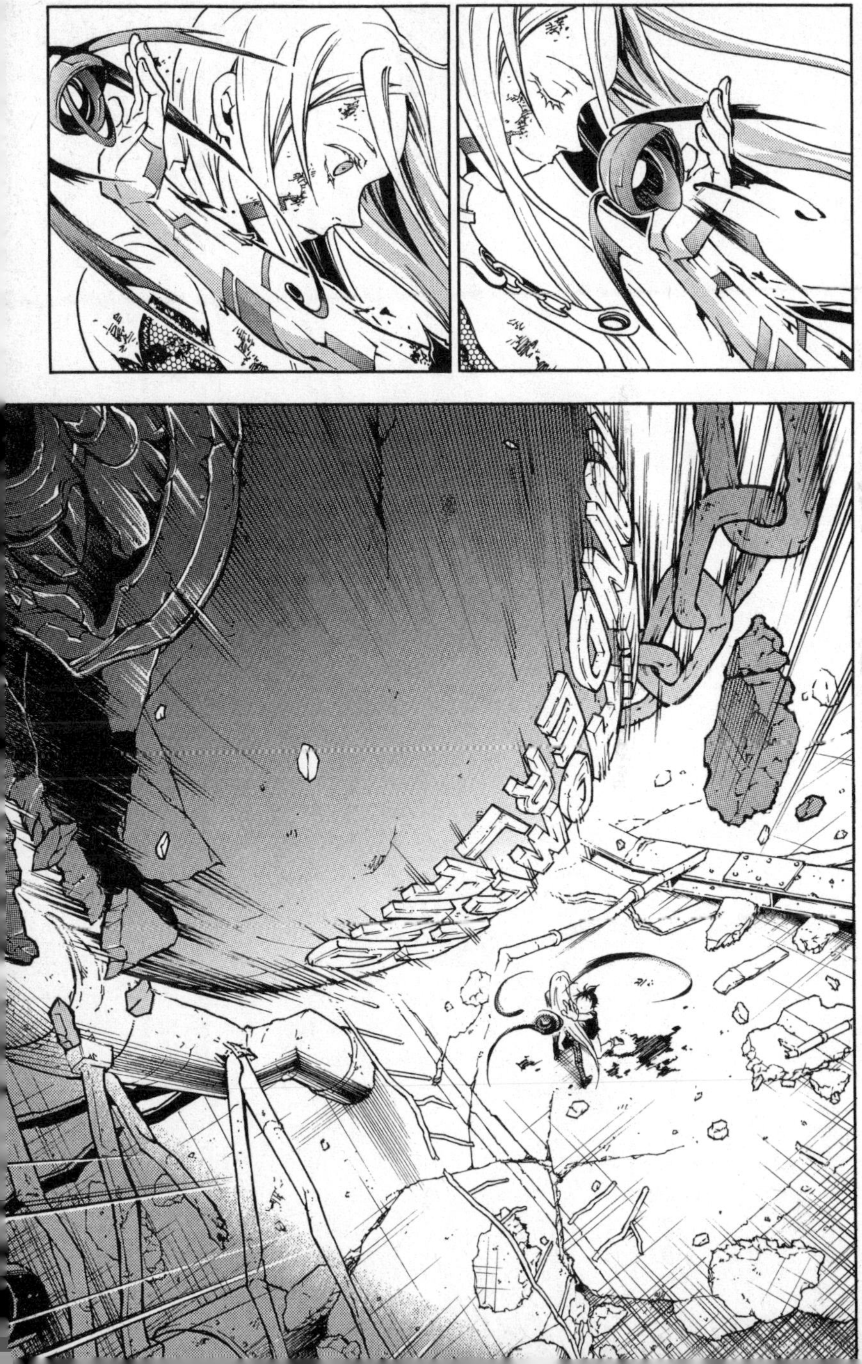

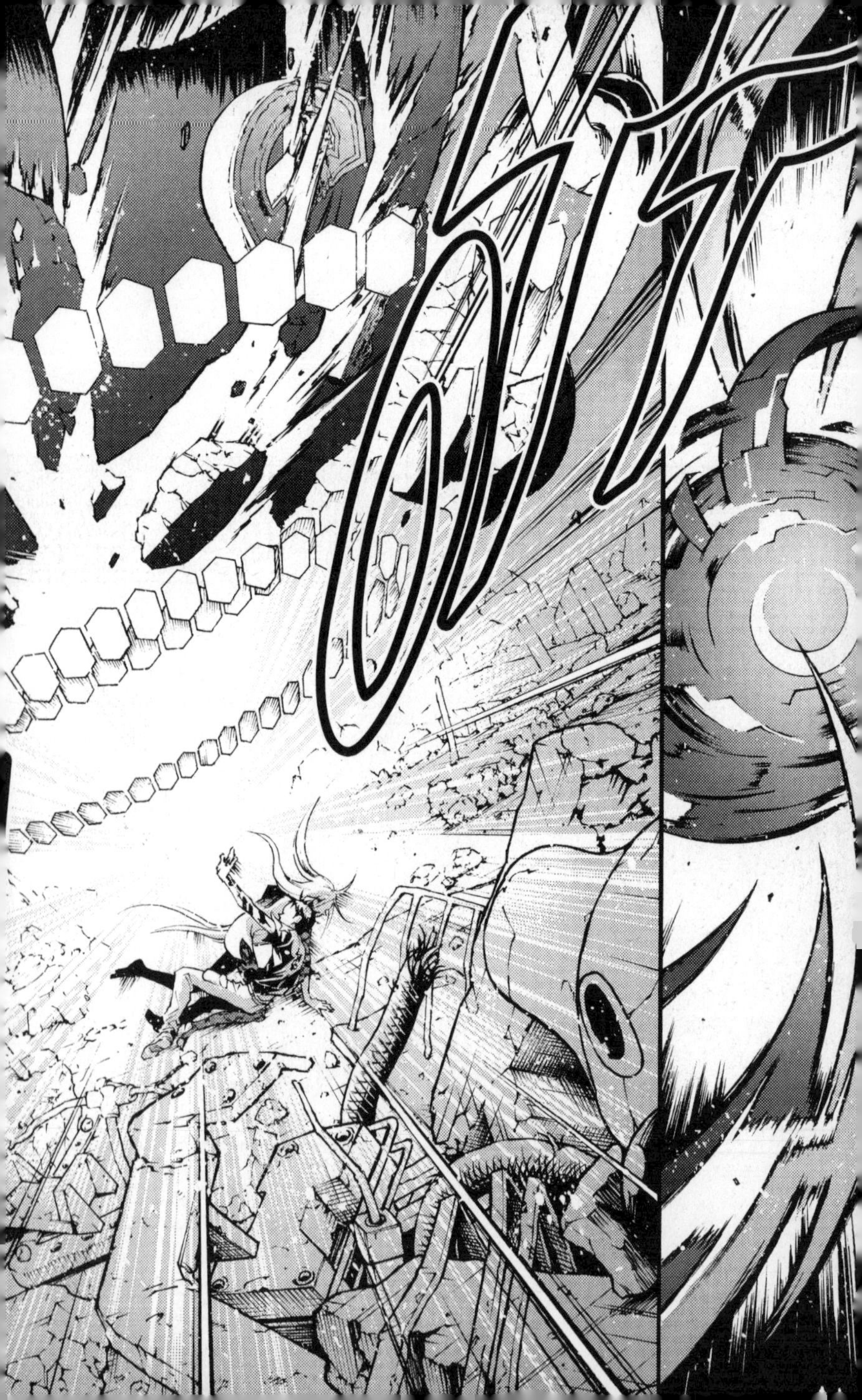

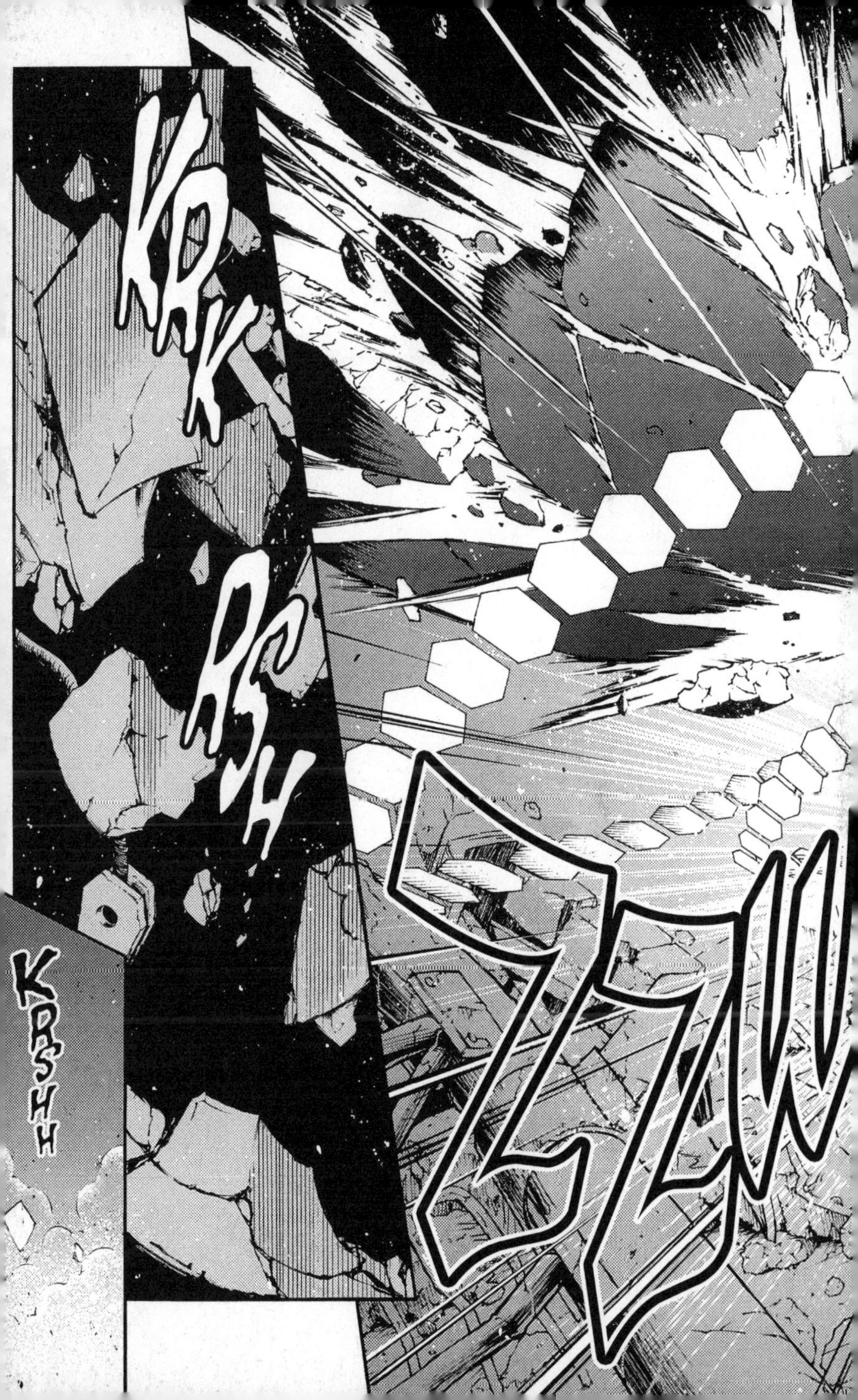
KRSHH

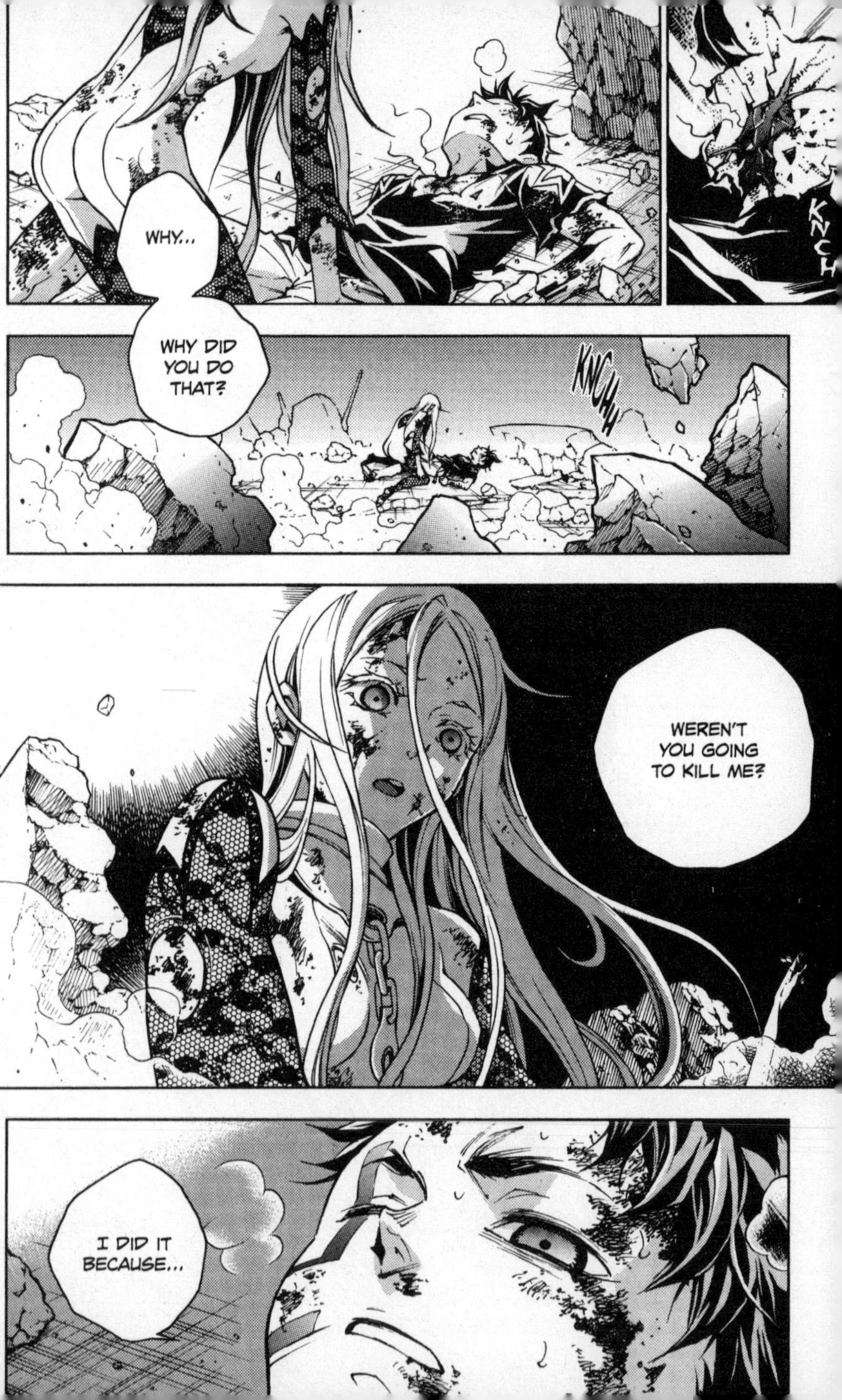
KNCH
WHY...
WHY DID YOU DO THAT?
KNCHH
WEREN'T YOU GOING TO KILL ME?
I DID IT BECAUSE...

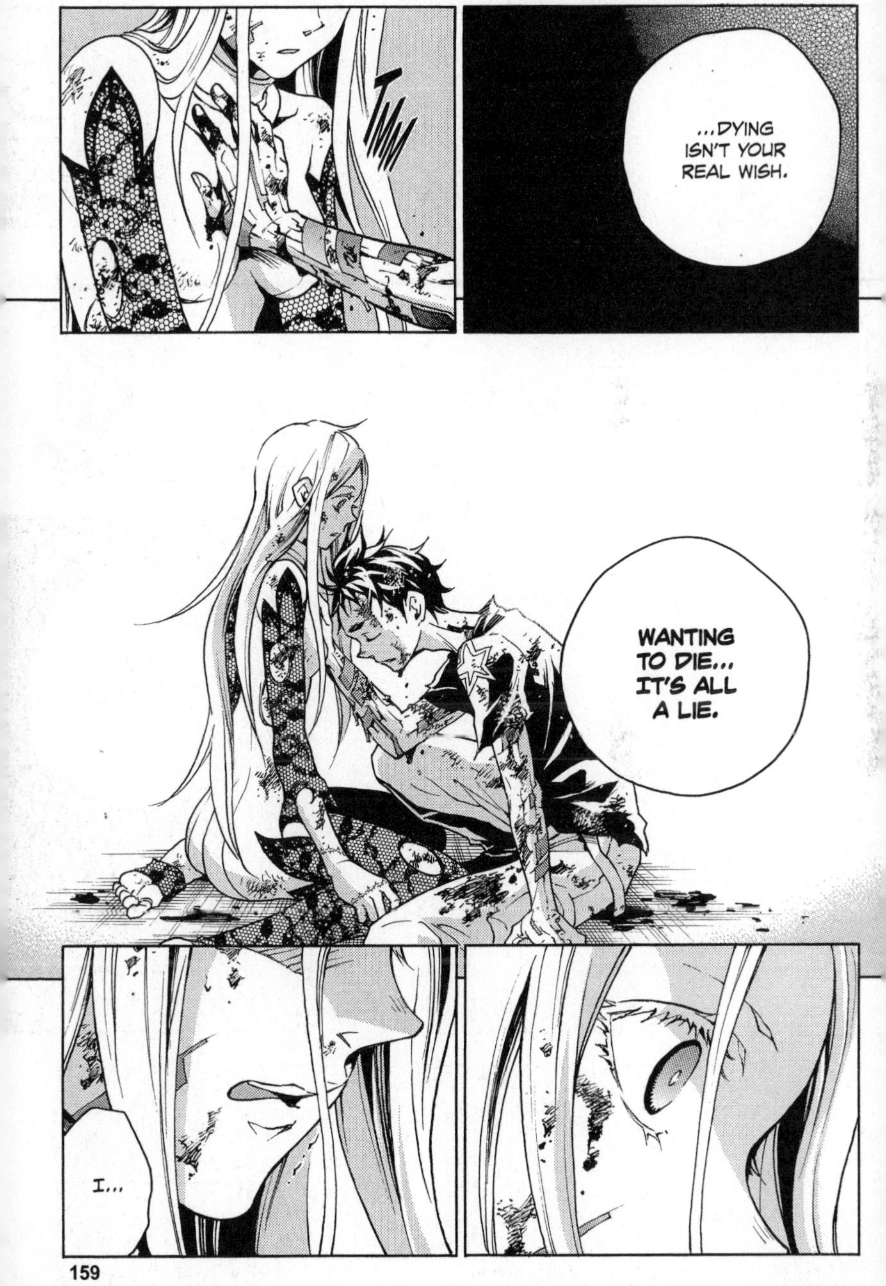
...DYING ISN'T YOUR REAL WISH.
WANTING TO DIE... IT'S ALL A LIE.
I...

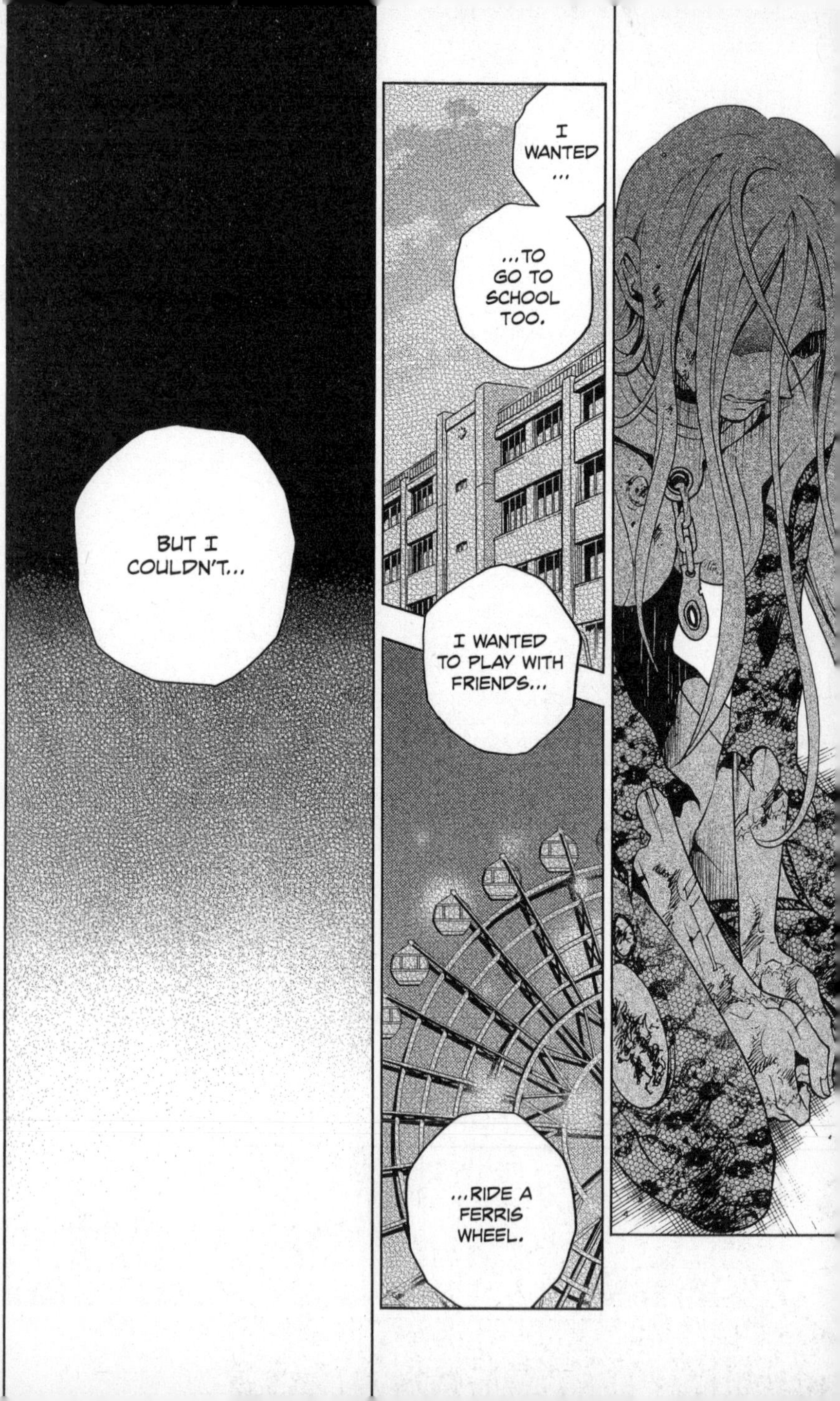
I WANTED ...
...TO GO TO SCHOOL TOO.
I WANTED TO PLAY WITH FRIENDS...
...RIDE A FERRIS WHEEL.
BUT I COULDN'T...

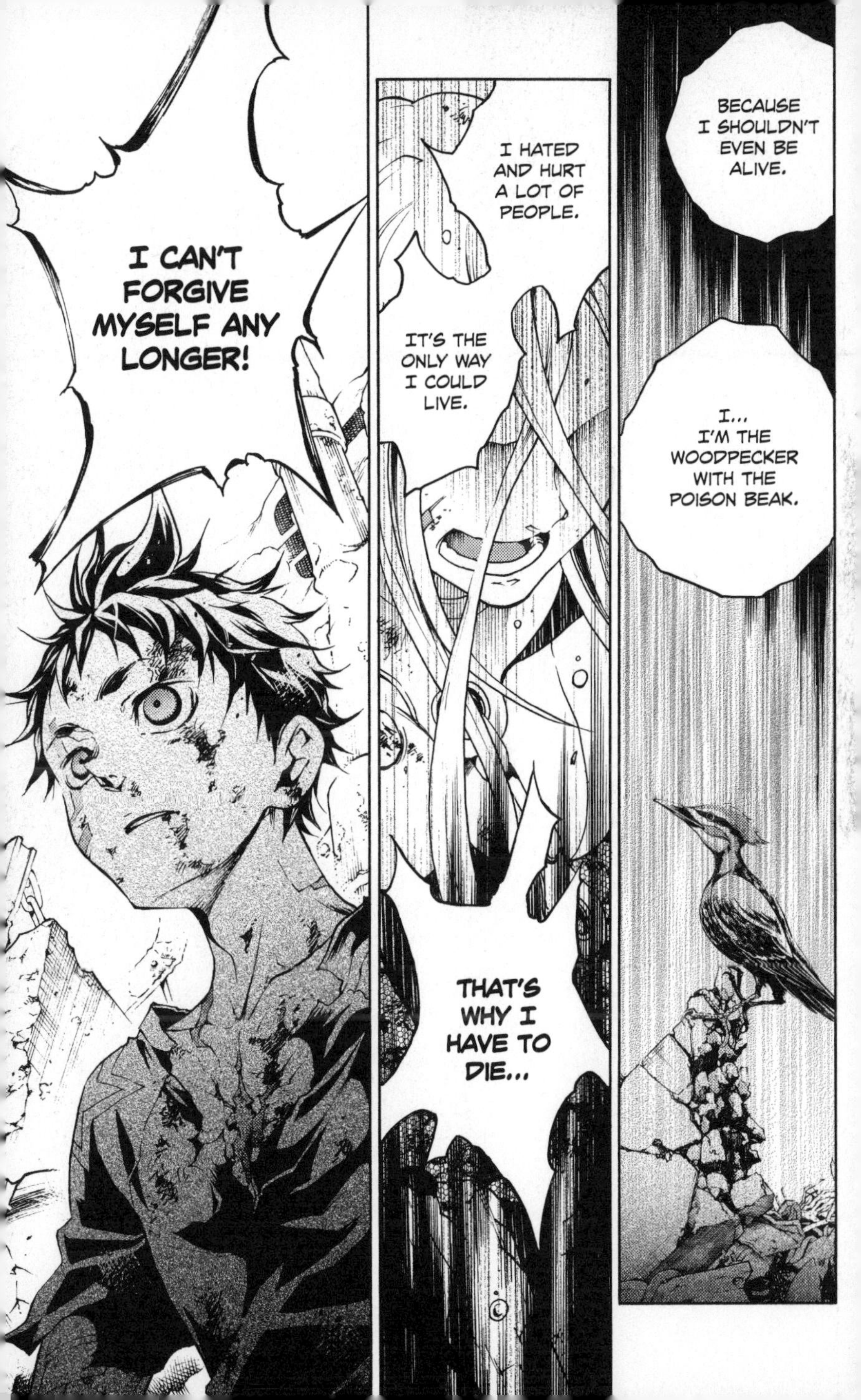
BECAUSE I SHOULDN'T EVEN BE ALIVE.
I... I'M THE WOODPECKER WITH THE POISON BEAK.
I HATED AND HURT A LOT OF PEOPLE.
IT'S THE ONLY WAY I COULD LIVE.
THAT'S WHY I HAVE TO DIE...
I CAN'T FORGIVE MYSELF ANY LONGER!

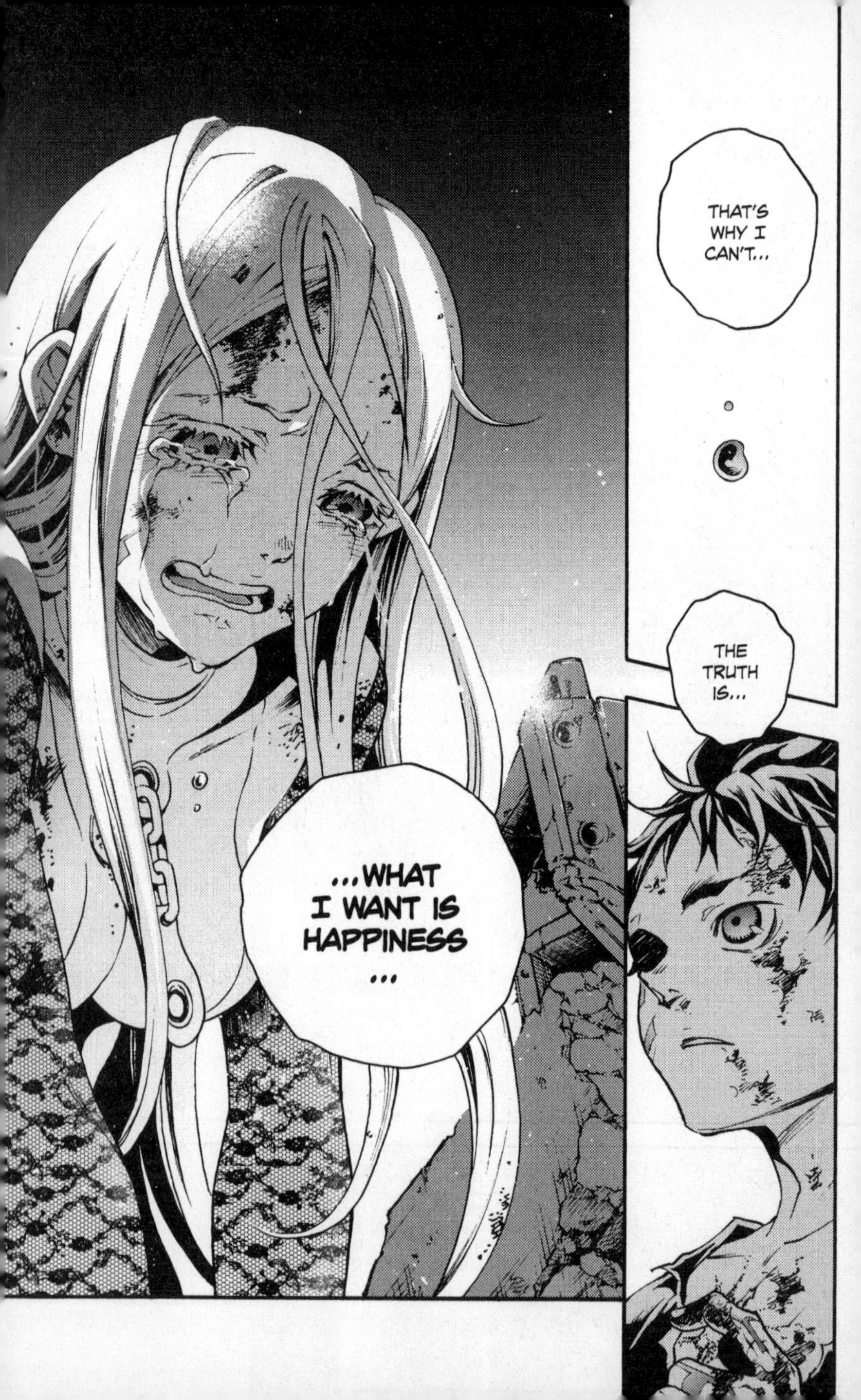
THAT'S WHY I CAN'T...
THE TRUTH IS...
...WHAT I WANT IS HAPPINESS ...

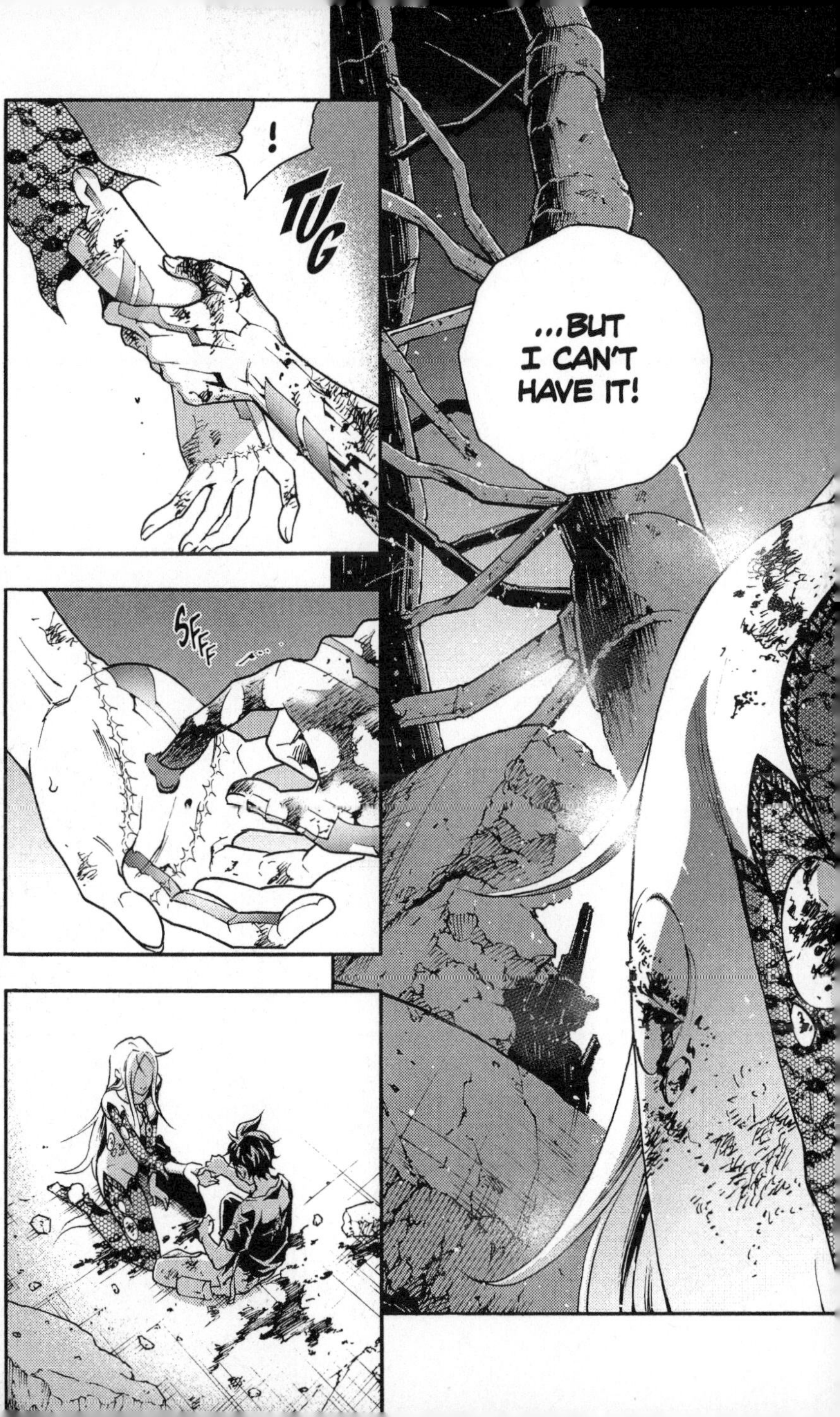
...BUT I CAN'T HAVE IT!
!
TUG
SFFF

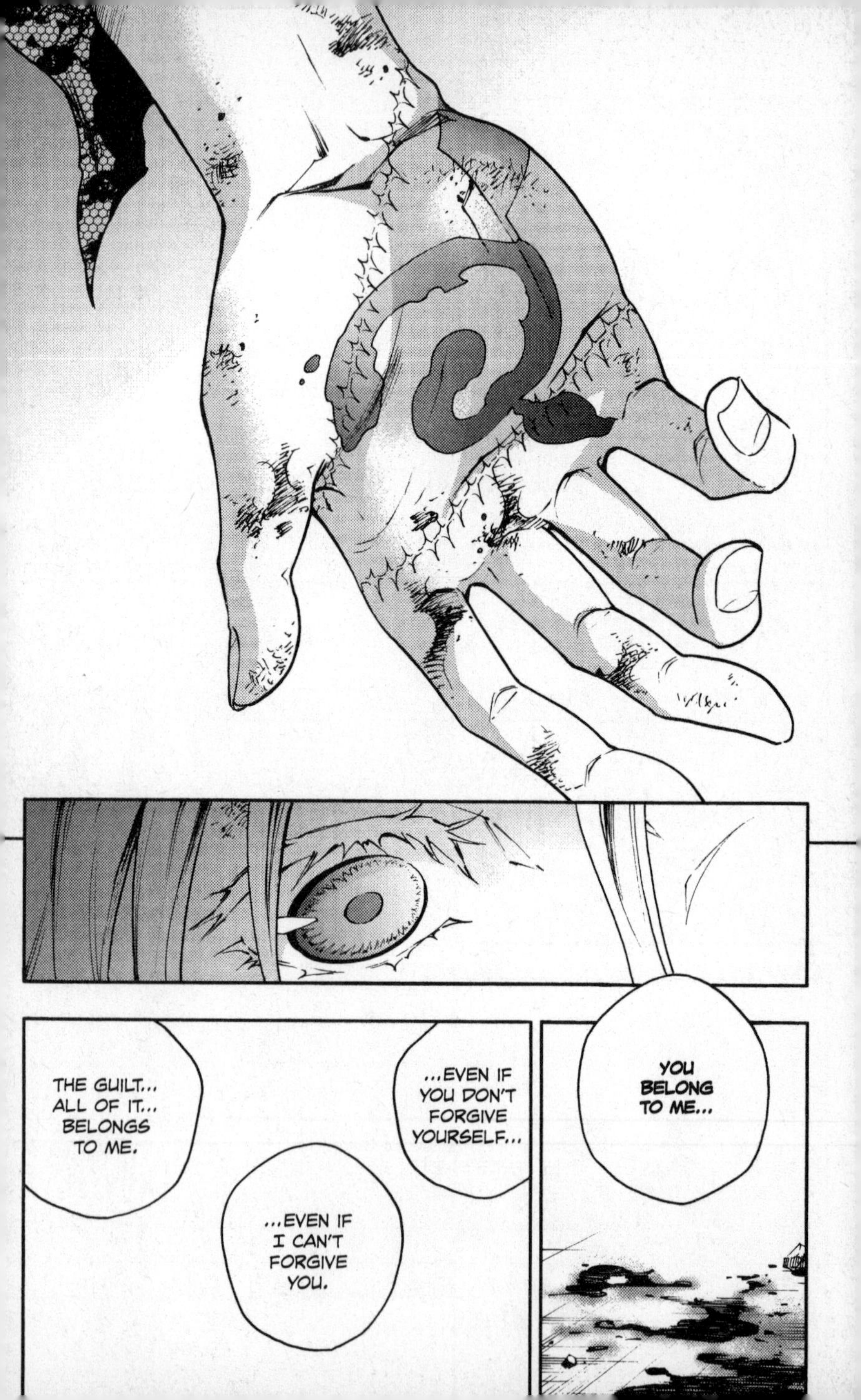
YOU BELONG TO ME...
...EVEN IF YOU DON'T FORGIVE YOURSELF...
THE GUILT... ALL OF IT... BELONGS TO ME.
...EVEN IF I CAN'T FORGIVE YOU.

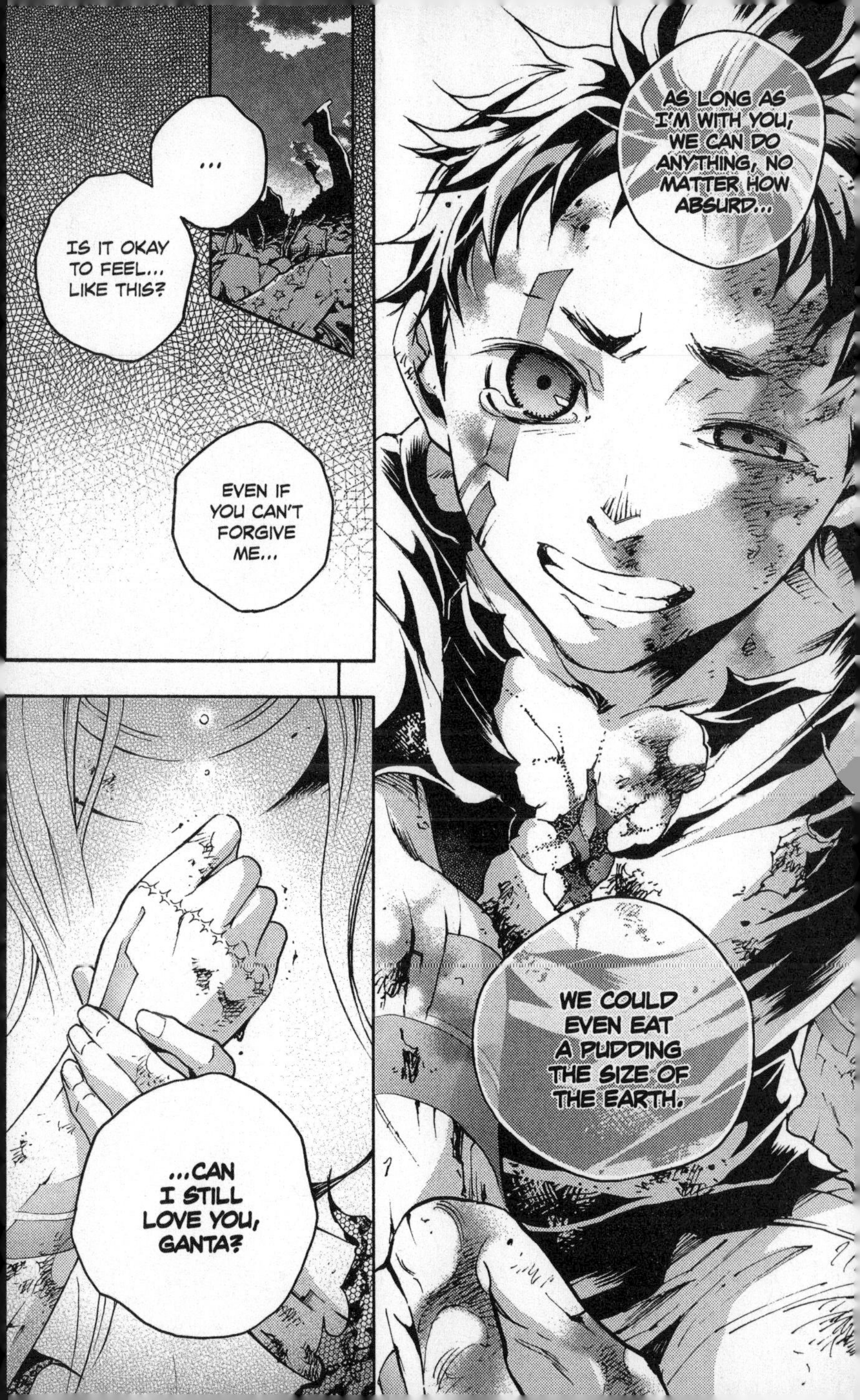
AS LONG AS I'M WITH YOU, WE CAN DO ANYTHING, NO MATTER HOW ABSURD...
WE COULD EVEN EAT A PUDDING THE SIZE OF THE EARTH.
...
IS IT OKAY TO FEEL... LIKE THIS?
EVEN IF YOU CAN'T FORGIVE ME...
...CAN I STILL LOVE YOU, GANTA?

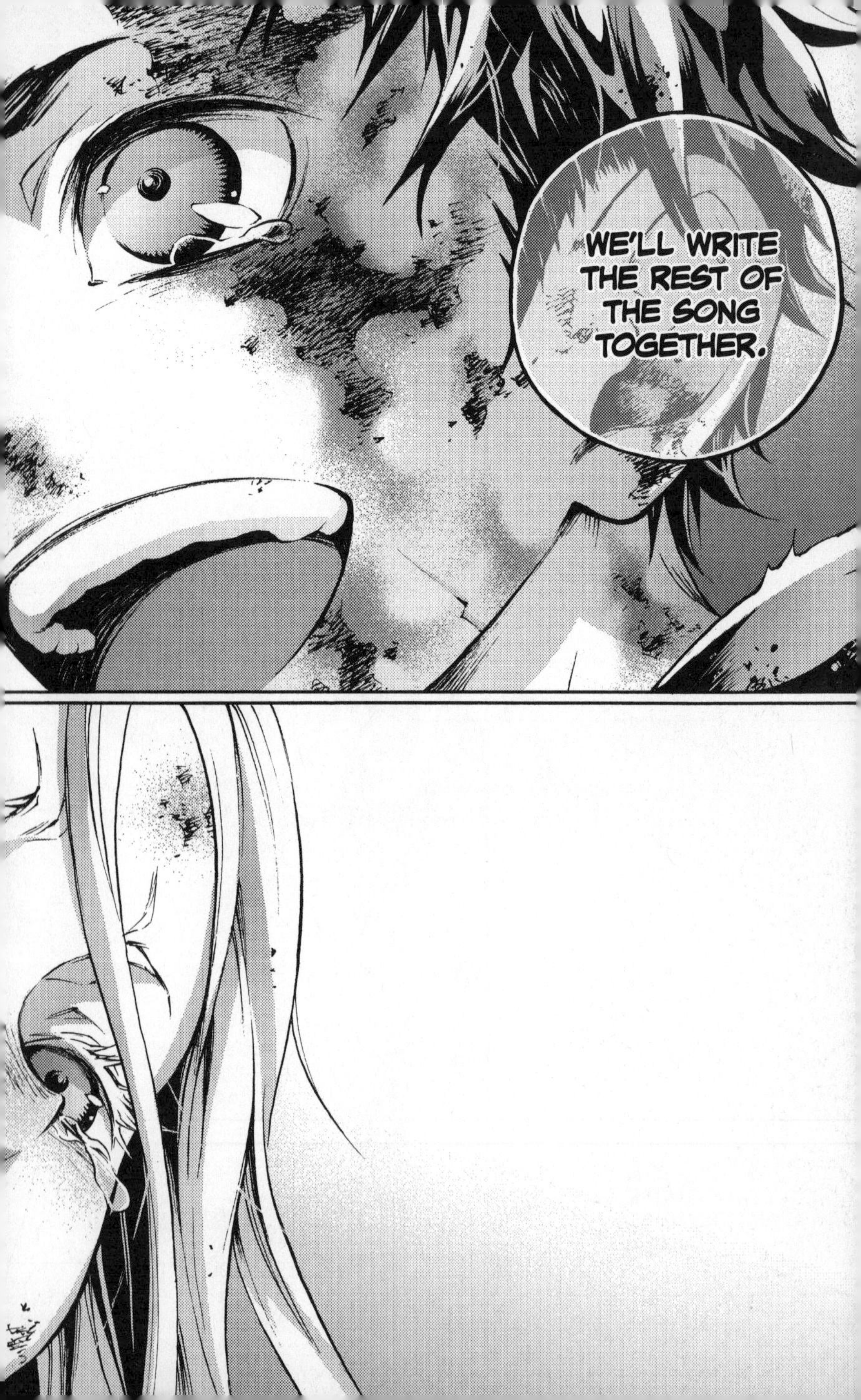
WE'LL WRITE THE REST OF THE SONG TOGETHER.

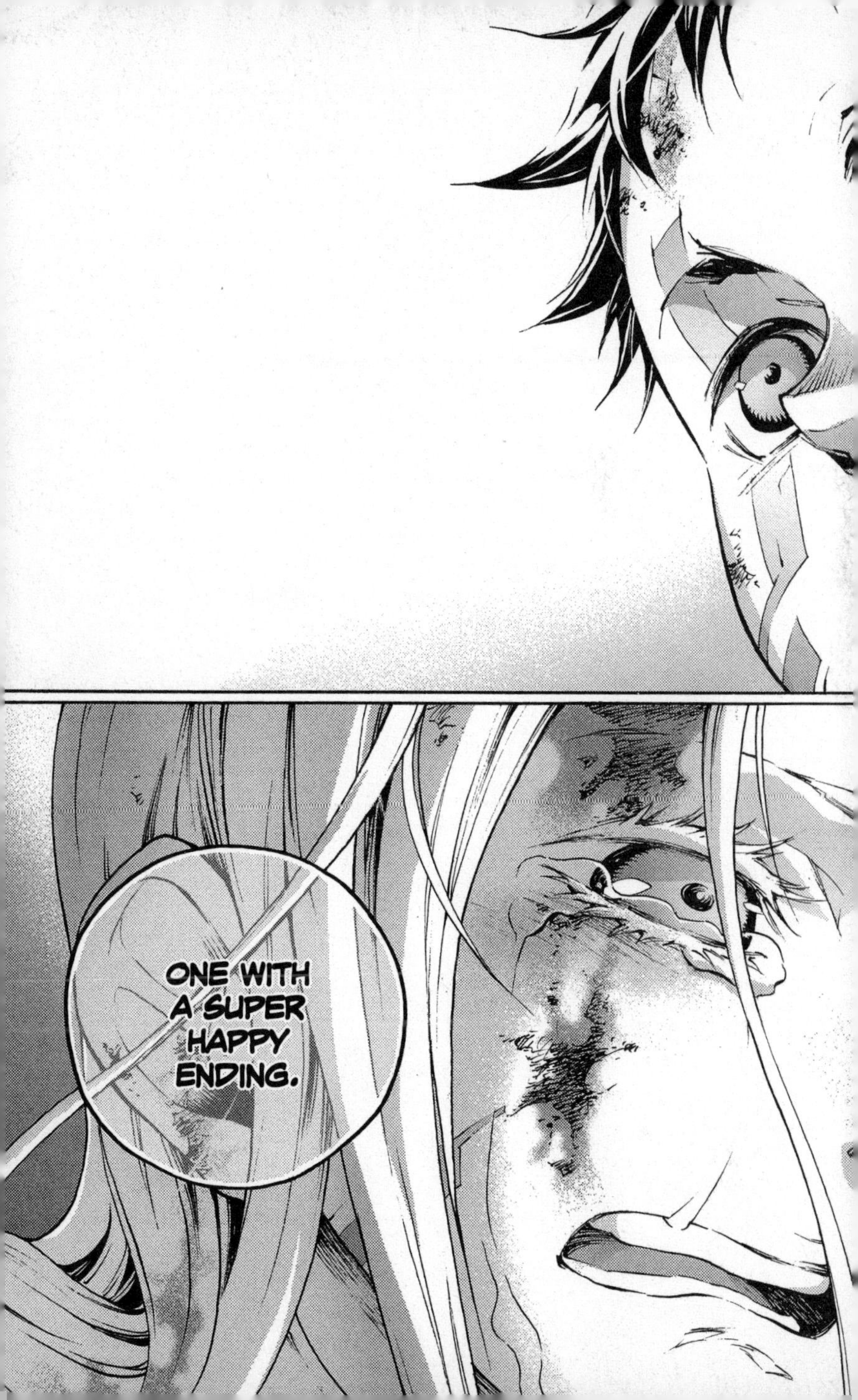
ONE WITH A SUPER HAPPY ENDING.

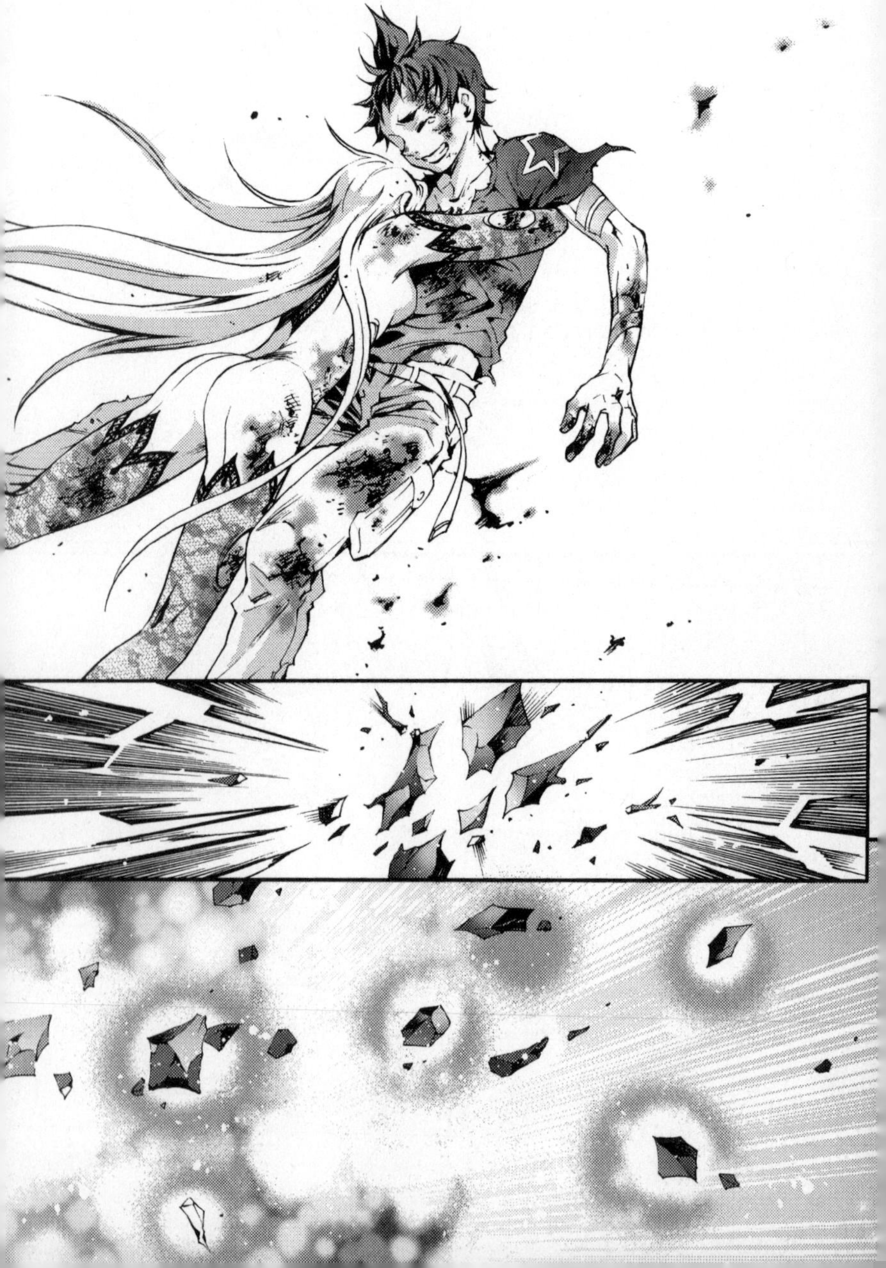

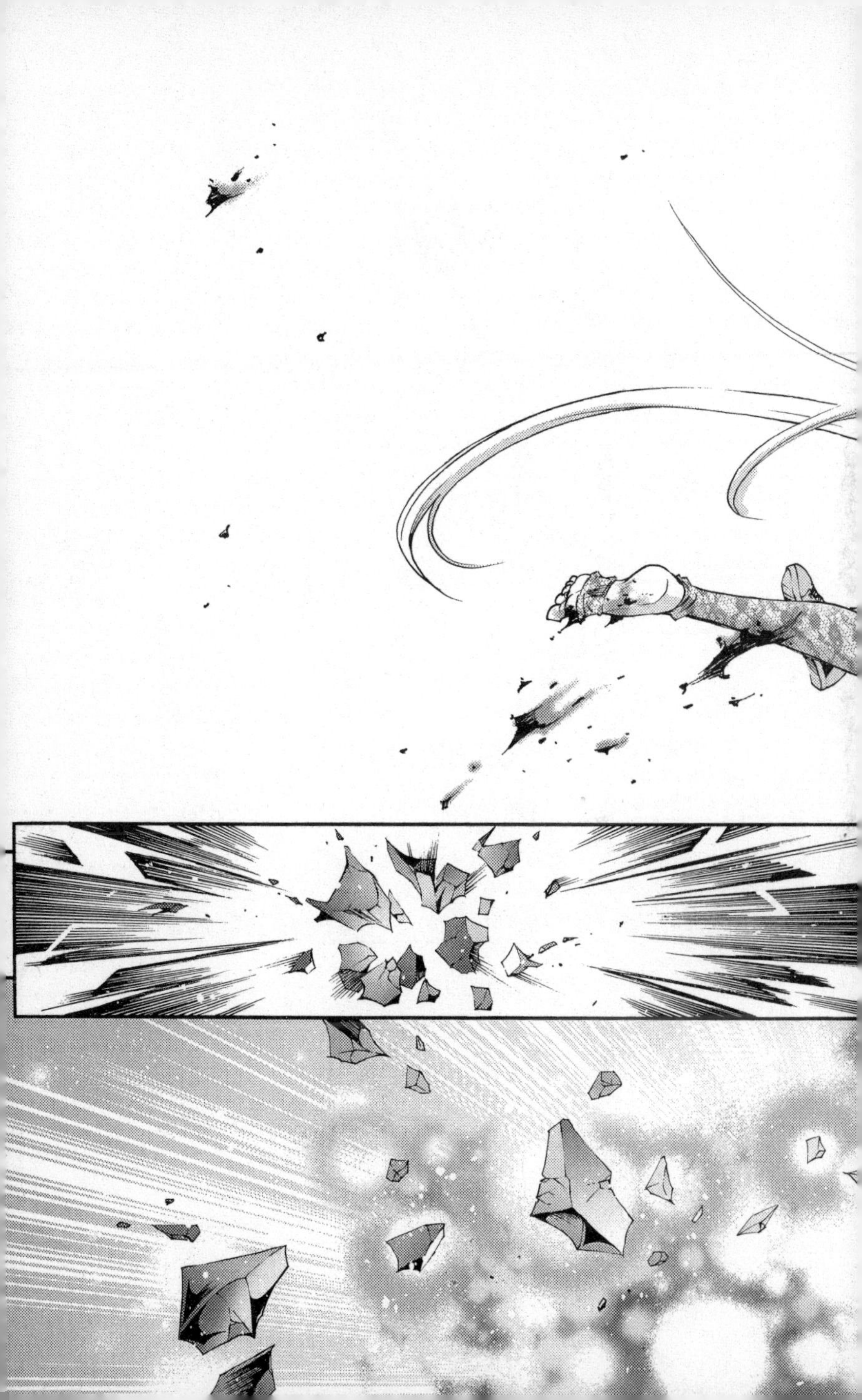

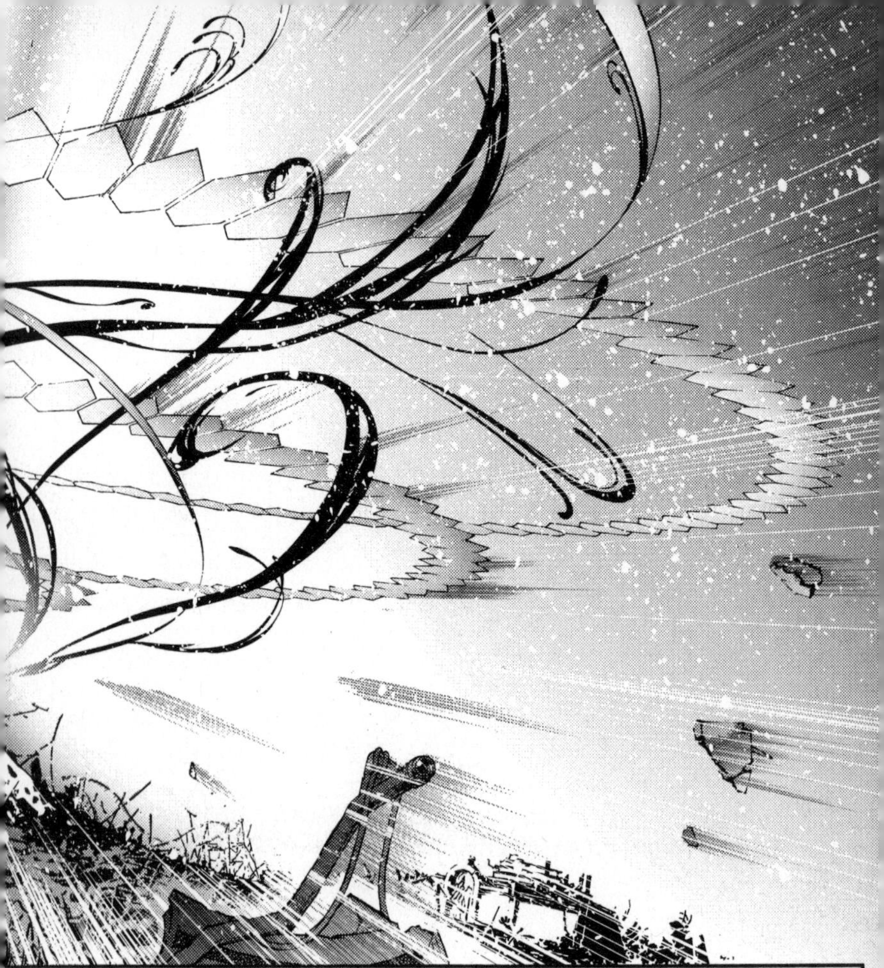

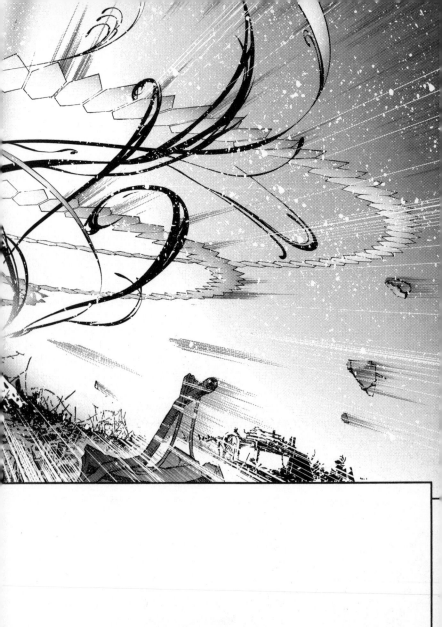

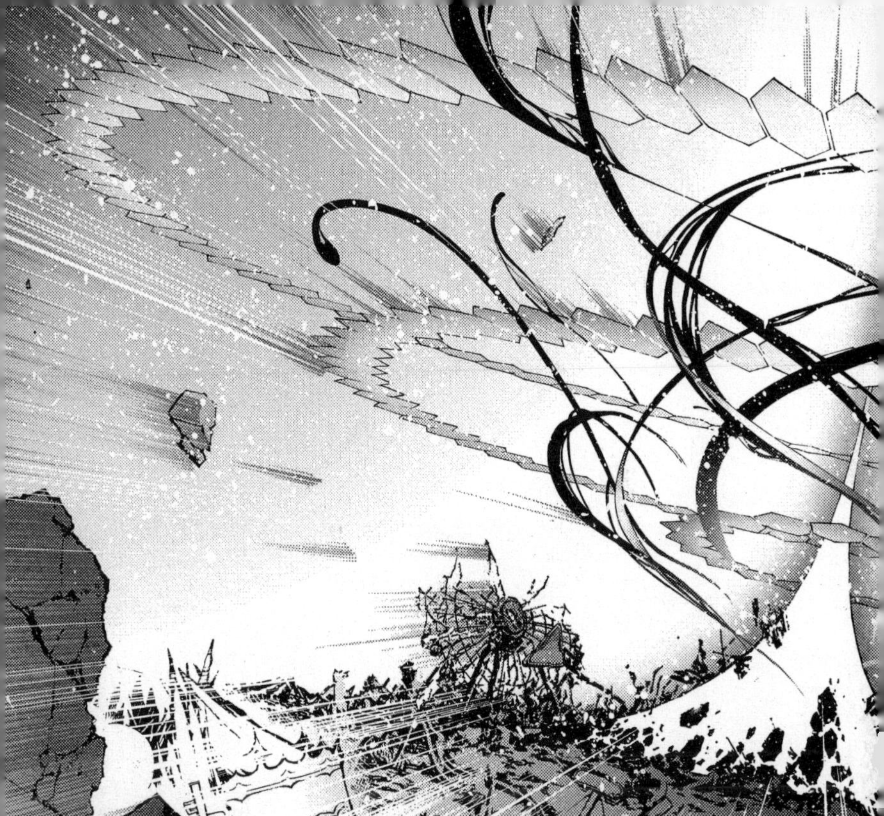

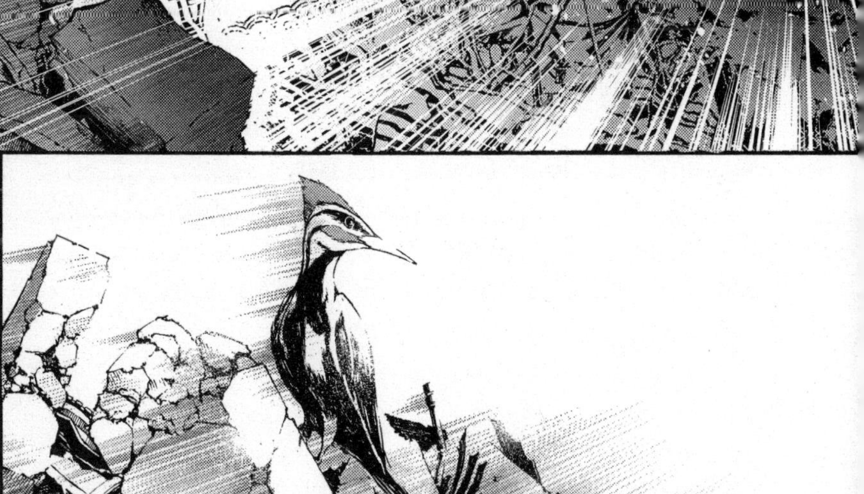

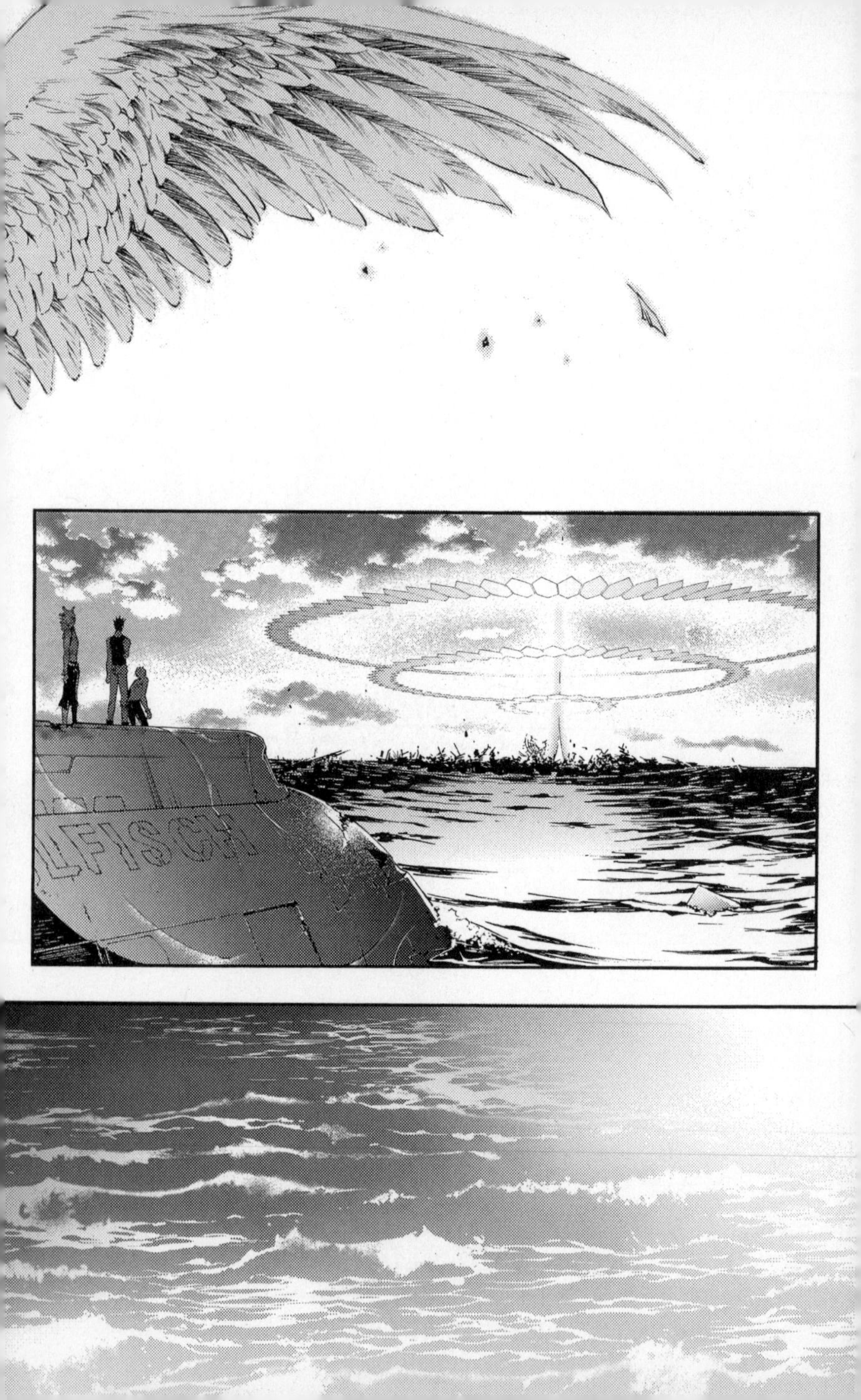
LFISCH

So was the
Dead
DEADMAN
WONDERLAND

So,
was the
Woodpecker
happy
after all?

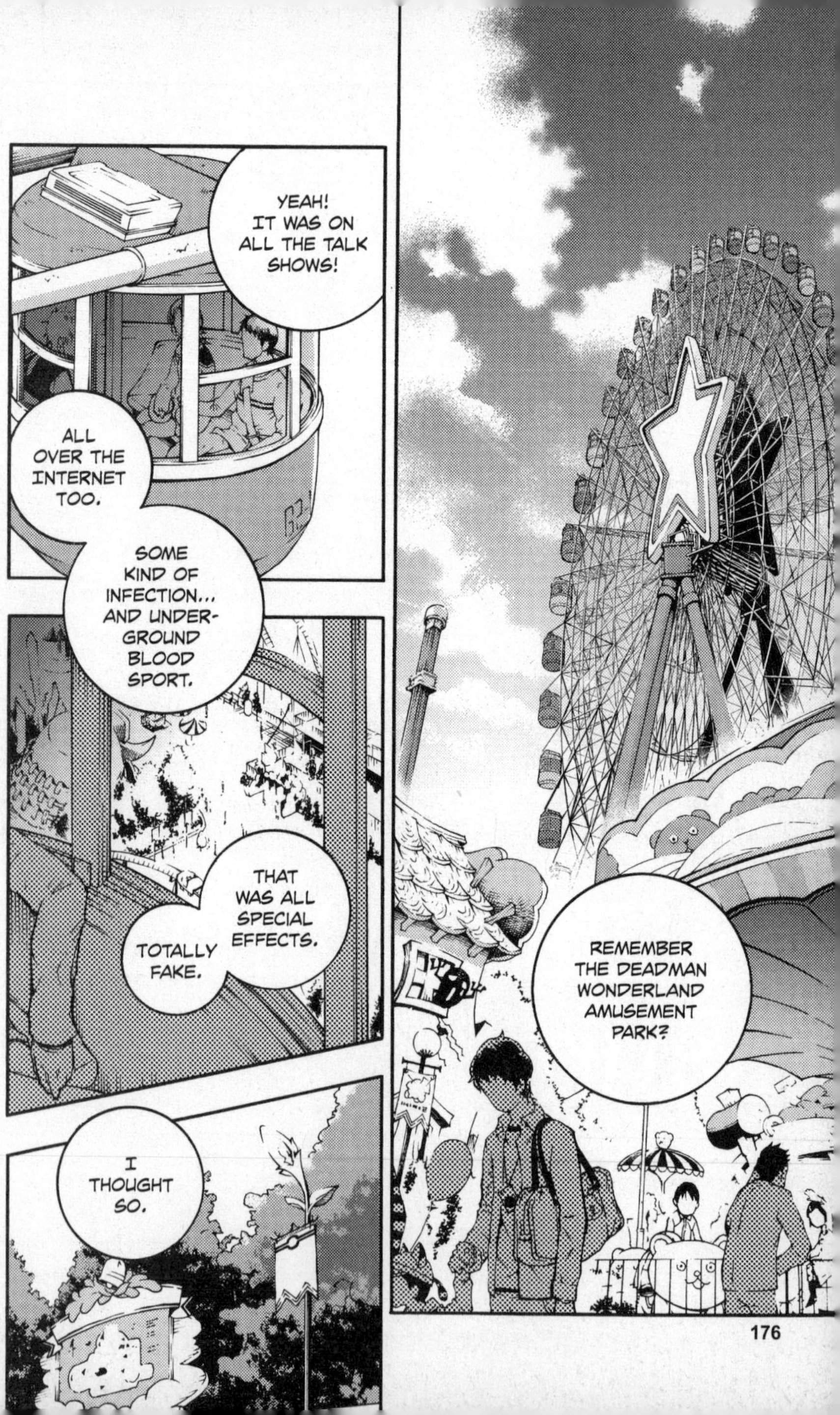
REMEMBER THE DEADMAN WONDERLAND AMUSEMENT PARK?
YEAH! IT WAS ON ALL THE TALK SHOWS!
ALL OVER THE INTERNET TOO.
SOME KIND OF INFECTION... AND UNDER-GROUND BLOOD SPORT.
THAT WAS ALL SPECIAL EFFECTS.
TOTALLY FAKE.
I THOUGHT SO.

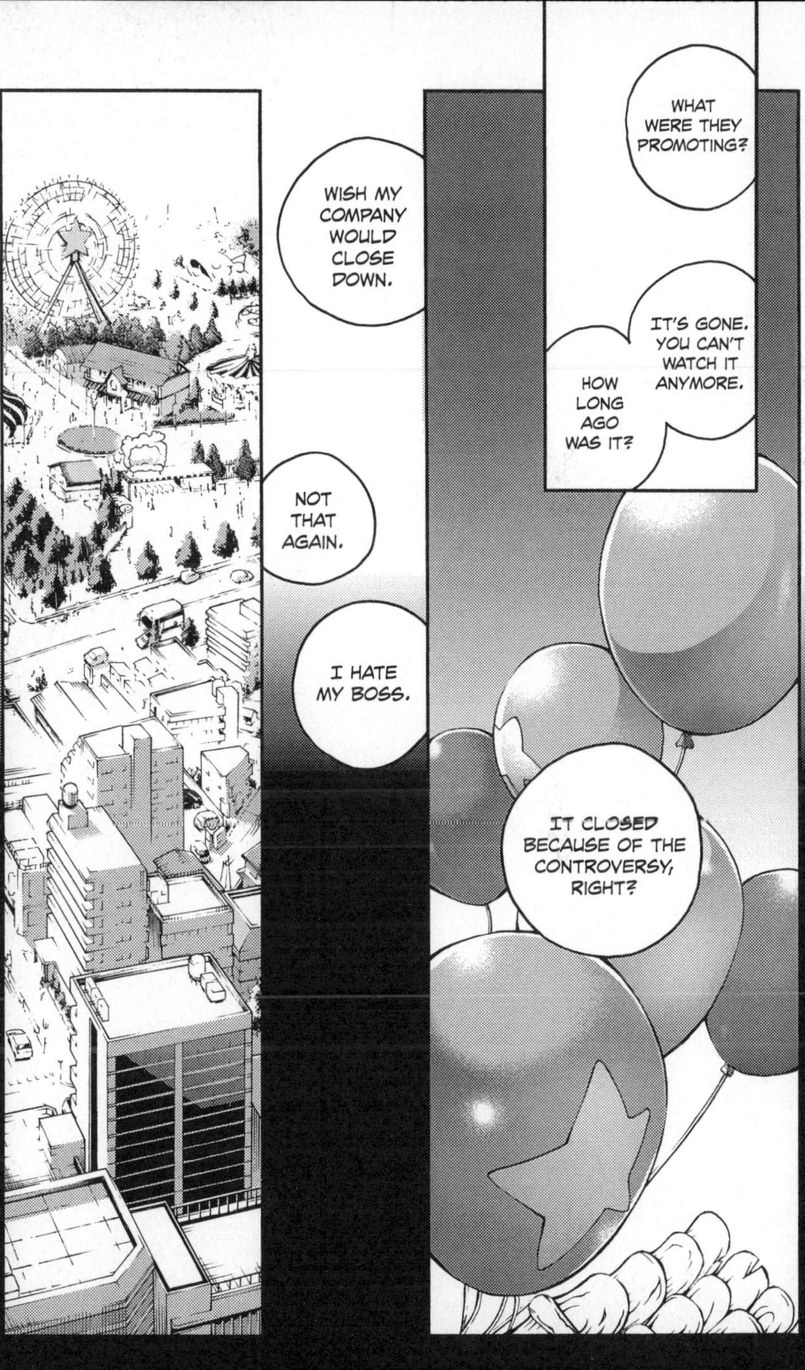
WHAT WERE THEY PROMOTING?
IT'S GONE. YOU CAN'T WATCH IT ANYMORE.
HOW LONG AGO WAS IT?
IT CLOSED BECAUSE OF THE CONTROVERSY, RIGHT?
WISH MY COMPANY WOULD CLOSE DOWN.
NOT THAT AGAIN.
I HATE MY BOSS.

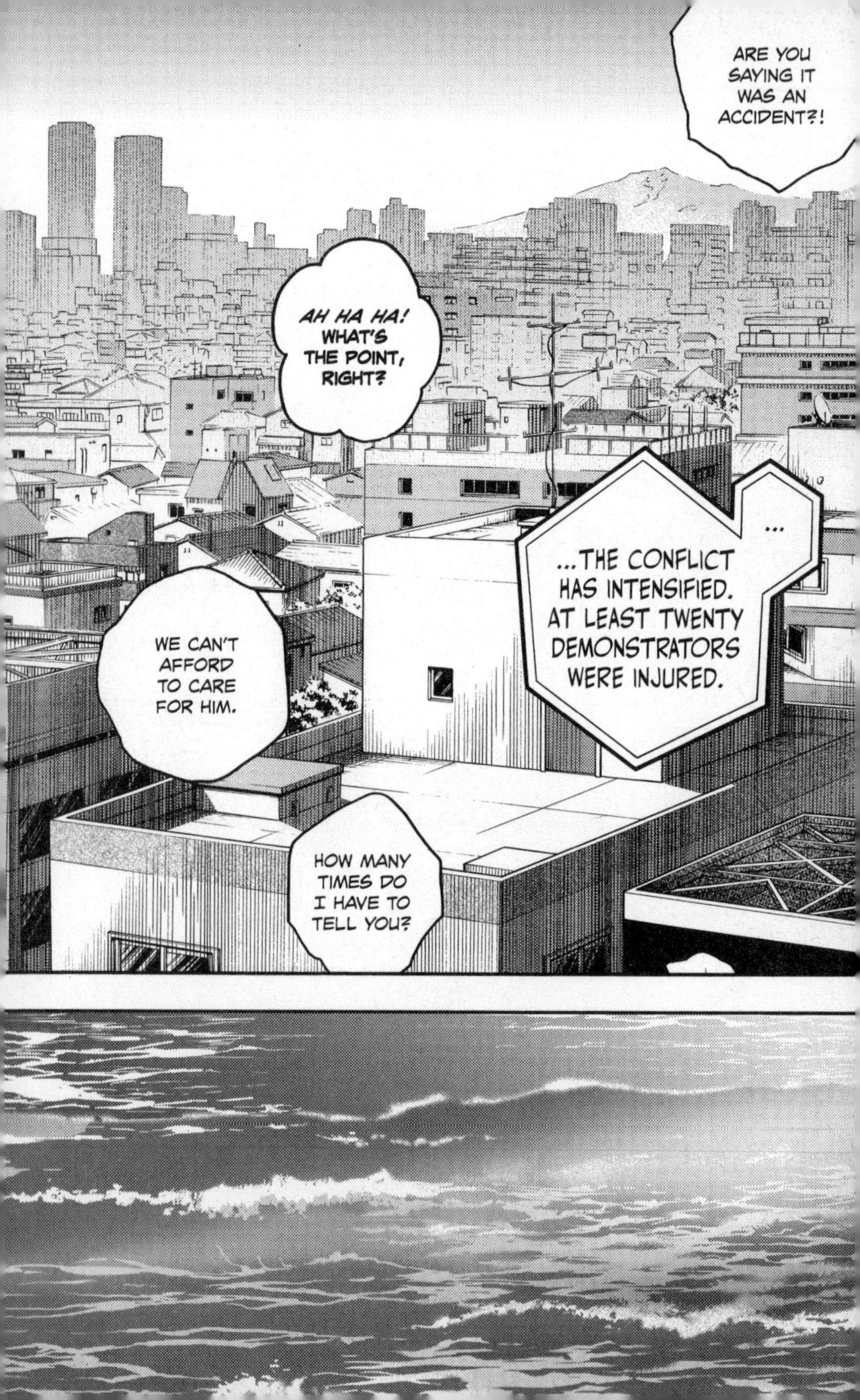
ARE YOU SAYING IT WAS AN ACCIDENT?!
AH HA HA! WHAT'S THE POINT, RIGHT?
...
...THE CONFLICT HAS INTENSIFIED. AT LEAST TWENTY DEMONSTRATORS WERE INJURED.
WE CAN'T AFFORD TO CARE FOR HIM.
HOW MANY TIMES DO I HAVE TO TELL YOU?

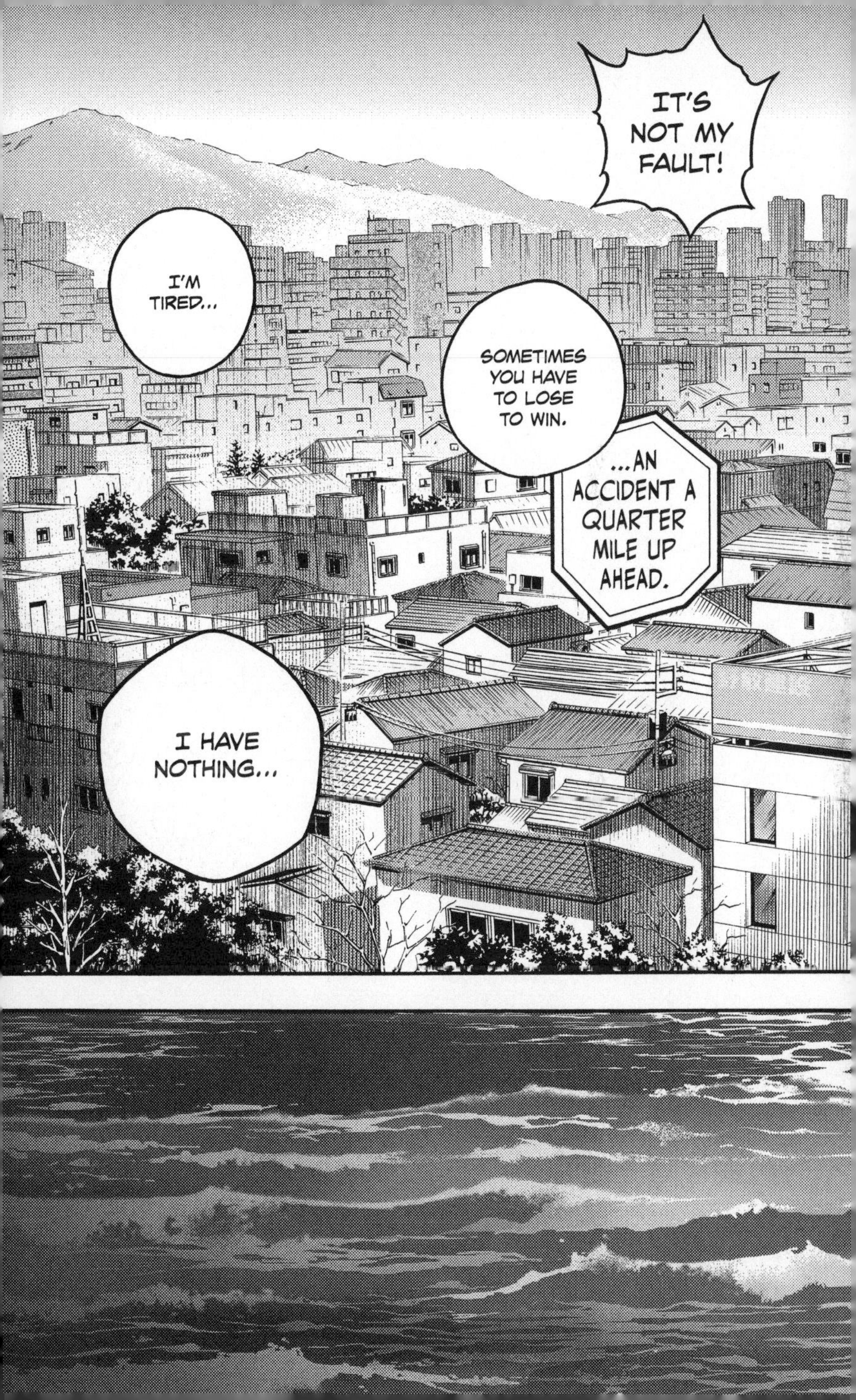
IT'S NOT MY FAULT!
I'M TIRED...
SOMETIMES YOU HAVE TO LOSE TO WIN.
...AN ACCIDENT A QUARTER MILE UP AHEAD.
I HAVE NOTHING...

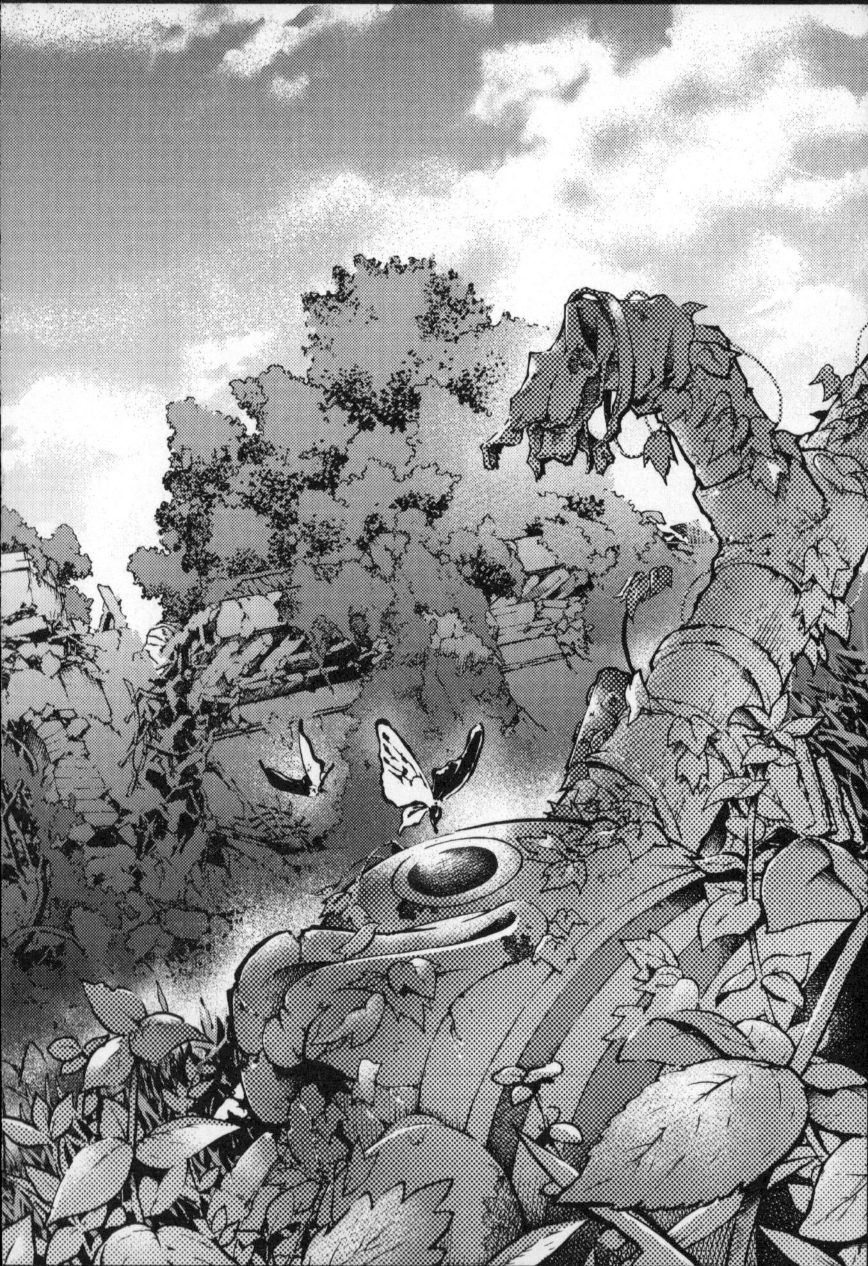

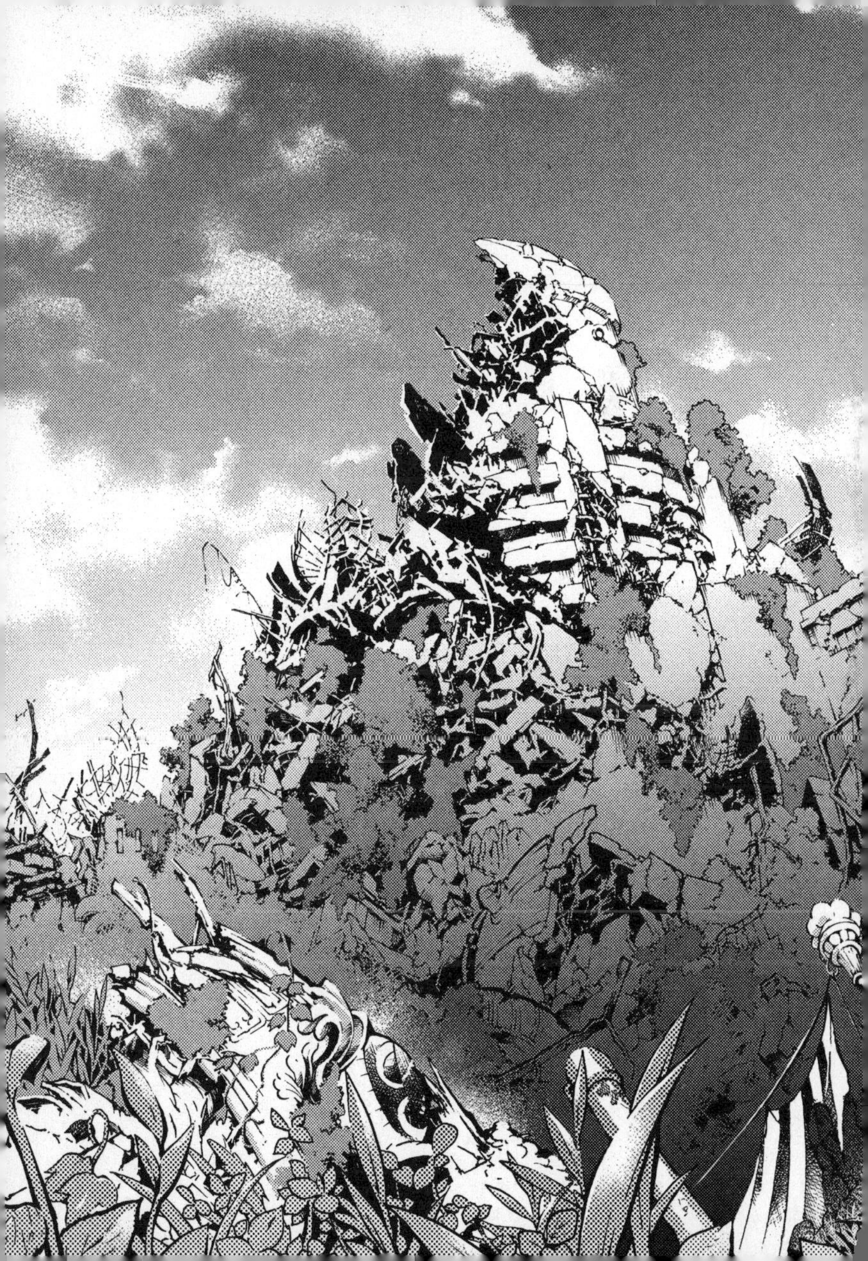

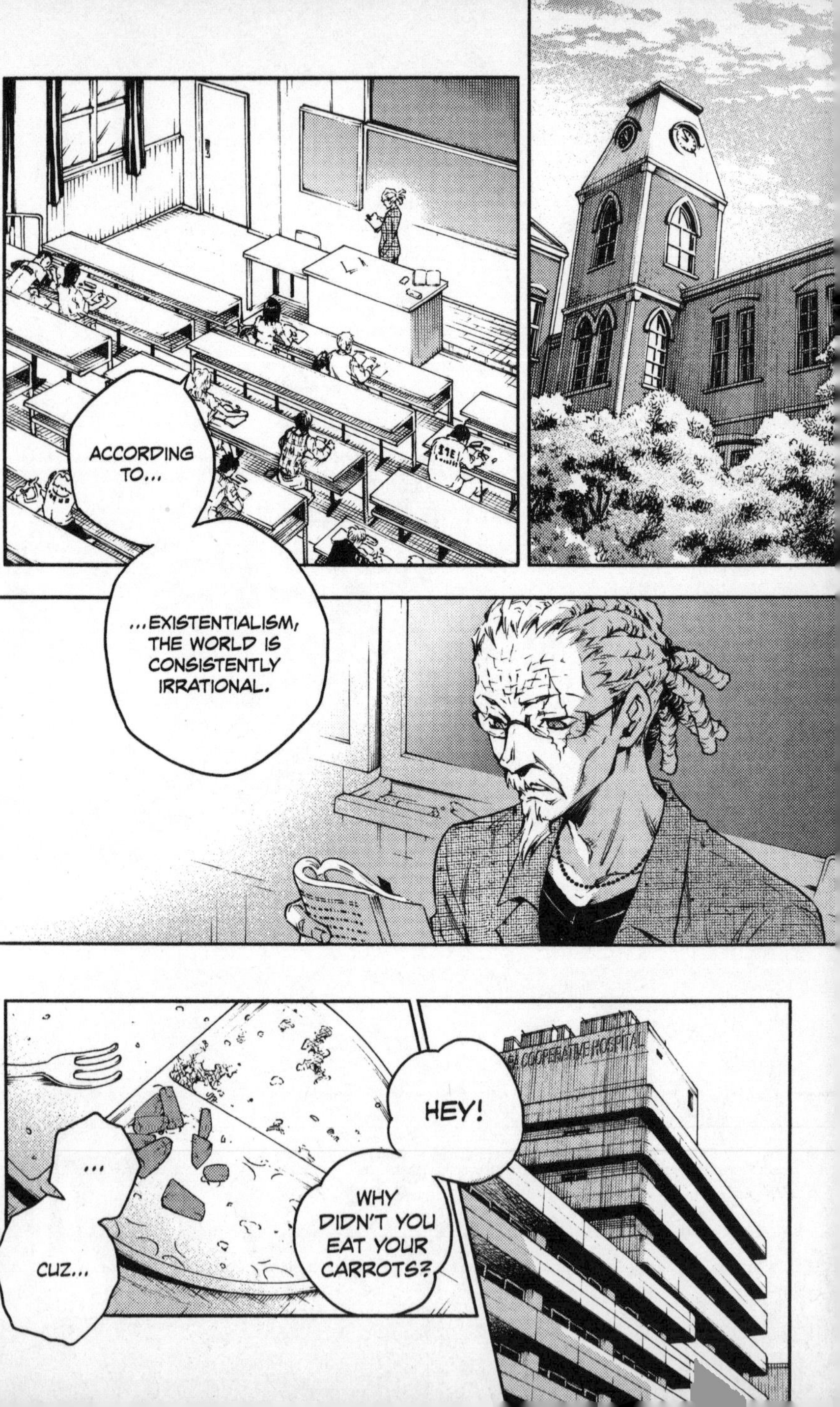
ACCORDING TO...
...EXISTENTIALISM, THE WORLD IS CONSISTENTLY IRRATIONAL.
COOPERATIVE HOSPITAL
HEY!
WHY DIDN'T YOU EAT YOUR CARROTS?
...
CUZ...

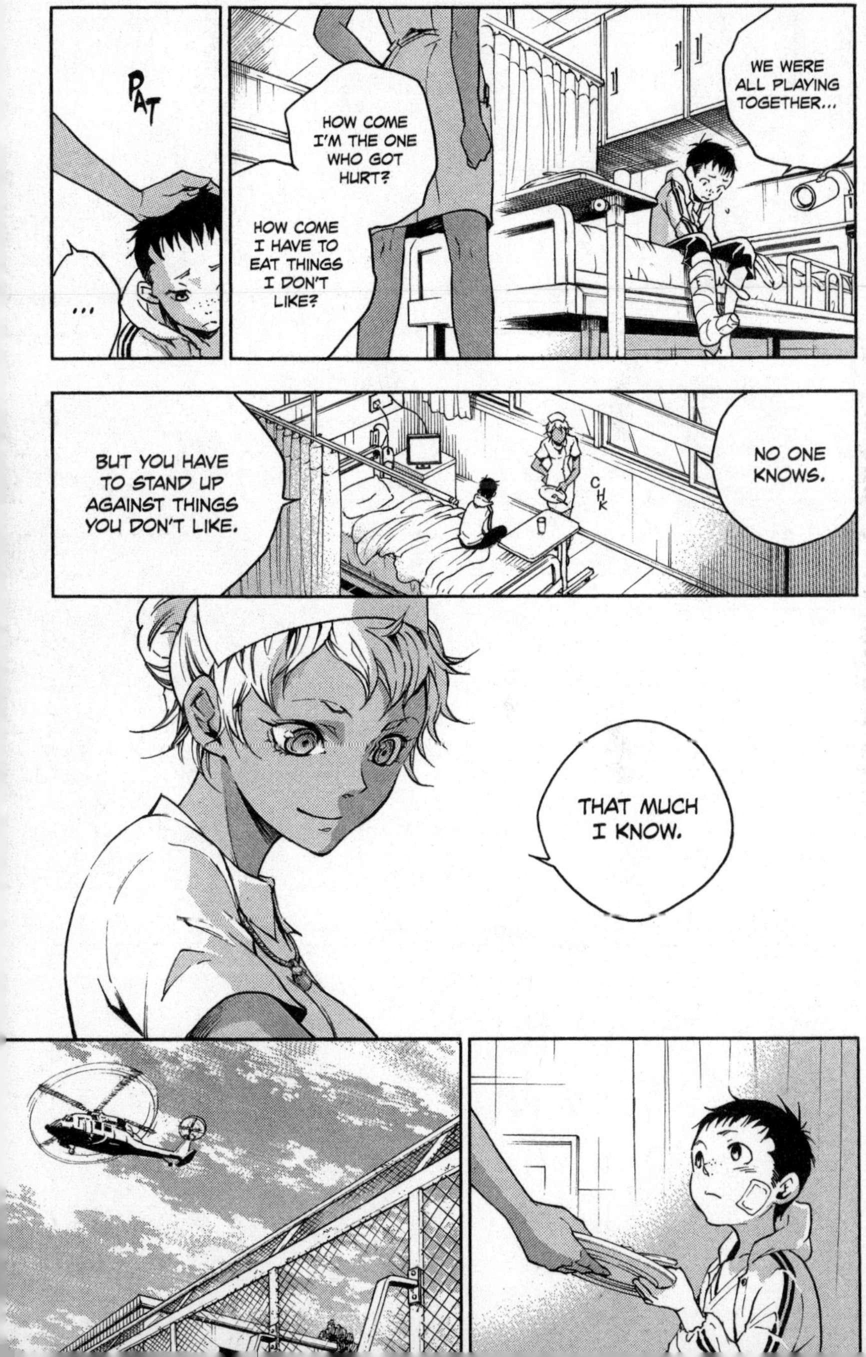
WE WERE ALL PLAYING TOGETHER...
HOW COME I'M THE ONE WHO GOT HURT?
HOW COME I HAVE TO EAT THINGS I DON'T LIKE?
PAT
...
NO ONE KNOWS.
CHK
BUT YOU HAVE TO STAND UP AGAINST THINGS YOU DON'T LIKE.
THAT MUCH I KNOW.

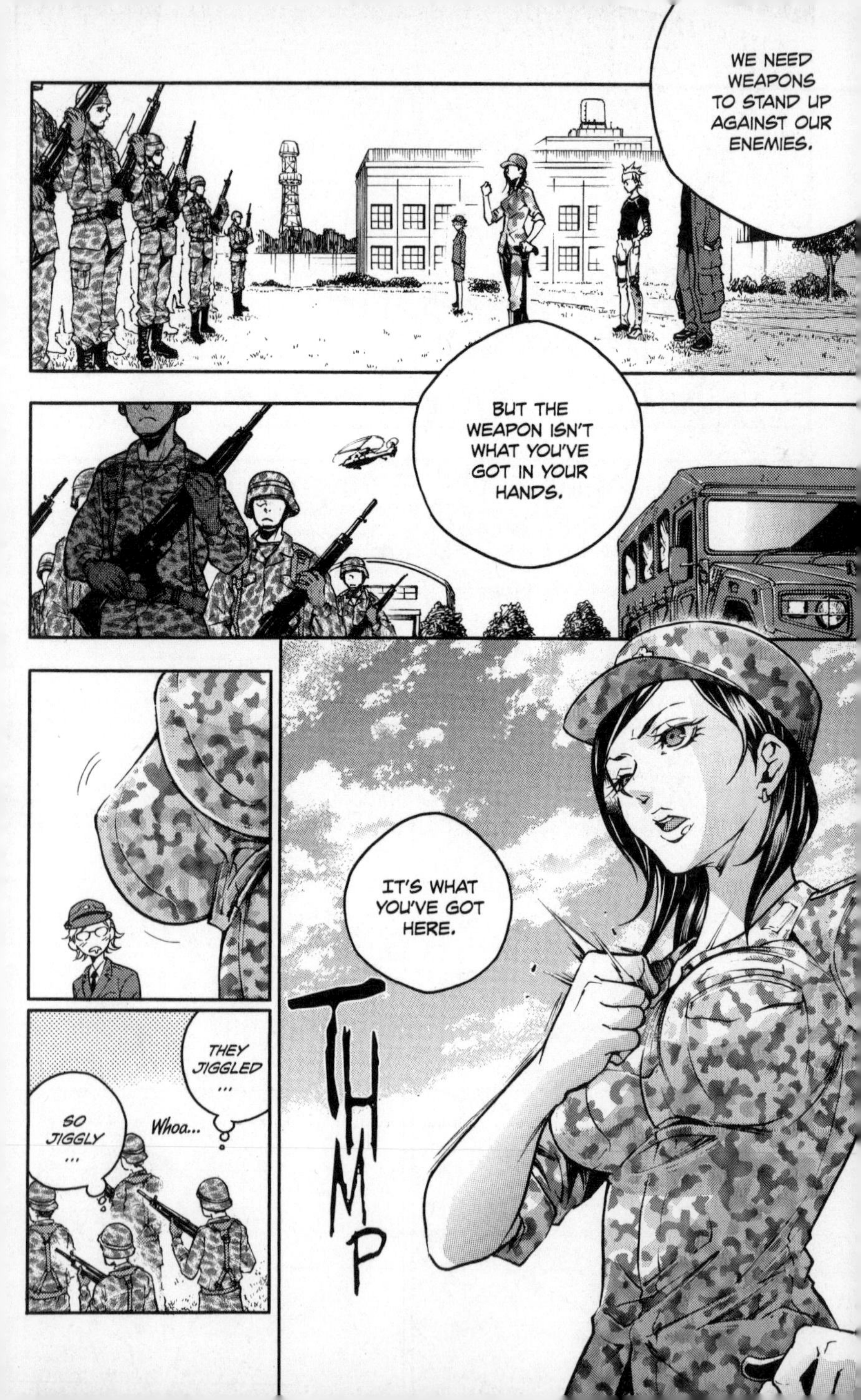
WE NEED WEAPONS TO STAND UP AGAINST OUR ENEMIES.
BUT THE WEAPON ISN'T WHAT YOU'VE GOT IN YOUR HANDS.
IT'S WHAT YOU'VE GOT HERE.
THUMP
THEY JIGGLED ...
Whoa...
SO JIGGLY ...

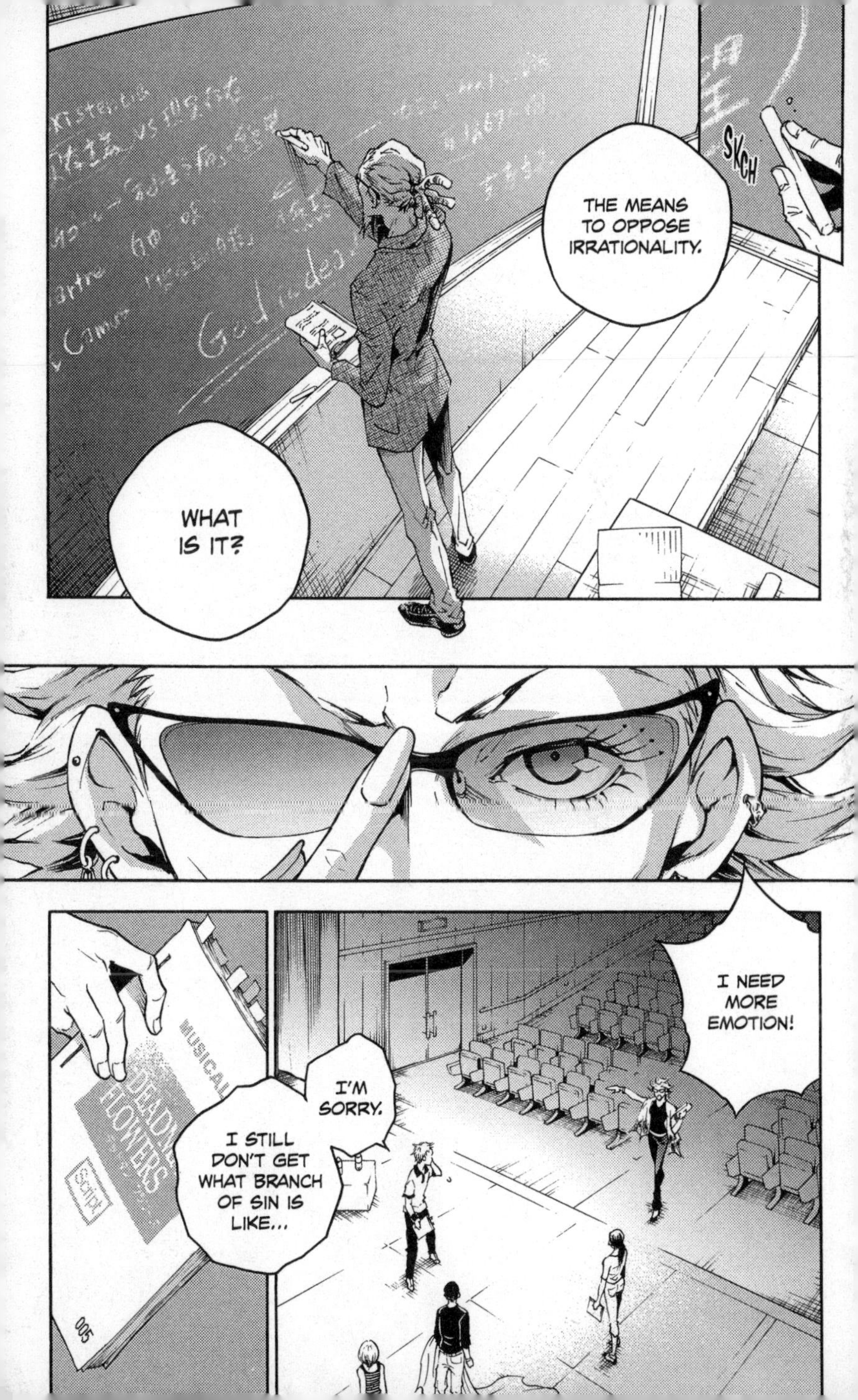
SKCH
THE MEANS TO OPPOSE IRRATIONALITY.
WHAT IS IT?
I NEED MORE EMOTION!
I'M SORRY.
I STILL DON'T GET WHAT BRANCH OF SIN IS LIKE...
MUSICAL
FLOWERS
Script
005

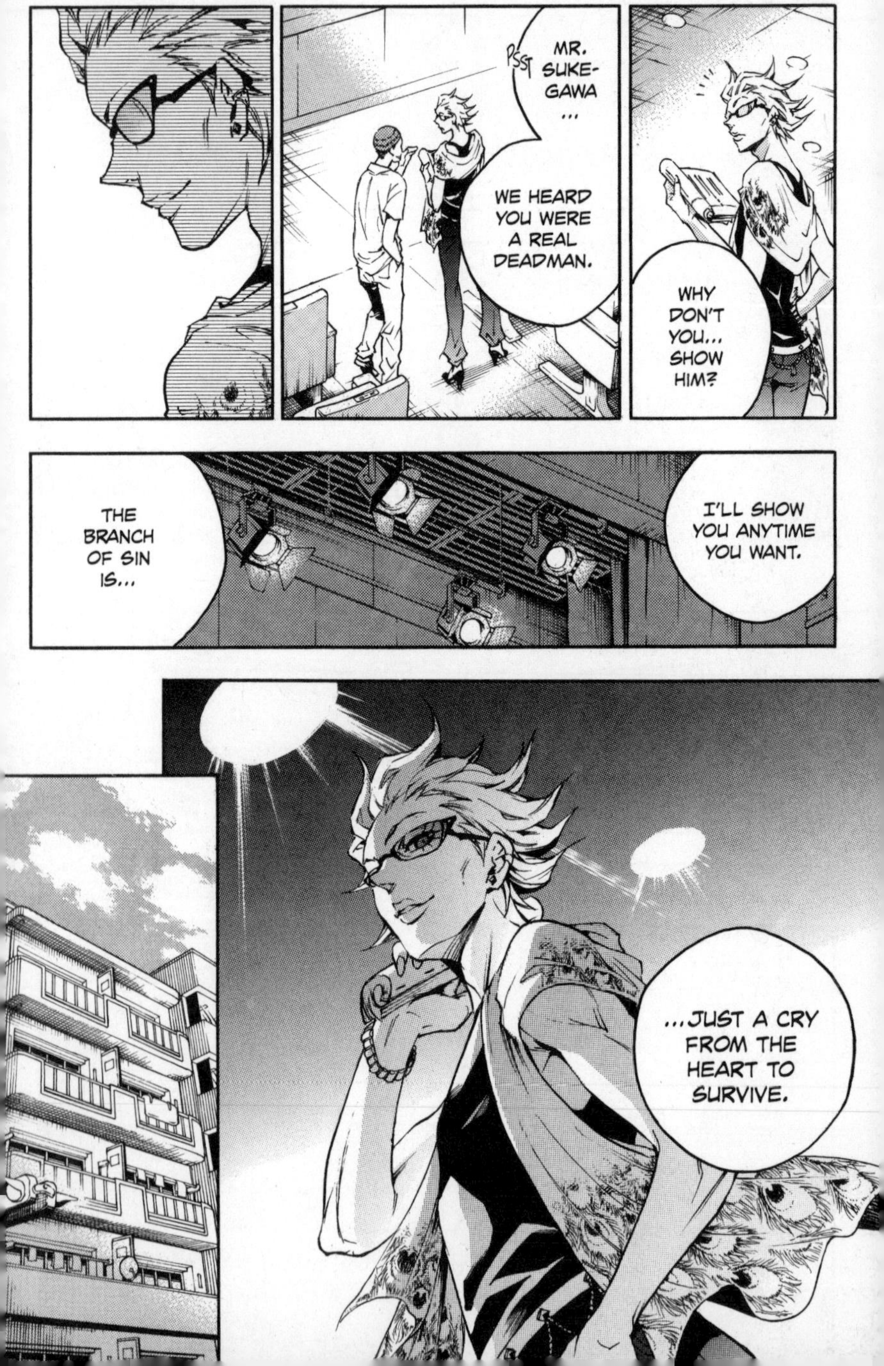
WHY DON'T YOU... SHOW HIM?
PSST
MR. SUKE-GAWA...
WE HEARD YOU WERE A REAL DEADMAN.
I'LL SHOW YOU ANYTIME YOU WANT.
THE BRANCH OF SIN IS...
...JUST A CRY FROM THE HEART TO SURVIVE.

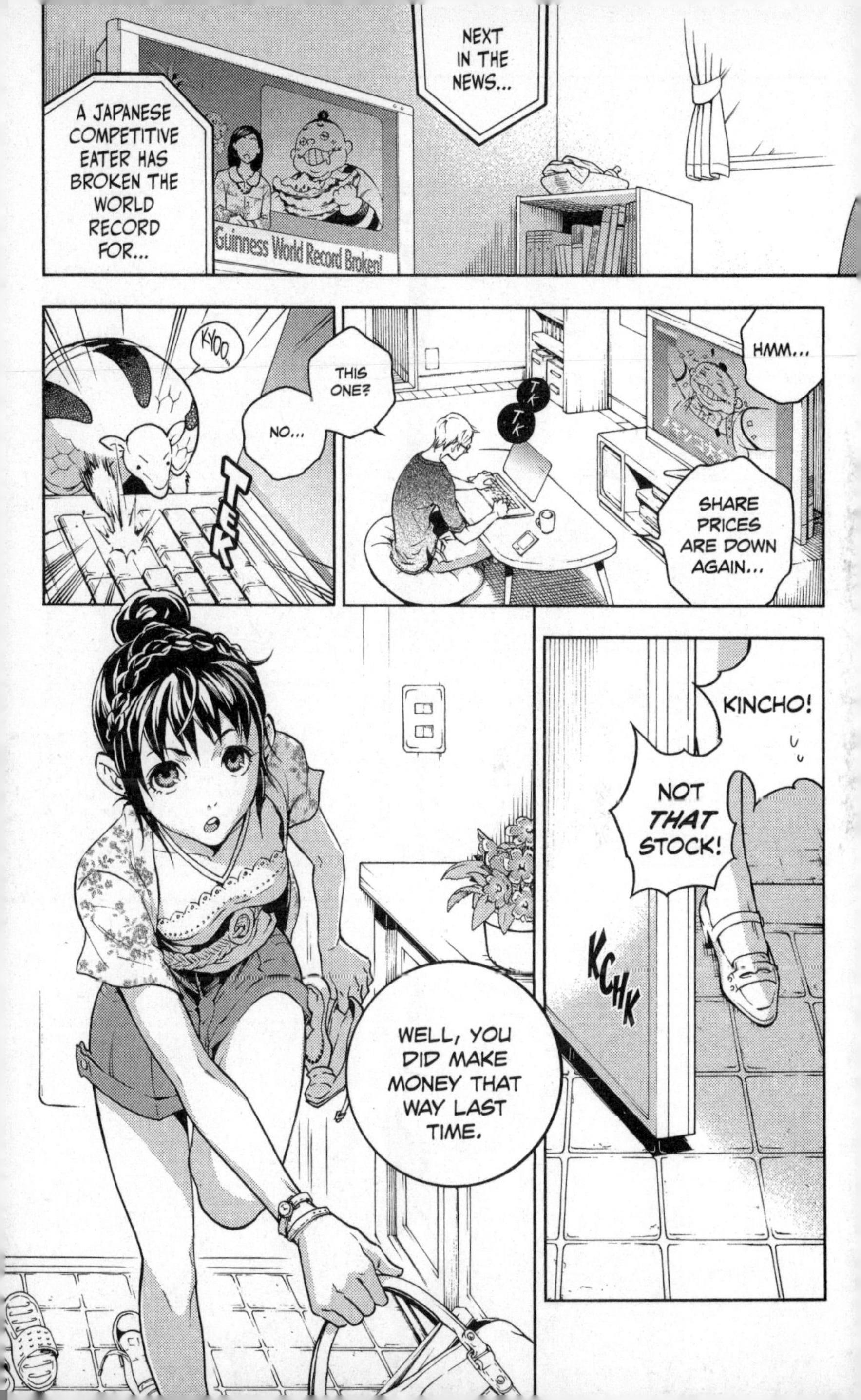
NEXT IN THE NEWS...
A JAPANESE COMPETITIVE EATER HAS BROKEN THE WORLD RECORD FOR...
Guinness World Record Broken!
HMM...
SHARE PRICES ARE DOWN AGAIN...
TK TK
THIS ONE?
NO...
KYOO...
TEK
KINCHO!
NOT *THAT* STOCK!
KCHK
WELL, YOU DID MAKE MONEY THAT WAY LAST TIME.

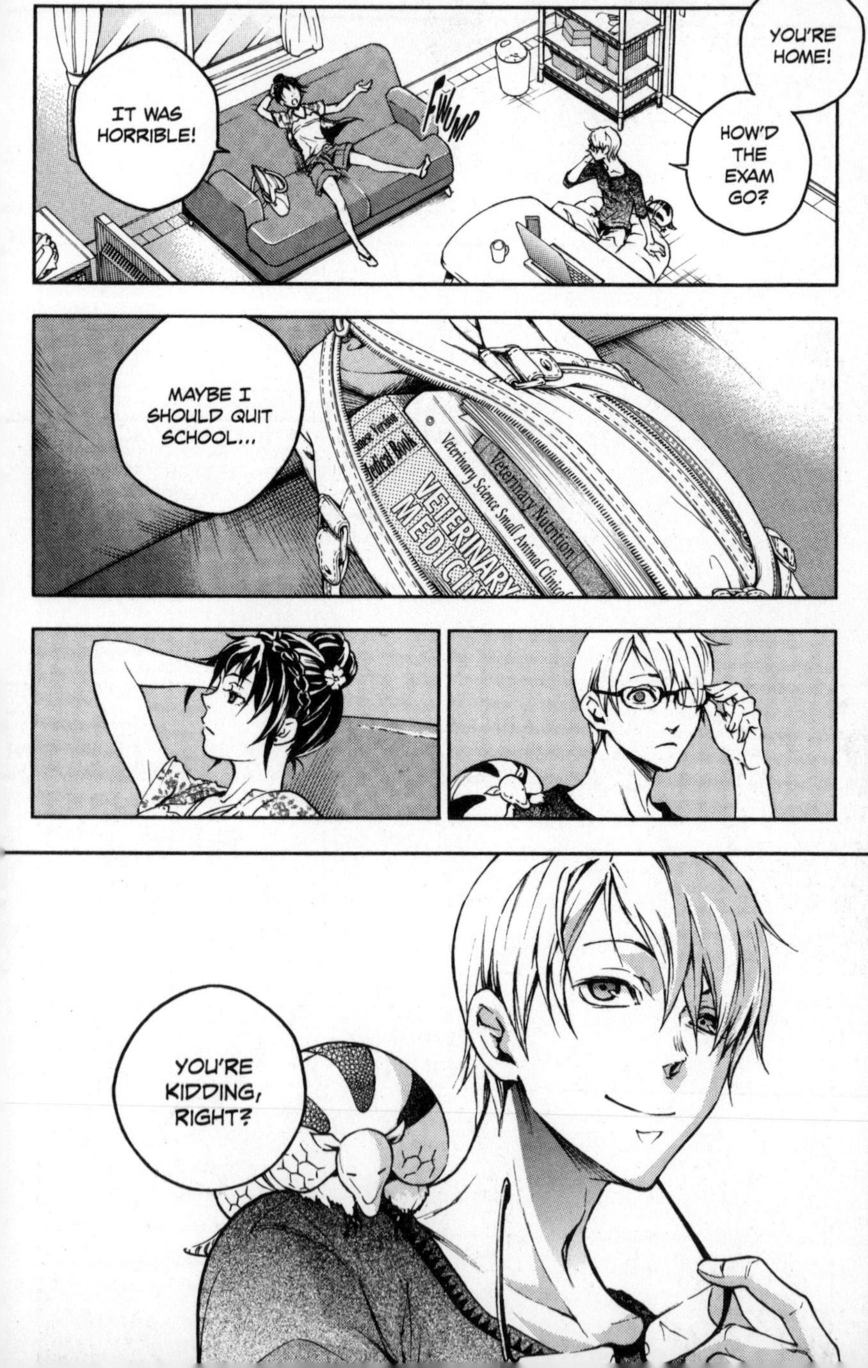
YOU'RE HOME!
HOW'D THE EXAM GO?
FWUMP
IT WAS HORRIBLE!
MAYBE I SHOULD QUIT SCHOOL...
Veterinary Nutrition
YOU'RE KIDDING, RIGHT?

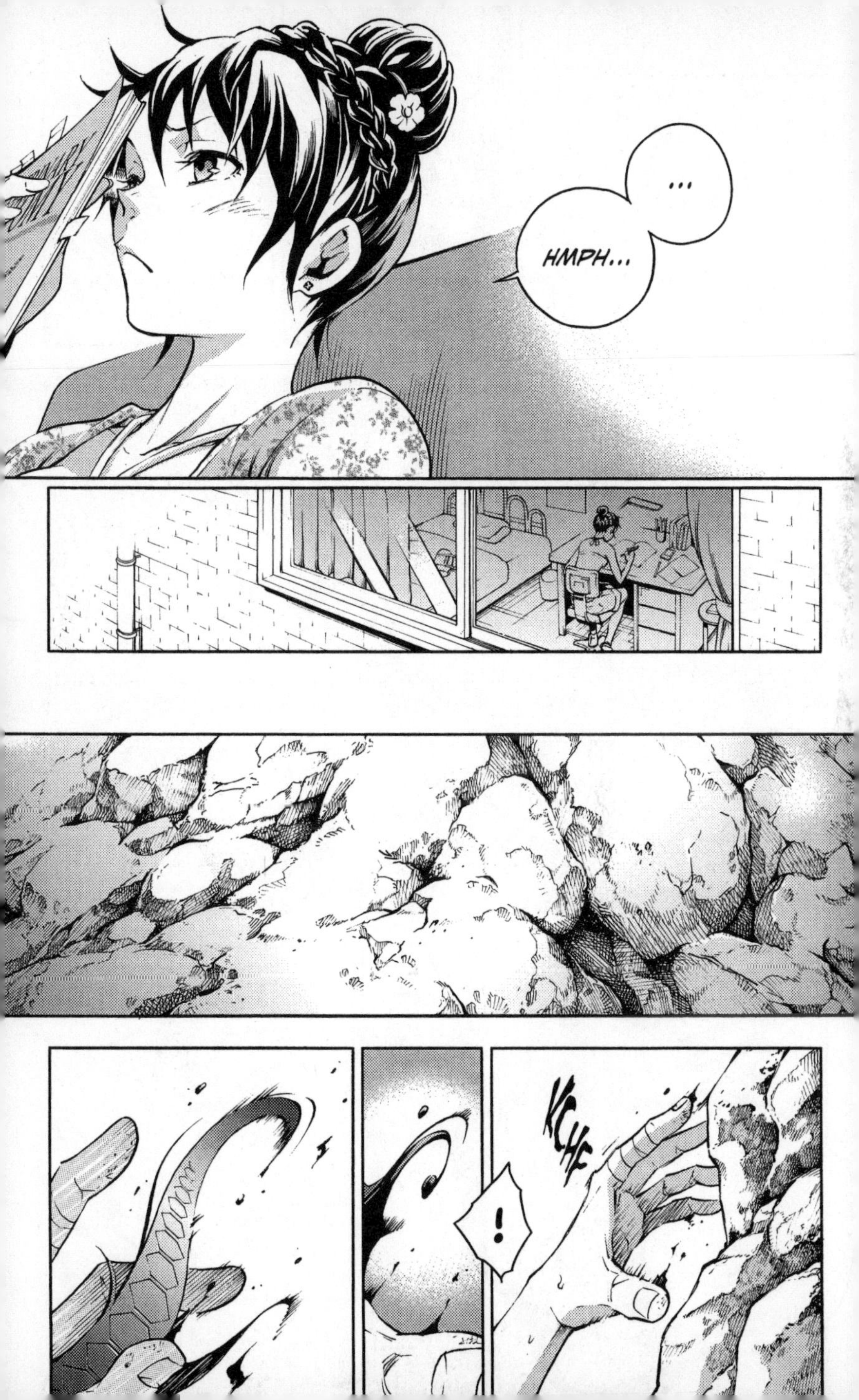
...
HMPH...
KCHF
!

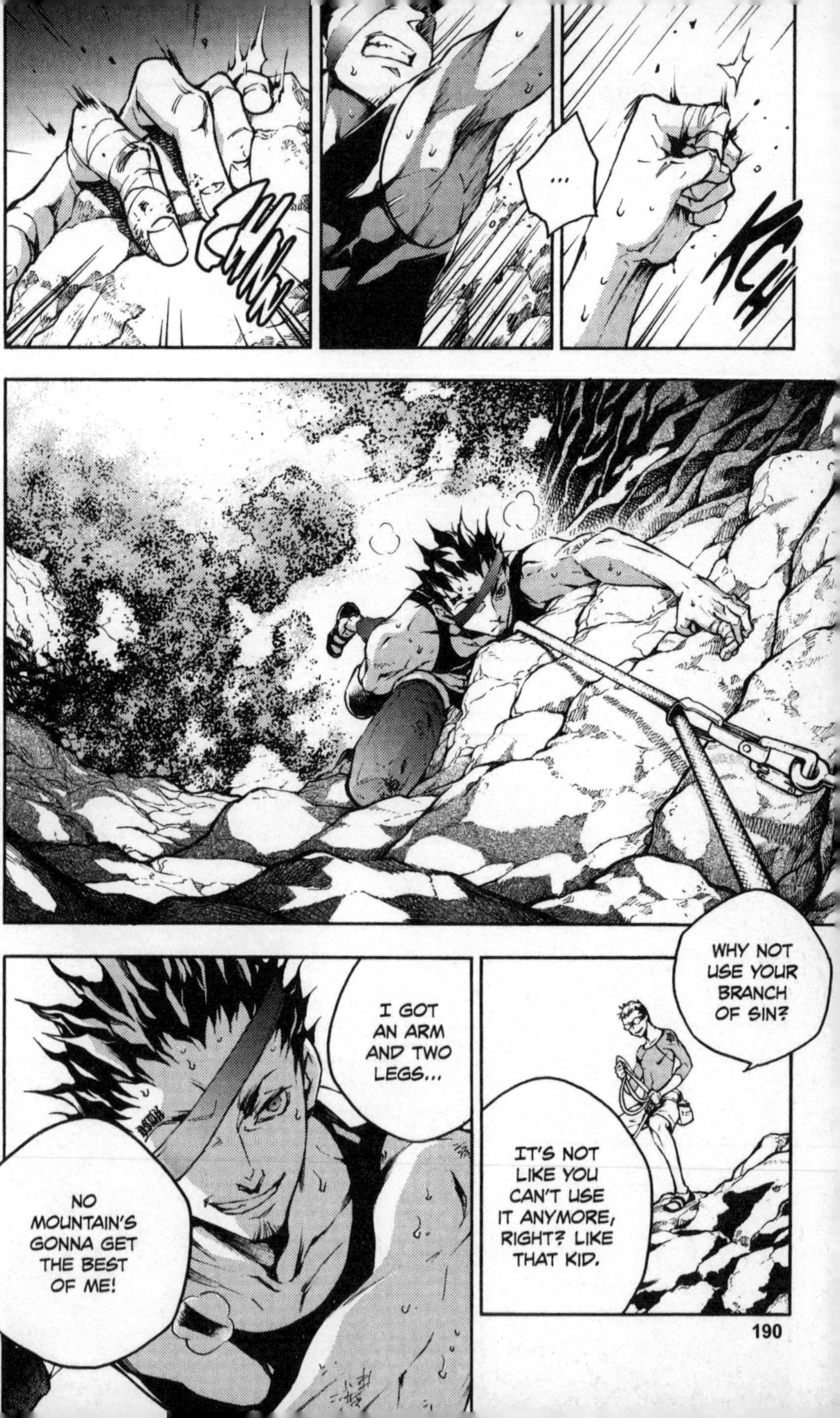
KCH
...
WHY NOT USE YOUR BRANCH OF SIN?
IT'S NOT LIKE YOU CAN'T USE IT ANYMORE, RIGHT? LIKE THAT KID.
I GOT AN ARM AND TWO LEGS...
NO MOUNTAIN'S GONNA GET THE BEST OF ME!

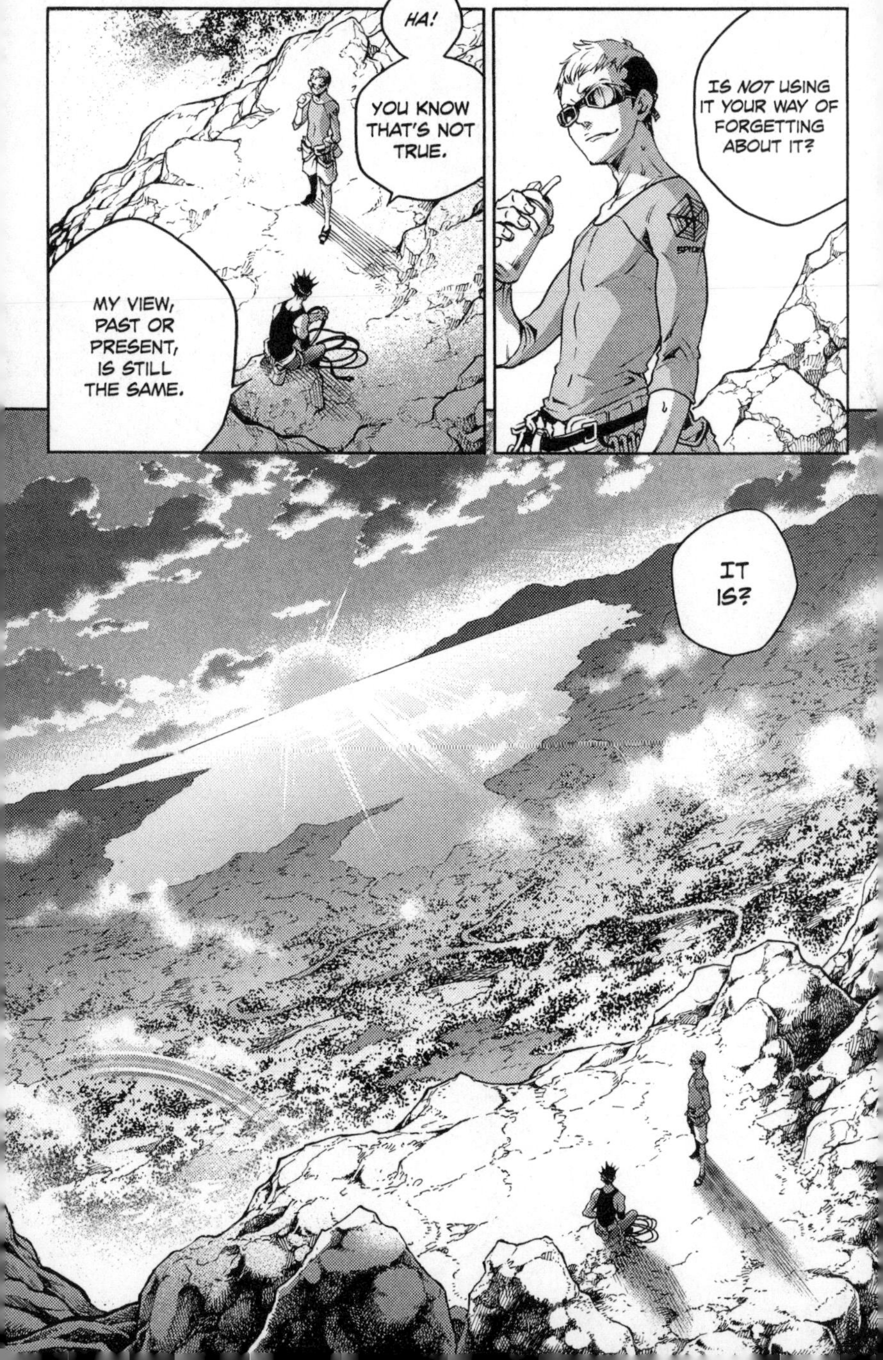
IS *NOT* USING IT YOUR WAY OF FORGETTING ABOUT IT?
HA!
YOU KNOW THAT'S NOT TRUE.
MY VIEW, PAST OR PRESENT, IS STILL THE SAME.
IT IS?

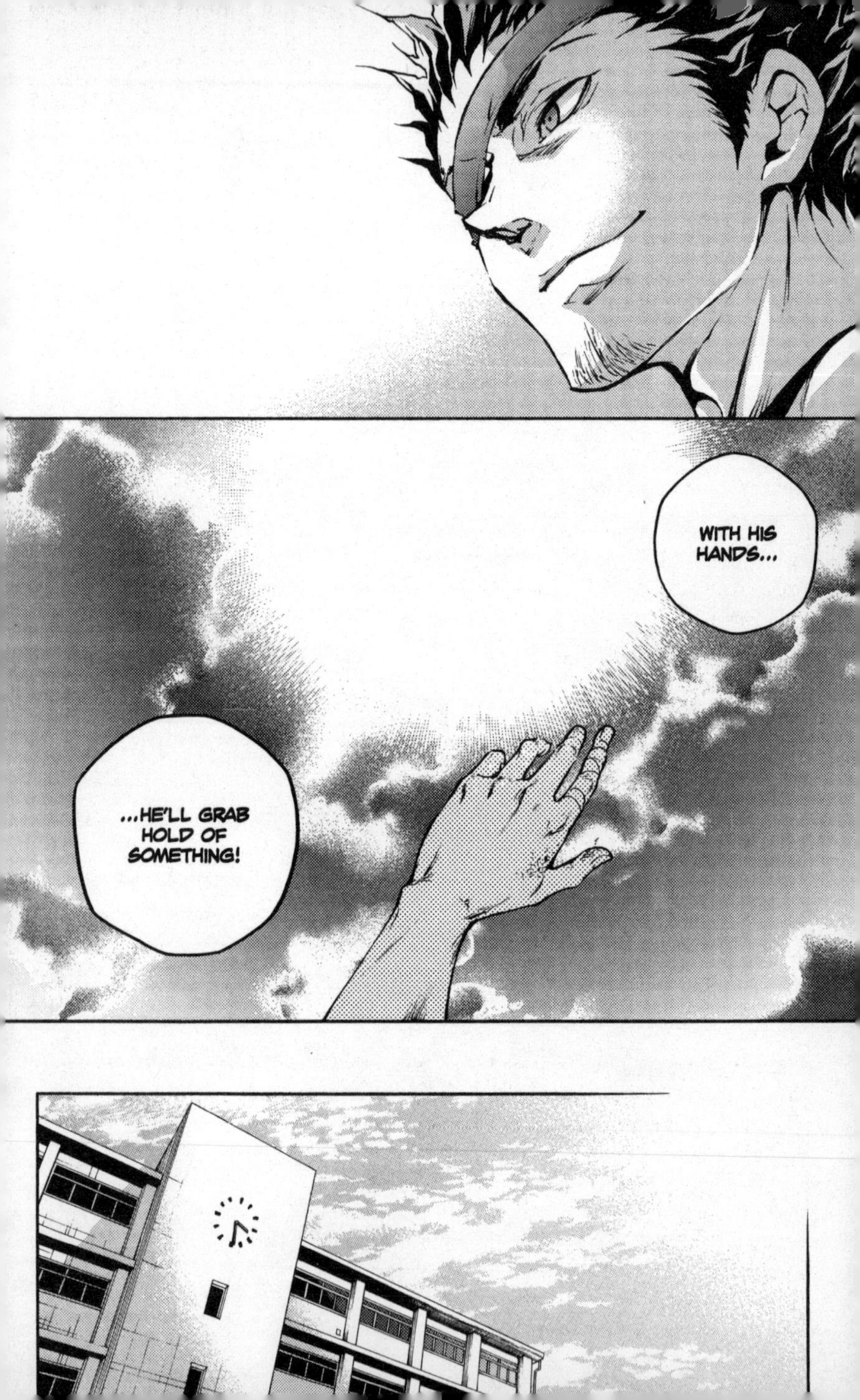
WITH HIS HANDS...
...HE'LL GRAB HOLD OF SOMETHING!

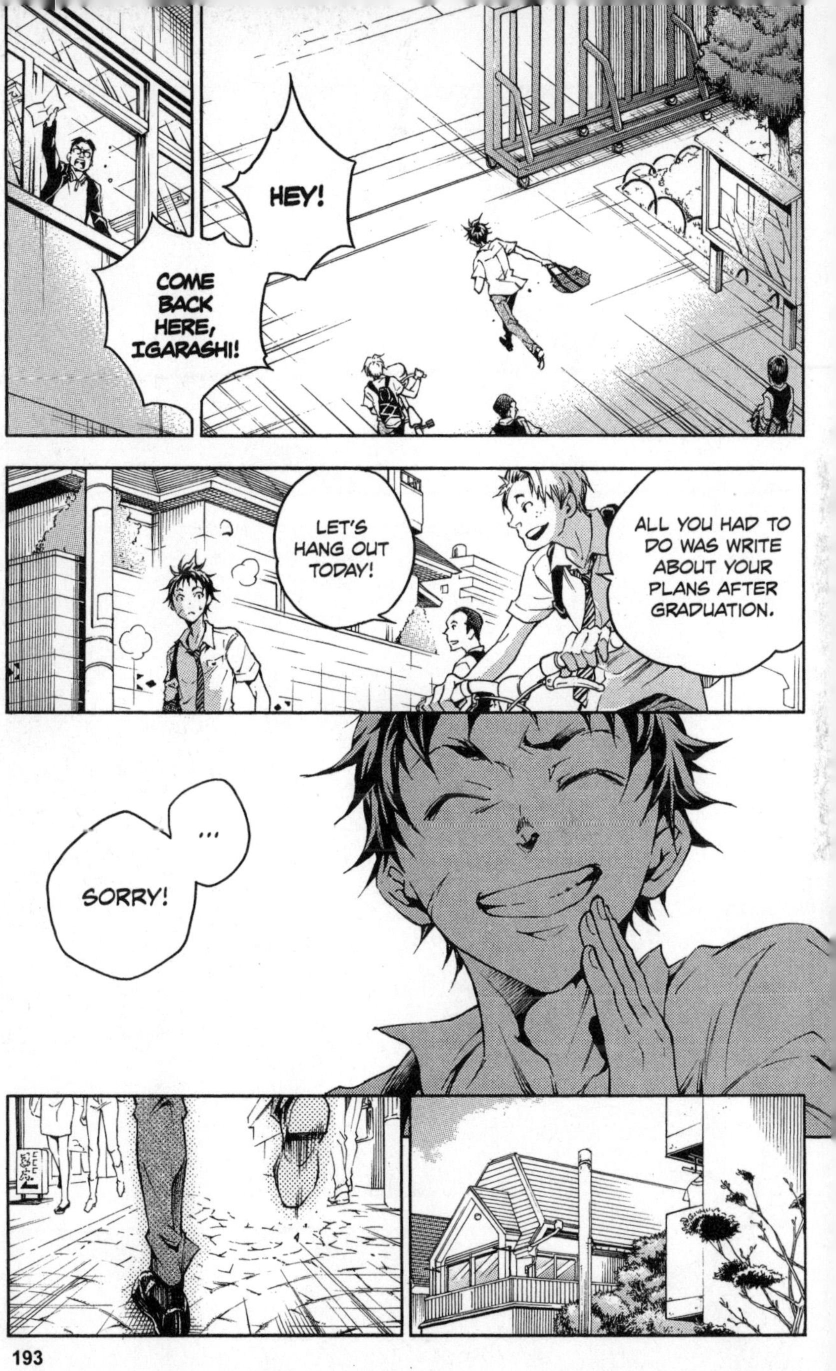
HEY!
COME BACK HERE, IGARASHI!
ALL YOU HAD TO DO WAS WRITE ABOUT YOUR PLANS AFTER GRADUATION.
LET'S HANG OUT TODAY!
...
SORRY!

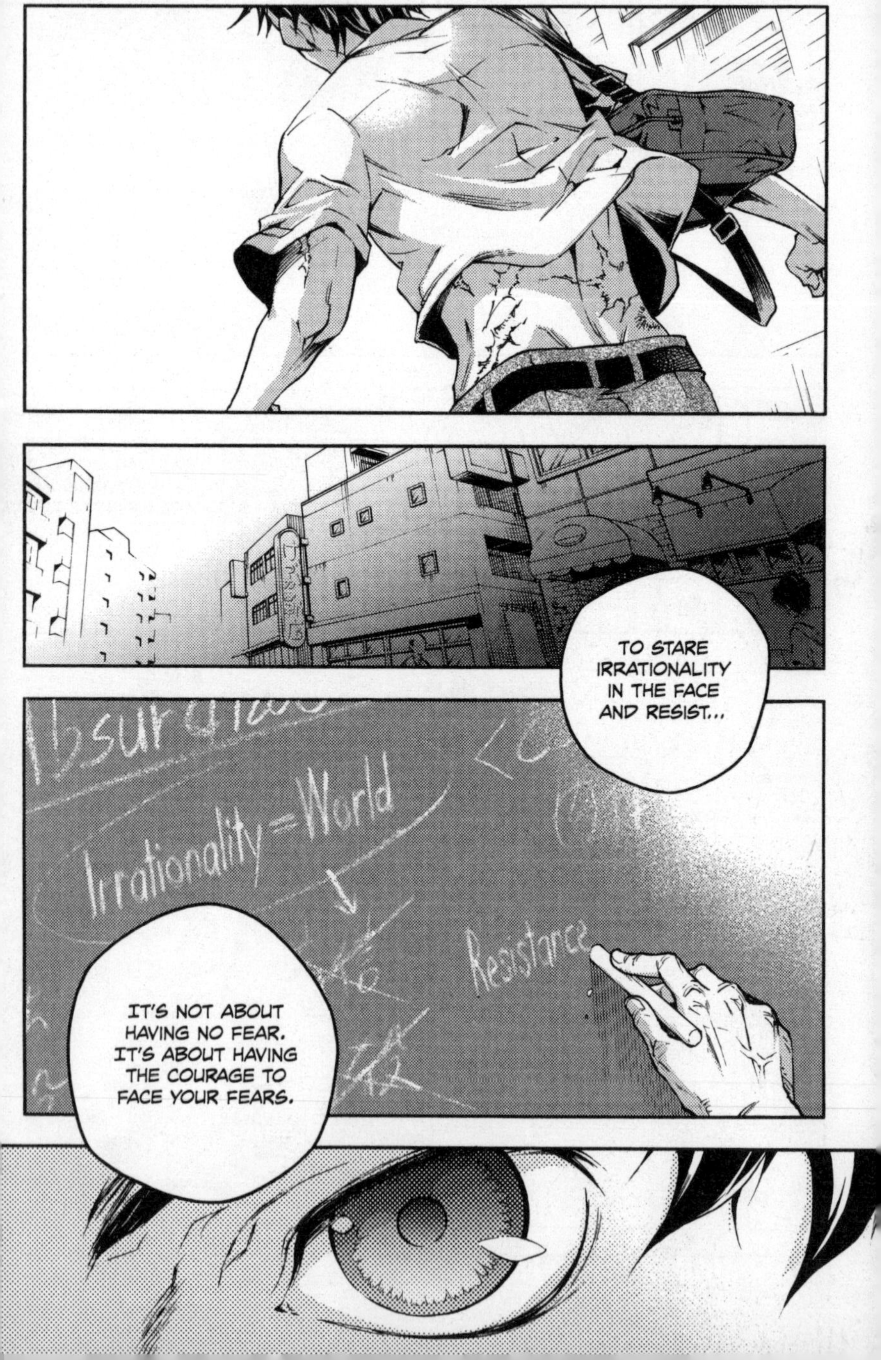
TO STARE IRRATIONALITY IN THE FACE AND RESIST...
Irrationality=World
Resistance
IT'S NOT ABOUT HAVING NO FEAR. IT'S ABOUT HAVING THE COURAGE TO FACE YOUR FEARS.

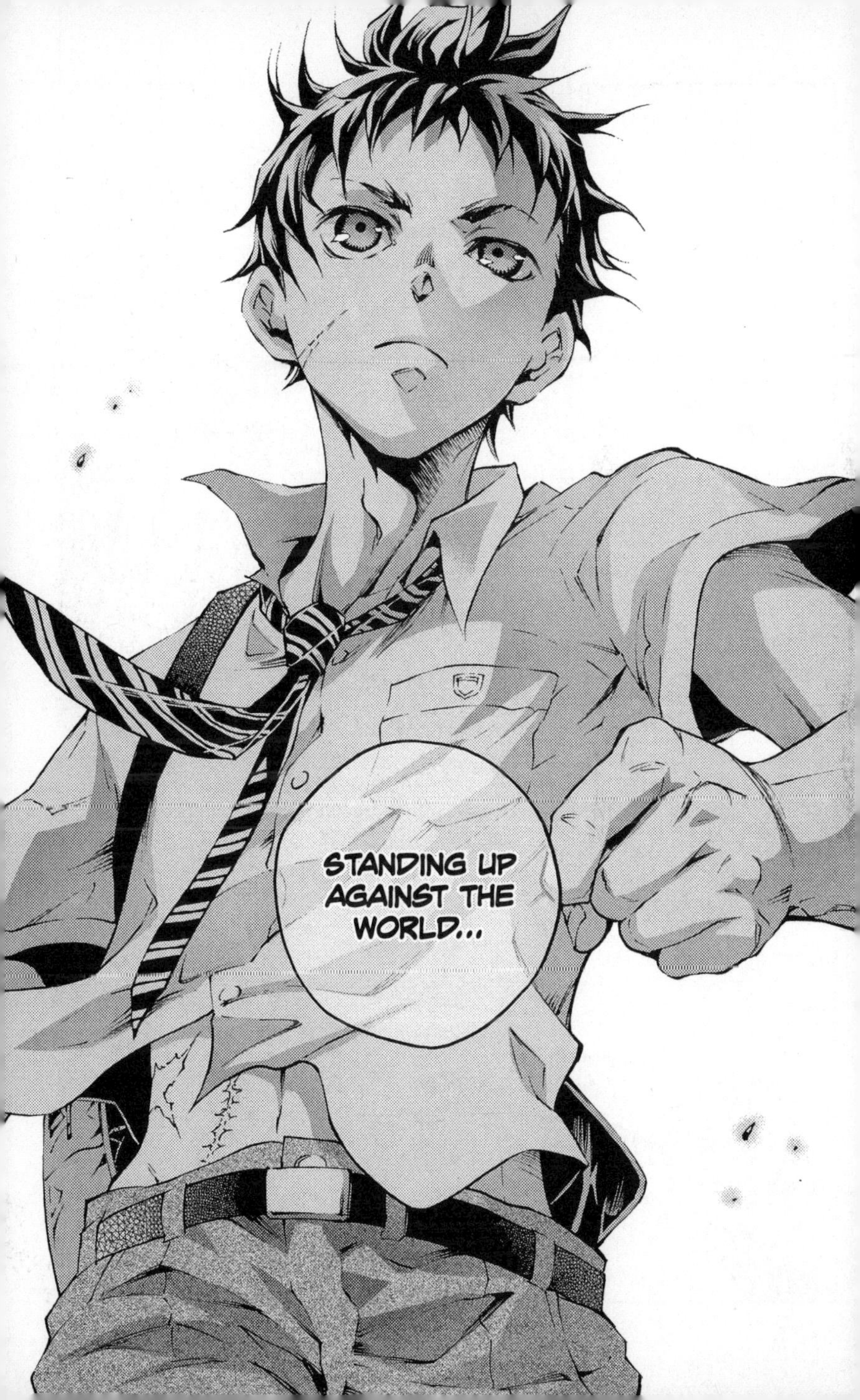
STANDING UP AGAINST THE WORLD...

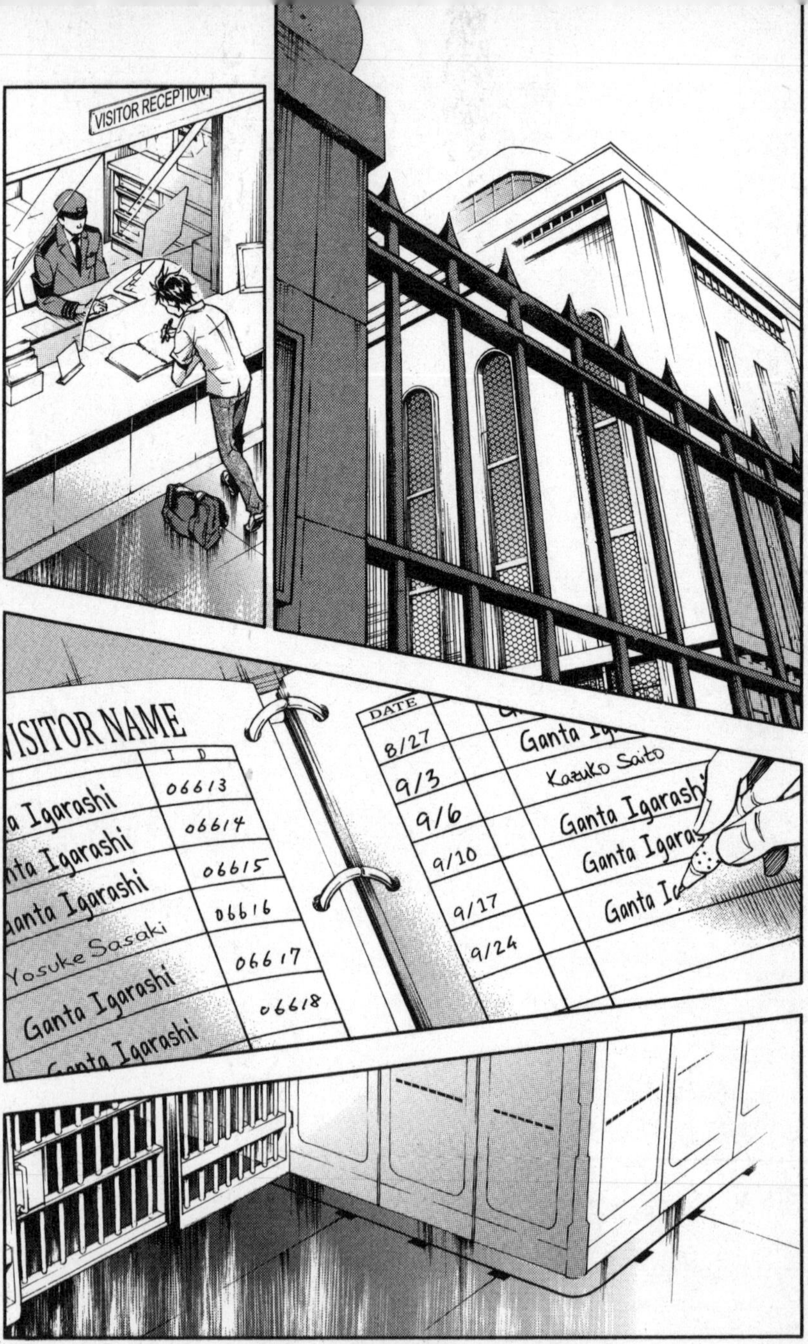
VISITOR RECEPTION
VISITOR NAME
ID
a Igarashi 06613
nta Igarashi 06614
anta Igarashi 06615
Yosuke Sasaki 06616
Ganta Igarashi 06617
Ganta Igarashi 06618
DATE
8/27 Ganta Ig
9/3 Kazuko Saito
9/6 Ganta Igarashi
9/10 Ganta Igara
9/17 Ganta Ig
9/24

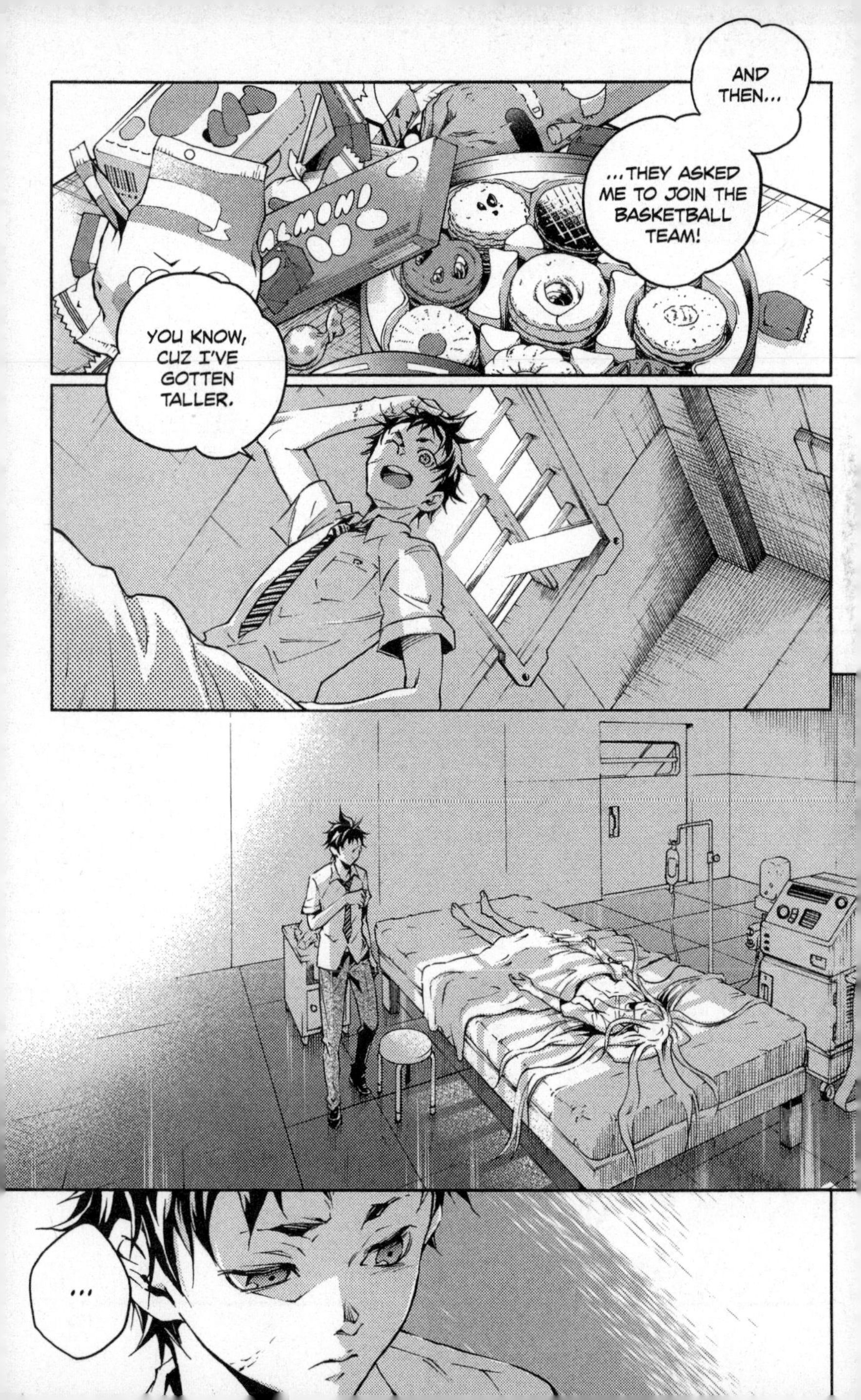
AND THEN...
...THEY ASKED ME TO JOIN THE BASKETBALL TEAM!
YOU KNOW, CUZ I'VE GOTTEN TALLER.
...

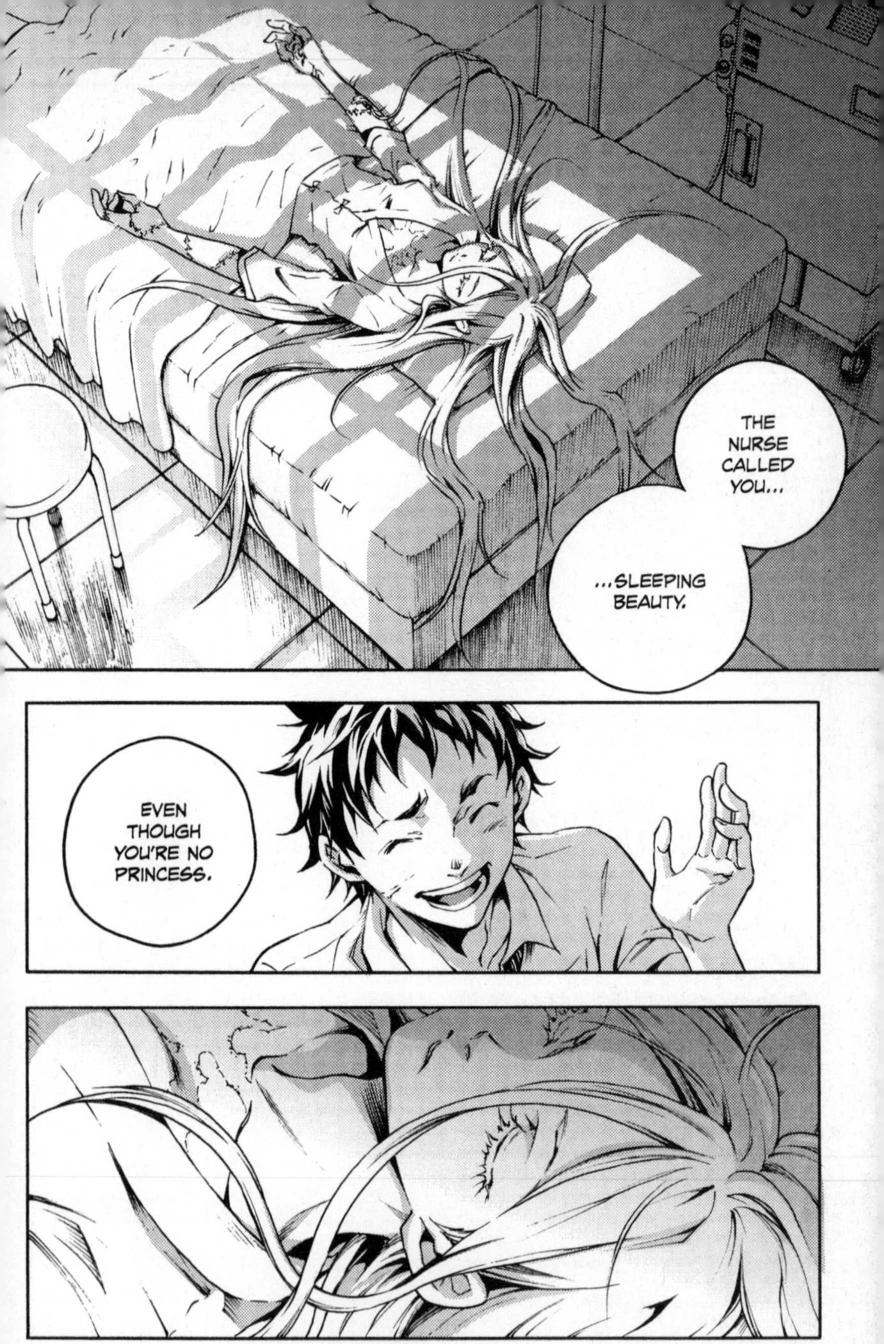
THE NURSE CALLED YOU...
...SLEEPING BEAUTY.
EVEN THOUGH YOU'RE NO PRINCESS.

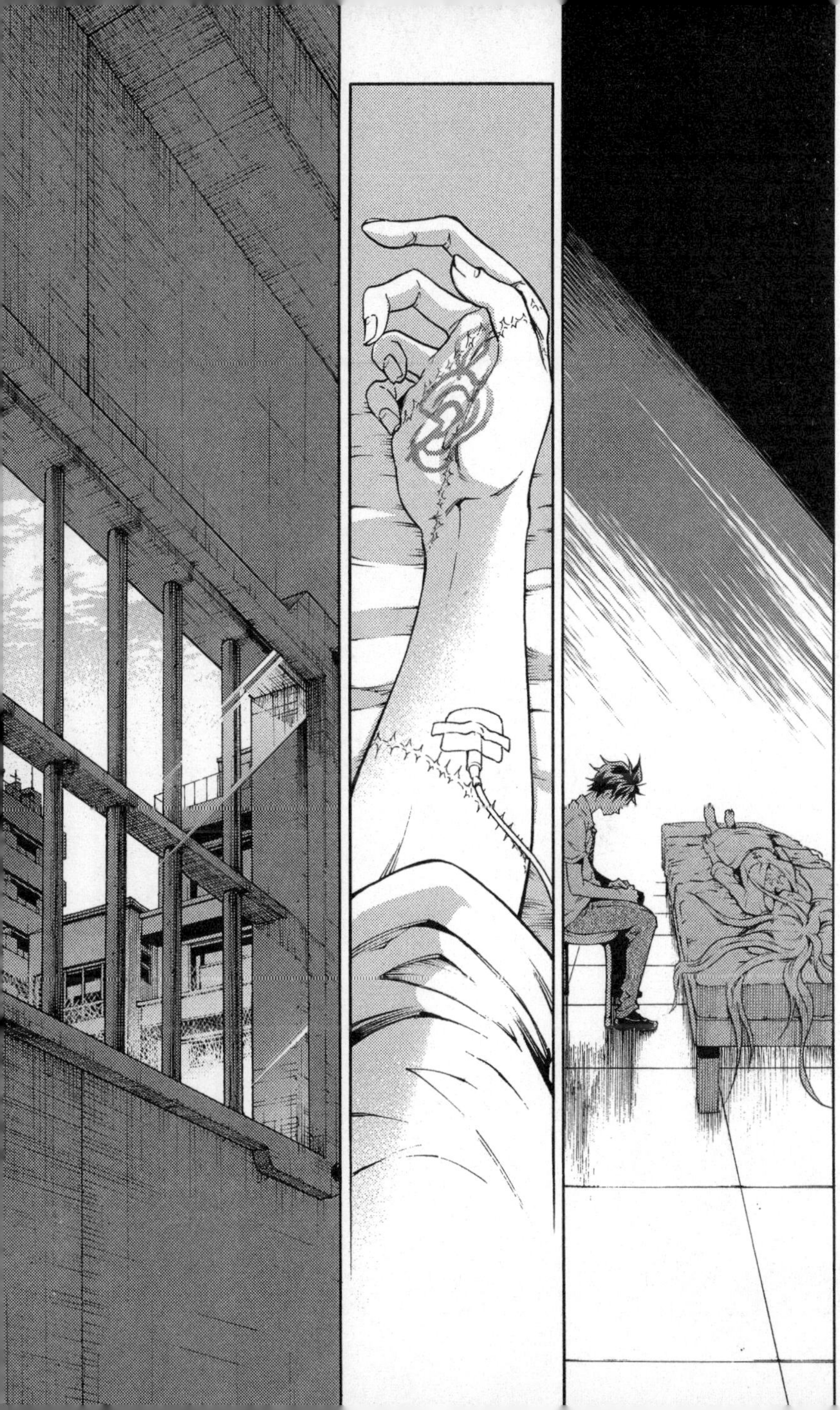

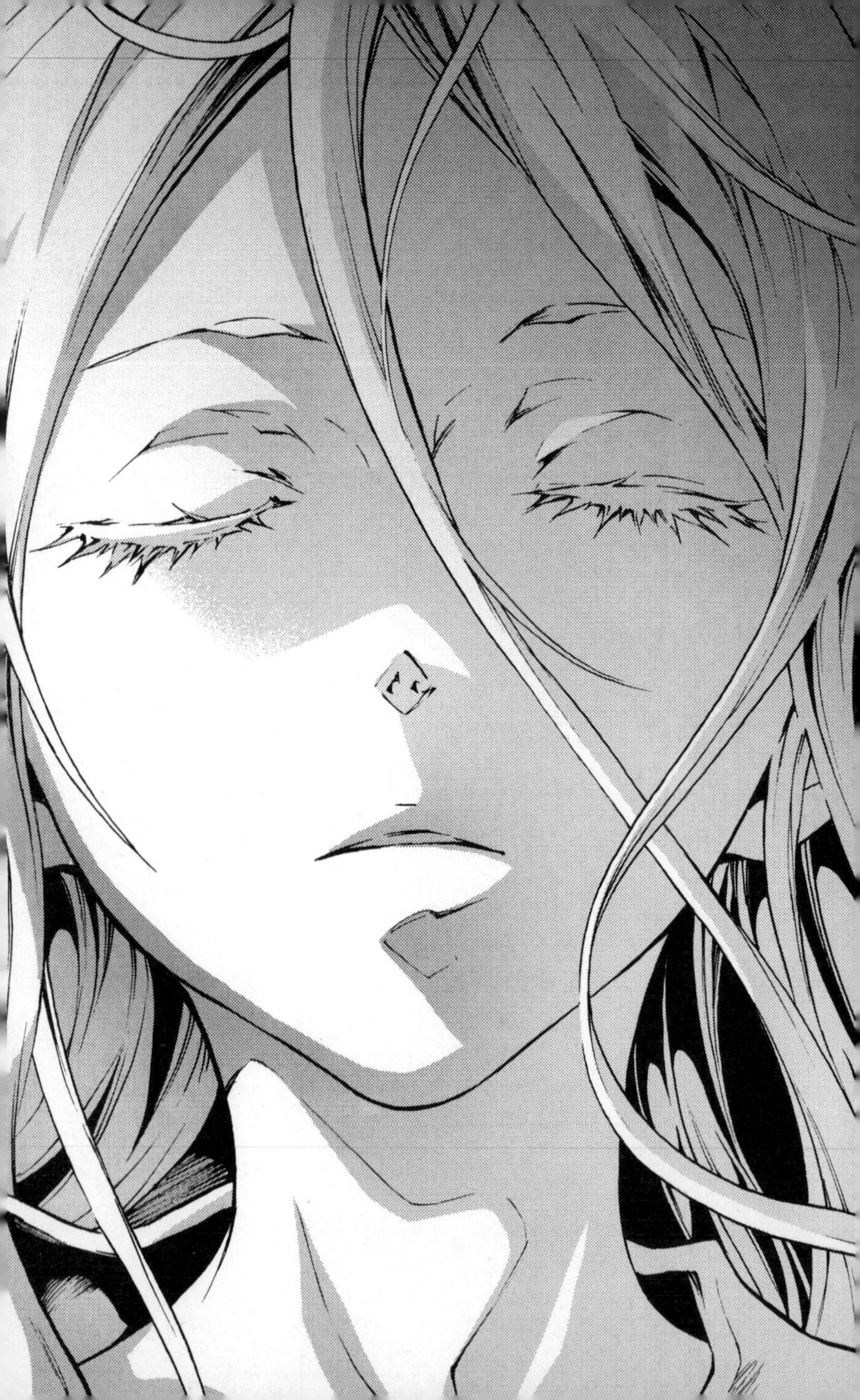

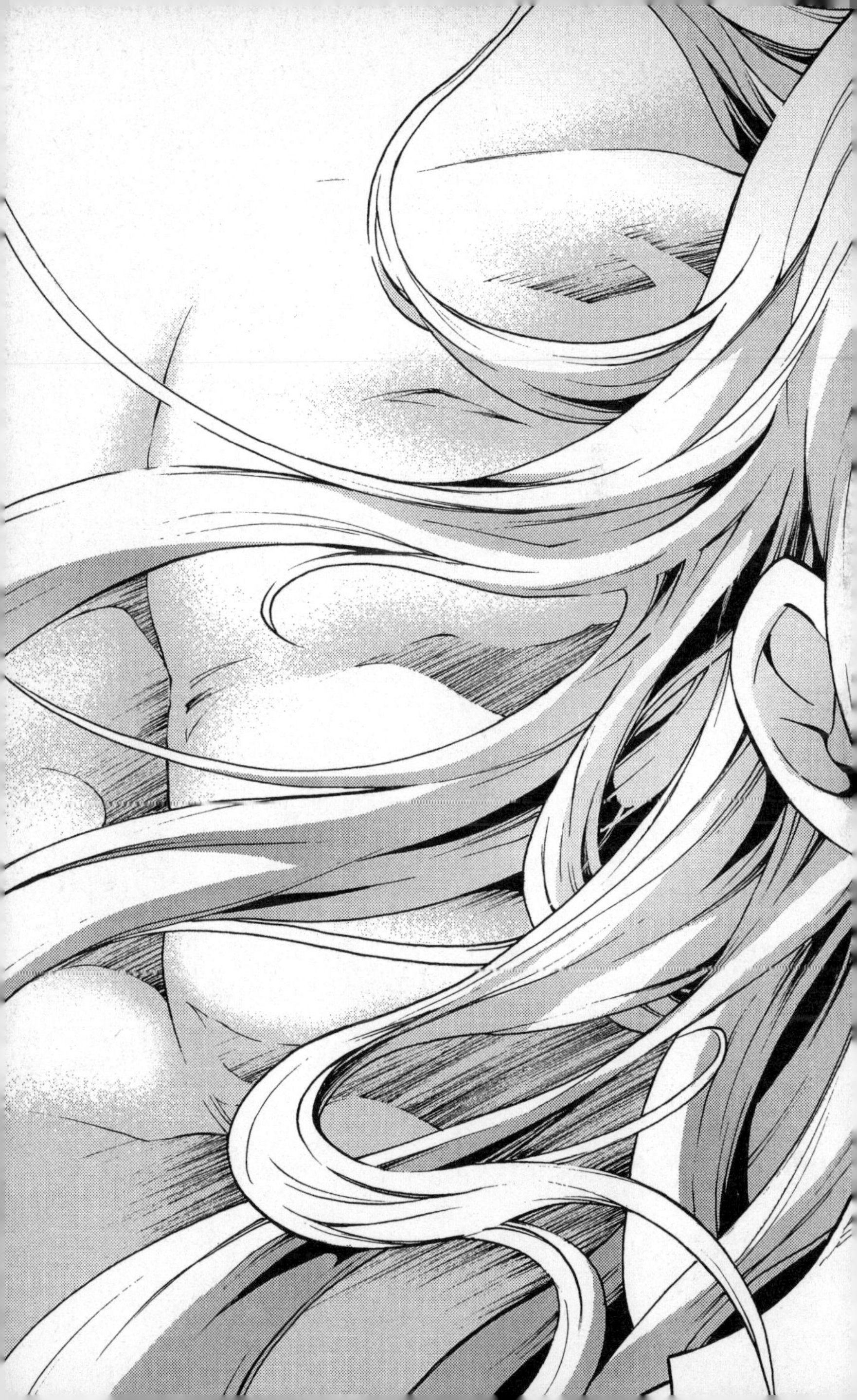

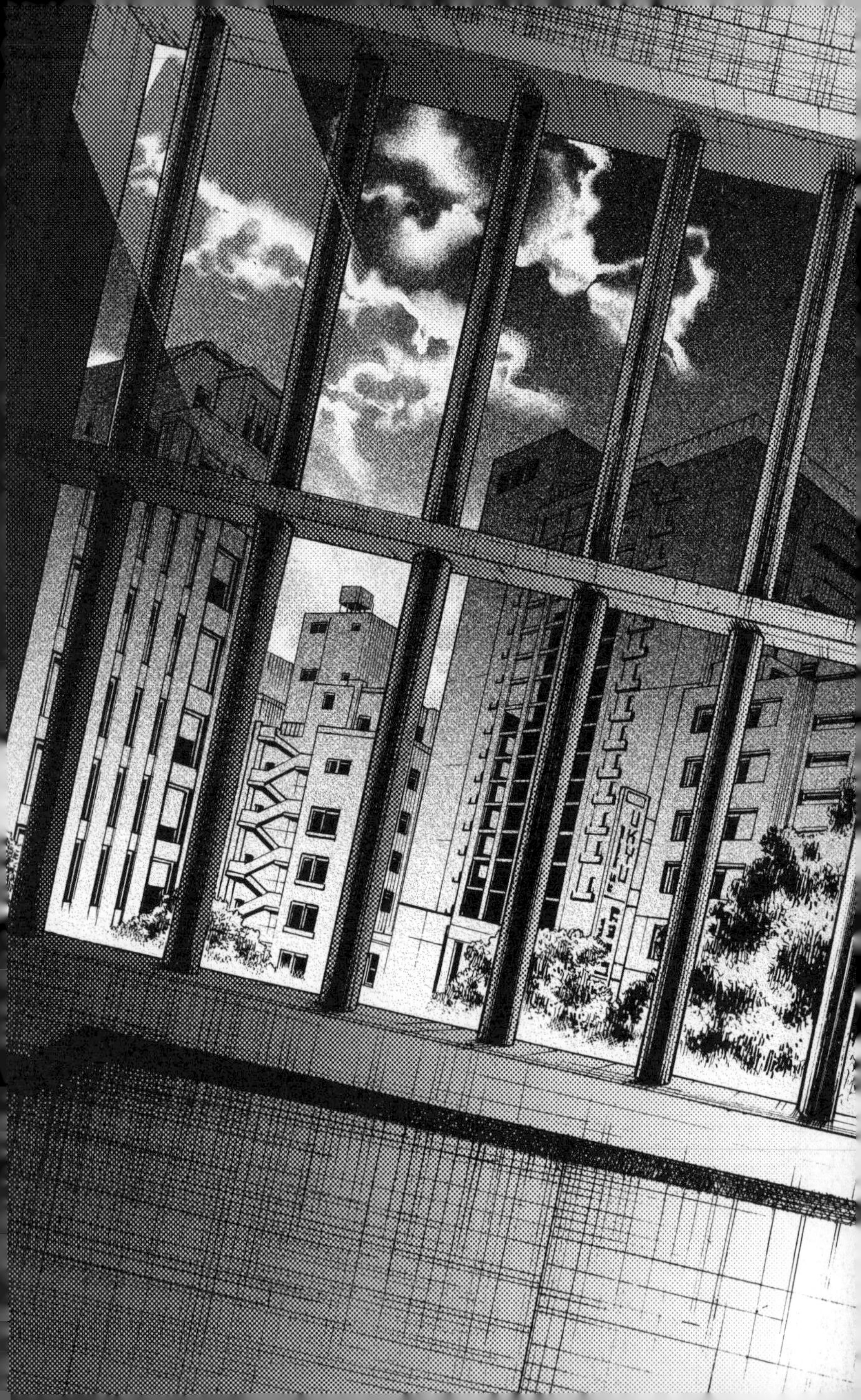

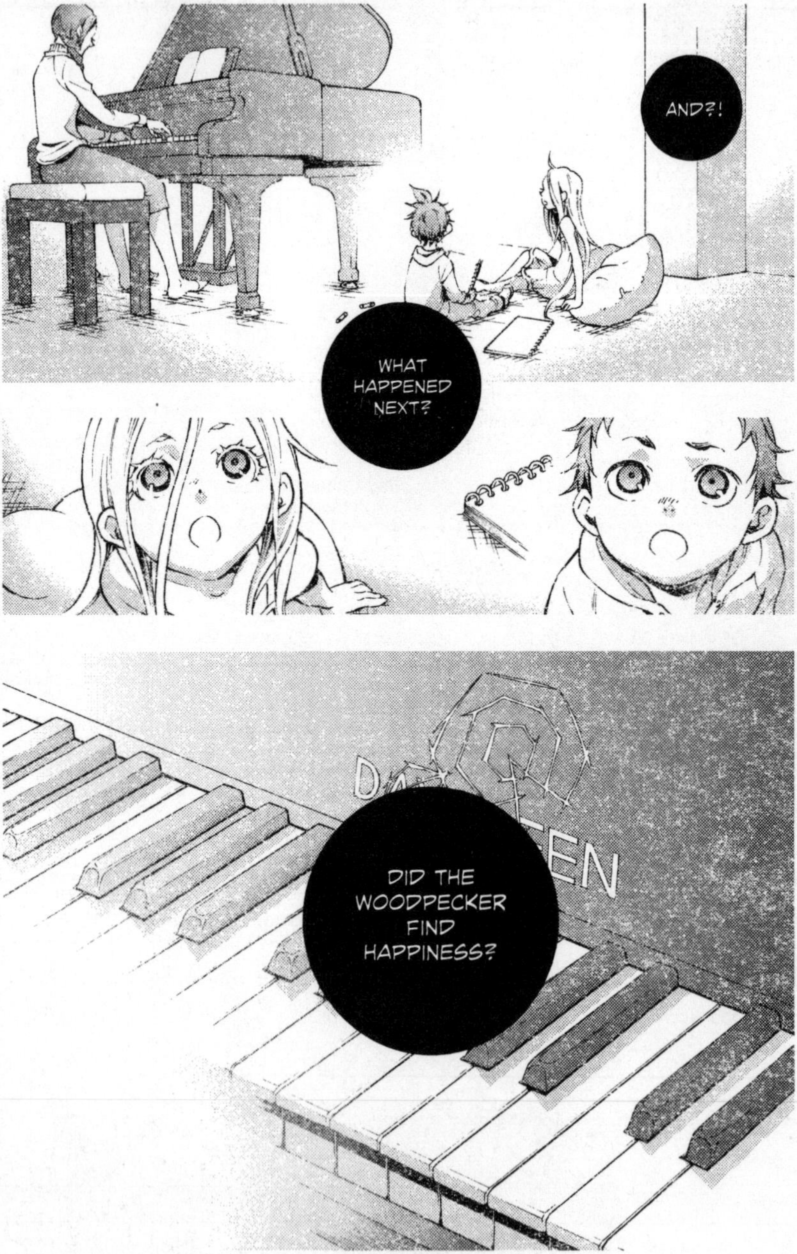
AND?!
WHAT HAPPENED NEXT?
DID THE WOODPECKER FIND HAPPINESS?

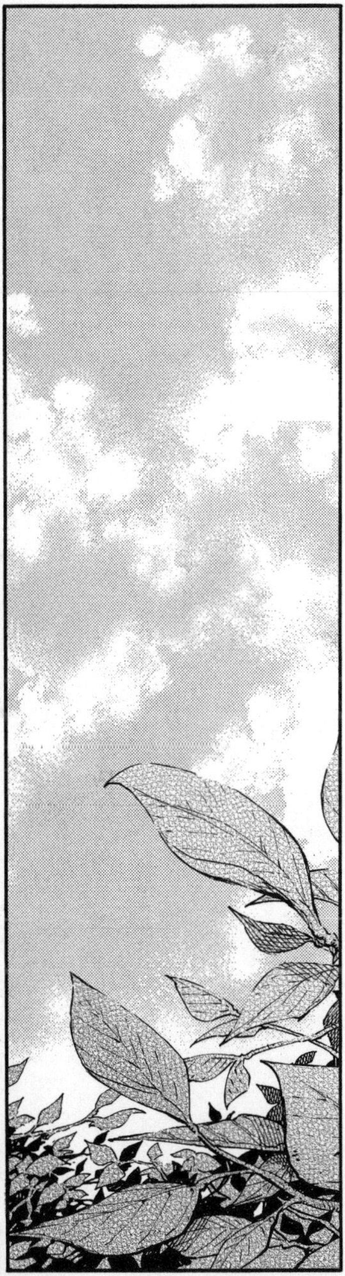
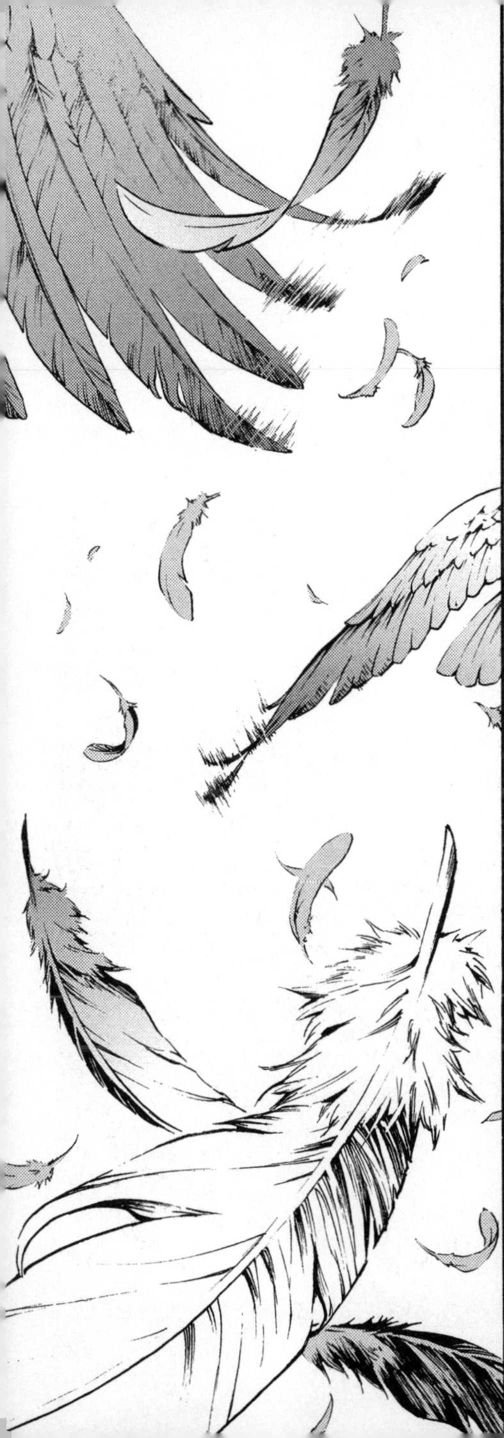

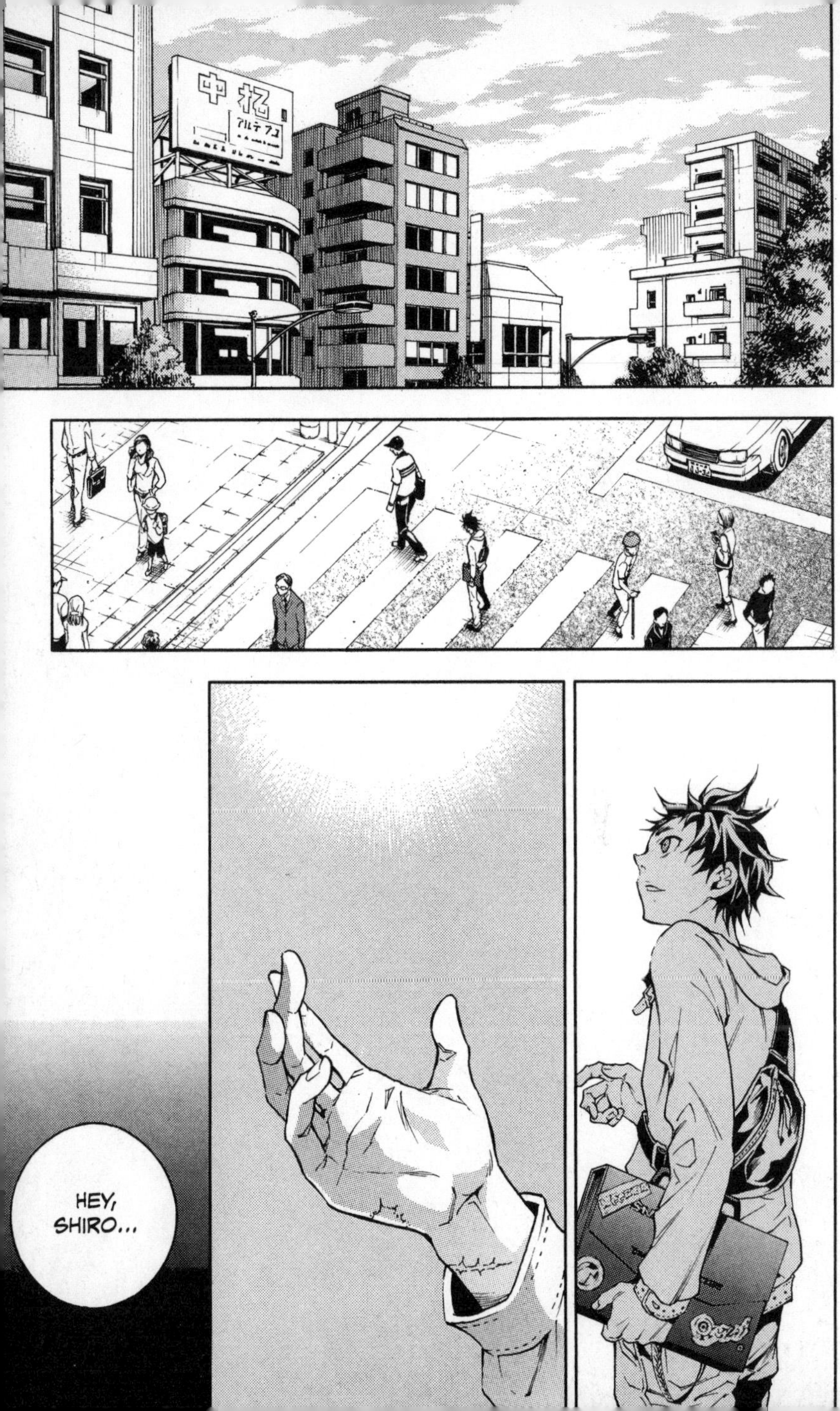
HEY, SHIRO...

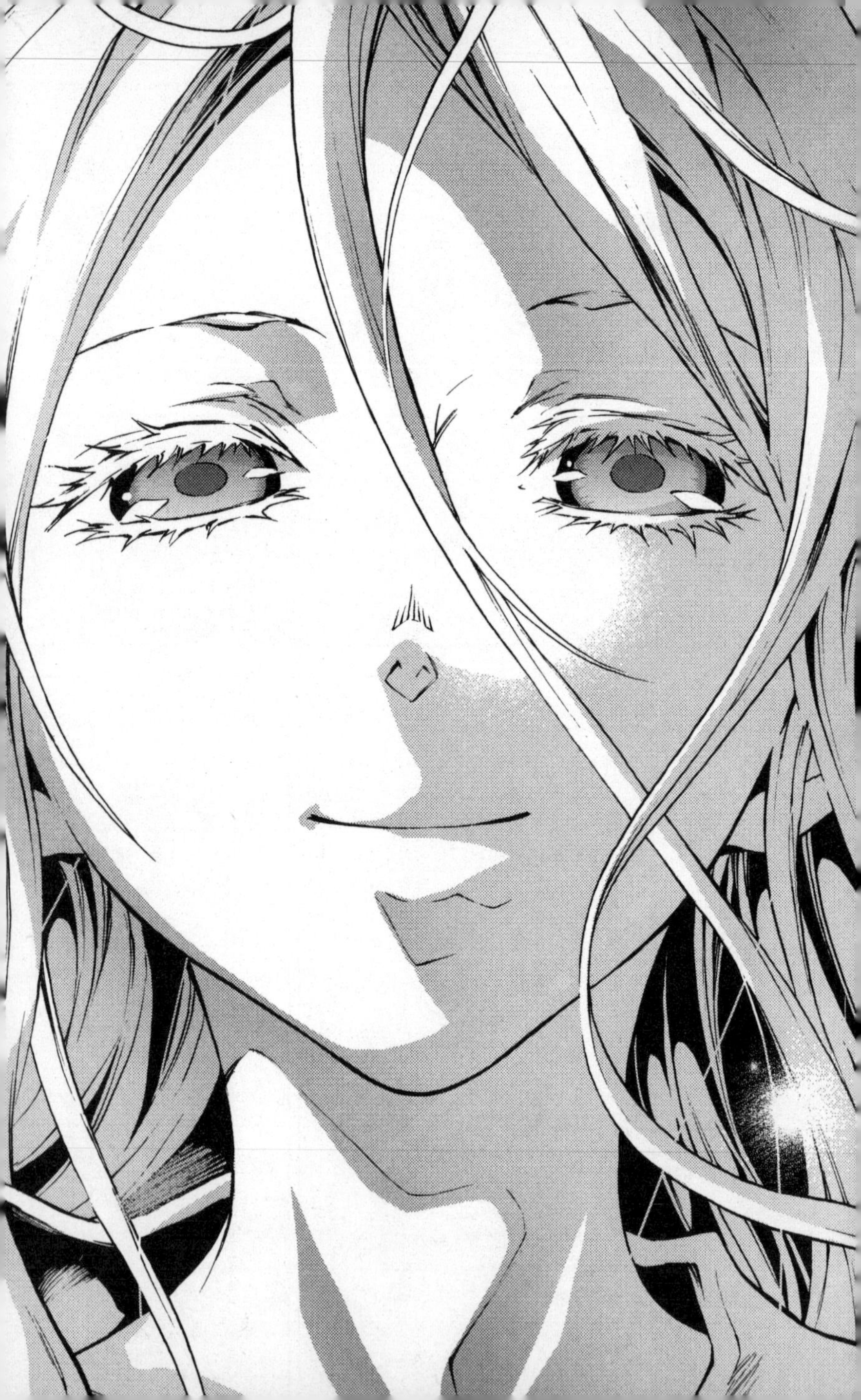

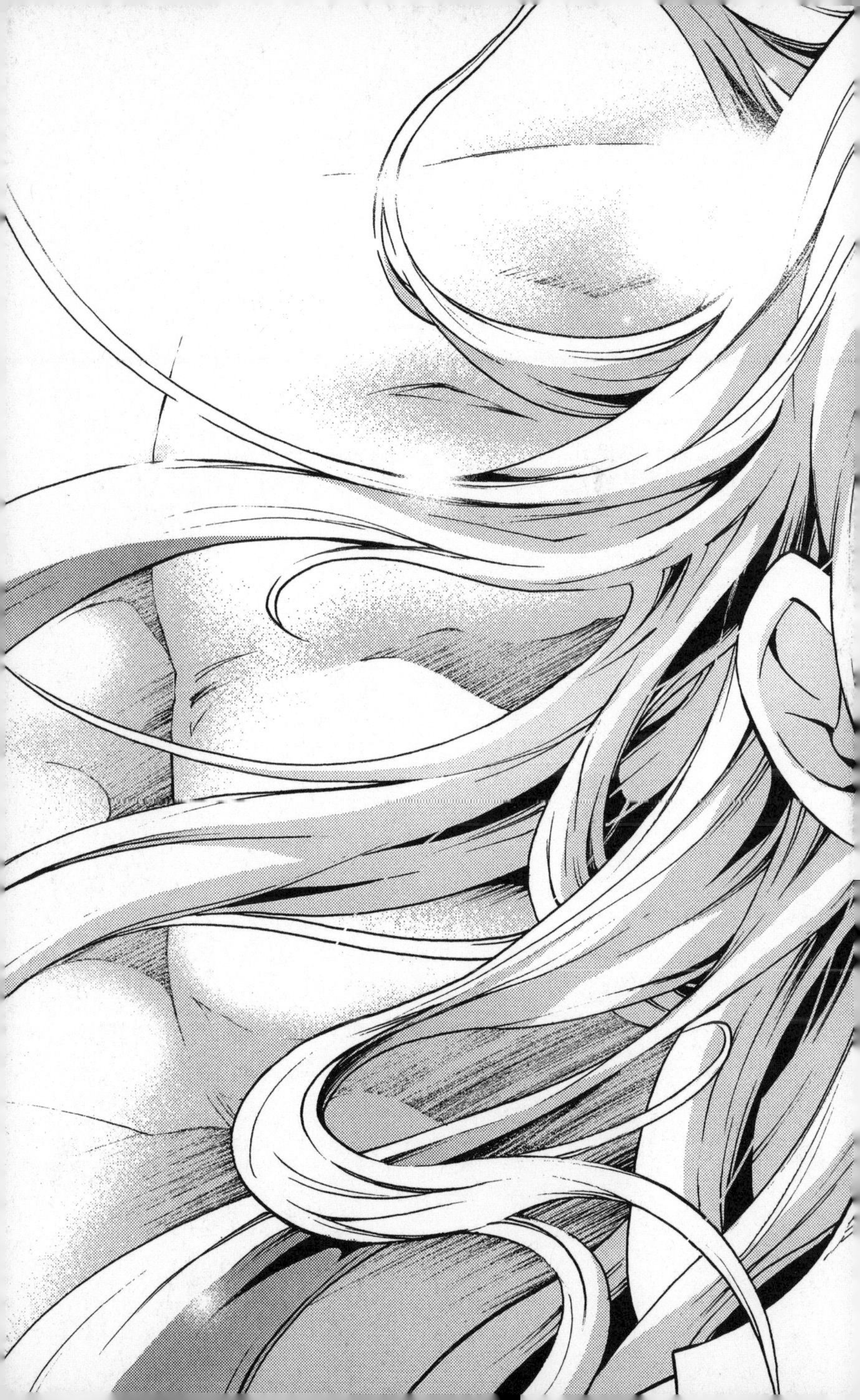

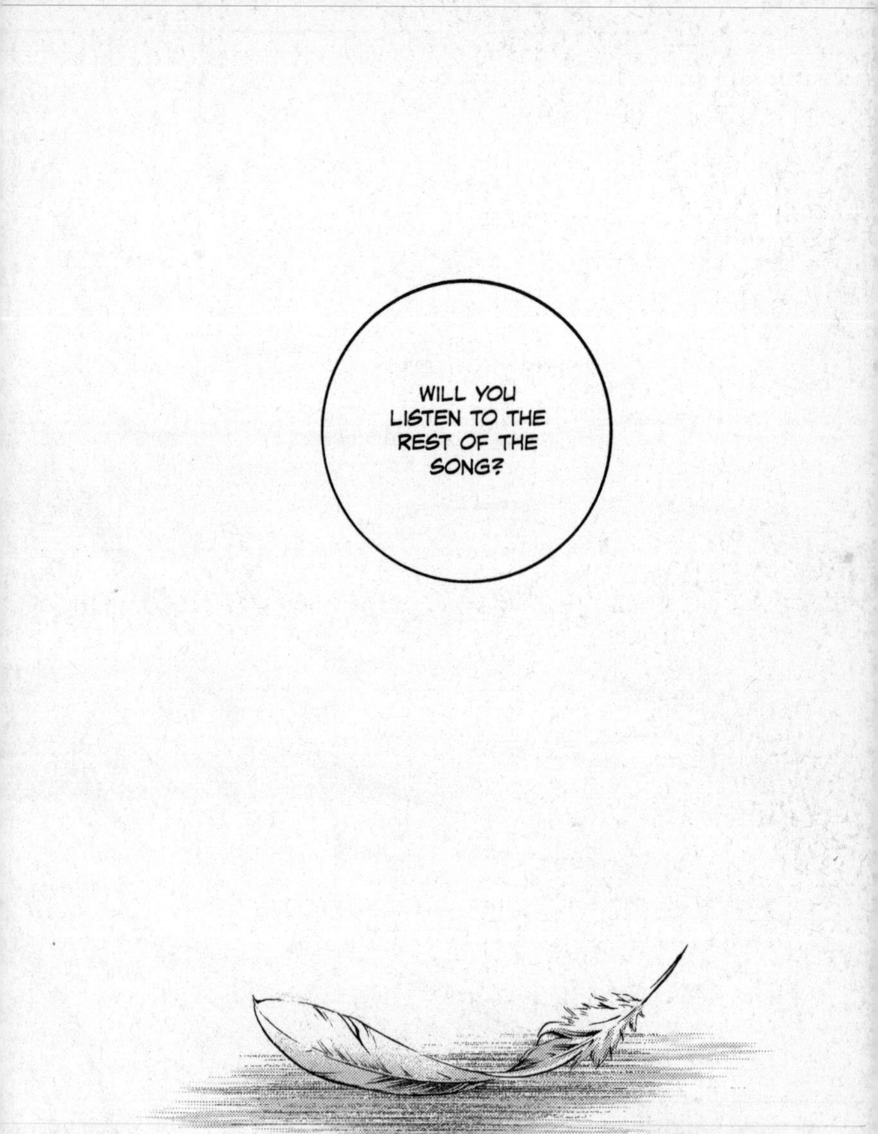
WILL YOU LISTEN TO THE REST OF THE SONG?

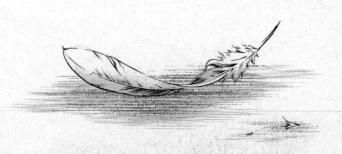

fin

DEADMAN WONDERLAND 13

Jinsei Kataoka
Kazuma Kondou

STAFF

Keiji Uchiyama

Karaiko

Shinji Sato

Taku Nakamura

Toshihiro Noguchi

DEADM☠N WONDERLAND

DEADMAN WONDERLAND
VOLUME 13
VIZ MEDIA EDITION

STORY & ART BY
JINSEI KATAOKA, KAZUMA KONDOU

DEADMAN WONDERLAND VOLUME 13
©JINSEI KATAOKA 2013 ©KAZUMA KONDOU 2013
EDITED BY KADOKAWA SHOTEN
FIRST PUBLISHED IN JAPAN IN 2013 BY KADOKAWA CORPORATION, TOKYO.
ENGLISH TRANSLATION RIGHTS ARRANGED WITH KADOKAWA CORPORATION, TOKYO.

TRANSLATION/JOE YAMAZAKI
ENGLISH ADAPTATION/STAN!
TOUCH-UP ART & LETTERING/JAMES GAUBATZ
DESIGN/SAM ELZWAY
EDITOR/JENNIFER LEBLANC

PRINTED IN THE U.S.A.

PUBLISHED BY VIZ MEDIA, LLC
P.O. BOX 77010
SAN FRANCISCO, CA 94107

10 9 8 7 6 5 4 3 2 1
FIRST PRINTING, FEBRUARY 2016

www.viz.com